Finance of International Trade

6th edition

Paul Cowdell and
Derek Hyde

The Institute of Financial Services
c/o The Chartered Institute of Bankers
Emmanuel House
4-9 Burgate Lane
Canterbury
Kent
CT1 2XJ
United Kingdom

Institute of Financial Services Publications are published by The Chartered Institute of Bankers, a non-profit-making registered educational charity and are distributed exclusively by Bankers Books Limited which is a wholly owned subsidiary of The Chartered Institute of Bankers.

Copyright © The Chartered Institute of Bankers 1997

ISBN 0-85297-473-6

Contents

iii

Acknowledgements

The authors and The Chartered Institute of Bankers would like to thank Barclays Bank plc for the kind permission to reproduce some of their specimen documents.

They would also wish to thank the following for their helpful comments on the fifth and sixth editions.

Peter Bamber - CIB Information Services

Colin Bower - National Westminster Bank

Dr David Goacher - Sheffield Hallam University

Simon Hyde - NCM Leeds Office

Ken Moss - Sheffield Chamber of Commerce and Industry

Ian Quinn - Barclays Bank

Peter Regan - NCM Cardiff

Preface

The sixth edition of *Finance of International Trade* has been extensively revised and incorporates all relevant developments since January 1994

The book is intended to assist all students and practitioners who seek to acquire the necessary background information to gain an understanding of the finance of international trade, foreign exchange and support services provided for exporters, importers and merchants by London's financial institutions.

It concentrates in particular on the needs of students studying for the following qualifications:

- The *International Trade Finance* option paper of the Associateship/Degree programme of The Chartered Institute of Bankers (CIB) in association with the University of Manchester Institute of Science and Technology (UMIST.);

- The Institute of Export: *International Trade and Payments*, and Advanced Certificate in Overseas Trade;

- British International Freight Association: *International Trade and Payments.*

This text also acts as a bridge between the retail banking option papers on the CIB/ UMIST qualification and those which deal with the corporate/international banking, e.g. *Banking Operations - Regulation, Market Practice and Treasury Management* or *Multinational Corporate Finance.* In addition, this text is one of the books cited in the Association of Corporate Treasurers' Manual for their Corporate Finance and Funding unit.

This book can be broken down into five parts:

- Part One consists of a single introductory chapter which sets out the rationale for the development and growth of international trade, including balance of payments issues.

- Part Two begins with an examination of the foreign exchange markets. It then analyses the practical applications of hedging techniques, both internal and external, and finally covers foreign exchange and settlement procedures.

- Part Three assesses the role of documents used in international trade and then analyses the way that documents are linked inexorably and logically with the shipping and payment terms agreed between importer and exporter.

- Part Four then examines the implications of the various financial and non-financial services from the point of view of exporters,

- Finally, Part Five analyses documentary credits from the applicant's point of view, and then evaluates the benefits and drawbacks of various specialist forms of documentary credit, such as transferable and back-to-back credits, together with services and facilities for importers.

For easy reference a list of learning objectives appears at the beginning of each unit and most units contain a multi-choice test and/or problem solving questions complete with indicative solutions. At appropriate stages of the book, a series of revision questions and answers have been included. In addition, there are appendices covering correspondent banking and electronic data interchange, and copies of various International Chamber of Commerce (ICC) rules covering documentary collections and documentary credits.

The sequence of topics in this book is set from a *teaching* point of view and therefore does not follow the syllabus topic order. Students are recommended to obtain copies of the examiner's reports from 1997 onwards for the CIB/UMIST *International Trade Finance* papers, as these are a first-class means of updating knowledge and acquiring a practical insight into the subject.

International trade is a rapidly changing subject; hence, careful study of publications such as *The Treasurer*, the *Financial Times*, *The Chartered Banker, Export Today*, and the various customer leaflets and circulars prepared by banks, is essential in order to keep up to date. In addition, both students and practitioners should regularly search the following web sites to keep abreast of new developments.

Department of Trade and Industry - http://www.dti.gov.uk

H M Customs and Excise - http://www.info.gov.hk/info/customs.htm

UN/ECE - http://www.unicc.org/unece/trade/facil

Electronic Commerce Association - http://www.eca.org.uk

Article Number Association - http://www.ana.org.uk

Electronic Commerce Information Resource - http://www.year-x.co.uk/ec/

Institute of Export - http://www.export.co.uk

SITPRO - http://www.sitpro.org.uk/

International Chamber of Commerce www.iccwbo.org

The aim of this book is to help readers acquire a sound understanding of relevant theoretical and practical concepts, coupled with an ability to apply the principles in a given practical situation.

You should find this subject to be a stimulating and enjoyable challenge.

Suggested further reading

The journals and web sites mentioned above are a first-rate source of information on changes to the subject. However, for readers who want to study the topics in greater depth the following are recommended:

Anon: *Financial Times*: July 1997, Survey FT Exporter

P. Fontaine: *Europe in Ten Points* (2nd edition) European Documentation Series July 1995 ISBN 92-827-4844-8

Anon: *The European Union and world trade*: Office for the Official Publications of the European Communities June 1995 ISBN 92-827-4375-6

Anon: *Second thoughts about globalisation*: *The Economist* June 21st 1997 p 108

A. Buckley: *Multinational Finance* (3rd Edition) 1996 Prentice Hall International

Anon: *The Foreign Exchange Market*: Fact Sheet May 1996; Bank of England

Anon: *Practical Issues Arising from the Introduction of the Euro* issues 1, 2, 3 Bank of England

Anon: *Introduction of the Euro, what does it mean for business?* January 1997: Bank of England

Anon: *Panorama of EU Industry 97*: European Commission

Anon; *Exporting 25 Years British Overseas Trade Board 1972-97* Annual Report and Forward Plan 1996-97

Anon: *Winning through exporting Overseas Trade Services:* Overseas Trade Services: DTI

International Chamber of Commerce Publications as follows:

Number	Title
497	Funds transfer in international banking
515	ICC Guide to Documentary credit operations for UCP 500
561	ICC Guide to Collection Operations for URC 522
461	Guide to ICC Incoterms 1990
533	The GATT Negotiations: A Guide to the results of the Uruguay Business Round
934	Trade Finance in Emerging Markets

Finance of International Trade

The Concept of the Course

This is a practical course written for students studying for banking and finance qualifications and also for practitioners in the financial services industry who are looking for a practical refresher. This study text is structured so that many will find it to be the most coherent way of learning the subject.

This book is the set text for the International Trade Finance option of the ACIB-Degree link.

Each chapter or unit of the Study Text is divided into sections and contains:

- Learning objectives;

- An introduction, indicating how this subject area relates to others to which the reader may have cause to refer;

- Clear, concise topic-by-topic coverage;

- Examples and exercises to reinforce learning, confirm understanding and stimulate thought;

- Usually, an exam-style question to try for practice.

Exercises

Exercises are provided throughout to enable you to check your progress as you work through the text. These come in a variety of forms; some test your ability to analyse material you have read, others see whether you have taken in the full significance of a piece of information. Some are meant to be discussed with colleagues, friends or fellow students.

Each of the main units consists of study notes designed to focus attention upon the key aspects of the subject matter. These notes are divided into convenient sections for study purposes.

At the end of most units there are self-assessment questions and revision questions have been inserted at appropriate stages of the book. These comprise a number of short-answer questions and often a full specimen examination question. The answers to all these questions are to be found at the back of the book in Appendixes VI and VII. Students should remain aware of the fact that the examination itself will comprise questions drawn from across the whole Chartered Institute of Bankers syllabus, the key sections of which for this subject are:

- The Meaning of International Trade Finance/Payment and Risk Management Services

- Financial Services from Banks and Other Sources

- Methods of Trading

Although the workbook is designed to stand alone, as with most topics, certain aspects of this subject are constantly changing. Therefore it is of great importance that students should keep up to date with these key areas.

It is anticipated that the student will study this course for one academic year, reading through and studying approximately two Units every three weeks. However, it should be noted that as topics vary in size and as knowledge tends not to fall into uniform chunks, some Units in this workbook are unavoidably longer than others.

The masculine pronoun 'he' has been used in this Workbook to encompass both genders and to avoid the awkwardness of the constant repetition of 'he and/or she'.

Study Guide

In the next few pages, we offer some advice and ideas on studying, revising and approaching examinations.

Studying

As with any examination, there is no substitute for preparation based on an organised and disciplined study plan. You should devise an approach which will enable you to get right through this Study Text and still leave time for revision of this and any other subject you are taking at the same time. Many candidates find that about six weeks is the right period of time to leave for revision, enough time to get through the revision material, but not so long that it is no longer fresh in your mind by the time you reach the examination.

This means that you should plan how to get to the last chapter by, say, the end of March for a May sitting or the end of August for an October sitting. This includes not only reading the text, but making notes and attempting the bulk of the illustrative questions in the back of the text.

We offer the following as a starting point for approaching your study.

- **Plan time each week to study a part of this Study Text**. Make sure that it is 'quality' study time: let everyone know that you are studying and that you should not be disturbed. If you are at home, unplug your telephone or switch the answerphone on; if you are in the office, put your telephone on 'divert'.

- Set a clearly defined objective for each study period. You may simply wish to read through a chapter for the first time or perhaps you want to make some notes on a chapter you have already read a couple of times. Don't forget the illustrative questions.

- **Review your study plan**. Use the study checklist a couple of pages on to see how well you are keeping up. Don't panic if you fall behind, but do think how you will make up for lost time.

- **Look for examples of what you have covered in the 'real' world**. If you work for a financial organisation, this should be a good starting point. If you do not, then think about your experiences as an individual bank or building society customer or perhaps about your employer's position as a corporate customer of a bank. Keep an eye on the quality press for reports about banks and building societies and their activities.

Revising

- The period which you have earmarked for revision is a very important time. Now it is even more important that you plan time each week for study and that you set clear objectives for each revision session.

- Use time sensibly. How much revision time do you have? Remember that you still need to eat, sleep and fit in some leisure time.

- How will you split the available time between subjects? What are your weaker subjects? You will need to focus on some topics in more detail than others. You will also need to plan your revision around your learning style. By now, you should know whether, for example, early morning, early evening or late evening is best.

- Take regular breaks. Most people find they can absorb more this way than if they attempt to revise for long uninterrupted periods of time. Award yourself a five-minute break every hour. Go for a stroll or make a cup of coffee, but do not turn the television on.

- Believe in yourself. Are you cultivating the right attitude of mind? There is absolutely no reason why you should not pass this exam if you adopt the correct approach. Be confident, you have passed exams before so you can pass this one.

The Day of the Exam

- Passing examinations is half about having the knowledge, and half about doing yourself full justice in the examination. You must have the right technique.

- Set at least one alarm (or get an alarm call) for a morning exam.

- Having something to eat but beware of eating too much; you may feel sleepy if your system is digesting a large meal.

- Don't forget pens, pencils, rulers, erasers and anything else you will need.

- Avoid discussion about the exam with other candidates outside the exam hall.

Tackling the Examination Paper
First, make sure that you satisfy the examiner's requirements.

Read the instructions on the front of the exam paper carefully. Check that the exam format hasn't changed. It is surprising how often examiners' reports remark on the number of students who attempt too few - or too many - questions, or who attempt the wrong number of questions from different parts of the paper. Make sure that you are planning to answer the right number of questions.

Read all the questions on the exam paper before you start writing. Look at the weighting of marks to each part of the question. If part (a) offers only 4 marks and you can't answer the 12 marks part (b), then don't choose the question.

Don't produce irrelevant answers. Make sure you answer the question set, and not the question you would prefer to have been set.

Produce an answer in the correct format. The examiner will state in the requirements the format in which the question should be answered, e.g. in a report or memorandum. If a question asks for a diagram or an example, give one. If a question does not specifically ask for a diagram or example, but it seems appropriate, give one.

Secondly, observe these simple rules to ensure that your script is pleasing to the examiner.

Present a tidy paper. You are a professional and it should always show in the presentation of your work. Candidates are penalised for poor presentation and so you should make sure that you write legibly, label diagrams clearly and lay out your work professionally. Markers of scripts each have dozens of papers to mark; a badly written scrawl is unlikely to receive the same attention as a neat and well laid-out paper.

State the obvious. Many candidates look for complexity which is not required and consequently overlook the obvious. Make basic statements first. Plan your answer and ask yourself whether you have answered the main parts of the question.

Use examples. This will help to demonstrate to the examiner that you keep up to date with the subject. There are lots of useful examples scattered through this study text and you can read about others if you dip into the quality press or take notice of what is happening in your working environment.

Finally, make sure that you give yourself the opportunity to do yourself justice.

Select questions carefully. Read through the paper once, then quickly jot down any key points against each question in a second read through. Reject those questions against which you have jotted down very little. Select those where you could latch on to 'what the question is about' - but remember to check carefully that you have got the right end of the stick before putting pen to paper.

Plan your attack carefully. Consider the order in which you are going to tackle questions. It is a good idea to start with your best question to boost your morale and get some easy marks 'in the bag'.

Read the question carefully and plan your answer. Read through the question again very carefully when you come to answer it.

Gain the easy marks. Include the obvious if it answers the question and do not spend unnecessary time producing the perfect answer. As suggested above, there is nothing wrong with stating the obvious.

Avoid getting bogged down in small parts of questions. If you find a part of a question difficult, get on with the rest of the question. If you are having problems with something, the chances are that everyone else is too.

Don't leave the exam early. Use your spare time checking and rechecking your script.

Don't worry if you feel you have performed badly in the exam. It is likely that the other candidates will have found the exam difficult too. Don't forget that there is a competitive element in exams. As soon as you get up and leave the exam hall, forget the exam and think about the next - or , if it is the last one, celebrate!

Don't discuss an exam with other candidates. This is particularly the case if you still have other exams to sit. Put it out of your mind until the day of the results. Forget about exams and relax.

Part One

Introduction

This first part of this book is intended to provide an overview of international trade. It analyses the rationale for the growth of International Trade and examines balance of payment issues.

Unit 1

International Trade: Introductory Overview - How it Differs from Domestic Trade and the Patterns and Reasons for its Growth, Implications for Balance of Payments

Objectives
On completion of this unit the student should be able to:

- understand why and how domestic trade and international trade differ;

- understand the concepts of absolute and comparative advantage, and how these concepts, in general, tend to support arguments for increasing the volume of international trade;

- appreciate the role played by GATT, WTO and SMP in promoting the growth of trade;

- understand the concept of the balance of payments and the implications of international trade for the balance of payments.

1.1 How International Trade Differs from Domestic Trade

Domestic trade has the following characteristics which apply to both parties:

- a common language and culture;

- the same laws;

- absence of customs formalities;

- usually relatively simple documentation;

- a single currency;

- relatively simple formalities to transport goods from buyer to seller.

International trade is much more complex in that, generally speaking, it has the opposite characteristics to those shown above.

Completing a sale of goods overseas can be much more costly than a domestic sale in terms of marketing efforts, coping with customs formalities, dealing with different legal requirements, and organising relatively complex transport arrangements. Further risk is involved if settlement is in a foreign currency since there is no guarantee of the value in domestic currency terms at the time settlement and conversion are effected. In addition to the risk of buyer default, which can obviously apply in domestic business but which may be more acute with an unknown buyer from overseas, there can be default caused by the overseas government's actions. One of the best-known examples of a change of government causing problems for exporters was that of Iran in 1979.

The immediate reaction to all this is to ask why anyone would wish to trade internationally when domestic trade is so much more simple. The purpose of this book is to explain the theoretical reasons which support the growth of international trade and then to show how organisations such as banks, the International Chamber of Commerce (ICC), and credit insurers can overcome the additional problems posed by overseas trade.

1.2 Why Do Countries Trade?

This question can best be considered by analysing the relationship between consumption and work. Men or women could possibly produce everything they needed by their own labour, but this would not be appealing to most people since they would find their consumption confined to a narrow range of goods. Thus individuals in modern economies do not try to produce exactly what they consume. Instead individuals work for money, which is then used for consumption purposes.

A person's work may help produce only a small range of goods, but the wages paid for that work help that person obtain access to a much wider range of goods and services. The well-known economic concepts of specialisation and division of labour, where people specialise in production of certain items and then obtain other goods through trade, evolved from the above concepts. Trade is therefore necessary if the full benefits of specialisation are to be enjoyed.

Even towns and cities are not normally completely self-sufficient. Those cities that might technically be capable of such self-sufficiency would be worse off without trade because the variety and quality of goods would be reduced if trade did not take place.

Since people gain by trading between each other, then trade will take place naturally without the need for any encouragement. Trade also takes place naturally between countries, since it would be illogical to expect gains from trade to stop at national boundaries.

In recent times, the increase in the importance of services, the political impetus from the development of free trade areas such as the North America Free Trade Agreement (NAFTA) and the Single European Market Programme (SMP), and pressure from organisations such as the World Trade Organisation (the successor to GATT) have resulted in an ever-increasing amount of trade in goods and services between different countries.

1.3 The Concept of Absolute Advantage and Comparative Advantage in International Trade

a) Absolute Advantage

Absolute advantage is an imperfect explanation for the reasons for international trade, but it paves the way for the more cogent argument of comparative advantage which is covered in b) below.

Let us take a very simple hypothetical example to illustrate absolute advantage. A country is said to have an absolute advantage in the production of a commodity if it uses fewer resources than another country to produce a given quantity. Thus for a commodity with only one factor of production, say labour, if one country uses less labour than another to make a given amount of the commodity, that country has an absolute advantage. This concept of absolute advantage assumes that one hour of labour in one country has the same characteristics as one hour in another country.

The following table illustrates this by comparing the hypothetical examples of wheat and car production in Canada and the UK. It assumes that the only factor of production is hours of labour and that an hour of labour in one country is identical to an hour of labour in another country. It also assumes that there are only two countries, only two commodities, and that the goods are of the same standard and quality in each country.

	Table 1	
	WHEAT-Hours to produce one ton	CARS- Hours to produce one
United Kingdom	300 hours	150 hours
Canada	200 hours	250 hours

Relying solely on the information above, it is clear that Canada has an absolute advantage in the production of wheat, since it takes fewer hours of labour in Canada to produce a ton of wheat, but the opposite applies to cars where the UK has an absolute advantage. In addition, 450 hours of labour in either the UK or Canada will produce one car and one ton of wheat in each country.

What happens if trade takes place and Canada exchanges one ton of wheat for one car from the UK?

Canada saves 250 hours by obtaining one car from the UK and not having to produce it itself, and it can use those 250 hours to produce 1.25 tons of wheat. Thus 450 hours of labour, after the trade shown above, leave Canada with one car and 1.25 tons of wheat. This is a net benefit to Canada of one quarter of a ton of wheat.

Conversely, the UK will obtain a ton of wheat from Canada and will then use the 300 hours saved to produce two cars, thus obtaining a net benefit of one car.

This phenomenon arises with international trade because each country specialises in producing the commodity in which it has an absolute advantage. In Canada, 450

oted to wheat, producing 2.25 tons of wheat, one of which is traded for
e UK, 450 hours are devoted to producing three cars, one of which is
. for a ton of wheat. Thus specialisation and division of labour, whether on
f individuals, towns or countries, will lead to a greater total output of goods
vices.

prices at which the trade is arranged will determine how the gains from trade are
ι between the two parties. From the point of view of the UK, the minimum amount
wheat to break even in exchange for one car is 0.5 tons, since 150 hours of labour
produce 0.5 tons of wheat or one car in the UK. From the point of view of Canada, the
maximum amount of wheat it can give in exchange for one car and still break even is
1.25 tons, since in Canada the 250 hours it takes to produce one car could be used to
produce 1.25 tons of wheat. Thus the expected exchange value of one car exported
from the UK to Canada would be somewhere between 0.5 and 1.25 tons of wheat. The
exchange value between these two parameters which is actually applied will determine
the actual split of the benefits of the trade between the UK and Canada.

b) Comparative Advantage

Whilst it is clear that, in principle, two countries can gain from trade when one has an
absolute advantage in the first commodity and the other has an absolute advantage in
the second commodity, this section will show how trade is beneficial in a two-good,
two-country economy even when one country has an absolute advantage in both
commodities. A country is said to have a comparative advantage in a good if its
opportunity cost of producing the good is lower than that of other countries. Likewise,
if the opportunity cost of producing the good is higher than that of other countries, a
country is said to have a comparative disadvantage in that good. In principle, a country
should export goods in which it has a comparative advantage and import goods in
which it has a comparative disadvantage.

Let us look at the following simplified example, where Canada is assumed to have an
absolute advantage in production of both wheat and cars:

Table 2

	WHEAT Hours to produce one ton	CARS Hours to produce one
United Kingdom	400 hours	375 hours
Canada	200 hours	300 Hours

Here Canada has an absolute advantage in both goods as it requires less hours of
labour to produce both cars and wheat in Canada. The opportunity cost of producing
these goods can be shown as follows:

Table 3

	Wheat One Ton	Cars One Car
United Kingdom	1.07 cars	0.94 tons of wheat
Canada	0.67 cars	1.50 tons of wheat

Explanation: If the UK uses 400 hours to produce cars instead of wheat, it will produce 400/375 of a car, i.e. 1.07 cars.

From the above, we can conclude that Canada has a comparative advantage in wheat production, having a lower opportunity cost than the UK, but the UK has a comparative advantage in the production of cars due to the lower opportunity cost of car production in the UK.

Similar principles to those shown in (a) above will apply in the determination of the exchange value of one car. However, if we assume for the moment that one car can be traded for one ton of wheat, what will happen if Canada exchanges one ton of wheat for one car from the UK?

Canada will utilise 500 hours of labour to produce 2.5 tons of wheat, and after exchanging one ton for one car, will have a total of 1.5 tons of wheat and one car. Thus Canada benefits by 0.5 tons of wheat.

What about the United Kingdom under this transaction? The UK will utilise 775 hours in producing 2.07 cars. One car will then be exchanged for one ton of wheat resulting in a net gain for the UK of 0.07 cars.

c)   Comparative Advantage with Money Inputs

Let us retain the two commodities, two countries, one factor of production model already used, but let us assume that the hourly rate of pay for labour is Can$ 40 in Canada and £20 in the UK. On this basis, and excluding any profit element, the price of the goods from our comparative advantage example would be:

Table 4

	Wheat (per ton)	Per car
United Kingdom	£8,000	£7,500
Canada	Can $8,000	Can $12,000

If the rate of exchange between the Canadian $ and the £ is: Can $1.5 = £1, then the cost in sterling terms of wheat produced in Canada is £5,333.33 per ton (i.e. £2666.67 cheaper than UK-produced wheat), and the cost of a car produced in the UK in terms of Canadian $ is Can $11,250 (i.e. Can $750 below the cost of a car produced in Canada).

Much, of course, depends on the rate of exchange between the two currencies, and on the hourly wage rates in the two countries. However, it can be seen that the Canadian $ equivalent of the UK hourly wage is Can $30 at the current rate of exchange, whereas the actual hourly rate in Canada is Can $40. The explanation for this could lie in the fact that the Canadian worker was, in this hypothetical example, more efficient than the UK worker and thus earned a greater hourly rate. In practice this efficiency could be an illusion since the Canadian worker could be better supported by capital equipment.

Whatever the reasons, traders will wish to buy wheat in Canada to sell in the UK and to buy cars in the UK to sell to Canada, ignoring transaction costs of the deal.

d) **Further Comments on the Implications of Comparative Advantage for International Trade**

The purpose of the preceding sections was to demonstrate, in general terms, that there is a gain from trade when countries export goods in which they have a comparative advantage and import goods in which they have a comparative disadvantage. If these 'rules' are followed, there is a total gain from international trade, because the total quantity of goods available expands as a result of more efficient resource allocation.

However, there are practical difficulties which can arise from the implementation of a policy of trade based on the principle of comparative advantage. When imports are suddenly allowed, there are immediate practical problems for the importing country:

- home-based producers could go into liquidation, with resultant unemployment;

- alternatively, home-based producers will reduce wages to compete;

- other sectors of the home economy which relied upon the defunct firms for their income will also suffer.

Logically, the unemployment and loss of trade caused by allowing imports will not last forever, as labour and resources will be moved into other industries with a comparative advantage, but there is considerable argument as to the size and duration of the immediate losses caused when imports are allowed. In general, countries which have liberalised trade have seen economic growth (the 'tiger economies' of the Far East, for example), but there are massive short-term problems when home industry is first exposed to external competition, as can be seen from recent events in Eastern Europe. The analysis of absolute advantage and comparative advantage ignores these issues, as well as ignoring the more obvious difficulties of whether goods produced in different countries are identical, the effects of transaction costs of trade and the implications of exchange rate movements.

This book is not the place for a full in-depth analysis of the various facets of the theory of comparative advantage as a driver of international trade, the purpose here is simply to demonstrate that international trade should normally result in economic growth due to more efficient resource allocation.

1.4 The General Agreement on Tariffs and Trade (GATT), The World Trade Organisation (WTO) and the Single European Market Programme (SMP)

a) **Introduction**

Now that we have studied the theoretical concept of comparative advantage as the basis of international trade, we shall look at how GATT, the WTO and the SMP have begun to overcome the obstacles to trade which exist in practice.

GATT was set up in 1948 and since that time it has initiated various sets of negotiations (known as 'Rounds') to try to reduce or, ideally, eliminate import tariffs and technical standard requirements with a view to encouraging economic growth through world trade. The final GATT Round, known as the Uruguay Round, began in 1986 and was successfully completed in 1995, at which time the WTO came into existence.

b)   The Uruguay Round of GATT

The negotiators' initial target was to reduce tariff barriers by at least a third within five years, but the world's major trading countries finally agreed to more substantial cuts. As a result, the final level of tariffs for industrialised countries fell from an average of 5% to 3.5%. The EU reduced customs duties from 6.8% to 4.1% and the United States from 6.6% to 3.4%. Before the first GATT negotiations in 1947, average tariffs stood at a far higher 40%.

As far as the EU is concerned, the concessions will affect exports valued at around £8.5b and EU imports valued at around £5.5b. More than 40% of EU imports are now duty-free.

The Uruguay Round also simplified non-tariff barriers by examining various rules and procedures that can lead to delays, extra costs and frustration in international trade. These cover such technical questions as customs valuation, pre-shipment inspection and procedures for securing import licences. The changes are aimed at making information on the various requirements more readily available, at keeping paperwork to a minimum and ensuring documents are processed speedily.

In addition, the negotiations examined health and safety regulations and quality standards to ensure these are not covert forms of protectionism. These must be better publicised and notified to the WTO where a more efficient procedure has been set up for handling complaints from aggrieved exporters.

Before the Uruguay Round, services such as banking, consulting and pop music were subject to very different national rules. Now, governments must in effect apply the same conditions to both domestic and foreign suppliers. As a result, a wide range of banking, securities and insurance activities will be answerable to multilateral rules for the first time. Services have been estimated to make up 20% of world trade.

Finally, the Uruguay Round made an attempt to clamp down on intellectual piracy, the copying of the rights of owners of ideas.

c)   The WTO

The WTO came into existence in January 1995. It enjoys equal status with the International Monetary Fund (IMF) and the World Bank and has a potential membership larger than the countries signed up to GATT. It also has a wider remit. GATT supervised just trade in merchandise goods, but WTO covers that and more, with responsibility over trade in goods, services and ideas, or in intellectual property.

One of the WTO's key roles will be to administer the new procedures for settling disputes between its members. Now strict deadlines are set for each stage of the process; non-confidential evidence is made public for the first time; interested parties like consumer groups can give evidence; and no single member can block the decision of the new Disputes Settlement Board.

The creation of the WTO has not entirely eliminated GATT. Countries, which were members of GATT prior to the Uruguay Round, but did not enter into the final Uruguay Round agreement, will continue to be members of GATT. However, they will be unable to make use of the WTO disputes mechanism if they feel that their exports are suffering discrimination under the Uruguay Round provisions.

At the time of writing, 131 countries are members of the WTO, while another 20 countries (including Russia, China, Taiwan and Saudi Arabia) are currently involved in accession negotiations.

d)   The SMP

Up to the mid-1980s, cross-border trade in the EU was subject to the same obstacles as cross-border trade outside the EU.

Examples of such obstacles were:

- all goods were stopped and checked at frontiers;

- most products had to comply with different laws in different member states;

- services, such as banking, transport and telecommunications, were largely insulated from competition from other EU states.

The SMP began with an agreement by member states, signed in February 1986, containing around 270 measures to create a single market. The measures currently adopted relate in the main to:

- the liberalisation of public procurement, which involved making the rules on works and supplies contracts more transparent, stepping up checks and extending the rules to important new areas such as transport, energy and telecommunications;

- the harmonisation of taxation, which meant aligning national provisions on indirect taxes, VAT and excise markets and financial services;

- recognition of the 'equivalence of national standards' harmonisation of safety and environmental standards;

- the removal of technical barriers;

- the creation of an environment which encourage business co-operation by harmonising company law and approximating legislation on intellectual and industrial property;

- the removal of the automatic need for customs clearance when goods cross EU boundaries, although customs authorities have a right to check goods if there are any suspicious circumstances.

e)   Future action on the SMP

The liberalisation of inter-community trade in the EU is by no means complete. In an article in the Financial Times Exporter July 1997 (p2), Margaret Beckett, the UK Trade and Industry Secretary, called for the following improvements:

- better and more even enforcement of the harmonisation rules;

- more liberal energy markets;

- a better single market in financial services and public procurement;

- further progress in telecommunications.

However, despite the problems of harmonisation within the EU, it is quite likely that the SMP will be widened to incorporate a Mediterranean Free Trade Area.

Several Arab and Southern Mediterranean countries are expected to join to create a free trade area which will have tremendous future potential.

1.5   The Balance of Payments (BoP)

a)   Introduction

The remainder of this chapter will focus on the concept of balance of payments, taking the UK position to illustrate what are widely applicable concepts.

We will examine the concept of the balance of payments as a record of international economic transactions. This provides the base for a discussion of the composition of the balance of payments accounts, and the crucial difference between the accounting balance (which must always occur) and economic equilibrium in the BoP. The concept of the terms of trade will then be considered, together with its relationship to the balance of trade. Finally, the problems involved in interpreting BoP statistics will be examined.

b)   The Concept of the Balance of Payments

The BoP may be defined as a systematic record, over a given period of time, of all transactions between domestic residents (including government agencies and military forces located abroad) and residents of foreign nations. For the UK, all transactions are recorded in sterling. When invoiced in foreign currency, the conversion is at the appropriate exchange rate at the time.

By convention, all credit items (i.e. those which increase net money claims on non-residents) enter the accounts with a positive sign (e.g. exports of goods and services, foreign investment in the UK); all debit items (i.e. those which decrease net money claims on foreigners) enter the accounts with a negative sign (e.g. imports of goods and services, UK investment abroad).

c)   The Structure of the Balance of Payments Accounts

The accounts may be divided into three parts:

i)   The current account comprises visible trade (exports and imports of raw materials, foods, manufactured goods, etc.) and invisibles (credits and debits for services such as insurance, banking, shipping, tourism, government expenditure on armed forces overseas and embassies; interest, profits and dividends; and current transfers including payments to/from the EU budget, foreign aid, immigrants' remittances, etc.).

The net balances on the visible trade and invisibles elements are added together to give the current account balance.

ii) Transactions in UK external assets and liabilities (the capital account) includes items such as direct and portfolio investment by foreigners in the UK and by UK residents overseas; sterling and foreign currency borrowing (+) and lending (-) abroad by UK banks; net values for other private sector external financial transactions; changes in UK official reserves and official borrowing from and repayments to the IMF, Bank for International Settlements and overseas central banks.

iii) The balancing item arises because of errors and omissions in the recording of payments, and it is simply the difference between the total value of recorded transactions and the recorded flows of currency. If the item is positive, this means that, in net terms, more foreign currency has come into the country than the total of recorded transactions shows. The value can be extremely volatile.

d) Official Financing

Prior to 1987, the UK BoP accounts were divided into four parts. The additional part arose from the sub-division of 'transactions in UK external assets and liabilities' into government capital flows, and 'official financing' (which included net transactions with overseas monetary authorities, foreign currency borrowing on international financial markets, and the usage of official gold and foreign currency reserves). Today, there remains a separate category for changes in UK official reserves, but it is somewhat more difficult to identify the other elements of official financing in the general capital account. Nevertheless, it should still be recognised that if the overall value of official financing is positive, then there is said to be a BoP deficit (i.e. all other items in the BoP, which are largely private sector items, but including certain amounts of non-financial government sector items, have a negative value in aggregate); conversely, a negative value for official financing means that the BoP is in surplus.

e) Accounting Equality and Economic Equilibrium

There can never be BoP accounts that do not balance in accounting terms, i.e. all negative items taken together exactly balance the sum of the positive items. The reason for this is that the accounts are constructed on the principle of double-entry bookkeeping. Effectively, each item is entered twice into the accounts: first to show the original transaction, and secondly to indicate how it has been financed.

There is an economic equilibrium only when official financing is zero. When a BoP surplus or deficit occurs, a disequilibrium position (an economic imbalance) exists. A persistent deficit or surplus on the BoP is referred to as a fundamental disequilibrium, and this concept is of importance in determining whether or not policy actions are required. However, in recent years there has been an increasing tendency for commentators to focus attention upon the current account of the BoP, in the light of its crucial importance in respect of the country's ability to pay its way internationally. Hence, both private and government sector capital items tend to be grouped together to give a broad measure of the level of net borrowing by the country as a whole.

f) The Terms of Trade and Price Elasticity of Demand

An important concept which affects the current account is the 'terms of trade'. This is defined as the ratio of an index of export prices to an index of import prices (for the UK, prices are expressed in sterling). If the index of export prices falls relative to the index of import prices, the terms of trade are said to 'deteriorate'. An 'improvement' in the terms of trade occurs when export prices rise relative to import prices. In effect,

BoP impact on exchange rate

movements in the terms of trade show changes in the real purchasing power of a given quantity of exports in terms of imports. However, whether an improvement in the terms of trade is good for the country (or a deterioration is bad) will depend upon the reason for the change.

If UK export prices rise due to increased domestic costs, then whilst this will cause the UK's terms of trade to improve (other things being equal), the effects on the balance of trade (and UK output and jobs) will depend upon the elasticity of demand for traded goods.

For most items traded, if the price falls, other things being equal, the quantity demanded will rise. In order to ascertain how trade values are affected by price changes, it is necessary to consider the price elasticity of demand for imported goods, and foreigners' price elasticity of demand for domestic exports. Price elasticity of demand may be defined as

$$e = \frac{\text{\% change in quantity demanded}}{\text{\% change in price of goods}}$$

The following sums up the implications of price elasticity of demand for the sterling values of UK imports and exports:

Table 4

Price elasticity of demand	Whether prices reduced/ increased	Effect on total revenue
e < 1	reduced prices	reduced revenue
e < 1	increased prices	increased revenue
e > 1	reduced prices	increased revenue
e > 1	increased prices	reduced revenue

Thus, if UK export prices can be reduced, then the price elasticity of demand for UK exports must be greater than 1 if the total sterling value of exports is to rise. To reduce the total sterling value of imports, following a rise in the sterling price of imports, the UK price elasticity of demand for imports must also be greater than 1.

The variables usually listed as being important to export/import flows are prices, income, the exchange rate, and the non-price attributes of goods and services (i.e. quality, after-sales service, delivery dates, etc.). The non-price attributes of goods and services are difficult to quantify.

To sum up, a higher price for UK exports may lead to a proportionately greater reduction in demand, thus having adverse effects on the balance of trade. Indeed, as imports become relatively cheaper, these may also increase in volume, thus making matters even worse. However, by contrast, if UK export prices rise in response to an increase in demand for UK goods overseas, this is much more likely to have positive effects on the balance of trade, and the UK economy as a whole.

Part Two

This part of the book commences with an overview of the foreign exchange market. It then analyses the techniques, both internal and external, which could be used by corporates to manage foreign exchange risk, and then assesses the arguments for and against the management of such risks. Finally this part examines the mechanics of money transfer across national boundaries.

Unit 2

The Foreign Exchange Market: Spot, Forward and Futures

Objectives

On completion of this unit the reader should be able to:

- understand that the basic operations of the foreign exchange market and its participants;

- appreciate the factors which influence the forward market in foreign exchange;

- understand how currency futures operate, the factors which affect their pricing, and how a currency futures contract differs from a forward exchange contract;

- appreciate the benefits and drawbacks of the various exchange rate regimes;

- understand the factors which affect foreign exchange rate movements in the spot market;

- appreciate the significance of the monetary arrangements within the EU;

- understand the broad significance of the developments concerning the single European currency, the euro.

Note:

1. The authors wish to acknowledge their indebtedness to various Bank of England Fact Sheets on the Foreign Exchange Market for parts of the section on foreign currency exchange markets in this unit.

2. The single European currency, which is currently due to commence in 1999, is to be called the 'euro'. Readers should take care not to confuse the word 'euro' in the context of a single currency with the word 'euro' in the context of 'eurodollar' or 'eurosterling' etc. The eurodollar market can be looked upon as the wholesale market for depositing and lending dollars, and the euro sterling market can likewise be looked upon as the wholesale market for the deposit and lending of sterling.

   If the 'euro' in the sense of a single currency ever comes into being, then the 'euro markets' for currencies of participating countries will cease to exist, but the 'eurodollar' market, for instance, will continue as the dollar will not be a participating currency.

2.1 Foreign Currency Exchange Markets

The foreign exchange markets enable companies, fund managers, banks and others to buy and sell foreign currencies, if necessary in large amounts. The Bank of England in its May 1996 Fact Sheet reported that global turnover in all currencies had been estimated at around US$ 1.2 trillion per day, with typical wholesale deals being in amounts of US $1m - US $5m and it also reported that the daily turnover in London's banks amounted to around US $464m per day.

These markets have no physical form, in the sense of there being an actual market place where dealers in currencies meet. Rather, the markets exist through a sophisticated network of communications, involving telephone, telex and computer links. London is the world's largest foreign exchange market , largely due to the business generated from other financial activities relating to products such as insurance and eurobonds and to shipping, commodities and banking. In addition, London benefits from its geographical location and time zone, which enables trade to take place with Europe throughout the day, with Japan, Hong Kong and Singapore in the morning and with the USA after 1p.m.

The markets in different countries are closely associated, and exchange market activity is today a truly international occupation. Further, it is often suggested that the foreign exchanges constitute almost perfect markets, with the prices of currencies (exchange rates) responding immediately to the finest changes in demand and supply conditions.

Broadly speaking, participants in the foreign exchange markets can be classified into four categories: customers, banks, brokers and official monetary authorities:

- Customers are companies which use the market because they require foreign currency in connection with their cross-border business;

- Some banks act as market makers who undertake at all times to quote buy and sell rates for foreign exchange transactions. Market makers profit from the spread between their buy and sell rates (bid/offer rates) but they must be ready to adjust prices very quickly to avoid being short of a rapidly appreciating currency or being over-stocked with a rapidly depreciating one;

- Brokers act as intermediaries and make their profit from commissions. Brokers have dedicated communication links with banks (telephones, telex, and computer-based links) and they should be aware at any given time of the trends in the market makers' prices and which market makers currently offer the best deal for their clients' needs;

- In many countries, the official monetary authorities are important participants in the markets, buying and selling currencies with the objective of either stabilising or altering currency exchange rates for economic policy purposes.

Dealings in the market may be 'spot' (where transactions take place at current market prices with settlement being within two business days of the deal being contracted) or 'forward' (where a price is agreed for currency to be delivered at a future date, with settlement being more than two business days after dealing). The Bank of England Fact Sheet (May 1996) gives the following example of how a deal might be carried out.

To execute a *spot* deal, a broker could contact a market maker and ask for the rate, for example 'dollar-mark' (i.e. deutschemarks to the US dollar). The market maker normally quotes a two-way price - that is, he stands ready to bid for or offer up to some standard amount. The *spread* is the difference between these two prices and favours the market maker against the price taker to whom the quote has been made. During interbank trading, where participants know the 'big figures' (i.e. dollars and cents, deutschemarks and pfennigs), the dealer might quote only the *points* (the last two figures of the price). For example, if the rate for dollars against the deutschemark was US$ 1 = DEM 1.5050 -1.5060 then the market maker would quote '50-60': he bids for dollars at DEM 1.5050 and offers them at DEM 1.5060. If the caller wishes to deal, he will *hit*, that is, accept, one side of the price. Confirmation of this oral contract will be exchanged and instructions concerning payment given, and passed on to the settlements staff, who ensure that the respective currency amounts are transferred into the designated accounts on the value date.

As an aside, it might be mentioned that as a precaution against internal fraud, the functions of dealing, confirmation and settlement are segregated to try and avoid problems such as occurred for Barings Bank when Nick Leeson was allowed to fulfil more than one of these roles for the same transaction.

2.2   The Forward Exchange Market

a)   Introductory Example
Example one
A forward deal is an agreement between two parties (usually a market maker and a customer) to set a rate at the outset for a deal (covering a set amount of foreign currency), which is to be settled at a future date (or between two set future dates).

Let us first of all take a highly simplified example to illustrate the principles which lie behind the relationship of the forward rate to the spot rate. Suppose a UK exporter who expects to receive US$ 1m in one year's time asks a UK bank for a forward rate. The following process could take place, given the following information:

> Spot Rate £1 = US$ 1.5
> Eurodollar one-year fixed-interest rates 6%
> Eurosterling one-year fixed-interest rates 10%

The eurocurrency interest rates for convenience can be considered as the wholesale rates of interest.

Action taken by the bank

1   At the outset, the bank will agree a forward rate of 1.4455 (after calculating the consequences of the actions shown below). This rate will ensure that the bank is not at risk from any subsequent exchange rate movements, provided the delivery of the US$ takes place to restore the bank's position to the status quo.

2   Today the bank will borrow US $ 943,396.23 and convert it to sterling £628,930.82 at the spot rate of 1.5.

3   The bank will pay debit interest of 6 % on the US $ funds, but will receive credit interest of 10% on its new sterling balances.

4   In one year's time the sterling balances will total £691,823.90 (with interest).

5   In one year's time the US $ debit balance will amount to US $1,000,000.00 (with interest).

6   At the end of the year, the exporter will deliver US $1m and the bank will pay him £691,823.90.

7   The bank will then use the customer's US$ 1m to repay its own dollar advance.

8   Thus the forward rate will have been calculated at the outset as

$$\frac{1,000,000.00}{691,823.90} = 1.4455$$

The purpose of the above example is to illustrate the general principle that the forward rate is derived from the spot rate and relative interest rate differentials. It does, however, make several simplifying assumptions, which do not apply in practice:

● It ignores the spread between the bank's bid and offer rates for foreign exchange transactions. In practice, these spreads apply to both spot and forward rates.

● It ignores the difference between deposit and lending rates of interest.

● it ignores transaction costs.

● It assumes that the above is the only transaction by the bank in the forward dollar market. In practice, there is endless scope for the bank to match its positions by other deals and by transactions in other markets, such as futures.

● It assumes that there are no government restrictions or tax distortions on such funds transfers.

Note on use of a swap to cover the bank's position
In practice, the bank would almost certainly have covered its potential liability under the forward contract by a swap, rather than by borrowing US $. Thus the bank would have 'swapped' (i.e. paid over to another, possibly American, bank) £ 666,667 in exchange for US $1m. At the end of the year, the principals would have been swapped back (i.e. the transaction would have been reversed) with the UK bank's exporter customer funding the US $1m and the American Bank providing sterling, which would be used to fund the purchase of the dollars from the customer. The two banks would have agreed at the outset an interest payment to cover the fact that the American bank was gaining interest from its increased sterling balances. The interest payment calculation would be based on the differential between the interest rates on dollar and sterling.

A summary of the swap now follows:

1   Today, as soon as the forward contract has been agreed, UK bank and American bank swap. UK bank pays £ 666,667 to the American bank and receives US$ 1m in exchange;

2   The two banks agree to reverse the transaction in one year, with the American bank to make an additional payment to the UK bank to compensate the UK bank for losing out on the higher sterling interest rates.

3   In one year's time, the following transactions take place:

- UK bank receives US $1m from its exporter customer and pays them over to the American bank.

- The American bank pays UK bank £666,667, plus interest as follows:

$$\frac{666,667 \times 0.04}{1.06} = £25,157$$

thus the total sterling paid is £ 691,824.

- Thus the forward rate would be agreed as

$$\frac{1,000000}{691,824;} = 1.4455 \text{ the same result as for currency borrowing.}$$

- For banks this method is more convenient than currency borrowing. In practice, the interest rate differential on the swap might be finer than for straight conventional currency borrowing.

b)   Simplified Explanation of Why Arbitrage will Support the Forward Rate Shown in the above

Example two

If the one-year forward rate had been agreed at a different figure, say, 1.60, and assuming that a large UK corporate could borrow and deposit at the rates shown in the above example, there would have been scope for a risk-free profit as follows:

1   The UK customer could have borrowed, say, US $ 1m for one year , and agreed a forward contract for the bank to sell US $ 1, 060,000 (the balance plus interest) at 1.60 one year forward.

2   The US$ would have been converted to sterling immediately at 1.5, giving a sterling equivalent of £666,666.67, which would have been deposited at 10%.

3   The US $ advance to be repaid after one year's interest would be US $1,060,000.

4   At the end of the year, the sterling balances would have amounted to £733,333.34 and only £662,500 would have been used to acquire the US $1,060,000 at the agreed forward rate of 1.60.

5   Thus there would have been a risk-free profit of £70,833 for the customer.

Obviously if a forward rate of 1.60 was on general offer in such circumstances, there would be an immediate demand by customers for US$ borrowing which would tend to raise the US$ interest rate and there would be a demand for spot sterling which would tend to make spot sterling appreciate. Thus by a process known as arbitrage, market forces would tend to remove this anomaly, thus moving the forward rate back to its logical interest rate parity figure.

Likewise, if the forward rate had been set at 1.40, a profit could be made by customers from borrowing £1m sterling, converting it to dollars, covering forward at 1.40, investing the dollars at 6% and then converting dollar principal in one year of $1,590,000 back to sterling. The resultant sterling sum of £1,135,714 would have exceeded the sterling advance of £1,100,000 (including interest).

c) The Determination of Forward Rates, by Way of Premium, or Discount

When a forward currency is more valuable than spot currency, then the forward rate is said to be at a premium. In the example above, the forward dollar rate would have been at a premium to spot rate because it required less dollars (1.4455 at the one-year forward rate) in exchange for one pound than the US $1.50 required in exchange for one pound in spot deals.

We shall see in Unit 3 that the forward premium is deducted from the spot rate when calculating the forward rate.

The following acronym can be used to determine when a forward currency is likely to be at a premium to spot:

LIP (The forward currency with the **L**ower **I**nterest rates will be at a **P**remium to its spot value)

If we look at the above hypothetical example of the US$ spot being at 1.50 and the one-year forwards being at 1.4455, we can see that the reason behind this is that the US$ interest rates are lower than sterling. Thus, in the course of the operation to cover (or hedge) its position under the forward contract, the bank 'gains' by borrowing at 6% in dollars, but investing the sterling proceeds at 10%. Hence, ignoring bid/offer spreads, the bank can afford to pay out more sterling against one-year forward dollars than against spot dollars. If there is more forward sterling than spot sterling against a given amount of dollars, then forward sterling is weaker and conversely the forward dollar is stronger. Hence the forward dollar is said to be at a premium to spot.

Conversely, when the forward currency is weaker than the spot, it is said to be at a discount to spot. Had the forward rate been at 1.60 at the time the spot rate was 1.50, then it would have required more one-year forward dollars than spot dollars in exchange for one pound. Thus, the forward dollar would have been at a discount to spot in £: $ deals.

We shall see in Unit 3 that a discount is added to spot rates in calculations of forward rates.

The following acronym can be used to decide when a forward rate is at a discount to spot.

HID (The forward currency with the **H**igher **I**nterest rates will be at a **D**iscount to this spot value).

If eurodollar interest rates had been higher than eurosterling (say 10% and 6% respectively) in the above example, the bank would have had to pay 10% interest on its dollar borrowing and would have received only 6% on the sterling deposit. Thus, the bank would have wished to pay out less sterling to its customer under the forward contract, than it would have paid out at spot rates. If there is less forward sterling than spot sterling against a given amount of dollars, then the forward pound is stronger than the spot pound and the forward dollar is weaker than the spot dollar in £: $ deals.

c)   Example of the Use of Premiums and Discounts to Calculate a Forward Rate

For convenience, forward rates are not always quoted outright (1.4455 in example one above). What is quoted is the differential between the spot and the outright forward (the premium or discount). Premiums and discounts are subject to much less fluctuation than spot rates, so quoting differentials requires far fewer changes to any published forward rates. Most writers show the forward premium or discount to be determined by means of the following general equation:

$$\frac{\text{Spot rate x interest differential x time in days}}{360 \times 100}$$

When the forward period is for less than a year, the number of days can complicate the calculation because some countries calculate interest on the basis of a 360-day year, whereas for sterling the number of days is taken as 365. In any event, to be strictly accurate, the effects of compounding should be taken into account for periods of less than one year. In addition, this equation requires adjustment to take account of whether the banks bid or offer rate is used.

Let us for convenience repeat the details in the original hypothetical example:

Spot Rate	US $ 1.50 - £1
One-year fixed eurodollar interest rate	6%
One-year fixed eurosterling interest rate	10%
One-year forward rate	US $ 1.4455 = £1

The forward dollar is at a premium to spot because of the nature of the interest differential, thus the above formula could be used, without concerning ourselves about the number of days since the period is one whole year, to calculate a premium of:

$$\frac{1.50 \times 4}{100} \quad = \quad 0.06$$

The premium will then be deducted from the spot to show an outright forward rate of 1.44.

To be strictly accurate, the formula could be re-written to calculate the premium as:

$$\frac{\text{Spot rate x interest differential x time in days}}{(1+i) \times 360 \times 100}$$

Thus, the premium to be deducted from the spot (ignoring the complexities of periods below one year) to show an outright forward rate is calculated as:

$$\frac{1.50 \times 0.04}{1.10} \quad = \quad 0.0545$$

The outright forward rate would then be	1.5000
less one-year forward premium	0.0545
	1.4455

When the forward rate is at a discount, the lower interest rate should be applied to the denominator of the above formula, and the resultant discount would be added to the spot rate to calculate the outright forward.

If the rate of exchange has a direct quote, that is, a number of home currency units equal to one unit of foreign currency, then the formula will have to be adjusted to take account of this change in quote.

d) The Premium/Discount as a Percentage of Spot

By simply re-arranging the above formulae, the premium or discount as a percentage of spot can be calculated. This percentage should equate to the interest rate differentials in the two centres, subject to the caveats expressed concerning the above calculations.

2.3 The Relationship between Spot, Forward, Relative Interest Rates and Relative Inflation Rates

a) Interest Rates and Inflation

There are many theories which explore the factors which determine the level of interest rates. However, for the purposes of this book we are concerned solely with the link between inflation, real rates of interest and nominal rates.

The nominal rate is the rate actually quoted in a transaction, and the real rate is the nominal rate adjusted to take account of inflation. For new transactions, the nominal rate will incorporate the real rate, plus an allowance for anticipated inflation over the relevant period of the transaction, so as to provide the lender with an anticipated real rate of return. This effect is often called the Fisher Effect, after Irvine Fisher, one of the pioneers of the theory of interest rate determination.

b) Interest Rate Parity

We have demonstrated in the examples in 2.2. above, that there is a link between the spot rate and relative interest rate differentials, and the forward rate for a given future period. If we then assume that real rates of interest are the same internationally, then the difference in the rates of interest on deposits of different currencies with equally creditworthy banks would arise solely from different inflationary expectations.

c) The Link between Interest Rates, Inflation, Forward and Spot Rates

When Fisher's link between inflationary expectations and interest rates holds, when real rates of interest are equalised between countries, and when interest rate parity holds, then spot and forward rates are linked to interest rates and anticipated levels of inflation in the two countries concerned.

There are many obvious limiting assumptions to this general principle, amongst which are:

- the effects of transaction costs;

- the possibility of government restrictions on funds transfer;

- the possibility of government intervention in the markets;

- differential taxation treatment of the transactions in different countries.

d)   The Forward Rate as an Unbiased Predictor of the Future Spot Rate

The forward rate is generally found to be an unbiased predictor of the future spot rate for the relevant period. 'Unbiased predictor' means that if the forward rate is used to predict the future spot rate at the end of the equivalent period of time , then in the long run the sum of the gains will equal the sum of the losses. However, empirical evidence has shown that in the short term the forward rate has consistently undervalued the future spot rate when the spot rate has been rising strongly , and conversely the forward rate has consistently overvalued the future spot rate when the spot rate has been falling rapidly.

2.4   Currency Futures

a)   Introduction

A currency future is a binding obligation to buy or sell a particular currency against another at a designated rate of exchange at a specified future date.

An essential feature of all financial futures contracts is that they are standardised and only the price (i.e. the rate of exchange) is negotiable.

One of the major exchanges for dealings in currency futures is the International Money Market (IMM), an offshoot of the Chicago Mercantile Exchange and the Singapore Mercantile Exchange (SIMEX). SIMEX and IMM jointly clear currency futures contracts, with SIMEX operating at the time when IMM is closed for the night.

Some of the main currency futures contracts on IMM/SIMEX are:

	Unit of Trading
Pound Sterling	£62,500
Japanese Yen	Y12,500,000
Deutschemark	DEM125,000

The quoted price for the currency futures contracts is the rate of exchange, and this is the number of US$ equivalent to one unit of the non US$. The US$ is known as the base currency and the other currency is known as the underlying currency. The rate (i.e. price) in the futures contract is always quoted as a number of base currency units against one unit of the underlying, irrespective of the convention in the cash market when for some currencies the rates may be quoted the opposite way round, depending on whether the rate quoted is direct or indirect (Unit 3 has a description of the meaning of the terms *direct* and *indirect quotes* in connection with rates of exchange).

In addition, there is a Yen/Deutschemark contract for which the quoted price is in a varying number of Japanese Yen (the base currency) against one Deutschemark (the underlying currency).

Other features of currency futures contracts are:

- Standard maturity dates are set for every contract, usually the third Wednesday of a particular month. On the maturity date, the position must be closed out and any resultant gains or losses must be settled between the parties to the contract.

- The designated exchange rate (price) of any particular contract on any particular day will be virtually the same as the forward rate of exchange which would apply for a forward contract with the same maturity as the futures contract. If that were not the case, arbitrageurs would take action to obtain a risk-free profit by taking a position in the forward market to be cleared from the futures market (or vice versa). Effectively, arbitrage brings the forward and futures prices into line.

  As the maturity period of the futures contract nears, the price will come closer and closer to the current spot rate in the same way as forward rates for short maturities are generally very close to spot rates, and at maturity the futures and spot prices would be virtually identical. Any difference could only arise because of different transaction costs.

- The net effect is that for futures contracts which are held until maturity, the overall gain or loss will be the difference between the designated rate on the purchase dates and what is effectively the spot rate at the closing date. However, instead of paying or receiving the net sum in one amount at settlement date, the holder of the futures contract will have arrived at the net profit and loss by way of a series of payments known as variation margins. On some days a gain may have been realised and on other days a loss could have arisen. The daily gains or losses are calculated by a procedure known as marking to market.

- Settlement of the obligation under a futures contract on the maturity date rarely consists of physical delivery of the foreign exchange between buyer and seller. Usually the position is offset by closing out, that is, taking an opposite position in the futures market. Thus, a person with a long position who had purchased a futures contract, would close out by selling a matching futures contract with the same expiry date, whilst a person with a short position would close out the position by buying a futures contract. This close-out is sometimes referred to as a round turn.

- For non-members of the futures exchange, the only way to deal is to do so via an authorised broker, who will charge a commission. There is only one price (i.e. quoted rate of exchange) on a futures contract, and dealing costs are by way of commission, as opposed to the cash market, whereby transaction costs are by way of the spread between bid and offer rates.

b)   Role of the Futures Exchange
The role of a futures exchange such as IMM/SIMEX is to:

- Bring together buyers and sellers in a single location;

- Guarantee the obligations of all parties by means of a clearing house which operates margin calls. This ensures that by means of mark to market operations the potential gain or loss on every contract is settled daily by variation margin payments. (Please see the numerical example which follows under the heading of variation margins.)

● Ensure that prices are transparent, because all transactions are conducted by open outcry on the floor of the exchange, or in a minority of cases by computerised dealing systems, which make prices readily available to all interested parties.

c)   Who Uses the Futures Market?

There are three main categories of users:

1   Hedgers who wish to take an exposure in the futures market which is equal and opposite to their exposure in the cash market. For hedgers, the aim is to ensure that any loss in the cash market due to adverse movements in the exchange rate is compensated for by a gain on the futures market, and vice versa if there is a gain on the cash market caused by favourable movements in the exchange rate. Financial services companies are the main users of the currency futures market as a hedge, although futures contracts are used as a hedge by non-financial services companies in some parts of the world more than in others.

2   Traders/speculators who take a position in the futures market without any matching exposure in the cash market. A buyer of a futures contract is said to have a long position and he will gain if the underlying currency strengthens (i.e. the quoted rate of exchange is higher so that a single unit of the underlying currency is now worth more units of the base currency, usually the US$). A seller of a futures contract is said to have a short position in the futures market. Such a person will benefit if the underlying currency weakens against the base currency and the quoted rate falls.

3   Arbitrageurs deal with the same contract on two separate exchanges with a view to benefiting from an difference in price. (Such arbitrage is said to be common between Osaka and SIMEX.) Arbitrageurs also take positions in the spot/forward market and the futures market if the price of the future does not reflect 'fair value'.

Thus the futures price will usually move in tandem with changes in the forward market. If the prices go out of line, arbitrageurs will undertake dealings which will give them a risk-free profit and these dealings will bring the forward market and futures prices back into line.

d)   Operation of Currency Futures as Speculation
1   *Long position*

A speculator believes that the German mark is likely to strengthen against the US$. He therefore buys (takes a long position) in the futures market. The position could be illustrated as follows: Let us ignore for the time being the complexity of margin calls and simply look at the overall outcome, assuming the futures position is maintained until the maturity date of the futures contract. In this example, the price of the futures contract on the date of purchase is US$ 0.70, and at maturity the price is US$ 0.695.

In this case the speculator has lost money from a long position on the futures market, because the DEM has fallen in value. The amount of the loss is:

125,000 x (0.70-0.695) = US $625 per contract.

A simple explanation of the above calculation is as follows:

- The speculator with the long position had an obligation under the futures contract to buy (or take delivery of) DEM125,000 in exchange for US $87,500 on the maturity date of the futures contract.

- When the contract matured, the spot rate would have been presumably US$ 0.695. Hence the spot value of the DEM125,000 would have been US$ 86,875. Thus the speculator will have acquired DEM 125,000 at a cost in dollar terms of US$ 625 more that their current market value.

2   Short position

A speculator who had expected the DEM to fall in value against the US $ would have sold a contract. Let us assume that this speculators activities covered the same period as those described for the speculator with the long position.

The 'short' would have had an obligation to take delivery of US $87,500 against DEM125,000 on the maturity and would have made a gain of US $625 on a single contract.

Here the 'short' would have had to purchase DEM125,000 on the market at a US$ cost of US $86,875.These DEM would then have been exchanged with the 'long' for US $87,500, giving the short a gain of US $625 under a single futures contract.

e)   Currency Futures as a Hedging Device

If the person with the long futures position had been a German exporter with receivables of US $87,500 due at the date of the maturity of the futures contract, he could have taken out a long position in the futures market in the same way as the speculator described above.

As regards the export proceeds, the exporter would gain from a strengthening of the US$ but would lose if the US$ weakened. However, as regards the position in the futures market, the 'long' would gain from the strengthening of the DEM (i.e. a weakening of the US $), but would lose if the DEM weakened and the US $ strengthened.

If we use the same example as above, the exporter on maturity of the futures position, assuming the US$ export proceeds were received, would have lost US$ 625 on the futures position, but would have gained the equivalent in DEM on the export proceeds due to the strengthening of the US$. These export proceeds would now be worth DEM 125,899.The 'profit ' of DEM 899 could be converted to US$ 625 at the spot rate to cover the loss on the futures position.

Likewise, a German importer with a similar but opposite monetary position would have made a loss in the cash market of approximately DEM899 due to the weakening of the DEM, but this would be compensated for by a gain in the futures market from the strengthening of the US $. The cost in terms of DEM of a payment of US $87,500 would be DEM125,899, but there would be a gain in the futures market of US$ 625, which could be converted into DEM 899 at the prevailing spot rate.

f)   Variation Margin Payments

The ultimate gain or loss of US$625 in the example above would be realised incrementally. Each day at close of business the contract is marked to market, and the resultant gain or loss is settled by the contract holder by way of what are called variation margin payments to the clearing house. If we look at the DEM currency futures contract described above, let us assume that the contract had been held for five business days only. and that we are looking at the position from the point of view of a long.

Day One close of business price is US$ 0.705.
Here the long would receive US$ 625 from the clearing house calculated as 125,000 x (0.705-0.700)

Day Two closing price is US$ 0.695.
Here the 'long' pays a variation margin to the clearing house of US$ 1250 calculated as 125000 x (0.705-0.695)

Day Three closing price remains unchanged thus no variation margin payments are made either way.

Day Four closing price is US$ 0.690.
Here the 'long' will pay a variation margin of US$ 625 calculated as 125,000x (0.0.695-0.690)

Day Five closing price is 0.695.
Here the position must be settled as this is the maturity date of the contract. In order to settle the position, the 'long' will receive US$ 625 calculated as 125,000 x (0.695-0.690).

The net position of the long will be as follows:

Day One   625
Day Two   (1,250)
Day Three   nil
Day Four   (625)
Day Five   625
Net Loss   (625)

The above demonstrates how the net profit or loss on a futures position is gained incrementally over the time that the contractual position is held, and that, ignoring the time value of money, the overall gain or loss will equate to the difference between the time the position was taken and the time when the position was closed out.

There is no obligation to hold the futures contract to maturity. The contract can be closed out any day, and the overall gain or loss will then be crystallised.

It should be noted that there is an initial margin payment to be made to the clearing house at the time a position is first taken in the futures market. The amount of this initial margin will vary from contract to contract, and it is the amount considered necessary by the clearing house to cover the maximum possible loss on the contract in a single day.

This initial margin can be looked upon as a refundable deposit held as security to cover the risk that obligations under the daily mark to market procedures will not be met.

The variation margin payments then adjust for daily changes in the value of the position, by means of mark to market calculations as shown in the previous examples. It should be noted that all futures contracts have minimum daily price change, sometimes called a tick. This is a relatively small amount. For example, in the case of the DEM contract which we have used for illustration purposes, the minimum daily price change in one contract is US $12.5.

2.5 Overview of the Difference between a Forward Exchange Contract and a Currency Future

Forward exchange contracts are the outcome of negotiations between a bank and a corporate. Normally the contracts will be exercised only on their expiry date, although it is possible to negotiate for early termination or extension, using a variation of the close-out procedure. These instruments are known as over-the-counter instruments, because of the need to enter into individual negotiations.

Futures contracts, however, are known as exchange traded instruments, because their terms and conditions are standardised and the only variable feature, the price, is publicly available during trading hours.

Gains and losses on futures contracts are settled daily, whereas with forward exchange contracts, the gain or loss is settled in a single amount, at the maturity of the contract. Forward contracts are a contingent liability which can reduce available borrowing facilities because of the possibility of a loss on a close-out. This cannot apply to futures as gains and losses are settled daily and obligations are guaranteed by the clearing house. (Full details of close-outs, with numerical examples, are given in Unit 4.)

In the UK, the use of currency futures by non-bank corporates to manage foreign exchange exposures is comparatively rare. Indeed currency futures are not traded on LIFFE. The main problems of futures are their inflexibility (although sophisticated corporates could construct a 'tailor-made' hedge by employing an appropriate combination of different futures contracts), their administrative complexity due to margin calls, and the tax and accountancy complications which can arise when a future and its cash flows do not exactly match the currency exposure for which they have been employed.

However, banks and other financial services institutions do employ currency futures as one of their range of techniques for managing currency exposure mismatch.

2.6 Different Types of Exchange Rate Regimes

The unit so far has largely ignored the potential effects of government intervention in the exchange markets. The remainder of the unit will analyse the effects of the different degrees of intervention by governments in the markets.

In theory, there are many different forms of exchange rate regimes which may be operated. At one extreme there is the rigidly fixed exchange rate regime, where currencies are given fixed parities by administrative edict. (In this case, the normal exchange market mechanism is by-passed entirely.) At the other extreme, exchange rates may be left to float cleanly, with no deliberate official interference, so that the market forces determine the exchange rates. Between the two extremes there are many variants of the basic forms, each involving differing degrees of official exchange market intervention.

a)   Clean Floating Exchange Rates

The advocates of clean floating exchange rates, where market forces alone determine the spot rates, argue that a country's monetary and fiscal policies should not be constrained by the need to defend a fixed exchange rate. They believe that exchange rates should be determined by the supply of and the demand for currencies in the free market.

The main disadvantages of clean floating are:

- It can cause uncertainty in relation to business transactions.

- Time lags in adjustment may make the BoP situation worse in the short run (i.e. when home currency has depreciated, relative export and import prices alter before relative quantities traded. This results in the J-curve effect where the BoP current account initially deteriorates and only subsequently moves into surplus.).

- Domestic inflationary pressures may be generated as import prices rise from a depreciation of home currency.

- Official financial discipline may be undermined as there will be no requirement to curb inflationary expectations to protect the exchange value of home currency.

The main advantages of a freely floating currency are that:

- It provides an automatic adjustment mechanism for dealing with BoP problems. Thus, in theory, a surplus on the BoP should result in an appreciating exchange rate which will then cause a rise in relative export prices resulting in the surplus being eroded. However, leaving aside the problems of elasticity of demand and the J-curve effect, it must be remembered that there are many factors other than the BoP position which cause exchange rate movements.

- There should be no need for restrictive measures by the authorities to interfere with trade because of the need to defend a fixed rate.

- At least in theory, international currency reserves are no longer required (except for occasional stabilisation of the exchange rate) since the government no longer has to choose the exchange rate that it believes to be 'correct'.

b)   The Factors which Influence Exchange Rate Movements in a Clean Floating Regime

In the short term, the most important factor affecting exchange rates is usually the relative levels of interest rates, or rather the anticipated short-term changes therein.

The following quote from an anonymous writer in the *Daily Telegraph Business News* of 5 July 1997 illustrates this phenomenon:

The pound soared yesterday as investors poured money into the currency in anticipation of an early rise in interest rates....Against the mark, the pound was up 1.5 pfennigs to 2.96, a six year high and against the dollar it rose 0.25 cents to 1.6875.

Obviously, at times such as when sterling was ejected from the Exchange Rate Mechanism (ERM) in September 1992, speculative pressures rather than factors such as relative interest rates (and expectations of changes therein) can affect the short-term value of a currency. However, under 'normal' economic circumstances, short-term interest rates play a major role in short-term currency movements.

To the extent that exchange rates are allowed to float freely, any factor which affects the component parts of the current account and/or capital account of the BoP, and hence which affects the supply and demand conditions on the currency markets, may potentially influence the pattern of currency exchange rates. The major factors affecting international trade and capital flows include:

i) Real economic variables, e.g. consumer tastes, real income levels, and technological innovation

ii) Relative inflation rates

iii) Relative interest rates, which must be viewed in real terms with expectations of inflation rates taken into account

iv) Non-economic factors, e.g. the social and political environment

v) Government policies, which may often affect the BoP indirectly.

c)   The Theory of Purchasing Power Parity.
This offers an explanation of movements in currency exchange rates in the long run. The theory states that the equilibrium exchange rate between any two currencies is that rate which equalises the domestic purchasing powers of the two currencies, e.g. if a bundle of goods has a price of £5 in the UK and $10 in the USA, then according to the theory the equilibrium exchange rate is £1 = $2. Trade flows will bring about this value by altering the supplies of and demands for currencies.

There are major problems with the theory:

● the theory ignores the existence of international capital flows, as well as the transport and transactions costs associated with trade;

● it fails to recognise the fact that many goods/services are not traded internationally;

● the role of news is not considered. In the real world major unpredicted events often occur and these unexpected events are often referred to as news. Exchange rates respond very quickly to new information, so news can often have an immediate impact on spot rates. However, prices of goods normally change much less quickly as a result of news, so the relevant price indices do not adjust as quickly as the spot rates.

A study by R. MacDonald (1988), *Floating Exchange Rates Theories and Evidence,* Unwin Hyman, reviewed 14 empirical studies of the purchasing power parity (PPP) theory.

Ten rejected the PPP as a long-run predictor of exchange rates, whilst four showed the PPP as being valid in the long term. The general consensus is that there are substantial deviations from the PPP in the short run, but the case is less clear in the long term.

On the other hand, the *Economist* uses the McDonalds hamburger as its benchmark for assessing the validity of the PPP on the basis that this is a standard product which is sold in over 100 countries. In April 1997 the *Economist* reported that the average American price of a 'Big Mac' cost US $2.42, whereas the dollar equivalent of the Swiss franc price at the current rate of exchange was $4.02, and the Chinese equivalent was only $1.16. Those who believe that the PPP holds and who are satisfied that the 'Big Mac' represents an adequate basket of goods will conclude that the Swiss franc is overvalued and the Chinese yuan is undervalued. The paper then reported that research by Robert Cumby of Georgetown University showed that the past year's 'Big Mac' survey had correctly forecast the direction of the movement of six out of seven currencies whose value had changed by 10% or more.

In the 1990s the growth of the markets in derivatives such as futures and options, has meant that only about 25% of spot deals now occur as a result of trade related transactions. Thus, factors other than the BoP and PPP theory must influence spot-rate changes.

It is therefore suggested that the main relevance of the PPP is when trading partners' inflation rates differ. In such cases it is likely that the exchange rate of the currency issued by the high-inflation country will depreciate in the long run.

d)   Adjustable Peg System (Bretton Woods System)

From the end of the Second World War until the early 1970s most countries were on the 'adjustable peg' system (often referred to as the Bretton Woods system). The basic notion was that a fixed-parity exchange rate system would provide a stable basis for international economic activity, but that allowance must be made for the occurrence of fundamental changes in the underlying real economic positions of countries participating in the scheme. Thus, although countries agreed to intervene in the foreign exchange market and to implement appropriate economic policies in order to hold the value of their currencies to within a narrow band around fixed-dollar par values, in the event of a 'fundamental disequilibrium' on the BoP they were allowed to adjust their exchange rates.

The problem of the adjustable peg system comes from:

●   the difficulty in defining what is meant by fundamental disequilibrium;

●   deciding when and by how much to adjust the exchange rate;

●   the risk of retaliation (including competitive devaluation when one currency has been adjusted downwards in value to try and improve the balance of payments position);

●   speculative pressure can also make the problem worse, as was seen when sterling left the European Monetary system in 1992.

The benefits of the adjustable peg, which were certainly apparent in the less volatile economic conditions prior to the 1970s , are that this type of 'fixed' rate system may encourage international trade (through the reduction of exchange rate risks), and longer-term business planning is made easier. Governments are also encouraged to pursue sound economic and financial policies (especially in respect of inflation) in order to support the existing exchange rate.

e)   Managed Floating

Since 1972, with the exception of the period October 1990 to September 1992, the UK has followed a regime of 'managed floating'. The Bretton Woods system had proved to be too inflexible, particularly when confidence was lost in its base, the US $. Initially, it was hoped that floating would be only temporary, until an alternative basis for a worldwide fixed-rate system could be found. However, managed floating has worked reasonably well, and is widely used throughout the world.

A serious practical problem with clean floating is that exchange rates may become unstable, and financial uncertainty may be created. With managed floating, the authorities intervene to iron out short-term fluctuations, leaving market forces to determine long-term trends; the problem here is in deciding when a movement is short-term. Furthermore, there are limits to the extent to which the authorities are able to intervene since their stock of foreign currency reserves is finite.

2.7   Monetary Arrangements within the EU

For many years, there has been much debate on the view that the EU should move towards full economic and monetary union (EMU). At the extreme, EMU may imply the introduction of a single EU currency, with monetary controls being implemented by a European Central Bank, and with a much greater power over economic policy being vested with EU institutions.

a)   The European Monetary System (the EMS)

The objectives of the EMS relate primarily to the stabilisation of EU currency exchange rates (i.e. the creation of a zone of currency stability in Europe), and mutual financial support for member states. Nevertheless, the successful operation of the EMS is generally seen as being an important first step on the road towards EMU, and the requirements for its operation are a necessary pre-condition for the successful implementation of a single European currency.

In the light of developments in connection with the single European currency (the euro, which is explained in detail in section 2.8 below)) there could be substantial changes in the operation of the EMS. Readers should study reputable financial journals to keep abreast of any changes which may arise. Currently, the main elements of the EMS are as follows:

a)   Limitation of EU members' currency exchange rate fluctuations. The ERM operates on the basis of two criteria:

    i)   A 'parity grid' arrangement sets upper and lower intervention rates for each pair of currencies - initially the grid allowed a maximum +/- 2¼% relative movement (with 6% for a small number of currencies). However, following extreme turbulence on the currency exchange markets in July 1993, the band was widened to +/- 15% for most currencies (officially as a temporary expedient). Once any two currencies reach their relative value limits the central bank of the country with the weak currency is required to sell the other country's (strong) currency on the foreign exchange markets, whilst the central bank of the country with the strong currency is required to buy the weaker currency. These purchases and sales, with supporting currency 'swaps' among central banks if required, continue until pressure is taken off the currencies' values and they are pushed away from their parity limits.

ii) The European Currency Unit Divergence Indicator - the ECU (see below) is used as the basis for calculating a central rate for each member's currency. Each currency is allocated divergence limits against its ECU central rate. In the event of a currency's value moving beyond 75% of the maximum deviation permitted, it is expected that the relevant government will take some form of remedial action. For a country with a weak currency this may involve the raising of domestic interest rates or perhaps a tightening of fiscal policy. For a strong-currency country, some form of expansionary policy might be expected. Thus, the ECU indicator relates to the broad position of a currency relative to all other EU currencies taken as a group.

In addition, the values of individual currencies may be realigned within the parity grid and in terms of the ECU central rate if the fundamental economic relationships underlying the exchange rates alter. However, the EMS rules are intended to impose a certain amount of financial discipline on member states; hence it has been argued that realignments should only take place as the very last resort.

Whilst all EU states are members of the EMS, the UK's membership of the ERM is suspended following the September 1992 currency crisis when sterling moved from its official central parity with the DEM of 2.95 to a market-driven rate of 2.35.

b) An exchange rate stabilisation fund provides both short- and medium-term financial support for EMS members with international payments problems. Members pool 20% of their gold and dollar reserves with the European Monetary Co-operation Fund (EMCF) in return for ECUs. These 'official' ECUs, created as a bookkeeping exercise by the EMCF, may be used for transactions between members' central banks (and certain other monetary institutions), for example, for settling debt incurred as a result of ERM operations. All EMS members participate in the EMCF swap arrangement, although members who are not a party to the ERM are not required to do so.

c) The Very Short-Term Financing Facility relates to arrangements whereby participants in the ERM open to each other very short-term credit facilities in their own currencies. The credit is provided for purposes of exchange market intervention, and is made available automatically and in unlimited amounts when currencies reach their official intervention limits. Repayment of funds may be temporarily deferred if the borrower's international payments position deems this to be appropriate.

b)   The Operation of the EMS and Recent Developments

Between its establishment, in March 1979, and September 1992, the EMS would appear to have operated reasonably successfully, although it was necessary to realign currency exchange values on a number of occasions. The benefits of the system could be summarised as:

- despite these realignments, the exchange rates of ERM participants were more stable than those of the other main Western currencies, and to the extent that this helps to support business confidence this is clearly a positive outcome.

- as the EU now accounts for over a half of all the UK's overseas trade, a more stable relationship between sterling and other EU currencies should help both exporters and importers in their business planning and pricing decisions.

- if UK producers were no longer able to rely upon a depreciating value for sterling in order to maintain their international competitiveness, they would be under greater pressure to hold down wage and price rises, in the face of generally modest inflation rates within the rest of the EU (failure to hold down UK inflation rates relative to other ERM members could have dire consequences for UK output and jobs, assuming that devaluation of sterling was not seen as an acceptable option).

- the political advantage of full membership of the EMS cannot be ignored, its supporters say, especially in the light of the Maastricht Treaty, which sees full participation of all EU members in the EMS as a vital part of the first stage for achieving EMU.

However, some critics of the ERM have argued that:

- its operation has tended to undermine economic growth within the participating countries. Immediately prior to September 1992, there was a strong body of opinion within the UK supporting a reduction in interest rates to stimulate economic growth to offset the effects of the recession. However, in order to keep sterling at its agreed central parity (commonly known by the DEM rate of 2.95), UK interest rates had to be kept relatively high.

- in order to achieve exchange rate stability in the longer term, it is necessary that the economic performances of the countries involved should be broadly similar. In practice, the UK, for example, seems usually to be at a different stage of the business cycle from its EU partners,

- the successful operation of the EMS may require the subordination of domestic policies within individual countries for the purpose of harmonising economic performance. That co-ordination of policies would be directed towards bringing inflation rates in member states to similar low levels, reducing interest rate differentials between the respective countries, and limiting the extent of BoP imbalances in the medium term. Whilst these objectives command substantial support, convergence of economic conditions is not easy to achieve in practice.

- when sterling was put into the mechanism in October 1990, there was much controversy over the parity chosen. Indeed the fears that, because of sterling's importance in international trade and investment, its entry into the ERM might generate instability within the mechanism (especially relative to the DEM) and thus require excessive exchange market intervention, proved to be well founded.

● excessive speculation against sterling caused it to be withdrawn from the ERM in September 1992. This had a damaging effect on the economic credibility of the UK government at the time.

b)   The European Currency Unit (ECU)

The ECU is a 'basket' of EU currencies, and may be regarded as a form of international money, performing all the functions which are normally associated with money assets. Thus, for example, the ECU is used as a means of payment between EU central banks; it is used as the unit of account for both the intervention and credit elements of the EMS; and it may be used for its medium of exchange, store of value, unit of account and standard of deferred payment properties in private sector financial transactions.

Since its introduction in March 1979, the ECU has developed along two distinct routes. The official ECU, as explained above, is a key element in the operation of the EMS. This is quite separate from the private ECU, which is created by private institutions out of the ECU's component currencies, and may be bought and sold on the foreign exchange market. Both individuals and companies may hold ECU assets (such as bank deposits and marketable securities) and incur ECU liabilities (such as bank loans and securitised debts). The major advantage in using the ECU is that its international purchasing power value is likely to be more stable than the corresponding values of the individual component currencies.

The value of the ECU is calculated as a weighted average of all EU members' currencies. The weights are set to reflect each member's relative economic size in terms of gross national product and the importance of its trade within the EU, and the access which each member has to short-term financing from the EMCF. Formerly, the weights were reviewed every five years, but since the ratification of the Maastricht Treaty the weights are to remain fixed at their current values, which were determined in June 1989.

2.8   The Single European Currency (the Euro)

a)   Background

The Maastricht Treaty envisaged that there could be irrevocable fixing of exchange rates within the EU, as the precursor to the introduction of a single EU currency. This move would be subject to a qualified majority of EU states being in favour (meaning that no one member state could veto the move) and at least seven member states meeting the economic convergence criteria. Amongst the convergence criteria are:

● annual inflation to be not more than 1.5 % higher than the average inflation rate of the three lowest inflation EU countries.

● annual budget deficit must not exceed 3% of gross domestic product (GDP), unless the ratio 'has declined substantially and continuously and comes close to 3%, or alternatively the excess is only exceptional and the ratio remains close to 3%'. It is unclear exactly what is meant by these additional clarifications to the 3% rule.

- total government debt must not to exceed 60% of GDP, unless the ratio is sufficiently diminishing at a satisfactory pace (again it is not too clear what the precise meaning is).

- the exchange rate must have been within the normal bands of the ERM for at least two years.

There have been some interesting financial manoeuvres as certain EU governments try to meet the fiscal criteria above, the most spectacular being the proposal in May 1997 by the German Finance Ministry to revalue the gold reserves and pass the paper gain off as public sector income.

An important aspect of the Maastricht Treaty is the proposal that a European Central Bank (ECB) will be established, and will take up its full powers when a single EU currency is introduced (within the conditions stated above). It is intended that the ECB will be politically independent, and will have as its main objective the maintenance of price stability within the EU.

Each member state's own central bank will be maintained as part of the European System of Central Banks, and will be expected to support the ECB in the implementation of agreed policy. Each individual central bank will also be required to be politically independent of its own country's government. The responsibilities of the ECB will include the conduct of EU monetary policy and control, foreign exchange market operations, the holding and management of member states' foreign exchange reserves, and the promotion of the smooth operation of EU payments systems.

However, as might be expected, there have often been substantial reservations expressed about such objectives, and in particular a number of EU governments have resisted strongly any proposal which would undermine their independent sovereign powers in respect of economic policy. Others have questioned the wisdom of having a single interest rate covering countries at different stages of economic development. A single interest rate could be set too low for countries where demand needs to be adjusted downwards to offset inflationary pressures (as with the UK's current situation), while in other parts of the EU the single rate of interest might be too high, because lower rates are needed to stimulate economic activity.

b)   Proposed Timetable for Implementation
At the time of writing developments are very fluid and readers must study the quality press and publications such as *The Treasurer Economist* and *Financial Times* to ascertain the current state of play. However, on current proposals the timetable for implementation is as follows:

- In Spring 1998, list of participants will be announced.

- In May 1998, a decision will be made regarding the conversion rates. These conversion rates are the rates at which national currencies will be exchanged irrevocably for the euro.

- From 1 January 1999, EMU is due to begin.

- From January 1999 to December 2001, there will be a three-year transition period during which national currencies and the euro could run in tandem. It would be up to individuals and companies to decide whether to adopt the euro or use national currencies, or to use a mixture of the two. Notes and coins of national currencies will continue to be legal tender.

● During the period January-July 2002, notes and coins in national currencies will be exchanged for the euro. From July 2002, national coins and notes of participating countries will cease to be legal tender.

c) Which Countries are Likely to Participate in the First Wave in January 1999?

It is difficult to predict, and political upheavals could easily change the position. However, at the time of writing, the acronym BAFFLING could be used to name the likely participating countries in the first wave in January 1999.

> Belgium,
> Austria,
> France,
> Finland,
> Luxembourg,
> Ireland,
> Netherlands,
> Germany

Countries which may wish to join, but may not meet the economic criteria are: Portugal, Italy, Greece, Spain. Countries which have the right to opt out are: Sweden, the UK and Denmark.

d) What Exchange Rates will be Used to Convert the Participating Currencies into the Euro?

There are three possible scenarios for the conversion rates:

● Market rates at 31 December 1998 could be used. The danger here is that countries might seek to engineer an artificial depreciation of their own currency to support exports. This could lead to 'competitive devaluations' by each participant, which would result in turbulence on the foreign exchange markets at the end of 1998.

● Alternatively, the choice could be the average rates over the two-year period leading up to 31 December 1998. The benefit here is that any artificial currency depreciation towards the end of 1998 would have a limited effect on the ultimate conversion rate, unless such depreciation was relatively large. It is difficult to predict likely consequences of this method, but average rates for the two-year period and spot rate on 31 December 1998 could be very different if the last few months were dominated by volatile markets.

● The final possibility to announce that the current central ERM parity rates would apply. If the market believed these rates to be credible, this would be the optimal method in that it would provide certainty. However, if towards the end of 1998 the market decided that these rates were not sustainable, there would be an incentive for massive amounts of currency speculation such as took place in 1992 when sterling was forced out of the ERM.

e)   What are the Implications of the Euro for Europe's Foreign Exchange Markets?

Once again it is hard to predict what could happen, but if the euro goes ahead on schedule the following could occur:

- The euro would replace the DEM as a reserve currency for central banks.

- The official ECU will be exchanged for euros on a 1:1 basis.

- Foreign exchange markets in participating currencies will ultimately cease to exist. This will mean that the participating banks and brokers will lose a lucrative source of income from the spreads on forward and spot rates, and from their trading in options and futures in the participating currencies. Research commissioned by the Geneva-based international trade union body FIET has predicted that large numbers of banking jobs could be lost throughout Europe if the single currency is fully adopted.

- The euro may become the unit of pricing for some commodities now denominated in US$, paper/pulp being possible examples as they are produced in Europe but currently priced in US$.

- The government bonds of participating countries, both those in existence as at 1 January 1999 and those subsequently issued, will be denominated euros. There will be a common basis for interest, that of the euro, but the different credit quality of the various governments will ensure that there is some difference in bond yields of participating governments.

f)   Issues for Consideration by Businesses Prior to 1999

Large companies involved in cross-border EU trade will switch as soon as possible, since most of their settlements will be by way of bank accounts denominated in euros.

However, retail and medium-sized companies will still use national currency during the transitional period of 1999-2002 and will only switch to the euro at the last minute. This is because retail customers will tend to use national currencies as there will not be any notes and coin denominated in euros until 2002.

Businesses which have dealings in national currencies issued by potential participants should ask these trading partners whether there will be a need to offer dual pricing for the transitional period from 1999 - 2001. Such businesses should check whether their cash management systems could cope with the transition. For instance, euros could be received for credit to a DEM account or vice versa.

Pricing will be transparent within countries which have adopted the euro. Thus, differential pricing of the same goods in different participating EU countries will ultimately be as difficult as it would be in two different American states. Indeed, differential pricing in participating countries will probably survive only for goods and services which are difficult to move across national boundaries. Examples are perishable food and services such as French television, which runs on a different standard from the rest of Europe.

The price transparency, accompanied by the existing single European market provisions, will make it easier for efficient and flexible companies in one participating EU state to take over less efficient companies which have traditionally concentrated on national markets. This assumes that there will be no EU directive restricting such actions.

Transaction costs will be lower with a single currency. Indeed, the European Commission has estimated that there will be savings of 0.4% of European GDP. This estimate is to some extent backed up by statistics from the IFO quoted in the *Economist* of 15 July 1997, which show that administrative costs have moved down as a percentage of foreign exchange transactions within the EU from just over 0.60% in 1986 to just over 0.45 % in 1995. The European Commission has estimated that transaction cost savings for one year will cover the cost of adapting IT systems to cope with the euro, but it is hard to see how these IT costs can be reliably estimated. It is particularly important to discuss lead times both internally and externally for any conversions required to the company's IT systems.

It may be as well for businesses to ascertain what facilities the company's bank is going to offer during this transitional period regarding the conversion of euros into and out of sterling. In addition, if the UK were to join the single currency, competition between UK banks and other participating member countries' banks would become more intense. For instance, a UK company could appoint a German bank as its main bank or German companies could appoint UK banks to this role, depending on the quality and price of service offered.

Naturally, from a UK perspective, much depends on whether the UK opts out and which countries, if any, actually participate.

2.9 Self-assessment Questions

Question 1
Define the term *spot* in connection with a foreign exchange deal.

Question 2
Briefly indicate the main benefits of clean floating exchange rate regimes.

Question 3
Briefly indicate the main criteria set out for economic convergence between participating states in connection with the single European currency?

Question 4
Why is it generally considered important that there should be economic convergence between participating states in connection with the single European currency?

Question 5
Name one potential business which, in the short term, may lose money and experience a fall in employment if the euro comes into being.

Question 6
What factor will, according to the European Commission, generate cost savings which will offset the costs of conversion of IT systems for the euro.

Question 7
What factors determine whether a forward currency is at a premium or discount to its spot value?

Question 8
What assumption is made about interest rates by those who link inflation, interest rates, spot and forward rates.

Question 9
Explain the difference in the way the monetary obligations of a forward contract are settled as opposed to those of a currency futures contract.

Question 10
What is meant by the initial margin paid on a futures contract and why is an initial margin required?

(Answers given in Appendix VI)

Unit 3

Spot Rates and Forward Rates

Objectives

On completion of this unit the student should be able to:

- **define a rate of exchange and appreciate how rates are quoted;**

- **differentiate between the bank's buy and sell rates;**

- **understand the difference between fixed forward exchange contracts and option forward exchange contracts;**

- **be able to calculate fixed forward rates and option forward rates using the spot as a base and adjusting for the premium or discount.**

3.1   Rates of Exchange and How They are Quoted

A rate of exchange is the price of one currency in terms of another. In the UK, rates of exchange are normally quoted as the number of foreign currency units, which are equivalent to one pound sterling. This method of quotation is termed the indirect quote. By contrast, most EU currencies are quoted as the number of units of home currency which are equivalent to one unit of overseas currency. This is termed the direct quote. In this book we concentrate on the indirect quote method.

Bank dealers normally quote two rates of exchange, one the buying rate and the other the selling rate. Since the bank wishes to make a profit on the 'turn' (i.e. the difference between the two rates), it will use the higher rate for buying and the lower one for selling. Thus, if the rate quoted for the US $ is 1.8525-1.8535, the bank will buy at 1.8535 and sell at 1.8525. The reason for this is quite logical. The bank wants to receive as many dollars for each pound as possible when it buys them and the bank wants to give out as few dollars as possible in exchange for every pound when it sells them.

When dealing with exchange rates, **always work from the point of view of the bank.** Hence the rule is:

BUY HIGH: SELL LOW

3.2   Spot Rates of Exchange and the Exchange Risk

A spot rate of exchange is a rate of exchange for a foreign currency transaction which is to be settled within two working days of agreeing the rate.

As you will know from your economics studies, spot rates of exchange can fluctuate violently from day to day or week to week. Hence, for example, UK traders who have receipts or payments denominated in foreign currency which are to be settled in the future, cannot be sure of the ultimate sterling amounts if the currency is simply converted at the spot rate ruling on the date of receipt or payment. This uncertainty as to the exact ultimate sterling receipt or payment is called the exchange risk. The exchange risk runs from the moment a commercial contract is entered into which involves receipt or payment of foreign currency, and it lasts until the currency receipt/payment has been converted into sterling. The management of exchange rate exposure in its widest sense is analysed in Units 7 and 8.

3.3 Forward Exchange Rates and Forward Contracts

A forward rate is a rate of exchange which is fixed now for a deal which will take place at a fixed date, or between two dates, in the future. Forward contracts can be arranged to cover periods for as long as 10 years ahead in some of the major currencies, but periods of between one and 12 months are the most common.

When a forward currency is more valuable than the spot currency, the forward is said to be 'at a premium'. Likewise when the forward currency is less valuable than the spot, it is said to be 'at a discount'. The term 'par', in connection with forward exchange, means that the spot and forward currencies are of equal value; hence, the spot rate and the forward rates are identical.

A forward exchange contract is a binding contract between a bank and its customer for a purchase or sale of a specified amount of a particular foreign currency at an agreed future date, at a rate of exchange fixed at the time the contract is made.

When the contract is a 'fixed' forward exchange contract, the future date at which the transaction will take place is a fixed date, whereas when the contract is an 'option' contract, the time at which the transaction will take place is any time within a specified future period. The customer has the 'option' to choose which day within the specified future period he will complete the transaction, but apart from this particular aspect the 'option' contract is just as binding as a fixed contract.

While the advantages of forward contracts will be considered later on in more detail, it should be briefly mentioned that the main purpose of a forward contract is to enable exporters to know what the home currency value will be for an amount of foreign currency which will be received at a future date, and likewise to enable UK importerss, say, to calculate the sterling cost of a foreign currency payment which is to be made in the future. When the exact timing of the receipt or payment is uncertain, option forward contracts could apply.

When traders do not take out forward exchange contracts or use some other method to cover known receipts or payments of foreign currency in the future, they are gambling. Nobody can predict with any accuracy what the spot rate will be on any future date, so that the amount of home currency received or paid will be an unknown quantity. The trader may, of course, benefit if the spot rate has moved in his favour when the transaction actually takes place, but he could equally well lose if the rate has moved against him.

3.4 How to Calculate Forward Rates for Fixed Forward Contracts

The forward rate is calculated by using the spot rate on the day of calculation and adjusting for the appropriate premium or discount. Let us consider two examples, bearing in mind that this book always works on the UK system of indirect quotes for exchange rates.

Example 1

On 1 January a UK bank quotes the following rates for the US $:

Spot	*One month forward*
1.9425-1.9435	0.53c-0.43c pm

The bank's one-month forward rates, quoted on 1 January for deals which will take place on 1 February, will be calculated as follows:

Buying rate

Spot (buy high)	1.9435
Deduct: Premium	0.0043
One month forward fixed buying rate	1.9392

Note

a) A premium is always deducted from the spot rate because if a currency is more expensive in terms of the pound, fewer units of it will be needed to be equivalent to a pound.

b) The bank must deduct when it quotes currency at a premium, but it can deduct either 0.53 cents or 0.43 cents. The bank will always use the premium which is most favourable to it. As the bank will wish to obtain as much currency as possible for every pound, given that it must deduct either 0.43 cents or 0.53 cents from the spot rate, the bank will deduct 0.43.

Selling rate

Spot (sell low)	1.9425
Deduct: Premium	0.0053
One month forward fixed selling rate	1.9372

Note

The premium is always deducted from the spot rate. The bank has a choice between deducting 0.43 cents or 0.53 cents. As the bank wishes to give as little currency as possible in exchange for a pound, it deducts the greater amount, 0.53 cents.

Example 2

On 1 January a UK bank quotes the following rates for the French franc:

Spot	*One month forward*
9.43-9.44	3c-4c discount

On 1 January the bank will quote its one month forward fixed rate for French Francs as:

Buying rate
Spot (buy high)	9.44
Add: Discount	0.04
One month forward buying rate	9.48

The bank must add the discount to the spot rate. It has a choice of adding 4 cents (or centimes) or 3 cents. Because the bank always acts in its own best interests, it will add 4 cents to the spot rate, thus buying as high as possible.

Selling rate
Spot (sell low)	9.43
Add: Discount	0.03
One month forward selling rate	9.46

The bank must add the discount to the spot rate. It has a choice of adding 4 cents or 3 cents. Because the bank always acts in its own best interests, it will add 3 cents, thus selling as low as possible.

Note
The basic rules can now be seen. Spot buy high sell low. Adjustment for premium or discount - deduct premium, add discount. Use the premium or discount which favours the bank.

3.5   The Importance of the Decimal Point

In the first US$ example above, the relevant forward premium was expressed as 0.43 cents. One dollar equals one hundred cents; hence, one cent is 0.01 of one dollar. Since 0.43 cents must be less than one cent, the expression of this amount in dollar terms must be 0.0043.

In the first French franc example, the relevant forward discount was expressed as 4 cents (or centimes). One cent is 0.01 of a franc, hence 4 cents must be expressed as 0.04 of a franc.

The following table should prove useful:

Table 1

Country	Name of Currency (with standard abbreviations)	Unit quoted for premium or discount	Relationship of Currency Unit to unit quoted for premium or discount
United States	Dollar ($) (USD)	Cent (c)	100c = 1USD or 1c = 0.01USD
Canada	Dollar ($) (CAD)	Cent (c)	100c = 1CAD or 1c = 0.01CAD
Netherlands	Guilder (NLG)	Cent (c)	100c = 1 NLG or 1c = 0.01NLG
Belgium	Franc (BEF)	Centime (c)	100c = 1BEF or 1c = 0.0lBEF
Ireland	Punt (IEP)	Pence (p)	100p = 1 IEP or 1p = 0.01 IEP
Germany	Deutschmark (DEM)	Pfennig (pf)	100pf = 1 DEM or 1 pf = 0.01 DEM
Portugal	Escudo (PTE)	Cent (c)	100c = lPTE or 1c = 0.01PTE
Spain	Peseta (ESB)	Cent (c)	100c = 1 ESB or 1c = 0.01 ESB
Italy*	Lira (ITL)	Lira (ITL)	1ITL = 1ITL = 1Lira
Norway	Kroner (NOK)	Ore (ore)	100ore = 1NOK or 1 ore = 0.0lNOK
Denmark	Kroner (DKK)	Ore (ore)	100ore = 1DKK or 1 ore = 0.01DKK
Sweden	Kroner (SEK)	Ore (ore)	100ore = 1 SEK or 1 ore = 0.01 SEK
Japan*	Yen (JPY)	Yen (JPY)	1JPY = 1JPY = 1 Yen
Austria	Schilling(ATS)	Groschen (gro)	100gro = 1ATS or 1gro = 0.01ATS
Switzerland	Franc (CHF)	Centime (c)	100c = 1CHF or 1c = 0.01CHF
France	Franc (FRF)	Centime (c)	100c = 1FRF or 1c = 0.01FRF

*   For the Italian lira and the Japanese yen, the unit of currency is also used for quotation of the premium and discount. For all other currencies, premiums and discounts are quoted in smaller units.

†   These standard abbreviations (e.g. USD) are used on international money transfers and in dealing transactions to show the name of the currency. These abbreviations are acceptable worldwide. The standard abbreviation for the £ is GBP and for the European currency unit is XEU.

3.6   How to Calculate Rates for Option Forward Contracts

An option forward contract means that the customer can select on which d⌐ complete the transaction, provided the choice falls within the option ⌐

The bank will calculate the forward rates which it woul⌐ maturing on the first and last days of the option contract rate which was more favourable to itself.

Example 1

On 1 January an importer enters into a contract to buy goods ⌐ $100,000. Payment has to be made when the goods are shipped an⌐ some time during March.

The rates ruling on 1 January are:

Spot	2 months forward	3 months forward
1.9425-1.9525	0.90c-0.80c pm	1.40c-1.20c pm

If the importer enters into a forward exchange contract to cover the exchange risk, he will require an option forward contract, with the option period of between two and three months. The bank will calculate the rates as follows:

Spot (sell low)	1.9425	Spot	1.9425
Less: Two months premium	0.0090	Less: Three months premium	0.0140
Two months forward rate	1.9335	Three months forward rate	1.9285

The bank will choose 1.9285 since this is the most favourable selling rate for the option period. Remember that a bank sells currency to importers, and buys currency from exporters.

Example 2

Using the rates quoted in Example 1, the bank would calculate its option buying rate for the proceeds of exports invoiced in dollars to be received in March as:

Spot (buy high)	1.9525	Spot	1.9525
Less: Two months premium	0.0080	Less: Three months premium	0.0120
Two months forward buy	1.9445	Three months forward buy	1.9405

The bank will therefore quote 1.9445 as its option buying rate since this is the higher rate and hence the one more favourable to the bank.

Note

In practice, bank dealers are involved in a very competitive market. For major customers, the bank may not quote the better of the two rates from its own point of view, but it may compromise by setting the rate somewhere between the two extremes. However, for exam purposes, you must complete the calculation as shown above.

3.7   Self-assessment Questions

Question 1
An importer needs to pay DEM50,000 today to his supplier. Spot rates are quoted as:

Spot 3.07-3.08

How much will the bank debit to the sterling current account of the customer to enable him to settle the amount? Ignore all commissions and any other incidental costs.

Question 2
An exporter has received DEM100,000 today and asks his bank to convert them to sterling and to credit his sterling account. What amount will be credited today? Ignore all charges and incidental costs and use the spot rates in Question 1.

Question 3
Calculate the bank's three months forward fixed buying and selling rates for French francs, using the following data:

Spot	9.2950	9.3055
1 month	1.75c pm	1.40c pm
2 months	3.90c pm	3.25c pm
3 months	5.50c pm	4.70c pm

Question 4
Using the rates quoted in Question 3, calculate the bank's forward buying and selling rates for a one to two months forward option contract.

Question 5
Suppose you were an exporter who anticipated receiving FRF 50,000 some time after one month but before the end of two months. Explain what is meant by the one to two months forward option buying rate which you calculated in Question 4.

Question 6
Express 0. l pfennigs in terms of Deutsch marks.

Question 7
Calculate the bank's one month forward fixed buying and selling rates for the Japanese yen using the following information:

Spot	235	236
1 month	1 JPY pm	0.5 JPY pm

Question 8
Calculate the spot to one month option forward buying and selling rates for the yen, using the information in Question 7.

Question 9
An exporter took out an option forward contract with his bank. Can the exporter avoid fulfilling his obligations because this is an option forward contract?

(Answers given in Appendix VI)

49

3.8   Past Exam Question

Your customers, International Venturers Ltd, act as middlemen and have received an order from a German buyer for motor vehicles to be supplied from the USA. Details of the orders are as follows:

Order from Germany to International Venturers Ltd

Date received	27 August
Quantity	30 vehicles
Price	DEM10,000 per vehicle
Delivery	One lot by 27 November
Payment terms	Three months after shipment

Order from International Venturers Ltd to USA

Quantity	30 vehicles
Price US	$3,500 per vehicle
Delivery	One lot by 17 November
Payment	Terms on advice of shipment

On the day on which the order was received by International Venturers Ltd, they covered their US $ commitments forward but decided to risk the difference in exchange on the DEM receivable. Using the following rates of exchange to the £ sterling, and ignoring interest or commissions, calculate International Venturers Ltd's profit or loss on the transaction. Assume that payment was made on 10 November in US $ and received on 20 February the following year in DEM.

27 August

Spot	*Forward*
US $ $1.7702-1.7722	1 month 1.20-1.10c pm
	3 months 3.40-3.30c pm
	6 months 6.60-6.50c pm
DEM DM4.46-4.47	1 month 3.10-3pf pm
	3 months 9-8.90pf pm
	6 months 17.50-17.40pf pm

20 February following year
DEM DM3.73-3.74

(Specimen Answer given in Appendix VI)

Unit 4

Close-outs and Extensions of Forward Contracts

Objectives

On completion of this unit the student should be able to:

● understand the contractual position between a bank and a customer as regards forward contracts;

● appreciate the close-out procedure which a bank must take if a customer fails to fulfil his contractual obligations under forward contracts;

● understand why the forward contract involves a contingent liability on the part of the customer, and why a bank 'marks a limit' on the customer's account when it grants a forward contract;

● be able to deal with extensions to forward contracts, as opposed to straight close-outs.

4.1 The Contractual Position

A forward exchange contract is a binding contract and the customer must ensure that he fulfils his obligations thereunder.

It can happen that a customer, through no fault of his own, cannot complete the agreed transaction. In this case the bank will have to 'close out' the deal.

If on the due date an exporter cannot provide the currency which the bank has agreed to buy from him, the bank will calculate the cost of the sale of the relevant amount of foreign currency at the spot rate ruling on the date of default. The bank will also calculate the amount which it would have credited to the customer had the forward contract been fulfilled. The bank will then pass the net debit or credit to the customer's account.

Likewise, where an importer is concerned, the bank will calculate the amount which would have been debited had the forward contract been completed; it will then calculate the value of the currency at the bank's spot buying rate ruling on the date of default. The net debit or credit will again be passed to the customer's account.

4.2   Examples of Close-out Procedures

Example 1

The bank agreed to enter into a forward contract to buy US $100,000 from an exporter. The contract was a fixed forward contract for a transaction due to take place in three months' time.

Unfortunately, the proceeds were not received by the exporter and he had to default. What action would the bank take? The rates on the date the forward contract was agreed were:

Spot	Three months forward
1.8525-1.8535	0.94c pm 0.89c pm

The spot rates three months later were 1.92-1.93.

Answer

The agreed forward buying rate would be:

Spot	1.8535
Less: Premium	0.0089
Three months forward	1.8446

On the due date the bank would calculate as follows:

(Dr) Cost of sale of $100,000 at 1.92	£52,083.33
(Cr) Proceeds of purchase of $100,000 at 1.8446	£54,212.30
Net credit passed to customer's account	£2,128.97

Example 2

Using the rates in Example 1, calculate the amount to be passed through the account of an importer where a forward exchange contract was made for the bank to sell US $100,000 for completion in three months and a close-out has to be effected.

Answer

The agreed forward rate would be:

Spot	1.8525
Less: Premium	0.0094
Three months forward	1.8431

On the due date the bank would calculate as follows:

(Cr) Proceeds of repurchase of $100,000 at spot rate 1.93	£51,813.48
(Dr) Amount which would have been debited had forward contract been completed ($100,000 at 1.8431)	£54,256.42
Net debit to customer's account	£2,442.94

Example 3 (Covers Partial Close-outs)

An importer had arranged a fixed forward contract for the bank to sell DEM50,000 at 3.94. On the maturity date the importer informed the bank that he only required DEM40,000.

The spot rates ruling on the date of the maturity of the forward contract were:

Spot   **DEM3.90**   **DEM3.91**

Answer

The bank will sell the DEM50,000 at the agreed forward rate, but will buy back any unwanted currency at the spot rate.

(Dr) DEM50.000 at 3.94	£12,690.36
(Cr) DEM10,000 at 3.91	£2,557.54
Net debit	£10,132.82

Example 4 (Covers Early Close outs)

If a customer realises that he will be unable to fulfil his obligations well before the expiry date, he can effectively fix the loss or gain under the close-out at maturity by arranging a matching forward contract with the same expiry date.

For example, an exporter may have entered into a three-month fixed forward contract for the bank to buy US $ 100,000. One month after the commencement of the contract, the underlying commercial deal may fall through. In this instance, the exporter could arrange a two-month fixed forward contract for the bank to sell him US $100,000.

Two months later, at maturity of the two forward contracts, the bank will notionally debit the customer with the sterling equivalent of the two-month forward contract, and will notionally credit him with the sterling equivalent of the original three-month forward contract. The net difference between these two amounts will be debited or credited to the account.

The net effect of such a transaction is to fix the loss/gain on the close-out from the time of the creation of the matching forward contract.

Note

Banks are developing new variations of the forward contract and, in practice, the customer should check out what the bank's procedures and advice would be for his particular circumstances, should this situation arise.

4.3   Why is it Necessary for the Bank to Close Out?

Many customers believe that the bank is somehow punishing them when they are debited on a close-out. (Their thoughts if they are credited on a close-out are no doubt different.) However, there is no element of punishment.

If the bank enters into a forward contract with a customer, the bank will take action to offset any exchange risk to itself. The action could take the form of a temporary 'swap', as described in Unit 2, or some other way of covering the exchange risk could be undertaken. However, the point is that once a bank agrees a forward contract with a customer, the bank itself enters into a contractual obligation with a third party so as to match or offset its own risk. The bank's customer must fulfil his obligations under the forward contract so that the bank can honour its 'matching' commitments with third parties.

If the customer cannot, or will not, fulfil his obligation under the forward contract, then the bank must take action to enable it to honour its matching obligation to the third party.

The procedure adopted is the close-out procedure shown in the examples above at 4.2.

In effect, the bank makes the customer fulfil his obligations under the forward contract by using the spot market. The resultant gain or loss is then credited or debited to the customer's account, as shown in the examples.

4.4 Why the Bank 'Marks a Limit' on the Customer's Account When it Agrees a Forward Contract

If the customer fulfils his obligation to deliver, or to take delivery of the appropriate amount of currency, then the bank is not in any danger. However, if the customer fails to fulfil those obligations, the bank is at risk, since there is a possible loss on the close-out. If the customer has insufficient funds to meet the loss on the close-out, then the bank will have incurred a bad debt.

Thus, banks usually mark up a limit when they agree a forward contract. The amount of that limit is the bank's estimate of the maximum possible loss on any close-out. This amount will depend on the length of time to the contract's maturity and on the volatility of the currency concerned. The limit which is marked is usually between 10% and 20% of the sterling value of the forward contract.

The risk involved in a forward contract is called a 'contingent liability', in that it is a liability which may or may not occur. The contingent liability, however, must be borne in mind by the bank, and that is why a limit is marked on the customer's account. Such a limit will reduce the scope for borrowing in other ways, say, by overdraft. Indeed, the bank's criteria for deciding whether to agree to a forward contract are very similar to those for granting an overdraft.

4.5 Close-out/Extension of Forward Contracts

When a customer cannot fulfil the transaction where a forward contract has been entered into, the bank will 'close out', as has already been described.

If the customer exports, the bank will buy the currency at the agreed forward rate and sell it to the customer at the spot selling rate ruling on the day the contract should have been completed.

The resultant profit or loss will be the customer's.

Likewise, if the customer imports, the bank will sell at the agreed forward rate and buy it back at the current spot rate.

It sometimes arises that the underlying commercial transaction is merely delayed instead of being totally frustrated. In such a case, the customer would be able to fulfil the contract in due course but after the date(s) specified in the forward contract.

In these cases, where the completion of the forward contract will merely be delayed, the bank will extend it. What happens is that the bank 'closes out' in the normal way but then arranges a new forward contract for completion at the time the customer expects to have the necessary currency.

In an extension the new forward rate is always based on the spot rate used in the close-out. Discount or premium is applied to the spot close-out rate in the normal way to calculate the new forward rate.

Example

The bank arranged a forward contract with its exporter customer to buy 40,725 DEM at 4 DEM = £1.00. The receipt of proceeds was delayed and the exporter asked for an extension of one month fixed. Show the transactions on the customer's account if the rates ruling on the maturity date of the forward contract were:

Spot	3.95-3.96
One month forward	2 pf-l pf premium
(Ignore commission.)	

Solution

a) On the date of maturity of the original forward contract, the bank will close out in the usual way:

(Cr) The bank will buy DEM40,725 at the agreed rate of 4.00 =	£10,181.25
(Dr) The bank will sell DEM40,725 at the spot rate of 3.95 =	£10,310.13
Net amount debited to customer's account	£128.88

b) On the same date as in (a), the bank will agree a new forward contract, one month forward fixed:

Spot close-out rate	3.95000
Deduct: Premium	0.01000
	3.94000

c) One month later, provided the exporter delivers the currency, he will be credited:

40,725 at 3.94 = £10,336.29

Notes

a) Those of you who have previously studied for this subject may have learned the 'diagonal rule' as a means of calculating forward rates. If you know this rule, and can apply it correctly to calculate the forward rate on an extension, then continue to use it. However, many students are totally confused when applying this rule to extensions. As a result, the diagonal rule is not used in this book.

b) The reason the bank applies the spot close-out rate to extension is that it has already made its 'turn' from the difference between buying and selling rates on the original contract.

4.6   Self-assessment Questions

Question 1

What is the name of the procedure which a bank adopts if its customer cannot or will not fulfil his obligations under a forward contract?

Question 2

An exporter customer had arranged a fixed forward contract for the bank to buy currency. The underlying export sale has fallen through. Briefly explain the procedure that the bank will follow.

Question 3

An importer has agreed a fixed forward contract for the bank to sell him currency. He does not now require that currency. Briefly explain the action which the bank will take.

Question 4

Would your answer to Question 3 differ if the forward contract had been an option forward contract?

Question 5

A customer who is involved in importing and exporting usually has a number of forward contracts with his bank at any one time. Does the fact that the bank has agreed forward contracts affect the amount which it is willing to lend on overdraft?

Question 6

The bank has agreed a forward contract with an importer to sell him DEM30,000 at 3.82. The importer does not require the DEM, because the underlying commercial deal has fallen through.

Set out the entries on the customer's account on the date of default, if the spot rates are:

Spot	DEM3.79	DEM3.80
One month	0.50pf pm	0.25pf pm

Question 7

Using the information in Question 6, set out the entries on the customer's account if he asks for a one-month forward fixed extension, instead of cancelling the contract entirely.

Assume he takes delivery of the DEM on the due date of the extended forward contract.

Question 8

Your exporter customer has arranged a forward contract whereby the bank will buy US $80,000 at 1.8875. On the due date, the customer can only provide $60,000. Set out the entries on the customer's account if the spot rates on the date of default are:

Spot	$1.88	$1.89
One month	0.43c discount	0.48c discount

Question 9

Using the forward contract details and the spot rates shown in Question 8 set out the entries on the customer's account if the customer delivered US $90,000 on the due date.

Question 10

Using the forward contract details and the spot rates shown in Question 8, set out the entries on the customer's account if he had to have the original forward contract extended by one month fixed. Assume the customer delivered the US $80,000 on the maturity date of the extended forward contract.

(Answers given in Appendix VI)

4.7   Past Exam Question

A London merchant contracts:

a) to buy 200 tons of chemicals in two equal shipments at DEM 479 per ton from Germany on terms which require an immediate payment of 50% and the balance on 1 August;

b) to sell at NOK900 per ton both shipments to a Norwegian buyer who agrees to pay during August when the goods are expected to arrive in Oslo.

On 1 July the merchant asks his bank to make the initial payment and to cover him forward for the other transactions.

The second transfer to Germany is subsequently made and a payment received from Oslo following arrival of the first shipment on 6 August. However, a fire partially destroys the chemical plant and the second shipment cannot be made. Its purchase price is refunded in full to the merchant, who sells it to his bank on 1 September, at the same time closing out the balance of the forward contract.

On the basis of the rates quoted below and exchange commission at 1.5 per mille maximum £25 per transaction (not to be charged on the close-out), calculate the net profit to the London merchant.

1 July spot	9.58-9.5825	17.0825	-	17.0875
one month forward	2 - 1 pf prem	7.75	-	3.75 ore prem
Two months forward	3 - 3 pf prem	12.5	-	8.5 ore prem
1 September spot	9.55-9.56	17.00	-	17.005

Please refer to the following note if you are not sure how to deal with commission.

Note on Commission

Rates vary between banks and you are not required to memorise actual rates. If the question gives a rate, it will usually be expressed as 'so much per mille (%o)'. This means £per £1.000, or $ per $1,000 etc.

a) Formula: Commission $= \dfrac{\text{P x Rate per mille}}{1,000}$

    Example: Commission on £5,000 at 2%o $= 5,000 \times \dfrac{2}{1,000} = £10$

b) If a question quotes a maximum amount of commission, take care not to exceed this.

c) **Add** commission when debiting a customer's account.

d) **Deduct** commission when crediting a customer's account.

(Specimen Answer given in Appendix VI)

Unit 5

Foreign Currency Options/Pure Options

Objectives

On completion of this unit the student should be able to:

- **appreciate the reasons for the development of currency options;**

- **understand the terminology which applies to currency options;**

- **appreciate how a currency option differs from a forward contract;**

- **evaluate the customer benefits of currency options;**

- **be aware of the competition which exchange traded options provide;**

- **understand the customer benefits of currency options provided by banks, as opposed to the customer benefits of exchange traded options;**

- **appreciate the implications of hybrid products, such as cylinder options, for both banks and customers.**

5.1 The Reasons for the Development of Foreign Currency Options

Foreign currency options give customers far more flexibility than is provided by the conventional, traditional forward contract.

Before defining these options, let us examine the main causes of customer dissatisfaction with the traditional forward exchange contract.

Customers' complaints when currency options were not widely available were as follows:

a) The customer could have lost money if he failed to comply with the forward contract and the bank had to close out. Customers conveniently chose to forget that, if rates had moved in their favour, they could be credited with the net profit on a close-out;

b) Customers did not appreciate that the term 'option' in an option forward exchange contract related solely to the period during which the agreed transaction could be carried out. Many customers wrongly thought 'option' in a forward contract meant that the customer could choose whether or not he wished to complete the transaction; in other words, the customer thought the word 'option' gave him the right to walk away from the forward exchange commitment if he so wished;

c) The following situation was a particularly strong cause of customer dissatisfaction:

    i) An option forward exchange contract was arranged;

    ii) The customer could not fulfil it because of a breakdown in the terms of the underlying commercial contract;

    iii) The bank had to debit the customer on close-out because the spot rates had moved against the customer;

d) Customers felt aggrieved when they took out forward contracts and were then unable to take advantage if spot rates on the date of execution had moved in their favour.

These complaints led to the development of the foreign currency option, which, at a price, overcomes all the real or perceived customer complaints regarding traditional forward contracts.

The development of the foreign currency option as a widely available foreign exchange risk management tool can indeed be said to be 'market-driven'.

5.2 What is a Foreign Currency Option?

It is an agreement whereby a customer can pay a premium to the bank for the right but not the obligation to buy from or sell to the bank a specified amount of a foreign currency at an agreed rate of exchange. Generally speaking, the option can be exercised, at the customer's discretion, at any time up to a specified expiry date, or it can be allowed to lapse by the customer at the expiry date.

As an alternative to exercising the option or allowing it to lapse, it may be possible to sell the option back to the bank. (This situation is covered later.)

Watch your terminology, and that of the exam question, when dealing with currency options (the common abbreviation of foreign currency options). In forward contracts the rates are always quoted from the bank's point of view so that the fixed forward buying rate relates to the rate at which a bank would buy, and the fixed forward selling rate relates to the rate at which a bank would sell to a customer. In currency options, however, it is the customer who purchases the right to buy from or sell to the bank the specified amount of foreign currency at the agreed rate of exchange.

5.3 Glossary of Terms Relating to Foreign Currency Options

Writer or Grantor

This is the bank (or any other organisation) which, in exchange for a fee, known as the 'option premium', grants the right but not the obligation for a purchaser to buy or sell the currency at the agreed rate during a specified period.

Purchaser

This is the person, usually a customer, who pays an option premium to bank for the right but not the obligation to deal under the terms of the option.

Holder

This can be the original purchaser of the option, or someone to whom the original purchaser has assigned the rights under the option.

Call Option and Put Option

A call option gives the purchaser the right to buy the currency from the writer whilst a put option gives him the right to sell to the writer. Exporters will normally require put options. Importers will normally require call options. You are reminded that the terminology differs from that of forward contracts.

Base/Counter/Underlying Currencies

The base currency (sometimes called the counter currency) is usually US dollars or sterling. The underlying currency is foreign currency, e.g. Deutschmarks, which the customer will wish to buy (call option) or sell (put option) to the writer. For example a sterling-based UK exporter who invoices in Deutschmarks would take out a put option in which the base currency would be sterling and the underlying currency would be Deutschmarks. The put option would give the customer the right but not the obligation to sell a certain amount of Deutschmarks to the bank during a specified period at a pre-set rate of exchange.

Strike Price

This is the rate of exchange which will be applied if the currency option is exercised.

Option Premium

This is the 'up-front' payment made by the purchaser to the writer and it is usually paid at the time the option contract is granted. Occasionally, however, for approved customers the 'up-front' condition can be waived so that the premium, plus interest, is paid on the exercise of the option or at maturity. The option premium is usually denominated in the base currency, i.e. US dollars or sterling, and is expressed as a percentage of the principal amount. The option premium is determined by the following main factors: the strike price and its relationship to the relevant spot and forward rates; the period of the option; and the volatility of the exchange rates of the underlying currencies.

Intrinsic Value at Maturity

An alternative to exercising the option is to sell it back to the bank at its intrinsic value (if any). The intrinsic value at maturity is the difference between the strike price and the current spot rate of the underlying currency.

For example, a call option may have the following characteristics on the expiry date:

Strike price	: 3.40
Base currency	: Sterling
Underlying currency	: Deutschmarks
Current spot rate	: 3.10
Amount of base currency	: £12,500
Type of option	: Call option

The intrinsic value on the expiry day would be:

a) Deutschmarks, which can be bought by the customer under the terms of the option:

(12,500 x 3.40) = DEM 42,500. at a cost of £12,500;

b) Sterling equivalent of DEM 42,500 which the customer could sell back at the current spot rate:

DEM 42,500 @ 3.10 = £13,710;

c) Intrinsic value:
£13,710 - £12,500 = £1,210.

Thus, on the expiry date, the bank would be prepared to pay £1,210 (ignoring dealing costs) if the holder decided that he wished to sell the option back to the bank, rather than exercise it.

Therefore, if the underlying commercial deal had fallen through, the importer could sell the option back to the bank for its intrinsic value.

Intrinsic Value and Time Value Prior to Maturity
Prior to maturity, the amount of the premium consists of two elements, the intrinsic value and the time value. For a European option prior to maturity, the intrinsic value (if any) in terms of base currency is calculated from the difference between the value of the underlying currency converted at the strike rate (the 'option value') and the value of the underlying currency converted at the forward rate for the unexpired period of the option (the forward value). The principles are similar to those shown in the intrinsic value calculation immediately above, except that for intrinsic values on the expiry dates, the spot rate, as opposed to the forward rate, is the one applied. Please refer back to Unit 2 (2.4 and 2.5), where similar principles are illustrated in the use of forward rates for the pricing of futures prior to maturity.

For a call option, when the option value is below the forward value, then the option is said to be 'in the money', as it has intrinsic value. When the option value of the underlying currency at the strike price is more than the value at the appropriate forward rate, the call option is said to be 'out of the money'. However, out-of-the-money options (whether puts or calls) can never have a negative intrinsic value, since the holder is not obliged to exercise them.

Put options work on the same principles, but they are in the money when the option value is above the forward value and they are out of the money when the option value is below the forward value. When the option value and the forward value are the same, then the option is said to be 'at the money'.

The other element of the premium is time value. The greater the time to maturity, and the greater the volatility of the exchange rate for the currency pairs, the greater the time value.

When an option is first arranged, the writer will use a computer program to calculate the 'fair value' of an option, but then the premium which is actually quoted is adjusted in the light of the writer's own position in the market and market demand.

Notification Date, Exercise Date, Expiry Date

These terms are synonymous. Once the expiry date has passed, the option will automatically lapse unless the holder has notified the writer that he intends to exercise his rights.

Settlement Date

Once the holder has notified the writer that he intends to exercise the option, he has up to two working days to settle the deal. For example, if a call option, with sterling as the base currency, expires on a Monday, the holder must notify the writer by that day of his intention to exercise the option. If notification takes place on the Monday, the holder has until close of business on Wednesday to provide the necessary sterling to purchase the underlying currency from the bank.

Note

It is too late to notify the writer on Tuesday of the intention to exercise, since the option will have lapsed at close of business on Monday.

American Options and European Options

With an American option, the holder can notify the writer of his intention to exercise the option on any business day, between the granting of the option and the expiry date. Notification can be for all or for part of the amount of currency covered by the option. The final settlement date for an American option will be two working days after the expiry date. Note that some banks may limit the number of drawdowns by placing a minimum drawing amount.

With European options, there is a single expiry date and a single settlement date. The holder can only notify the bank of his intention to exercise on the one expiry date, and he must then complete the underlying deal within two working days.

The option premium is higher for American options because of the greater flexibility for the customer, and the greater risk to the writer of the option who must manage the overall options book.

American options are readily available in the UK.

Over-the-counter Options (OTC Options)

These are foreign currency options which are negotiated as separate, individual contracts between the purchaser customer and the writer bank. Thus the OTC option can be tailor-made to meet a customer's specific needs. Each bank has a minimum amount below which it will not grant currency options.

Exchange Traded Options

These are currency options which are dealt with on organised exchanges. At one time such options were available via London International Financial Futures Exchange (LIFFE), but LIFFE no longer offers this type of option. However, exchanges in the USA and other parts of the world offer currency options.

Exchange traded options are standardised and cannot be tailor-made to meet specific customer needs. Quite often banks themselves take out exchange traded options to cover their own obligations on OTC options which the banks have written.

5.4 Comparison of Forward Exchange Contracts and Foreign Currency Options

Table 1

Forward Contracts	Foreign Currency Options
a) These are firm and binding contracts between the customer and his bank, whereby the customer has an obligation to deliver or take delivery of the foreign currency in accordance with the terms of the contract.	a) This is the right but not the obligation, for the customer to deliver or take delivery of foreign currency in accordance with the terms of the agreement.
b) If a customer fails to fulfil the terms of the forward contract, the bank will 'close out'. In this case the customer will have to stand the loss, or he will receive the gain, depending on the spot rate of exchange on the day of close-out.	b) The currency option gives the holder the right but not the obligation to deal on the terms set out. There is no question of a close-out taking place. The holder has three choices on the expiry date of a currency option: i) exercise it ii) abandon it iii) sell it if the currency option has an intrinsic value.
c) If a bank grants a forward contract, the bank usually marks up a contingent liability facility of between 10% and 20%, of the full contract value. This facility is marked to cover the fact that, if the customer defaults, the bank may need to debit the customer with a loss on the close-out. Thus the granting of a forward contract will reduce the available credit facilities for the customer.	c) A currency option is not classed as a contingent liability, since the customer is under no obligation to deal on the terms set out. Thus, the currency option does not affect the available credit facilities for the customer.
d) From a customer's point of view, the forward contract eliminates the exchange risk, but he cannot gain the benefit if spot rates move in his favour. However, if the underlying commercial deal falls through, the customer will make a gain or loss on the close-out. Thus, forward contracts which are not matched by an underlying currency deal will create an exposure.	d) Under the currency option, the holder can take full advantage if spot rates move in his favour. If the holder has the underlying currency, he can deal spot and abandon the option.

Table 1 (Continued)

Forward Contracts	Foreign Currency Options
e) A forward contract is inflexible and affects the credit facilities of the customer. However, the cost of arranging forward contracts is relatively low compared to the cost of a currency option (usually just the bid offer spread).	e) The currency option gives a holder much greater flexibility. Hence, the cost (the option premium) will be much more than for a forward contract
f) A forward contract is a contract between a customer and his bank. A customer cannot normally sell his rights to a third party.	f) It may be possible for a holder to sell his rights under a currency option, depending on whether it has an intrinsic value. The right to sell is an alternative to the other two rights the right to exercise the option or the right to abandon it.

5.5 The Customer Benefits of Currency Traded Options

The benefits to the customer can be summarised as follows:

a) The purchaser can choose the strike price. (One of the factors which influences the option premium is how far the strike price differs from the relevant forward rate.)

b) The currency option provides far more flexibility than forward contracts or other methods of covering exchange risks. The option period can be chosen by the purchaser.

c) There is no question of marking a limit on the customer's account with currency options, since there is no obligation whatsoever for the customer to deal in accordance with the terms of the option. Hence, currency options do not affect the available borrowing facilities, since they are not a contingent liability. However, settlement risk must be considered upon exercise of the option. The bank must be sure that the customer will deliver or take delivery of the relevant currency prior to the end of the settlement period.

d) The purchaser can take advantage if spot rates move in his favour, by simply abandoning the option.

e) If the underlying commercial deal falls through, the purchaser will be able to sell the option back to the bank, provided the option has an intrinsic value.

f) The purchaser's costs are known at the outset, and are limited to the amount of the option premium.

g) The documentation required to set up the option is simple and straightforward.

5.6 Customer Benefits of OTC Options as Opposed to Exchange Traded Options

As we saw in the definitions at 5.3, OTC options are provided by banks whereas exchange traded options are obtained on organised exchanges, such as the Philadelphia Exchange in America.

The main customer benefits of OTC options as opposed to exchange traded options are:

a) OTC options are tailor-made whereas exchange traded options are standardised and may not match the customer's requirements.

b) OTC options involve less administration on the part of the purchaser. With exchange traded options it is necessary to deal via authorised brokers. In addition, purchasers of such options are required to deposit cash margins, and there may be extra cash margins required during the life of the option. None of this is required with bank OTC options, which have simple documentation and no cash margin requirements.

5.7 Cylinder Options

A cylinder option is a combination of an option and a forward contract. In exchange for a reduced premium, the holder acquires some, but not all, of the benefits of an option. Let us first of all look at a particular situation when cylinder options could be used.

Example

i)   Today

- X plc expects to have to pay out US $100,000 in 3 months.

- X plc buys a call option from its bank, strike price US $1.45.

- X plc writes a put option in favour of its bank, strike price US $1.55=£1.

- Both options cover an underlying principal of US $ 100,000.

- Both options have an expiry date in three months and are European.

- The premiums net out exactly. (This is not always the case, it depends on the terms of each option . Sometimes the bank's premium as writer will exceed that for the customer as writer, but the opposite could equally apply).

Table 2

	Outcome i)	*Outcome ii)*	*Outcome iii)*
Spot Rate	*US $1.30 = £1*	*US $1.50 = £1*	*US $1.60 = £1*
Sterling value at spot	£76,923	£66,667	£62,500
Sterling value of call	£68,966	£68,966	£68,966
Sterling value of put	£64,516	£64,516	£64,516
Action by call holder	exercise	abandon	abandon
Action by put holder	abandon	abandon	exercise
Result	X plc obtain the US $ at a cost of £68,966 using call rate of 1.45 If the US $ are not required, the call will be sold for its intrinsic value.	Both options are abandoned. X plc acquires the US $ at spot rate, cost £66,667, if the dollars are needed.	The bank sells US $100,000 at 1.55. The cost is £64,516.

ii)   At maturity in three months the outcome depends on the spot rate

From the above example, we can see the features and benefits of the cylinder option from this customer's point of view are:

- the premium will be lower than for a conventional option, since the customer can offset the premium on the option written by him against the premium on the option written by the bank. In this case the net premium is nil.

- if the spot rate at maturity is in between the two strike prices (i.e. within the 'cylinder'), both options will be abandoned, and the US $ payment, if made, will be settled at spot. If the US $ are not required, then no action is required on the part of the customer.

- if the rate is outside the cylinder (i.e. above or below the two strike prices), the call will be exercised if the underlying currency has strengthened, and the put will be exercised if the underlying currency has weakened. Likewise, the put will be abandoned if the underlying currency has strengthened and the call will be abandoned if the underlying currency has weakened.

- provided the customer still has the underlying currency position at maturity, (e.g. to make a payment of US $100,000) then the deal will be transacted as follows:

    - at call strike rate if the currency has strengthened at maturity;

    - at spot rate if this falls within the cylinder;

    - at put strike rate if the underlying currency has weakened at maturity;

- banks look upon a cylinder option as a credit facility, for the same reason that the forward contract is deemed to carry default risk in the case of a close-out. In this instance, if the underlying currency had weakened at maturity, the bank would need to be sure that X plc would honour its obligations under the put.

- cylinder options are useful where:

- the underlying currency position in the cash market at maturity is 'certain'

- the customer wishes to take advantage (to a limited extent) of the upside potential if the spot rates do move in his favour, but will not pay the full option premium

- the customer wishes to cover himself by setting the 'worst rate' which can be applied if rates have moved adversely at maturity;

● thus in exchange for a reduced premium, the customer gains a limited maximum upward potential, coupled with the danger of exposure to risk should the underlying currency receipt/payment not come to fruition.

Conclusion on Cylinder Options
There are infinite variations on the way in which banks can use 'financial engineering' skills to offer a hybrid product which combines the features of options and forwards. The net effect is that in exchange for a lower premium the customer forgoes some of the benefits of an option.

5.8   Self-assessment Questions

Multi-Choice Questions (Tick correct answer(s))

Question 1
Your customer is an importer. Which type of currency option would you expect him to require?

a) Call option.

b) Put option.

Question 2
Your customer exports to Germany and will be paid in DEMs. Which option is applicable for him?

a) A call option, base currency sterling, underlying currency DEMs.

b) A put option, base currency sterling, underlying currency DEMs.

c) A put option, base currency DEMs, underlying currency sterling.

Question 3
Your customer has an option which gives him the right, but not the obligation to exercise all or part of the option at any time up to the stated expiry date. Which type of option is this?

a) American.

b) European.

Question 4
Which type of option can only be exercised on the stated expiry date?

a) American.

b) European.

Question 5
Which type of currency options is written by banks?

a) Exchange traded options.

b) OTC options.

Question 6
Which type of options can be 'tailor-made' to meet the customer's own particular needs?

a) Exchange traded options.

b) OTC options.

Question 7
Which option will require the higher option premium?

    a) American options.

    b) European options.

Question 8
Your exporter customer has a currency put option whereby he can sell DEM 100,000 to the bank at a strike price of 3.40. The base currency is sterling and the underlying currency is DEMs. The customer has now received the DEMs and today, the expiry day, the spot buying rate quoted by the bank is 3.50. What will the customer do?

    a) Exercise the option and deal at 3.40.

    b) 'Walk away' and deal at spot.

Question 9
Suppose the customer in Question 8 does not have the DEMs. What will he do?

    a) Walk away.

    b) Sell the option to the bank at its intrinsic value.

Question 10
Suppose the spot rate in Question 8 is 3.20, not 3.50. What will the customer do if he has received the DEMs?

    a) Exercise the option.

    b) Walk away and deal spot.

Question 11
Suppose the customer in Question 10 does not have the DEMs. What will he do?

    a) Walk away.

    b) Sell the option back to the bank at its intrinsic value.

Question 12
Your importer customer has a call option to deal in DEMs at 3.40. What will he do, assuming he does require the DEMs, if the bank's spot selling rate on the expiry date is 3.10?

    a) Walk away.

    b) Deal at 3.40.

Question 13
Suppose the customer in Question 12 did not actually require the DEMs. What would he do if the spot rate was 3.10?

    a) Walk away.

    b) Sell the option to the bank at its intrinsic value.

Question 14

Which facility eliminates the 'downside' of the exchange rate risk, but still enables the customer to benefit if spot rates move in his favour?

a) Option forward contract.

b) Currency option.

Question 15

A UK exporter expects to receive DEM 100,000 in three months' time. He enters into the following arrangements to hedge the exposure:

The bank writes a European put option in favour of the customer, strike rate 2.80

The customer writes a European call option in favour of the bank, strike price 2.90.

In each case the base currency is sterling and the underlying currency DEM.

Each option expires on the same date and the amount of underlying currency is the same.

At the maturity dates the spot rate is 2.95 (ignore the bid/offer spread)

a) What will the customer's position be if the sale has fallen through and there is no possibility of receiving any DEMs in the future?

b) What will the customer's position be if the DEMs are received on the maturity date of the options?

c) Why did the bank treat these two options as a contingent liability and mark up a limit on the customer's account?

(Answers given in Appendix VI)

Unit 6

Alternatives to Forward Contracts and Currency Options, and Benefits of Foreign Currency Invoicing for Exporters

Objectives

On completion of this unit the student should be able to:

- **understand the benefits of forward contracts;**
- **appreciate the alternative techniques for covering the exchange risk;**
- **understand the benefits and drawbacks of foreign currency invoicing for exporters.**

6.1 The Benefits of Forward Contracts for Sterling-based Importers and Alternative Methods of Covering the Exchange Risk

a) The sterling cost of the imports is fixed; thus, the importer can set his prices and profit margins more accurately.

b) In theory, there is no limit to the amount of sterling the importer could require on the due date, if he has not covered the exchange risk, since the £ floats freely. The forward contract eliminates this exchange risk.

c) Failure to take any action to cover the exchange risk amounts to gambling. The importer will be legally liable to acquire the necessary foreign currency from the date he signs a commercial contract.

Some major corporate customers deliberately allow themselves to be exposed to the exchange risk in certain currencies, because they expect spot rates to move in their favour. However, such companies are quick to cover the exchange risk if the outlook for the currency in question changes adversely.

Normally, smaller companies should cover the exchange risk, since they probably could not survive a catastrophic change in spot rates.

Alternative forms of hedging are:

i) Currency call options which are more expensive than forward contracts and may not be available for the currency and amount required. However, the currency option enables the importer to deal at the spot rate on the due date, without penalty, if the rates move in his favour. (Full details of currency options are given in Unit 5.)

ii) The bank could sell the importer the necessary currency immediately at the current spot rate. The currency could then be kept on deposit until required. Much depends on the post-tax value of the deposit in the two countries as to whether this method is worthwhile.

iii) Open a foreign currency account but only if there are receipts and payments in the currency. The importer can then take out a forward contract to cover the anticipated balance, or he can delay conversion of the balance until rates move in his favour, or he can buy a currency option to cover the anticipated balance. It is possible to have a cheque book for a currency account.

iv) When a trader has receipts in one foreign currency and payments in another, he can convert the receipts directly into the currency of the payment, using cross rates. Forward contracts may well be available for cross rates.

6.2 Exporters: Means of Protection against Exchange Risk

The following methods of protection may be adopted:

a) Forward contracts.

b) Borrow foreign currency now, let the bank then convert it at the current spot rate to sterling and then credit the current account with the proceeds at once. The currency loan is subsequently repaid from the currency proceeds of the exports. The interest rate is based on the interest rates ruling in the overseas centre.

c) Foreign currency account but only if there are receipts and payments in the currency.

d) Currency put options.

Note
A more detailed analysis of the wider issues regarding exchange rate risks can be found in Units 7 and 8.

6.3 Advantages of Foreign Currency Invoicing for Exporters

The basic benefit is that currency invoicing gives a product a competitive advantage. The product is more attractive to the buyer because:

i) The buyer does not run any exchange risk;

ii) The buyer can easily understand the price implications if quoted in local currency;

iii) It is easier for the buyer to compare the price quoted by local competitors.

Note

a) Where the exporter has both receipts and payments in currency, it will be more efficient to open a foreign currency account. Forward contracts could be arranged to cover the anticipated net balance.

b) Where applicable, a currency option can cover the exchange risk whilst allowing the customer to 'walk away' if the spot rates move in his favour. Alternatively, a less flexible method, such as the forward contract, could be used.

6.4   Disadvantages of Foreign Currency Invoicing

The following four disadvantages should be borne in mind:

a) The exporter runs the exchange risk, which runs from the moment the commercial contract is signed until conversion of the currency;

b) Although the exchange risk can be covered, there is a cost involved (for example, the management time and/or the cost of the premiums for options);

c) Currency invoicing creates problems for the accounts staff, unless specialist help such as export factoring is employed (covered in Part Four of this book);

d) Published price lists may need frequent revision.

6.5   Self-assessment Questions

Question 1
A UK exporter invoices a US buyer in US $. Who runs the exchange risk?

Question 2
A UK importer is invoiced in £ by the Italian exporter. Who stands the exchange risk?

Question 3
An Arab exporter invoices a UK buyer in US $. Who stands the exchange risk?

Question 4
A UK, sterling-based merchant is due to receive the equivalent of CHF 50,000 denominated in DEMs. On receipt, he is obliged to pay CHF 50,000 to his supplier. What rate of exchange should be used?

Question 5
Would you use the spot rate or arrange a forward contract for the transaction in Question 4?

Question 6
A UK exporter sells to Germany and invoices in DEMs. He has no other foreign currency receipts or payments. Is a foreign currency account in DEMs an appropriate method of avoiding the exchange risk?

Question 7
A UK exporter invoices in DEMs and there is usually a three-month delay between date of invoice and date of payment. The exporter has been advised to borrow DEMs in anticipation of the proceeds, and to take out forward contracts to cover the exchange risk. Briefly comment on this advice.

Question 8
An exporter has borrowed foreign currency in anticipation of his export proceeds which are invoiced in that currency. Unfortunately, the buyer has defaulted and the exporter is obliged to repay the currency borrowing. What loss, over and above the loss of the sale proceeds, might the exporter make?

(Answers given in Appendix VI)

6.6   Past Exam Question

Tiger Moth Ltd, customers of your bank, are a sterling-based aircraft charter company operating in the UK, Western Europe and the Caribbean. They have been awarded a contract to provide freight and passenger services for a number of remote islands in the mid-Atlantic and the Caribbean.

The contract, which is guaranteed by the governments of the various territories, is to be signed on 1 June 1993. The value of the contract to the customer is US $1.5 million, and it will be necessary for Tiger Moth Ltd to charter three aircraft at a total cost of US $900,000. Payment and receipt terms are as follows:

Payments by Tiger Moth Ltd

a) One third upon signing the contract;

b) One third six months after signing the contract;

c) One third 12 months after signing the contract.

Receipts by Tiger Moth Ltd

a) One third ($500,000) three months after signing the contract (guaranteed);

b) One third ($500,000) six months after signing the contract (guaranteed);

c) One third payment of up to $500,000 (one third of the contract value) 12 months after signing the contract. (According to the contract, this payment may be reduced if Tiger Moth Ltd generate extra business on their own account.)

Your customers ask you to make the best possible financial arrangements to obviate any risks to them.

US dollar rates on 1 June 1993 are as follows:

Spot	1.3195	1.3210
Three months	0.16c disc	0.21c disc
Six months	0.44c disc	0.72c disc
Twelve months	0.85c disc	1.05c disc
Spot 1 June 1994	1.4610	1.4670

Additional Information and Assumptions

i)   The full expected net receipts are sold forward on 1 June 1993 for delivery on 1 June 1994.

ii) For the purpose of this question, ignore the possibility of any other forward contracts which might be arranged.

iii) The contract is performed in its entirety except that, when the third payment falls due on 1 June 1994, it is calculated that Tiger Moth Ltd has generated extra business on its own account which requires a reduction in the contract payment from US $500,000 to US $250,000. (The 'extra earnings' should be ignored for the purpose of the calculations required in c) below.)

iv) All commercial risks, such as chartering risks, credit risks, etc., which may be included in the commercial contract, may be ignored.

v) Any changes or interest payable in connection with any overdraft or transfers may be ignored.

Required

The advice you would give to the company covering the following:

a) The nature and duration of the exchange rate risk that the company has to face in accepting the contract which is awarded to them. (4 marks)

b) The method that you would recommend to Tiger Moth Ltd in order to minimise the risk mentioned in (a). (5 marks)

c) A statement of the currency account you would operate on behalf of the customer, including a calculation at the end of the period showing the total sterling proceeds which would be credited to the customer's sterling account. (11 marks)

(Total 20 marks)

(*Note* Assume that Tiger Moth Ltd are unwilling to purchase currency options.)

(Specimen Answer given in Appendix VI)

Unit 7

Overview of Management of Foreign Currency Exposure

Objectives

On completion of this unit the student should be able to:

- **differentiate between the three basic classifications of foreign currency exposure;**

- **understand the difference between the three main corporate hedging philosophies;**

- **appreciate the link between hedging philosophy and business and operating risk;**

- **differentiate between internal and external techniques;**

- **understand the wider practical and theoretical issues relating to whether, and if so how, companies should manage foreign exchange exposures;**

- **appreciate the relevance of the budget rate of exchange in the formulation of projections.**

7.1 The Three Main Classifications of Foreign Currency Exposure

In the preceding units, we have simply looked at techniques which can be employed to manage exchange rate risk. Now is the time to formally define what is meant by exchange rate risk and to differentiate between the three main categories.

Foreign currency exposure can be defined as the vulnerability of a company to changes in its profit and loss and balance sheet position arising from exchange rate movements. 'Foreign currency' is any currency other than the company's reporting currency in which the company's published accounts are denominated.

Foreign exchange exposure is usually classified under three main categories; transaction, translation and economic. In this unit, we shall concern ourselves with transaction exposure and its various subdivisions.

7.2 Transaction Exposure

This can arise out of normal overseas trading activities. For exporters who invoice in foreign currency, the transaction exposure exists between the date of the commercial contract and the date of conversion of the receivables into home currency. For importers who are invoiced in foreign currency, the transaction exposure exists between the date of the commercial contract and the date of conversion of home currency into the requisite sum of foreign currency. Transaction exposure also arises in respect of any cash transfer between domestic currency and overseas currency, thus cash expenditure or capital receipts, such as dividends denominated in foreign currency, will give rise to transaction exposures.

The above is the traditional definition of foreign exchange transaction exposure. However, another view is that, over and above the traditional exposure, there is an 'extended transaction exposure', which applies whenever a company is committed to selling to certain countries or to buying from certain countries. This exposure will last for the period of time required before the corporate could switch to other countries. (Some authorities would classify extended transaction exposure as 'economic' exposure).

A third category of transaction exposure, 'pre-transaction' exposure, occurs when a company is committed to receiving payment in a foreign currency if buyers decide to purchase. The two major manifestations of pre-transaction exposure are:

i) When a company has submitted a tender for a contract which is to be settled in foreign currency. If the contract is awarded, the company will incur a foreign currency transaction exposure and the spot rate of exchange may well be different from the one ruling on the day of tender. However, taking out a forward contract at the time of the tender could be unwise, since, if the tender proves unsuccessful, the forward contract will have created an exposure.

Readers will no doubt recall from Unit 4 that the close-out procedure will mean that a corporate which is a party to a forward contract has created an exposure when there is no underlying transaction to facilitate the fulfilment of obligations.

ii) A similar exposure applies when a company issues price lists denominated in foreign currency. There is no guarantee of the amount of sales that will actually be made, but the company is committed to fulfilling any sales which may arise at the price set out in the published list.

7.3   Corporate Hedging Philosophies

a)   Introduction

A hedge is some action taken by a company to cover itself against risk. The techniques of hedging can usually be categorised as either internal or external. For the moment let us consider only external techniques. These are usually instruments known as 'derivatives', which are available from external providers, such as banks and organised futures exchanges.

A derivative is simply a financial instrument whose value depends on (or is derived from) another financial instrument or commodity. When a company wishes to hedge an underlying transaction exposure, it can take a position in the derivatives market which is equal and opposite to the underlying transaction exposure. Examples of the use of derivatives such as currency options have already been seen in Units 3, 4 and 5.

However, it is difficult to hedge transaction risks for long periods ahead. For example, a UK-based car maker may incur most of its costs in sterling and about half of its sales revenue in US $. Obviously, the company will suffer if the US$ falls against the £. In theory, the company could have sold its anticipated dollar receipts forward for five years, but the problem then arises of how the company can accurately predict its dollar sales over such a long period. If forward contracts were arranged, the company would incur an exposure on a close-out if it could not fulfil the contracts.

b) Hedging Philosophies

The three main philosophies are:

i)   hedge nothing;

ii) hedge everything;

iii) hedge selectively.

i)   Hedge nothing

Small companies which are new to overseas trade often hedge nothing because they are unaware of the risks of exchange rate exposure and because they do not know about the techniques of hedging. This situation is clearly dangerous since a small firm is unlikely to have the capacity to absorb any significant exchange rate losses.

In theory, there is a case for larger companies to hedge nothing, since academic economic studies indicate that in the long term a 'no-hedge' policy should produce the same results as a fully hedged policy. The arguments for and against corporate hedging will be discussed at the end of this unit

If a company is a 'price maker' in the overseas market, or if demand for its products is inelastic, then it may decide not to hedge extended transaction exposure. Such a company can simply raise the price of its goods in foreign currency to cover currency depreciation.

ii)   Hedge everything

Such a policy can eliminate transaction exposures, but it cannot eliminate economic exposures, and it gives rise to an 'opportunity cost'.

For example, if the spot rates were to move in favour of the company between the date of the invoice and the conversion of the currency, the company will have 'lost out' or incurred an opportunity cost if it has hedged the exchange exposure. A hedge-everything philosophy is common in heavy engineering companies when currency transactions are large and 'one-off' and where profit margins are tight.

In practice, many corporations with a hedge-everything philosophy use forward contracts to cover 'certain' cash flows in foreign currency and use options to cover cash flows which may arise but cannot be considered as 'certain'.

iii)   *Hedge selectively*

Selective hedging involves taking a view on the future movements of exchange rates, the object being to hedge only those exposures where the anticipated risk of loss exceeds the opportunity for gain.

One system of selective hedging is to set a maximum permissible exposure, which will be based on the company's capital base, cash flow and profitability, and also the degree of the company's risk aversion. Any exposure above the maximum would have to be hedged. Any exposure below the stated maximum would either be left uncovered or it would be hedged, depending on the treasurer's perception of exchange rate movements.

In practice, limits on the size of an individual exposure and on the size of exposure to a particular currency will be set, so that the company does not 'use up' its exposure 'allowance' in just one uncovered position.

An open currency position should be monitored on a daily basis and a level set at which cover will be taken. One mechanism for doing this is the use of a stop loss order. For example, if a UK company is due to receive FRF10m from its overseas customer in three months' time, it may set the stop loss so as to sell the FRF in the forward market if the exchange rate is 5% above the original rate. The stop will be moved downwards but never upwards. If the exchange rate starts to move up from a low, the stop will be triggered close to although not at the lowest rate. (If the rate 'moves up', it means that the French franc is depreciating, because there are more francs than previously required to equal £1.)

A policy of selective hedging makes heavy demands on executive time and professional expertise. It requires a treasury system which is integrated into the budgetary control system so that future exchange exposures can be identified in a systematic way.

Many small and medium-sized companies will lack the expertise to hedge selectively, and in practice such companies will hedge everything. On the other hand, some MNCs will hedge selectively, unless they are mainly in heavy engineering or similar industries with large, one-off transactions and tight margins.

c)   The Link between Hedging Philosophy and Business and Operational Risk

Companies which have a high business risk (e.g. contractors) or high operating risks (where there are high fixed costs which cannot be easily reduced in an economic downturn) should tend towards a 'hedge-everything' policy. The riskier a business, the greater its cost of capital. These companies with a high business and operating risk cannot usually afford a high financial risk from foreign currency exposure. (Similar principles apply to gearing and interest rate exposure.)

Whatever hedging philosophy is adopted, there must be clear internal documentation setting out the general philosophy and detailing the techniques which can be used.

7.4 Internal Techniques for Hedging Transaction Exposures

a) Matching

This involves the use of foreign currency bank accounts when a company has both receipts and payments in overseas currency. When payments are due before receipts, the company can arrange overdraft facilities, subject to creditworthiness, and when there are receipts due before payments, interest can be negotiated for the credit balances. Interest rates will be based on those ruling in the overseas centre.

Companies can arrange to hedge the anticipated balances at periodic intervals.

The major benefit of foreign currency accounts is that the company can avoid consistently buying and selling the same currency. In other words, the company avoids the bank's spread between its buying and selling rates.

b) Multilateral Netting

This system is useful for large groups of companies with a centralised treasury function. Each operating subsidiary must report the following details to the centre:

a) anticipated receipts and payments in every currency other than its own domestic currency;

b) an estimate of the subsidiary's exposed position in every currency other than its own domestic currency.

The central treasury will then act as a clearing house and will hedge the group's net exposure in any particular currency. This system is only really applicable in large MNCs which have an efficient centralised treasury function. The requirements for successful implementation are:

a) the budget periods for all operating subsidiaries must be synchronised, otherwise the reported net exposures of the group could be distorted;

b) the savings from netting must be sufficient to cover the costs of the information system between the group and its subsidiaries;

c) the system must not contravene any local exchange control or tax regulations.

Note

If the single European currency comes into effect, then UK companies which operate a multilateral netting system for currencies of participating member countries will no longer require such a system.

c) Leads and Lags

This technique applies when a company has not purchased a bank product such as a forward exchange contract to hedge a transaction exposure in foreign currency. In other words, this is not really a hedging technique at all, but simply an attempt to forecast exchange rates and then to take action based on the forecasts.

If the company has to make a payment in, say, three months in a foreign currency which is expected to appreciate in value, it will 'lead', i.e. it will attempt to pay early so as to reduce the home currency cost of the payment. Naturally, the company will attempt to negotiate a discount to compensate for the early payment.

Obviously, the converse would apply if the foreign currency were expected to be about to fall in value. In that case, the company would attempt to 'lag', i.e. delay payment for as long as possible, subject to contractual obligations.

A similar process applies with exporters who try to lead, i.e. speed up, receipts if the foreign currency is expected to fall and who try to lag when the currency is expected to rise in value.

When the underlying commercial transactions are between different operating subsidiaries of the same group, there could be tax complications in leading and lagging. Expert tax advice is required; in addition, care must be taken to ensure that any overseas exchange control regulations are not contravened.

In order to decide whether leading or lagging is a viable proposition, the treasurer needs to know:

i)   the amount of discount to be paid or received in the leading or lagging;

ii) the forward rates which are currently available;

iii) interest rates;

iv) tax and exchange control implications.

The treasurer can then compare the benefits of leading or lagging with the benefits of using other hedging techniques.

d)   Invoicing in Composite Currencies

At the present time, the main examples of composite currencies are the SDR and the ECU. There are active foreign exchange markets in ECUs, and it is possible for companies to open ECU accounts with their banks. Obviously, ECU invoicing does not hedge an exposure, but it can facilitate the management of exposures, where a company is selling to or buying from a number of EU companies. If and when the single European currency ever comes into existence, then this Euro currency will replace the ECU as the plan is for the ECU to be exchanged for the euro on a one-for-one basis on 1 January 1999. (Please see Unit 2 for a more detailed assessment of the implications of the single currency.)

e)   Other Internal Techniques

i)   Local suppliers may be prepared to invoice in a different currency from their home currency, e.g. UK-based subsidiaries of USA multinationals may be happy to invoice in US $ to UK purchasers.

ii) The company may, as a long-term strategy, switch its manufacture to other locations, to change the currency of its cost base.

7.5 Theoretical Arguments concerning Foreign Exchange Exposure Management by Corporates

Introduction

There has been considerable academic debate as to whether foreign currency exposures should be managed by corporates. If foreign exchange exposure should be managed by corporates, which principles apply and what techniques could be used ?

a) **Summary of Arguments against Foreign Currency Hedging**

i) *Purchasing power parity theory*

Movements in foreign exchange rates will be offset by changes in relative price levels. (This is a simplistic summary of the PPP theory. A more detailed explanation has already been given in Unit 2.)

If the above version of the PPP theory applied in practice, without any time lags, there would be no such thing as foreign exchange exposure, since any loss due to foreign exchange rate movements would be compensated for by a gain in price, and vice versa.

ii) *Capital Asset Pricing model (CAPM)*

Unsystematic risks are risks which apply to particular individual companies.

If exchange rate risk (and interest rate risk, for that matter) can be considered as unsystematic risks, then investors can eliminate such risks by holding a diversified portfolio of shares. Gains on some shares due to exchange rate movements would be offset by losses on other shares which would be adversely affected by the same exchange rate fluctuations.

If, however, foreign exchange risk is considered as a systematic risk, which is one which is embodied in the market as a whole, then hedging instruments will be priced in a rational way to take account of the volatility of the relevant currencies. Hence, there will be no added value from hedging, and indeed the cost of hedging, as represented by option premiums, management time and bid/offer spreads, will destroy shareholder value. When hedging instruments are priced in a rational way, the market can be said to be 'efficient'.

iii) *Modigliani and Miller (M & M) propositions 1958*

M & M argued, in connection with corporate gearing, that shareholders could obtain 'home-made leverage' by borrowing on their own account instead of leaving the borrowing to be carried out by the companies in which they owned shares. Taking this proposition a step further, it could be argued that investors should obtain 'home-made hedging' by hedging on their own account. Individual shareholders could each make their own personal arrangements to hedge currency exposures from their own portfolio of shares. Hedging by individual corporate entities from the investors' portfolio would be counterproductive, since this corporate hedging would counteract the hedging of the individual investor.

iv) *Market efficiency*

Currency markets do not provide bargains; rather they provide fair gambles based on fair prices. In the long run, gains and losses on unhedged foreign exchange exposures will tend to average out. Thus, in the long run, there will be no benefit from hedging. The argument concludes that corporates could 'self-insure' by simply allowing gains and losses to cancel out in the long run.

Hedging, so the argument says, will reduce the value of the firm since the premium paid will exceed the potential loss after taking into account the probability of that loss actually occurring.

b) Summary of Arguments which Contradict the Above

i) *Purchasing power parity*

Major deviations have occurred in the PPP (see Unit 2). If relative inflation and relative exchange rates do not immediately offset each other, then corporates are exposed to exchange rate risk. Even if the relative levels in the countries concerned did immediately offset each other, the input and output prices of a particular company may not adjust in line with the general change in price levels in the countries concerned.

ii) *CAPM and market efficiency*

Even if the CAPM is considered valid with regard to foreign exchange exposures, and even if it can be accepted that foreign exchange markets are efficient, there could still be adverse consequences from failure to manage a corporate's currency exposure. If large adverse changes in exchange rates coincided with the receipt or payment of a large sum of foreign currency, then the exchange rate movement could give rise to serious liquidity problems.

Although in the long run, all such gains and losses should cancel out, that would be of little consolation to shareholders, managers and creditors if the liquidity crisis had forced the corporate to go into liquidation.

iii) *M & M*

Individual investors are unlikely to be able to diversify exchange risk as efficiently as corporates. There are minimum amounts for hedging instruments such as forward exchange contracts, options and futures, so it may not be possible for an individual investor to tailor a hedge to meet his own requirements. Major corporates also might have access to techniques such as accelerating or delaying inter-company payments in accordance with foreign exchange market conditions. In addition, the managers have access to information on their companies' foreign exchange exposures which is just not available to the private investor. Finally the cost of hedging may be far lower for corporates than it is for individual shareholders.

It may be that the above arguments are less cogent in the case of institutional investors such as pension funds, which should have the same 'bulk power' as major corporates. In addition, the managers of institutions may be capable of hedging the foreign exchange risk from their portfolio of investments in a more cost-effective manner than relying on the managers of the various companies to hedge the risk of each corporate entity independently.

c) Other Arguments Supporting Management of Currency Exposures by Corporates

i) Corporate hedging reduces the volatility of earnings and the volatility of future cash flows. This in turn reduces the risk of incurring the costs of financial distress (a technical term describing the costs incurred in a liquidation from legal fees and other transaction costs).

ii)   Lower risk should result in a lower cost of capital. The cost of capital (after some adjustments) is the basis of the discount rate applied to future cash flows when valuing the business; thus, the lower the discount rate the higher the value of the firm.

iii) Lower risk of financial distress may increase debt capacity for a hedged company.

iv) Managers and employees cannot hold a diversified portfolio of jobs. Good managers should be attracted to firms which manage foreign currency exposures, as such firms are likely to be affected to a lesser extent by the costs of financial distress.

v)   In some tax regimes, fortuitous foreign currency gains may be liable to taxation, whereas foreign currency losses may not be tax-deductible.

vi) Suppliers and customers will prefer to deal with less risky firms.

Note

In a major international survey conducted by Price Waterhouse in 1995, it was found that 96% of companies undertake some form of hedging.

7.6   The Use of a 'Budget' Rate of Exchange in Projections

a)   How Budget Rates are Used

Nowadays even the smallest businesses must plan, and one essential basic planning tool is the projected profit-and-loss account (known as an operating budget) and a projected cash budget. For a business with anticipated receipts or purchases denominated in foreign currency, there is an added complication: the projected spot rates at which the receipts or payments will be converted.

A typical planning exercise would take place in October, and would cover the twelve months starting in the following January.

Most businesses decide upon a 'budget rate of exchange' and this rate is used to convert all anticipated currency receipts or payments into home currency for the purposes of the operating and cash budgets. The company can select any rate it wishes for this exercise but, in practice, the three-month or six-month or twelve-month forward rate is usually chosen. The forward rate does not claim to predict what the spot will be at the end of the relevant period, it simply reflects the current spot rate today and the current interest rate differentials in the two countries. However, the forward rate is usually selected, simply because it is the one that is available at the time the budget is prepared.

If all other parts of the budget are totally accurate (which is most unlikely in practice!), then any actual conversions which are made at more favourable rates will result in extra profit and more cash than that projected in the budgets, and the converse will apply if the actual rates used for conversion are less favourable. By making regular comparisons between the actual rates of exchange used for conversions and the budget rate, companies should be able to assess the likely effect of exchange rate movements on the company's year-end profits and cash position, and should be able to evaluate the success of any hedging action taken.

b) How Internal Communication Can Help Contain Transaction Exposure

Transaction exposure arises from decisions taken by purchasing and sales personnel who cannot be expected to have a detailed knowledge of the treasury function.

However, it is essential that sales and purchasing personnel are broadly aware of the impact of their decisions on the company's exposure position, and to this end they require a broad understanding of:

- hedging techniques and forward rates;

- how to use forward rates in comparison to leading and lagging.

Likewise the treasurer must be made aware of the likely long-term sales volumes in different currencies and how sensitive such sales are to price changes. This information will be particularly important in monitoring 'extended transaction exposure'.

Treasurers should also liaise on a regular basis with sales and purchasing staff to ensure that these people know the current rates (spot or forward) and can therefore quickly calculate whether a particular deal will be profitable in home currency terms.

Note

There will not be any short-answer questions at the end of this unit. Instead there will be an integrative case study at the end of Unit 8 which will examine transaction, translation and economic exposure.

Unit 8

Foreign Currency Translation Exposure and Foreign Currency Economic Exposure

Objectives

On completion of this unit the reader should be able to:

● understand the nature and implications of translation exposure;

● differentiate between profit-and-loss and balance sheet translation exposure;

● understand how currency borrowing and swaps can be used to manage translation exposure;

● evaluate the benefits and drawbacks of managing translation exposure;

● understand the nature of foreign currency economic exposure;

● appreciate the difficulties in the management of foreign currency economic exposure.

8.1   Translation Exposure

a)   The Nature of Translation Exposure

This exposure arises from the changes in the value in home currency of overseas assets and liabilities from one balance sheet date to the next. It also relates to the consolidations of the year's profits and the effect on earnings per share when some of the profits relate to an overseas subsidiary.

This unit does not seek to provide a detailed understanding of the accountancy treatment of translation gain or loss, but merely seeks to explain the broad principles..

b)   Translation Exposures and Balance Sheets

The largest translation effect for most international groups is the result of translating the net worth of overseas subsidiaries into the company's reporting currency for the purpose of producing consolidated accounts. The value in the reporting currency of the group would be calculated by using the rate of exchange which applied at the balance sheet date. Hence, even if the net worth of the subsidiary remained unchanged between balance sheet dates when denominated in the currency of that subsidiary, there would be a translation gain or loss in the reporting currency of the consolidated accounts, depending on the movement of exchange rates between the two balance sheet dates.

c)   Translation Exposure and its Effect on the Profit and Loss Account

This is easily explained by an example. A UK-based company may have a subsidiary located in the USA. Naturally the year's profits, which will be denominated in US $, will have to be included in sterling terms in the consolidated accounts. This consolidation will occur even though the profits may be retained in the subsidiary. (Under SSAP 20, UK companies can use period end exchange rates or average exchange rates for the year. The American equivalent, FASB52, in practice allows a weighted average exchange rate to be applied to the profit-and-loss statement)

The sterling figure produced in the consolidated profit and loss account will affect the group's annual reported earnings and the reported earnings per share.

8.2   Specific Examples of Translation Exposure on Profit-and-loss Accounts

In this example we shall look at a UK company with a French subsidiary, which uses the year-end rate to translate its overseas profits for the published accounts.

The profit forecasts by City analysts for the current financial year are £95m, based on forecast UK profits of £45m and forecast profits of the French subsidiary of FRF 500m at a forecast exchange rate of FRF10=£1.

The following table shows the various outcomes at different year-end exchange rates, assuming that the UK profits are actually $45m and the French profits are actually FRF 500m.

Year-end Rate/£	FRF8=£1	FRF10=£1	FRF12=£1
UK profits £m	45	45	45
French profits FF500m	62.5	50	41.7
Group total	107.5	95	86.7

There are various possible solutions to overcome this potential translation exposure.

i)   Arrange a forward contract for the bank to buy FRF 500m at the year end. This contract will not be fulfilled, but will be closed out on maturity at the year end.

   If the FRF has weakened at the year end, the paper loss on consolidated earnings will be matched by a cash gain on the close-out of the forward contract. However, if the FRF has gained in value at the year end, there will be a paper gain on consolidated earnings matched by a cash loss on close-out.

ii) Arrange a currency put option for FRF 500m. If the FRF has weakened, the currency option can be sold for its intrinsic value to offset the paper loss on consolidated earnings. If the FRF has strengthened at the year end, the option will be abandoned, with the cost of the premium having been paid by the company.

iii) It may be possible to change accounting policy if the auditors and the accountancy rules allow this, so that, instead of using year-end spot rates to convert the profits in the consolidated accounts, average rates for the year are used. In this case, likely exchange rate to be applied on consolidation of profits should be capable of a reasonably accurate estimate well before year end.

Most accountancy conventions insist that assets and liabilities are translated at closing rates, but in some countries, for example, the UK, average rates can be used for conversion of the annual profits. Auditors will normally allow only occasional changes in the basis of consolidation of profits and companies will certainly not be allowed to chop and change at will, depending on which method proves more favourable each year.

iv) The company should undertake a serious public relations exercise to educate analysts to understand the effect of exchange rate movements on the profit stream.

v) For 'strong' companies, treating the investment community with respect and avoiding the use of a 'cash' hedge must be the preferred course, but this may not be possible for a company which is not considered to be a 'blue-chip' company, due to potential adverse reactions from shareholders, bankers and creditors.

8.3 Specific Examples of Translation Exposures on Balance Sheets

Example

A UK company has just acquired an American subsidiary at a cost of US $150m. The payment was funded by a sterling loan of £100m, which was converted to US $150m at the spot rate of 1.5. There was a net worth of £100m immediately before the transaction and no currency assets or liabilities existed until this acquisition. Immediately after the acquisition, the group balance sheet would look like this:

	Assets £m	Liabilities £m	
(US $150m) Dollar Assets	100	Debt (Sterling)	100
Sterling Assets	100	Equity	100
	200		200

The gearing is 100% (Debt/Equity)

Net worth £100m

In many loan agreements there are covenants under which banks require companies to pass 'health checks'. In the documentation, financial targets may have to be met. Two of the most common are the 'gearing test' and the 'maintenance of net worth' or 'consolidated net worth' tests. Let us assume that the bank insisted that this company agreed to a loan covenant which requires a minimum net worth of £80m and a maximum gearing ratio (debt/equity) of 125%.

Let us now look at the year-end balance sheet in one year's time, making the unlikely but necessary assumption that the only change was the closing spot rate between the pound and the dollar.

There will be various alternative outcomes depending on the year-end spot rate: Assumption one :   All sterling debt and dollar rises to US $1 = £1.

	Assets £m	Liabilities £m	
(US $150m) Dollar Assets	150	Debt (£)	100
Sterling Assets	100	Equity	150
	250		250

Gearing   67% (100 ÷ 150 x 100)
Net worth   £150m

Assumption ii) :   Dollar falls to $2 = £1 and debt is all sterling

	Assets £m	Liabilities £m	
(US $150m) Dollar Assets	75	Debt (£)	100
Sterling Assets	100	Equity	75
	175		175

Gearing   133% (100 ÷ 75 x 100)
Net Worth   £75m

What we find from this simple example is that the reported gearing and net worth of the company will be changed each year, depending on the exchange rate prevailing at the year end. As the company had agreed a 125% gearing covenant and a maintenance of net worth test at £80m, there would be a problem. This is all the worse because the movement in exchange rates may well only be temporary.

8.4   Use of Foreign Currency Borrowing to Hedge Balance Sheet Translation Exposure

In the above example, the solution to the net worth problem is straightforward. All that is required is to match foreign currency assets with foreign currency liabilities. In this case, both sides of the balance sheet will be equally affected, as shown in the following example:

We repeat, for convenience, the opening balance sheet of the previous example when the spot rate was $1.50 = £1

	Assets £m	Liabilities £m	
(US $150m) Dollar Assets	100	(US $150 loans)	100
Sterling Assets	100	Equity	100
	200		200

Gearing   100%
Net Worth   £100m

Let us now examine the outcome if the borrowing had been denominated in US $(150m at 1.50).

The next year's balance sheet assuming all conditions are as before (i.e. the only change is that the year-end spot rate is $1 = £1 (outcome 1).

	Assets £m	Liabilities £m	
(US $150m) Dollar assets	150	(US $150 at $1 = £1)	150
Sterling assets	100	Equity	100
	250		250

Gearing   150%
Net Worth   £100m

Let us now see what happens when the closing rate at the next balance sheet date is US $2 = £1 (outcome 2).

	Assets £m	Liabilities £m	
(US $150m) Dollar Assets	75	(US $150 @ $2 = £1)	75
Sterling Assets	100	Equity	100
	175		175

Gearing   75%
Net Worth   £100m

This currency borrowing achieves the desired effect on maintenance of net worth, but gearing increases as sterling weakens (outcome 1), and reduces gearing as sterling strengthens (outcome 2). Thus, matching the net foreign currency assets of the company with foreign currency borrowings will stabilise the reported net worth, but will not stabilise the reported gearing. Treasurers should seek to negotiate loan covenants which will not be affected by translation exposures. Where these covenants are not available, seek covenants which relate only to net worth, or match the assets by 50% only by currency borrowing if there are gearing covenants (see examples below).

8.5   Managing Translation Exposures by Matching 50% Currency Borrowings and 50% Sterling Finance

Suppose the US $ assets of 150m shown in the previous three balance sheet examples had been originally matched with half sterling and half dollar debt when the spot rate was US $1.50. The balance sheet would have looked like this:

	Assets £m	Liabilities £m	
(US $150m) Dollar	100	Loans	100
		(US $75 @ 1.5 = £50 +£50)	
Sterling	100	Equity	100
	200		200

Let us now look at the outcome for the next balance sheet when $1= £1, i.e. sterling has weakened.

	Assets £m	Liabilities £m	
Dollar assets	150	Loans	125
		(US $75 @ 1= £75 + £50)	
Sterling assets	100	Equity	125
	250		250

Gearing   100%
Net worth   £125m

Now let us see the outcome when sterling has strengthened at the next balance sheet date to US $2 = £1:

	Assets £m	Liabilities £m	
Dollar assets	75	Loans	87.5
		(US $75 @ 2 = 37.5 + 50)	
Sterling assets	100	Equity	87.5
	175		175

Gearing	100%
Net worth	£87.5 m

Thus, it is possible to hedge translation exposures as regards net worth or gearing by currency borrowing. However, it is not possible to hedge both simultaneously by this method.

8.6 Considerations to Bear in Mind When Using Currency Borrowing to Hedge Translation Exposures

a) Borrowing in the Currency of the Assets to Hedge Balance Sheet Exposures

The company can initially eliminate the translation net worth exposure by financing the overseas asset purchases with borrowings in the same currency. Thus, any increase in the asset value because of exchange rate movements will be matched by an increase in the domestic currency equivalent of the loan, and vice versa.

While the initial purchase can be hedged in this way, this technique cannot entirely eliminate the exposure in future years. The net worth of the subsidiary in terms of local currency will increase or decrease because of profits, or losses and dividend or interest payments. It is difficult to predict year-end net worth in advance.

b) Other Problems which can Arise from Foreign Currency Borrowing to Hedge Translation Exposure:

i) Foreign currency borrowings will have to be rolled over at maturity and the borrower will have to pay the current market rate of interest at the renewal date.

ii) The borrowing may contravene local exchange controls.

iii) If the foreign currency appreciates and the assets are sold, there will be capital gains tax to pay. In some tax jurisdictions, there will be no tax relief against the extra cost of the loan.

iv) Servicing costs will be denominated in foreign currency, and this will create a transaction exposure unless the overseas assets are generating sufficient foreign currency to cover this servicing.

v) Foreign currency borrowing facilities are not available in certain soft currencies.

vi) If the asset does not require borrowings to fund its purchase, then borrowing to hedge translation exposures will artificially inflate the balance sheet and create unnecessary borrowing.

vii) If the asset is funded by an inter-company loan, there may be withholding tax complications.

8.7   Currency Swaps

a)   The Use of Currency Swaps as an Alternative to Direct Currency Borrowing

We have already seen in Unit 2 how banks utilise short-term currency swaps to cover their own exposures in connection with forward contract commitments. We now examine how, as an alternative to direct currency borrowing, longer dated currency swaps can be used to effectively switch the currency in which a loan is denominated. A typical swap works as follows:

i)   In a typical currency swap, two different currencies are normally exchanged at the outset.

ii)   During the life of the currency swap, the counterparties agree to exchange interest payments on the principal amounts originally exchanged.

iii)   At maturity, the principal amounts on the currency swap are re-exchanged at a rate agreed at the outset. This pre-set rate is often agreed as the same rate as applied to the original exchange.

Note

There may be subsidised rates of interest available (e.g. export finance from a government-backed export support scheme) and companies could borrow in their own currency from this source and swap into the desired currency.

b)   Numerical Example of Currency Swap

A UK company, X plc, wants to borrow US $24m, repayable over 10 years to finance its US subsidiary. It is not well known in the USA and does not have a credit rating. However, the company is well known on the UK markets.

Let us assume that the company can issue a sterling debenture at 8%, fixed for 10 years, and that the following bank swap quote is available:

Rate US $	1.5 to £1
Interest on US $	5% fixed
Interest on £	8% fixed

The swap will operate as follows:

i)   Day one: X plc borrows £16m in the market and swaps it for US $24m.

ii)   Annual interest payments: X plc will receive £1.28m and will pay US $1.2m.

iii) At maturity: X plc will pay the bank US $24m and will receive £16m in exchange.

c)   Cash Flow Diagrams

i)   Day one

To purchase subsidiary
US$ 24m

£16m
from debenture issue

ii)   Annual interest payments

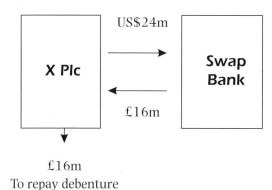

£1.28m
interest on debenture

Note

It is assumed that the subsidiary will generate US$ income to service the swap interest commitment.

iii) Maturity

£16m
To repay debenture

The company has created a synthetic US $ loan in this case, but the rate of interest could well be much lower than that which would have been payable on direct US $ borrowing, if the company has access to subsidised export finance for its sterling borrowing, or if the company was a well-respected borrower on the sterling debenture markets.

At maturity, X plc will be obliged to use £16m sterling towards the purchase of

US $24m. However, if X plc remains creditworthy, the bank will almost certainly extend the swap, using the interest rates ruling at the time of maturity as the basis of the subsequent interest rate exchanges.

Note
Particular care must be taken to obtain specialist tax advice.

8.8 Is It Necessary to Manage Translation Exposure?

Translation gains or losses do not result in any cash gain or loss. These changes are recorded in the reserves of the group and represent unrealised gains or losses on conversion of the net worth of overseas subsidiaries, or of other foreign currency denominated assets and liabilities. However, such gains or losses affect the reported gearing and net worth of the consolidated position and as such they affect the attitudes of lenders, creditors and investors. Thus, translation gains or losses can ultimately result in a cash effect if the behaviour of creditors, bankers and shareholders is changed. For a strong company with a first-class international reputation (e.g. BP) the 'paper' gains or losses from translation exposure are not too important. Such companies can simply explain the true nature of the exposures to analysts and bankers, and there will be no adverse effects. However, companies which are not in the BP league need to take banker/market perceptions much more seriously.

In addition, truly world-wide MNCs can afford to ignore translation exposure, as paper translation losses in some currencies will be offset by paper translation gains in other currencies.

Some companies do not attempt to manage translation exposure at all because:

● There is no cash inflow or outflow.

● The effect on the balance sheet can be likened to the effect of a revaluation of a factory in the balance sheet of a company with no foreign exchange commitments. If the factory is revalued, the increase in fixed assets in the published accounts is matched by an increase in reserves and a reduced gearing ratio. However, there is no change in the actual cash position of the company.

● If hedging techniques are used, companies are paying money to hedge what is purely an accounting exercise. Many writers feel that it is not in the shareholder's interest to hedge paper gains and losses.

● In addition, hedging techniques involve a cash inflow or outflow (e.g. the gain or loss on a close out of a forward contract) which is not justified when the translation gain or loss is of a non-cash nature.

● Investing in overseas assets is essentially a strategic decision, and investors may have invested in a particular company to take advantage of its overseas investments. Any form of hedging would nullify that strategic exposure.

Indeed, when a company purchases assets in a country with a weak currency, it should ensure that the return on those assets is likely to be sufficient to compensate for the translation exposure.

The main argument for managing translation exposure is that, especially in the case of 'weaker' companies, changes in gearing or net worth, however caused, affect the attitudes of lenders, shareholders and creditors. This must ultimately affect the cash position. In addition, in many countries translation losses are not allowable for tax purposes. Thus, such losses can affect reserves by more than would the equivalent trading loss.

A survey by Price Waterhouse in October 1995 reported that 39% of the companies surveyed applied local currency borrowings to hedge foreign asset exposures while 32% used forward contracts. Respondents in the Scandinavian countries indicated relatively high levels of translation exposure hedging, but Canada, the Netherlands and Hong Kong indicated significantly lower levels.

Whenever any hedging action is taken to cover translation exposure, always:

i)   take specialist tax advice.

ii)   make sure that the hedge is cost-effective. It is pointless spending precious management time in trying to construct a perfect translation exposure hedge. A hedge which approximately covers the translation exposure will be more cost-effective than a 'perfect hedge'.

iii). In some countries, companies can now denominate their capital in currencies other than home currency if they wish. Hence, a major MNC could have part of its equity capital denominated in overseas currency to match overseas assets. However, there are major problems in having equity denominated in a cocktail of currencies:

-    There will be a need to explain and justify this, to the market.

-    What happens if the currency base of assets changes?

-    The tax position is unclear.

-    Separate dividend streams would be needed.

-    Essentially, there would be separate companies for each type of equity.

iv)   Hedging profit-and-loss translation exposure is always worthwhile in the following circumstances:

-    if the corporate has tight loan covenants covering reported gearing or reported net worth that might be breached because of translation losses.

-    if the Chief Executive has given in profit forecast to the share analysts for earnings that are exposed to translation fluctuations. It may be important to protect this commitment to retain credibility with the capital markets.

-    if the company enjoys a high price earnings ratio because of steady growth of reported accounting profits. This record may be an asset which is worth preserving, even though it means hedging a paper gain/loss with a cash gain/loss.

8.9   Economic Exposure

a)   Overview

This arises from the structure of the business, the currency of competitors and the way in which costs and prices respond to change. A brief definition could be 'the risk that long term movements in relative exchange rates will cause structural changes which undermine profitability'.

Foreign currency economic exposure risks are often not managed because they are:

a)   not reported in the accounts;

b)   difficult to quantify;

c)   sometimes unhedgable.

However, nowadays there are sophisticated computer techniques which can provide a logical and quantifiable analysis of economic exposure, but many large companies tend not to make full use of these developments.

When such computer techniques are not available, the treasurer can prepare a schedule showing the currencies to which the company is economically exposed.
However, a major problem in trying to quantify economic exposure is :

i)   In addition to forecasting exchange rate movements, it is necessary to forecast movements in relative inflation rates (or, better still, changes in input costs and output prices). If the move in exchange rates is caused by relative inflation differences, then presumably the effect of the change of exchange rate will be cancelled out by way of increased or decreased costs or prices.

ii)   It is not easy to know exactly what the currency of cost base is for competitors. For instance, Japanese car manufacturers have a sterling cost base to the extent that they manufacture cars in the UK.

iii) It is even more difficult to ascertain whether and to what extent competitors have hedged their currency positions. Such hedging will nullify the effect of exchange rate movements for the amounts so covered.

b)   General Points on Economic Exposure

A company which is entirely home-based and which makes all its payments and receipts in domestic currency, can still have an economic exposure to foreign exchange risk if its market is subject to foreign competition.

A typical example could be a UK-based coal-mining operation with all its costs and revenues denominated in sterling. In the case of imports from Australia, the foreign currency economic exposure could arise if the Australian $ were to depreciate against sterling, without a corresponding change in relative price levels. In that situation, assuming the Australian's costs were denominated in Australian $ and assuming it did not hedge its sterling receipts, then there would be scope for a price reduction in £ sterling terms for Australian coal.

c)   Minimisation of Economic Exposure

The best methods are internal techniques such as:

- The company must have a high level of efficiency with good profitability. This makes the company less vulnerable to adverse economic changes.

- Diversification of suppliers, products, markets and countries of manufacture is essential. MNCs are well placed in this respect.

- There must be active research on new products and new materials to help maintain diversity.

- The company may be able to exert political pressure to reduce competition via imports (e.g. prove that the competitor's products do not meet safety standards).

- The company must not become over-borrowed, otherwise its room for manoeuvre is restricted.

- The company may be willing if necessary to switch its manufacturing location to match the cost base of its competitors. However, this would be a major strategic decision involving company policy in areas other than foreign currency management.

Note

Hedging instruments which create a cash gain or loss (e.g. forward contracts which are closed out) are not suitable for hedging foreign currency economic exposure. These cash gains or losses are to be sudden large one-off amounts which are to be offset against a long-term exposure which is difficult to quantify and which will tend to develop gradually over time.

8.10   Brown Construction: Case Study

Brown Construction plc is a UK-based company which specialises in undertaking major projects in the USA. Some three years ago the company acquired a subsidiary in the USA in order to help in overcoming the problems which can prevent UK firms from obtaining contract work in North America.

Recently the company purchased a quarry in the UK so as to be assured of a supply of raw materials which are required in the manufacturing process. The purchase cost, £10m, was funded out of a medium-term sterling loan with interest at 1% over London Inter-bank Offered Rate (LIBOR).

In addition to the raw materials extracted from the UK mine, the company purchases raw materials from France and also from UK suppliers. The supplies from France make up about 20% of the company's costs of raw materials.

At the present time, there is strong competition from Japanese companies for the contracts in the USA.

The USA subsidiary has a current net worth of US $12m and the asset is translated into sterling for the purposes of Brown's accounts, using the closing rate method. The US $ has strengthened since acquisition, so the group treasurer has been content to leave the translation exposure unhedged. However, he would like to 'lock in' the existing translation gains.

Brown Construction have a policy of taking out forward contracts once firm commercial contracts have been agreed for USA sales.

Required

Assess the practical and theoretical issues which could be considered in connection with the management of foreign exchange exposures of Brown Construction.

8.11   Issues for Brown Construction to Consider

Practical Issues for Brown Construction

a)   Transaction Exposure

It is assumed that the company is in a highly risky industry with large one-off payments. In addition, there will probably be a high ratio of fixed costs to variable ones. As Brown Construction is certainly not a price maker, and as dollar receipts will tend to be large 'lumpy' amounts, it cannot afford to take the risk of not hedging. Thus, a hedge-everything policy would seem wise.

Brown's should first of all try internal techniques :

- Possibly a larger proportion of the preparatory work could be switched to the USA to switch the cost base. This would be a major, long-term decision and strategic factors over and above transaction exposure will be involved in such decisions.

- Ascertain whether any UK suppliers will be prepared to invoice in US $. Some suppliers, for example, subsidiaries of USA multinationals, may be willing to co-operate. However, check that the dollar prices are still competitive in sterling terms,

- Obtain quotes for cross rates to convert some US $ receipts to French francs, crediting the proceeds to an FFR bank account. The benefit here is that FFR credited to this account can cover the FFR payments to French suppliers. In addition, the impact of the bank's bid/offer spread will be reduced, since it avoids converting dollars to sterling, and then converting sterling to FFR to pay French suppliers.

After netting as far as possible by means of internal techniques, external techniques can be considered for managing the remaining transaction exposures.

- Use forwards for 'certain sums', then use options to cover potential, but not certain sums. Thus if 70% of the sales forecast was considered 'certain', then forward contracts could be utilised. The remaining 30% could be covered by options.

- Hedge the pre-transaction exposure by way of options or seek other methods (see Unit 20 for a more detailed explanation of the problems of tender bonds etc.).

b)   Translation Exposures

The treasurer wishes to 'lock in' his translation gains which have arisen as a result of the appreciation of the US $. The past gains could be 'locked in' if the US $ asset were to be matched by a US $ liability. This switch could be achieved by borrowing US $ and converting the proceeds to sterling to pay off the sterling loan. However, a currency swap would be a more appropriate technique, as this leaves the existing sterling borrowing undisturbed and thus avoids any penalties for early repayment of the sterling loan (which in any case may well be at a subsidised rate for export finance).

If there are gearing covenants in the loan agreements, it may be wise to match around half the US $ assets with a currency swap. If net worth covenants apply, then consider matching the full dollar value of the subsidiary by means of a currency swap.

The US $ interest cost will help hedge some of the US $ transaction exposure.

Take specialist tax advice to ensure the swap and the assets are matched for tax purposes.

Many academic writers consider that translation exposures should not be managed as they are merely 'paper' gains and losses. However, 'weaker' companies do need to monitor translation exposures, as the perceptions of bankers, creditors and shareholders could be affected.

If any profit forecasts have been made to market analysts, the company should take out a currency option to ensure credibility is not lost by adverse exchange rate movements. This will be less necessary if the average rate is used for consolidation of profits.

c) Economic Exposure

On the face of it, the relevant rates are £:US $ and Japanese yen:US $. If the yen depreciates faster than the £ against the $, and if there is no change in relative inflation, then the Japanese will gain a competitive advantage (vice versa if sterling depreciates faster).

However, in practice this economic exposure probably cannot be quantified. Brown's may not know the currency cost base of their competitor nor whether the competitor hedges.

In practice this exposure may not be hedged as it will not be reported in the published accounts.

Other Arguments to Support the Hedging of Exchange Rate Risks by Brown Construction

These arguments are summed up as:

i)   Corporate hedging reduces the volatility of earnings and the volatility of future cash flows. This in turn reduces the risk of incurring the costs of financial distress.

ii) Lower risk should result in a lower cost of capital. The cost of capital (after some adjustments) is the basis of the discount rate applied to future cash flows when valuing the business; thus, the lower the discount rate the higher the value of the firm.

iii) Lower risk of financial distress may increase debt capacity for a hedged company.

iv) Managers and employees cannot hold a diversified portfolio of jobs. Good managers should be attracted to firms which manage foreign currency exposures as such firms are likely to be affected to a lesser extent by foreign exchange fluctuations.

v) The theoretical arguments against hedging (CAPM, PPP, market efficiency and self-insurance), even if valid in general terms, are all applicable over long periods of time. However, a single large loss on foreign currency could be enough to put Brown Construction into liquidation.

For more detailed explanation of points iv) and v) above, please see Unit 7.

Other Matters Regarding Internal Controls
The board of directors should ensure that there are clear written rules for the following internal aspects of currency management:

- hedging philosophy;

- which derivatives can be used;

- details of authority for company officers to transact derivatives business on behalf of the company (who is authorised, maximum amounts, which instruments and the extent to which the derivative must exactly match an underlying future cash commitment);

- separation of dealing, confirmation and settlement duties to avoid a 'Nick Leeson' situation;

- details of the banks with which derivatives business can be transacted.

Unit 9

Methods of International Settlement through Banks

Objectives

On completion of this unit the student should be able to:

- **differentiate between nostro and vostro accounts;**

- **understand the bookkeeping involved in funds transfer;**

- **appreciate the different methods of international settlement, i.e. SWIFT, telegraphic transfer, mail transfer and bank draft;**

- **appreciate the problems involved in the use of personal cheques for international settlement;**

- **appreciate the issues set out in the EU directive on cross-border payments.**

Note: Dangers of fraud or illegality when transferring money abroad

Under the Drug Trafficking Act 1994 and under the Prevention of Terrorism Act 1989, banks must disclose to the authorities any suspicions regarding the location of funds which might be used for possible offences under these Acts. It is implied that banks making disclosures in good faith under the 'money laundering' provisions of these Acts will be protected from potential liability under the duty of secrecy to customers.

Many banks have a compliance office or a fraud office which is a central point, the function of which is to prevent fraud or illegal transfers taking place. It is important to identify examples of potential fraud and to refer them to the fraud office. Instances which could involve fraud are:

- large round amounts going abroad from a relatively new account, which is fed by many small payments coming in. Obviously, there may be legitimate reasons for the transactions but, where the account is new, its proprietors are not well known, and its business is not too clear, then it may be worth a reference to the fraud office. It is important to take and follow up references on new accounts.

- attempts to transfer money in contravention of internationally agreed sanctions.

- unauthenticated instructions to make large sums available to a beneficiary abroad. Be particularly careful as regards messages via fax, telex or a computer link, which purport to authorise such transfers. It is essential that proper authority is held, by way of signatures or by way of computerised code.

- transfers which would contravene the laws of other countries, for example payments for exports which the exporters' government has banned by law. Involvement in such transfers could mean that the bank could be 'blacklisted' by the other government.

- status replies from other banks which are unauthenticated and cannot be verified as being genuine.

- requests from customers to pass messages to overseas businesses, usually by means of telex. Take care as to the wording of such messages and refer them to the compliance office if there seems to be any danger that the message could commit our bank in a way which may not be intended.

9.1 Nostro and Vostro Accounts

The word **nostro** means our and **vostro** means your.

From the point of view of a UK bank, a nostro account is our bank's account in the books of an overseas bank, denominated in foreign currency. An example would be an account in the name of Midland Bank, in the books of Chemical Bank New York, denominated in US $. Midland is a customer of Chemical Bank.

From the point of view of a UK bank, a vostro account is your bank's account with us, denominated in sterling. An example of a vostro account would be an account in the name of Chemical Bank maintained in the books of Midland Bank. The account would be denominated in sterling and Chemical Bank would be a customer of Midland.

When funds are remitted from the UK, nostro accounts are used if the payment is denominated in foreign currency, and vostro accounts are used if payment is denominated in sterling.

Banks treat their nostro accounts in the same way as any other customer would treat his bank account. The bank will maintain its own record of the nostro account, known as a mirror account, and it will reconcile the bank statements against these mirror accounts.

In order to maintain accurate records, the bank tries to **value-date** all transactions. The bank estimates the date on which authorised transactions will actually be debited or credited to the nostro account, and it uses these dates in its mirror account.

9.2 Book-keeping for Transfers of Funds

When a UK bank customer wishes to transfer funds denominated in sterling to the bank account of a beneficiary abroad, the book-keeping is as follows, assuming that an account relationship exists between the respective banks:

a) Debit the UK customer with the sterling amount, plus charges, and credit the sterling account of the overseas bank. This is a vostro account from the UK bank's point of view.

b) On receipt of the advice, the overseas bank will withdraw the sterling from the vostro account, convert it to currency, and then credit the beneficiary with the currency equivalent, less its charges.

If the transfer is denominated in foreign currency, the book-keeping is:

i) Debit the customer with the sterling equivalent, plus charges, of the required currency amount, and credit the currency to the nostro account. (If the UK customer maintains a foreign currency account, then the appropriate currency amount can be debited to that account, and there will be no need to arrange for conversion into sterling.)

ii) Advise the overseas bank that it can debit the nostro account with the requisite amount of currency and credit the funds to the account of the beneficiary.

The various methods of settlement all involve the same book-keeping. The only difference is the method by which the overseas bank is advised about the transfer.

9.3   Bank Drafts

A bank draft is in effect a cheque drawn by one bank on another. If sterling payment is required, the draft will be drawn on the vostro account; if currency payment is required, then the draft is drawn on the nostro account.

The UK bank will place sterling in the vostro account, or currency in the nostro account, to meet the drafts. The customer's account will be debited in reimbursement and charges will be passed.

The UK customer will forward the draft to the beneficiary, who will pay it into his bank for credit to his account. Ultimately, the draft will be debited to the appropriate nostro or vostro account.

There are major disadvantages to the use of drafts for large transfers:

a) The remitter is debited at the time the draft is issued, but there is a delay before the beneficiary can pay the draft into his bank account and obtain cleared funds.

b) If the beneficiary does not bank at the bank on which the draft is drawn, the funds will be treated as uncleared.

c) The draft could be lost or stolen, and banks are reluctant to 'stop' a bank draft because it amounts to dishonour of the bank's own paper. In any case, the bank will require an indemnity from the customer authorising the bank to debit the customer's account if it should suffer any loss by stopping the draft and issuing a duplicate.

9.4   Mail Transfer (MT) and Telegraphic Transfer (TT)

The UK bank will need to know whether to credit the account of the beneficiary with a named bank (in which case, request the bank account number) or whether it is instructed to request the overseas bank to advise and pay the beneficiary, if the beneficiary banks elsewhere. In the case of transfers of funds to a private individual, the overseas bank can be asked to pay the beneficiary on application and identification.

Please refer to the customer order forms (Figures I and 2).

On receipt of the customer's instructions, the book-keeping shown above at 9.2 will be applied. The UK bank will advise the overseas bank of the transaction by airmail, and the instruction must be signed by authorised signatories.

If a TT is used, the same procedure as for MT is adopted. However, the instructions to the overseas bank are sent by cable or telex, and the overseas bank will require a special authenticating code word before it will act.

9.5   SWIFT (Society for Worldwide Interbank Financial Telecommunications)

SWIFT is a computerised method by which banks are able to remit messages using British Telecom or international lines. SWIFT is similar to cable or telex, except that it is a computerised link and is totally secure. Not all banks are on the SWIFT system, and indeed 50 banks world-wide represent 70% of the SWIFT turnover.

Urgent SWIFT is an alternative to a TT. The accounting entries and procedures are identical for TT or for urgent SWIFT. The only difference is the method whereby the message is remitted to the overseas bank. These SWIFT transfers are sometimes known as 'express international money transfers'.

Ordinary SWIFT is used as an alternative to MT. These transfers are sometimes known as 'international money transfers'.

The distinction between 'priority' and 'non-priority' SWIFT occurs in the speed of action undertaken by the overseas bank, not in the time it takes to deliver the message. For ordinary SWIFT, the UK bank will ask the overseas bank to value-date the transaction forward to the date when an airmail instruction, sent at the same time, would be expected to arrive.

9.6   Application of Charges to SWIFT, TT and MT

The UK customer can instruct the bank as to who is responsible for charges.

This is best shown by an example. Suppose the transfer was for sterling £10,000, and the UK bank's charge was £20. The customer's authority would state who was responsible for the charges. There are three combinations:

BARCLAYS BANK PLC
INTERNATIONAL PAYMENT ORDER
(formerly Mail Payment Order)

Please complete this form by
TYPEWRITER or in BALL PEN in
BLOCK CAPITALS. NO CARBON
PAPER IS REQUIRED.

	Amount (State £ Sterling or Currency Required)
	Amount in words and Name of Currency

BENEFICIARY'S FULL NAME
(State Mr., Mrs., Miss, Ms. or other title)
AND ADDRESS
(Instructions to USA require Street and Zip Code)

Name
Street
Town
Country

If instructions B, C or D below apply please insert **BENEFICIARY'S BANKERS**
(Instructions to USA require Street and Zip Code)

Bank
Branch
Town
Country

REMITTER'S NAME
and
DETAILS (e.g. invoice)

Name

REQUEST PAYING BANK TO

A. Notify and Pay
B. Advise and credit beneficiary's account
C. Pay to the beneficiary upon application
D. Place to the credit of a new account to be opened in the beneficiary's name. – *Specimen signature(s) and Banker's reference required.*

TO BE SENT IN

S. £ Sterling
F. Foreign currency
(Please state currency if other than local currency)

CHARGES INSTRUCTIONS

G. Debit me/us with all charges
H. Deduct all charges
I. Deduct me/us with your charges. Correspondents' charges to be paid by the beneficiary. SINCE SOME CORRESPONDENTS HAVE NO MAXIMUM TO THEIR TARIFF

Please transmit the above instructions in cypher or otherwise. At your discretion or the discretion of your agent and ENTIRELY AT MY/OUR RISK you may use any method of transmitting the payment which you consider appropriate and in this connection I/we specifically release and indemnify you and your agent and your correspondents from and against the consequences of their failure to receive the message in the form in which it was despatched and of any delay that might occur during the course of transmission.

Should you, your agent or correspondents be uncertain as to the correct interpretation of the instructions given above then you, your agent or correspondents are specifically authorised to retain the funds transmitted pending further confirmation from me/us as to the instructions in doubt.

Signature

This part of formset is for Customer's guidance and should be detached by branch before submission.

425 (TFR 202) 4/85

---

1 | **TO BARCLAYS BANK PLC** | **2**

FOR CUSTOMER USE   DATE _____

PLEASE TRANSFER DIRECTLY OR INDIRECTLY BY AIRMAIL OR OTHER MEANS AS APPROPRIATE

Name of Currency		Amount in Figures

State or Province

State or Province

Beneficiary Account Number

Please transmit the above instructions in cypher or otherwise. At your discretion or the discretion of your agent and ENTIRELY AT MY/OUR RISK you may use any method of transmitting the payment which you consider appropriate and in this connection I/we specifically release and indemnify you and your agent and your correspondents from and against the consequences of their failure to receive the message in the form in which it was despatched and of any delay that might occur during the course of transmission.

Should you, your agent or correspondents be uncertain as to the correct interpretation of the instructions given above then you, your agent or correspondents are specifically authorised to retain the funds transmitted pending further confirmation from me/us as to the instructions in doubt.

FOR BANK USE ONLY

Vet.	Branch Code No.	Branch Ref.	Customer's Sterling A/C No.	Special Codes
Input	20 – –			

TO THE DEBIT OF MY/OUR ACCOUNT

Check — STERLING ACCOUNT   CFC ACCOUNT   AGAINST FORWARD CONTRACT

Release   Date _____

Signature(s) - SEE OVERLEAF FOR BANKS STANDARD TERMS AND CONDITIONS

ADDRESS (if not already known) _____

DATE SUBMITTED

Figure 1

This is a Multipart Set   Please use a Ball Point Pen

TELEGRAPHIC TRANSFER ORDER

| | I.S.B. REF |

TO BARCLAYS BANK PLC   **STAFF TRAINING CENTRE**   BRANCH

SORTING CODE NUMBER   BRANCH REF   DATE
A 20 - 07 - 94 **B** 127 **C** 21-4-XX

BANK USE ONLY

AMOUNT REMITTED	
Check against Para 6 below	
RATE	£
COMMISSION	
CORR CHARGES	
CABLE CHARGES	
TOTAL	£
CREDIT	

ACCOUNT NO   BENEFICIARY (short name)

DATE E P   CHECKERS' INITIALS

IF CURRENCY BOOKED   Rate

Ref

Confirmed with

| Value date | Date Booked | Initials |

CABLE TO   Route

TELEX NO OR ADDRESS

1	TT REF No
2	TEST
3	WE CREDIT
	WE PAY
	DEBIT
4	VALUE
5	CABLE PAY YOUR
6	CURRENCY AND AMOUNT LESS EXPENSES / CHARGES OUR ACCOUNT

CCY SYMBOL   AMOUNT   DECIMAL

CABLE ORDER (Delete words not to be sent.
Check Para 6 against Amount Remitted above).

Authorised by

DESPATCH   TELEX NO OR ADDRESS
CHECKED   CHECKED

TO BARCLAYS BANK PLC
   INTERNATIONAL SERVICES BRANCH

ORIGINAL CABLE ORDER   CONFIRMATION OF TELEPHONE ORDER

BRANCH AUTHORISATION

CUSTOMER'S INSTRUCTIONS

D Please complete this side of the form by TYPEWRITER or in BLOCK CAPITALS USING BALL PEN. NO CARBON PAPER is REQUIRED. Instructions must be indicated by an 'X' in the appropriate box. This form is NOT TO BE USED FOR PAYMENTS AGAINST SHIPPING DOCUMENTS

E AMOUNT IN FIGURES   **£ 7000**

AMOUNT IN WORDS   **SEVEN THOUSAND POUNDS STERLING**

F TO BE SENT IN
☐ STERLING
☒ FOREIGN CURRENCY
NAME OF CURRENCY   **SWISS FRANCS**

G CHARGES
☐ ALL CHARGES TO BE DEBITED TO PAID BY ME US
☐ ALL CHARGES TO BE DEDUCTED FROM AMOUNT
☒ YOUR CHARGES TO BE DEBITED TO PAID BY ME US BUT CORRESPONDENT'S CHARGES TO BE PAID BY BENEFICIARY

BENEFICIARY'S BANKER'S (if known)

CABLE RATE
☐ URGENT (If available)
☐ ORDINARY

7 ☐ ADVISE AND CREDIT   ☒ NOTIFY AND PAY   ☐ PAY ON APPLICATION

8
K BENEFICIARY (full name and address)
**SIMON BURNAGE
RAEMISTRASSE 4
8001 ZURICH SWITZERLAND**

9
L REMITTER
CURZON COMMUNICATIONS

10
M   **INV 71594**

Please transmit the above instructions at my risk and use and or expense. I agree and consent that at your discretion you may use the Test system and that I acknowledge your and your Correspondents from and against the consequences of their failure to receive the message and of any resulting delay mistake or alteration. I also undertake to indemnify you and against any loss which may be incurred through your Correspondents using powers to modify the terms named in the above instructions or retaining the funds should your or your Correspondents deem such retention expedient pending confirmation of the identity of any person or of the above instructions or retention of identity.

☐ PAYMENT BY CHEQUE CASH ☒ DEBIT MY ACCOUNT   70395612

IF APPLICABLE INDICATE
☐ CFC A/C   ☐ FORWARD CONTRACT   rate / deal reference

N *T. Curzon*

SEE REVERSE FOR THE BANK STANDARD TERMS AND CONDITIONS
SIGNATURE

2-3-2R

Figure 2

	UK Bank's Charges	Australian Bank's Charges
a)	Remitter	Beneficiary
b)	Remitter	Remitter
c)	Beneficiary	Beneficiary

a) Account entries for remitter/beneficiary charges:

Debit UK customer	£10,020
Credit commission	£20
Credit vostro account	£10,000

The Australian bank will deduct its charges from the amount credited to the beneficiary.

b) Account entries for all charges remitter:

Debit UK customer	£10,020
Credit vostro account	£10,000
Credit commission	£20

The Australian bank will credit its customer with the full £10,000, and will claim its charges from the UK bank who will debit the UK customer's account in reimbursement.

c) Account entries for all charges beneficiary:

Debit UK customer	£10,000
Credit vostro account	£9,980
Credit commission	£20

The Australian bank will deduct its own charges from the £9,980 before crediting the beneficiary.

9.7 The Advantages and Disadvantages of TT, MT and SWIFT

All these systems are secure, in that the payments cannot be stolen in the same way as a bank draft could be. However, with mail transfer, there is always the danger that the instruction itself could be lost in the post.

The main disadvantage of TT or urgent SWIFT is that there is an extra cost involved for remitting an urgent message. However, the beneficiary can receive the funds much sooner, and this reduction in float time can save interest for both remitter and beneficiary. For large sums, TT or its equivalent will save far more in interest than will be lost by the extra costs.

9.8 The Disadvantages of the Buyer Using his own Cheques in Settlement of Overseas Debt

This course of action is not to be recommended because:

a) In some countries (but not in the UK), sending a cheque abroad may contravene the exchange control regulations of the buyer's government.

b) The buyer's bank and the beneficiary's bank usually impose heavy charges for handling such cheques.

c) There is an inevitable delay between the time the cheque is collected and the time funds are actually remitted by the buyer's bank. One method of speeding up the process of clearing cheques is to use a 'lockbox' facility and this system is particularly useful for UK exporters who sell to the USA and who are paid by the buyer's cheque. The buyer is instructed to post his cheque to a post office box address in the USA. A local bank opens the 'lockbox' at least once a day and initiates the clearing of the cheques. This process dramatically reduces the clearing time, since the cheque itself does not have to go from the USA to the UK and back again. UK banks can organise 'lockbox' facilities by making arrangements with correspondent banks abroad.

Lockbox facilities are also widely available within the EU. Arrangements can be made for the proceeds of the cheques collected via the 'lockbox' system to be held in a collection account with the overseas bank. The funds can then be drawn down as and when required to meet the local currency needs of the UK seller.

d) From the beneficiary's point of view, there is no guarantee that the cheque will be paid.

9.9 Special Problems with Value-dating Of TTs

The problem with value-dating TTs is best illustrated by the following question:

Question
At 9.30 a.m. your customer instructs you to transfer FRF50,000 to a beneficiary in Rouen, France and US $50,000 to a beneficiary in Look out Mountain in Tennessee, both payments to be made by TT. The customer says that he telexed both beneficiaries the previous day and received replies from them. He therefore assumes that the funds will be received by the beneficiaries by close of business today.

a) Advise him whether it is likely that the beneficiaries will receive the funds today.

b) Are there any particular points which could help speed up the transfer of funds?

Answer: Part One

a) Many overseas banks have cut-off times, sometimes as early as 8.00 a.m. Any instructions received after this time are processed on the next working day.

b) It is most unlikely that the UK bank will have a nostro/vostro account relationship with the bank in Tennessee; likewise, the French transfer will most likely have to be routed through a bank in Paris. The funds will therefore have to be transmitted through intermediary banks.

c) The messages between intermediary banks have to be authenticated, causing further delay.

d) On the Continent there are often local holidays where banks are closed on a particular saint's day. Hence, there is no guarantee that funds will be received by the beneficiaries today.

Answer: Part Two

a) If there are any particulars that can be quoted, e.g. bank branch and account number of the beneficiary.

b) The intermediary banks must be advised to remit all instructions by telex or telephone, or TT.

Note

Section 9.13 of this unit explains some of the initiatives taken by the European Commission to speed up settlements and reduce costs of cross-border transfers.

9.10 Settlement of Inward Payments to UK Beneficiaries

One possible cause of delay in the crediting of cleared funds into the account of a UK beneficiary could be the time taken between receipt of the funds from overseas by a London office of a UK bank and the transferring of those funds from that London bank to the branch bank of the beneficiary. The methods used depend on whether the payment is denominated in sterling or in foreign currency.

i)   Inward Sterling Payments

Sterling will have been credited to the vostro account of the UK bank by the remitting overseas bank. Usually this vostro account will be maintained at the London office of the UK bank or at one of the major International Division branches in the provinces. Provided the beneficiary's bank account details as quoted on the incoming transfer show the account as being held at one of the branches of the bank holding the vostro account, there should be no problem regarding delays. The payment would normally be credited as cleared funds through the bank's internal systems on the date of receipt, or on the value date advised by the remitting bank.

Where the beneficiary's bank account details show a branch of a different bank, the CHAPS system could be used to transfer the funds on receipt of payment or on the value date quoted by the remitting bank. In theory, CHAPS involves a same-day transfer of sterling funds between bank accounts in the UK. However, there are cut-off times after which the transfer cannot be effected until the next working day. Some banks have built an interface between SWIFT and their CHAPS gateways to facilitate rapid processing of international sterling payment instructions.

Usually payments of under £1,000 are made by banker's payment, which is, for all practical purposes, a cheque drawn on the head office of the bank holding the vostro account. For transfers by this method, delay is inevitable both on account of postal time and on account of the time required to clear the banker's payment. While such banker's payments are certain to be honoured if drawn on a reputable bank, there will be a delay before the payment is treated as cleared for interest purposes.

As an alternative to banker's payment, the bank holding the vostro account may use the bank giro system to transfer the funds to the beneficiary's bank account. This method is superior to banker's payment because the beneficiary will receive cleared funds on the second working day after the transaction has been initiated. Bank giro transfers can be for any amount.

Where the overseas remitting bank's advice merely quotes a name and address of the beneficiary, without bank details, the bank holding the vostro account will usually send a bank draft to the address shown. Once again, postal and clearing delays could apply.

ii) Inward Currency Payments

Initially such payments will be made into the nostro account in the name of the UK bank. Where the beneficiary banks at a branch of the same bank as that holding the nostro account, the relevant branch must be contacted for confirmation that the beneficiary requires the funds to be converted to sterling. Once that confirmation has been received, the currency will be converted to sterling, and the beneficiary will receive the funds in the same way as has already been detailed for the sterling funds in section i) above.

Where the beneficiary banks at another bank, the bank holding the original nostro account would simply transfer the funds to the nostro account of the beneficiary's bank. That bank would then be responsible for transferring the funds into the relevant account of the beneficiary.

9.11 How a UK Beneficiary Can Reduce Delays within the UK in Respect of Funds Received from Abroad

i) Always specify bank account details on the contracts and invoices sent to the buyer.

ii) Whenever possible, insist that the buyer quotes the beneficiary's bank as the correspondent bank through which settlement is to be made by the remitting bank.

iii) Where currency payments are to be received, the beneficiary should ensure that his bank is given clear instructions as to the disposal of funds. The bank should have been instructed in good time as to whether to convert the currency into sterling or whether the monies should be credited to a currency account in the customer's name.

iv) The beneficiary should, whenever possible, insist that the buyer telexes the remitting bank's remittance reference. In the event of any delay in receipt of funds, the UK bank can be advised of this detail to help it trace the payment.

v) Whenever cash flow and interest considerations justify the expense, arrangements should be made to have all transactions advised by the quickest possible means. This will ensure that internal UK transfers are made by CHAPS. However, for smaller amounts where the CHAPS fee is not justified, arrangements should be made for internal transfers to be made by bank giro, rather than by banker's payment.

9.12   Recent Developments within the EU Regarding Payments

i) For some time now, corporate treasurers have been able to initiate CHAPS transfers from their own desktop terminals. This facility is now available for international transfers by way of SWIFT or TT. In addition, the payment details of regular suppliers can be retained on computer so that the corporate treasurer merely needs to input the amount and value date to initiate a payment. Naturally, appropriate security procedures are laid down to cover direct payments.

ii) The direct debit system has existed for many years in the UK. This has now been extended to international payments in parts of the EU. Thus, a UK importer could authorise his bank to accept claims from his suppliers, subject possibly to maximum amounts and frequencies, at the debit of his account.

iii) Strategic alliances of national clearing houses may well set up in competition with SWIFT.

iv) Suppliers, purchasers and bankers are becoming linked in Electronic Data Interchange (EDI). This enables simultaneous real-time transfers to be made with automatic advice and reconciliation against invoice for the supplier (see also Appendix II).

v) Lockbox systems can be used to speed up the collection of cheques.

vi) Different giro systems are being linked in different countries to speed up international bank giro transfers.

vii) Credit cards are being developed to facilitate person-to-person and person-to-company transfers.

viii) Banks are increasingly seeking to develop new networks and links throughout the EU.

ix) There are currency clearing systems in London whereby cheques drawn on foreign currency accounts by UK drawers may be cleared.

117

9.13 The EU Directive on Cross-border Payments within the EU

Towards the end of October 1994 the EC Commission announced a package of measures designed to improve cross-border banking services. The most significant initiative was a proposal to introduce a council directive setting minimum standards for fund transfers within the EU.

Under the directive the maximum time limit for banks to complete a cross-border payment will be six working days. Banks failing to make payment within the six day time limit will have to pay interest charges. The directive will also ban double-charging and require banks to supply clear written information about their cross-border payment services, including details on how long a transfer of funds will take, how much it will cost and notification that payment has been made.

Discussions about the overall financial threshold for which the directive will apply are still being held. Once these discussions have been concluded, the directive will be submitted for final approval by the European Parliament and the EU Council of Ministers. Member states will then have to prepare binding legislation to implement the Directive.

Indications are that full implementation may be delayed until mid-1998 to ensure that all member states have the necessary legislative framework in place.

The EC Commission obviously regards the improvement of cross-border payments in the EU as being central to facilitating the work of the single market.

9.14 Self-assessment Questions

Question 1

Suppose Barclays Bank, London, holds a sterling account in the name of Chemical Bank, New York. What sort of account is this from the point of view of Barclays Bank?

Question 2

What sort of account is the account in Question 1 from the point of view of Chemical Bank?

Question 3

A UK importer wishes to settle an invoice denominated in Deutschmarks. From the point of view of the UK bank, which bank account will be used?

Question 4

Which bank account will apply to the transaction in Question 3 if the invoice is denominated in sterling?

Question 5

How does the book-keeping differ between an urgent SWIFT transfer and an MT?

Question 6

A UK importer asks the bank to remit £10,000 to an overseas beneficiary, with all charges to be passed to the beneficiary. Set out the book-keeping for an MT where the UK bank's charge is £30.

Question 7

Is it a good idea for a buyer to send his own cheque in payment for imports from abroad?

Question 8

Is a beneficiary of a TT 'guaranteed' to receive cleared funds on the same day as the remitter's bank account is debited?

Question 9

Name one customer benefit and one customer drawback to the use of TTs as opposed to the use of MTs.

Question 10

What are the disadvantages of bank drafts as a means of settlement of international debts?

(Answers given in Appendix VI)

9.15 Specimen Question

Your bank has a customer whose payment terms are **cash with order**. This has resulted in a large number of cheques, drawn in sterling by buyers in Europe, and in dollars from others in the USA, being paid into your bank for collection by this customer.

Required

a) Detail the various steps taken by banks in both cases, whereby funds are eventually received for the sterling account of the company.

b) The parent company has expressed concern as to the cost and delay involved in obtaining these funds and seeks your advice. It is understood that while it might be possible to persuade customers in Europe to adopt other methods, any attempt to make a complete change in the USA would seriously affect the business. Their buyers in the USA insist on sending the actual payments in dollars with orders and in a few cases would not be prepared for any alteration whatsoever.

What advice would you give the parent company regarding payments by customers, with a view to reducing cost and delay in the availability of funds:

i) in Europe?

ii) in the United States?

State any possible disadvantages for your customers which your suggestions in relation to ii) might involve.

(Specimen Answer given in Appendix VI)

Revision Questions 1

You are advised to attempt the following questions before you proceed to Part Three of this book.

Currency Option Test
General Revision Questions

Currency Option Test

There is only one correct answer to each of the following questions. The answer is either: exercise the option, sell the option to the bank at its intrinsic value, or 'walk away' (abandon the option) or walk away and deal spot. Write the correct answer.

Question 1
An exporter has a currency put option to sell dollars to the bank at a strike price of 1.80. The exporter receives the dollars from his buyer on the expiry date of the option, when the spot rates are 1.90-1.91.

Question 2
The facts are the same as in Question 1, but the spot rates on the expiry dates are 1.70-1.71.

Question 3
The exporter holds the currency option specified in Question 1, and the spot rates are as in Question 1. However, he has not received the dollars.

Question 4
The exporter does not have the dollars, but he holds a put option to sell to the bank at 1.80. What will he do if the spot rates are 1.70-1.71 on the expiry date?

Question 5
An importer holds a call option to buy US dollars at 1.80. What will he do, if on the expiry date of the option:

a) Spot rates are 1.90-1.91 and he requires the dollars?

b) Spot rates are 1.70-1.71 and he requires the dollars?

c) Spot rates are 1.90-1.91 and he does not require the dollars?

d) Spot rates are 1.70-1.71 and he does not require the dollars?

(Answers given in Appendix VII)

General Revision Questions

Question 1
Your customer complains because he was recently debited with the close-out cost on a forward contract which he was unable to fulfil. He says it is unfair that he should have to pay a 'penalty'. How would you reply?

Question 2
Your customer entered into a forward contract for the bank to sell him DEM400,000 six months fixed. on that day the rates were:

Spot	3.9270-3.9430
Six-months premium	9.3 pf-8.6 pfg

On the maturity date of the forward contract, you are advised that the customer requires only DEM360,000 because he did not receive the full amount of goods which were expected.

Show how you would deal with this transaction on the maturity date when the rates were:

Spot	3.9225-3.9415

Question 3
Your customer has today signed a contract to export 1,000 tons of material at $100 a ton.

Payment is due two months after shipment and shipment is any time over the next month.

The rates of exchange ruling today are:

Spot	1.7755-1.7775

One-month forward 0.36 cents discount 0.41 cents discount

Two-months forward 1.18c discount 1.23c discount

Three months forward 2.40c discount 2.45c discount

The customer covered his exchange risk forward today.

a) Calculate the forward rate to be given.

b) Shipment is made two weeks later and payment is received in two months and two weeks time. However, only $95,000 is received because there is a slight defect in the goods.

Show the entries on the customer's account when the money is received, ignoring commission.

The rates ruling on that day are:

Spot   1.7950-1.8000

One-month forward 0.40c premium-0.30c premium

Question 4
The bank arranged a forward contract to sell DEM400,000 to a customer six-months forward fixed.

Rates of exchange on the day the forward contract was arranged are: 3.9225-3.9415.

Six-months forward: 0.860pfg premium-0.830pfg premium.

At the completion date of the forward contract, the customer asks you to extend it by one-month fixed. Show the entries on the customer's account, assuming he takes up the DEM400,000 in accordance with the extended forward contract.

Rates ruling on the date the forward contract is extended are:

Spot   DEM3.9215-3.9395

One-month forward 0.15pfg premium-0.07pfg premium

(Answers given in Appendix VII)

Part Three

Introduction

You will recall that at the very outset it was claimed that students would find *Finance of International Trade* a stimulating and enjoyable challenge. In Part Two you applied sensible logical principles to practical aspects of foreign exchange and money transmission. No doubt you can now see that the claim made at the beginning of the book was perfectly valid.

In Part Three of the book we examine the documents which are used in international trade. The selection of documents is inexorably and logically linked with the shipping and payment terms agreed between exporter and importer, and this link is carefully analysed.

Finally, we consider the main methods of payment for exports, together with their attendant risks and methods of containing that risk. These methods of payment are analysed in detail purely from the point of view of the exporter and his bank. A detailed analysis of the considerations of importers and their banks will be given in Part Five of the book.

125

Unit 10

Transport Documents Used in International Trade

Objectives

On completion of this unit the student should be able to:

- **understand the basic meaning of open account payment terms;**

- **appreciate the role of the bill of lading in international trade;**

- **differentiate between transport documents which are documents of title and those which are not.**

10.1 The Meaning of Open Account Payment Terms

When a buyer and seller agree to deal on open account terms, it means that the seller will despatch his goods to the buyer and will also send an invoice requesting payment. The seller loses control of the goods as soon as he despatches them. He trusts that the buyer will pay in accordance with the invoice. However, if the buyer does not pay, then the seller is in a difficult position, since the goods are now in the buyer's possession.

Despite the problems from the exporter's point of view, open account terms are quite common, especially for trade within the EU. The role of documents as discussed in this unit will relate solely to their use under open account payment terms. The changes which apply for documentary collection or documentary credit are described in Units 15 and 16.

10.2 Specimen Bill of Lading

A bill of lading normally embodies the following details, the numbers of which correspond to those on the specimen bill of lading (see Figure 1).

1   The name of the shipping company (sometimes known as the carrier).

2   The name of the shipper, who is usually the exporter, or the exporter's agent.

3   The name of the consignee. If the word 'order' appears here, then the shipper (exporter) must endorse the bill of lading. When the bill of lading has been endorsed in this way, then it is transferable by delivery. Once the goods arrive at their destination, they will be released to the bearer of one original bill of lading (see also item 11 below).

BILL OF LADING FOR COMBINED TRANSPORT SHIPMENT OR PORT TO PORT SHIPMENT

Shipper	B/L No 45969648

Shipper (2)
Speirs and Wadley Ltd.
Adderley Road
Hackney
London E8 1XY
England

B/L No 45969648
Booking Ref 1234567
Shippers Ref Job 5678

OVERSEAS
(1) CONTAINERS
LIMITED

OCL

Consignee
To Order (3)

SPECIMEN

Notify Party Address
Woldal Ltd. (4)
New Road
Kowloon
Hong Kong

Place of Receipt (Applicable only when this document is used as a Combined Transport Bill of Lading)
Speirs and Wadley Ltd.
Adderley Road
Hackney
London E8 1XY
England

Intended Vessel and Voy No
Cardigan Bay (5)

0415

Intended Port of Loading
London

Place of Delivery (Applicable only when this document is used as a Combined Transport Bill of Lading)
Woldal Ltd.
New Road
Kowloon
Hong Kong

Intended Port of Discharge
Hong Kong (6)

Marks and Nos. Container Nos (7)	Number and kind of Packages, description of Goods	Gross Weight (kg)	Measurement (cbm)
WL 124 HONG KONG 1/5	5 Wooden Cases containing 400 ELECTRIC POWER DRILLS Model LM 425 2 Speed (900RPM/2400RPM) 425 Watt high-torque motor 2 chucks – 12.5mm and 8mm supplied with each drill (8)	950	2.376

ABOVE PARTICULARS AS DECLARED BY SHIPPER

✱ Total No. of Containers/Packages
Packages or pieces (9) 5

Movement
LCL. Depot/LCL. Depot

Freight and Charges (Indicate whether prepaid or collect)

Origin zone transport charge — Prepaid
Origin Terminal Handling/LCL Service Charge — Prepaid
Ocean Freight — Prepaid (10)
Destination Terminal Handling/LCL Service Charge — Prepaid
Destination zone transport charge — Prepaid

ICS
CTBL
April /8

Number of Original Bills of Lading
(11) Two (02)

Received by the Carrier from the Shipper in apparent good order and condition (unless otherwise noted herein) the total number or quantity of Containers or other packages or units indicated✱ stated by the Shipper to comprise the Goods specified above, for Carriage subject to all the terms hereof (INCLUDING THE TERMS ON THE REVERSE HEREOF AND THE TERMS OF THE CARRIER'S APPLICABLE TARIFF) from the Place of Receipt or the Port of Loading, whichever is applicable, to the Port of Discharge or the Place of Delivery whichever is applicable, in accepting this Bill of Lading the Merchant expressly accepts and agrees to all its terms, conditions and exceptions, whether printed, stamped or written, or otherwise incorporated, notwithstanding the non signing of this Bill of Lading by the Merchant. When this document calls for Combined Transport it is a negotiable Combined Transport Document the terms of which are based upon the Uniform Rules for a Combined Transport Document (ICC Publication No 298)

Place and Date of Issue
London (13) 01 08 19..

IN WITNESS of the contract herein contained the number of originals stated opposite has been used, one of which being accomplished the other(s) to be void

For the Carrier A.J. S[illegible] (12)

COBRA B/L 2 9/831

Figure 1: Specimen Bill of Lading

As an alternative to 'order', the name and address of the importer can appear as consignee. In such cases, the importer can obtain the goods, once they have arrived at their destination, by presenting an original bill of lading, together with identification.

Normally bills of lading are made out to order and endorsed by the exporter. It is unusual for the importer to be shown as consignee.

4   The notify party is the person whom the shipping company will notify on arrival of the goods. Usually this is the importer or his agent.

5   This is the name of the carrying vessel.

6   These are the two ports. In this case the goods are to be transported from Hong Kong port to the premises of Woldal Ltd in Kowloon, and thus a place of delivery is mentioned in addition to the two ports.

7   The marks and numbers will appear on the cases in which the goods are contained, so that it is quite clear which cases are covered by this bill of lading.

8   This gives a brief description of the goods.

9   This shows how many cases. In this particular shipment, the goods are packed into five cases.

10   This shows whether the freight costs have already been paid, as they have in this case, or whether payment of freight is due on arrival at the overseas destination.

11   This shows how many original bills of lading have been issued. An original bill of lading is one which is signed by the ship's master, or by an agent of the shipping company.

12   This bill of lading is an original, having been signed on behalf of the company.

13   This is the date on which the shipping company received the goods for shipment and/or loaded the goods on board the ship.

10.3   How the Specimen Bill of Lading Would be Used in an Open Account Transaction

A UK exporter, Speirs and Wadley Ltd, has agreed to sell electric drills to Woldal Ltd, with Speirs and Wadley Ltd being responsible for all costs and risks until the goods are delivered to Woldal's premises in Kowloon.

The transaction will proceed as follows, assuming open account terms have been agreed:

a)   Speirs and Wadley will pack the drills into cases and will arrange a contract with the shipping company to deliver the goods.

b)   Speirs and Wadley will deliver the cases to Ocean Containers Ltd, who will issue two signed original bills of lading in exchange for the goods. The bills of lading will be given to Speirs and Wadley.

c)   Speirs and Wadley will airmail one of the original bills of lading to Woldal Ltd, along with any other necessary documents. The other original will probably be sent by a later mail in case the first happens to go astray, although this is unnecessary if a courier is used.

d)   When the goods arrive at Hong Kong port, Ocean Containers will notify Woldal, and will make arrangements to move the goods from the port, overland, to the Kowloon premises of the importer.

e)   Ocean Containers will release the goods to Woldal only against an original bill of lading.

f)   Woldal will then pay Speirs and Wadley in accordance with the arrangements which they have made between themselves.

10.4   The Functions of a Bill of Lading

There are four main functions:

a)   A bill of lading acts as a receipt for the goods from the shipping company to the exporter. Note the words 'received by the carrier from the shipper in apparent good order and condition' at the bottom right hand part of the front of the specimen bill of lading.

When there is no indication of damage to the goods, a bill of lading is said to be clean. The specimen bill is a clean bill of lading since the words 'received in apparent good order and condition' are not qualified in any way.

b)   The bill of lading is evidence of the contract of carriage between the exporter and the carrier. In the specimen (Figure 1) we can see the basic details of the journey (by the ship *Cardigan Bay* from London to Hong Kong and thence overland to Kowloon).

The full contract details appear on the back of the bill of lading. A detailed knowledge of these conditions is not required for the purpose of this syllabus.

c)   A bill of lading is a quasi-negotiable document. Any transferee for value who takes possession of an endorsed bill of lading obtains a good title to it, provided the transferor had a good title in the first place.

d)   A bill of lading acts as a document of title for goods being shipped overseas. The goods will be released from the overseas port only against production of one of the original bills of lading.

Original bills of lading are usually issued in sets of two or three (the number of originals will be indicated on the bill of lading).

As any one original bill of lading will enable the possessor to obtain the goods, possession of a complete set is required before control of the goods is assured. Shipping companies often issue unsigned copies of the bill of lading for record purposes. These unsigned copies are not documents of title.

10.5 The Different Types of Bill of Lading

There are many different types of bill of lading, but the main ones we need to consider are:

a) Combined Transport Bills of Lading and Similar Documents
A combined transport bill of lading may evidence that goods have been collected from a named inland place and have been despatched to a port or inland container depot in the country of import.

Depending on the terms of the sales contract (known as Incoterms and explained in Unit 12), the importer may have to make separate arrangements to have the goods collected from the port or inland container depot in his country and delivered to his factory or warehouse.

A through bill of lading is a similar document which may evidence despatch of goods to a named destination, for example the importer's warehouse. Strictly speaking, where the two parties agree that goods will be sent at the expense of the seller to the buyer's own premises, then a through bill of lading should be used if any part of the journey is covered by a sea voyage.

In practice, combined transport documents are sometimes used in place of a through bill of lading, as can be seen from the Speirs and Wadley combined transport bill of lading (Figure 1). In this document, it appears that the delivery point is the warehouse of Woldal Ltd.

Finally, it must be noted that when we come to examine documentary credits, the words 'multi modal transport documents' may be used in certain circumstances.

b) Transhipment Bills of Lading
These are used when the goods have to be transferred from one ship to another at a named transhipment port. Once again, the carrier has full responsibility for the whole journey, and these documents are usually considered to be documents of title if the appropriate **negotiable** wording appears.

c) Container Bills of Lading
When goods are packed in containers, shipping companies will issue bills of lading, which simply act as a receipt for a container. Container bills of lading can be issued to cover goods being transported on a traditional port-to-port basis, or they can cover transport from an inland container depot in the exporter's country to an inland container depot in the importer's country.

Palletised cargoes, and cargoes contained on **lash** barges which are loaded onto larger vessels, qualify for the issue of container bills of lading.

Once again the shipping company is responsible for the whole journey, and these bills of lading are considered to be documents of title, provided they contain the appropriate **negotiable** wording.

d) Marine Bills of Lading or Conventional Ocean Bills of Lading
These bills of lading are issued when the goods are being transported from one port to another by ship.

e) Short Form Bill of Lading

These bills of lading do not contain the full details of the contract of carriage on the back. However, they fulfil all the other functions of bills of lading and, in particular, they are considered to be documents of title.

f) Liner Bills of Lading

These documents fulfil all the normal functions of a bill of lading, including that of document of title. The liner bill of lading indicates that goods are being transported on a ship which travels on a scheduled route and has a reserved berth at destination; thus the exporter can reasonably assume that his goods will reach the buyer's country by a set date.

An alternative name for these documents is 'bill of lading (liner)'.

g) Charter Party Bill of Lading

A charter party bill of lading is issued by the hirer of a ship to the exporter. The terms of the bill of lading are subject to the contract of hire between the ship's owner and the hirer. Such bills are usually marked **subject to charter party.**

Because of the legal complexity involved, charter party bills of lading are not usually considered to be documents of title.

10.6 Sea Waybills

A sea waybill (sometimes known as a ship's waybill) is a transport document which can be issued by the shipping company as an alternative to bills of lading.

The functions of a waybill are similar to those of a bill of lading, except that a waybill is not negotiable and it is not a document of title. On arrival at their destination, the goods will be released by the shipping company to the named consignee against identification.

When exporters agree to sell on open account terms, it follows that the exporter should ask the shipping company for sea waybills rather than for bills of lading.

The objective with open account is for the goods to reach the importer with the minimum formality, and waybills can meet that objective. As soon as the goods reach their destination, the shipping company will notify the consignee, who will be the importer. The importer can then collect the goods, without the need to produce the waybill.

If bills of lading go astray, there are problems for the importer in collecting the goods, whereas it is immaterial to the importer whether or not he has possession of a waybill.

Sea waybills are very similar in scope to air waybills, a specimen of which we will examine at 10.7.

10.7 Specimen Air Waybill (also Known as an 'Air Consignment Note')

Air waybills are issued by airlines when goods are sent by air freight. There is no such thing as a bill of lading with air transport and the only transport document which can be issued is an air waybill.

Examination of the Air Waybill

The numbers correspond to those on the specimen air waybill (Figure 2).

1 This shows the names and addresses of the exporter (shipper), importer (consignee) and the carrier, Oriental Air. The words **not negotiable** indicate that this is not a document of title.

   In this particular example, the airline will notify the consignee, Woldal Ltd, when the goods arrive. Woldal will then be able to collect the goods without the need to produce this waybill.

2 This shows the names of the airports of departure and destination together with details of any special route.

3 This shows the declared value for customs purposes. A detailed knowledge of customs procedures is not required for this syllabus.

4 These marks fulfil the same function as the shipping marks on a bill of lading. The marks will appear on all the cases and on all other documents relating to this transaction.

5 This shows details of the freight charge.

6 This gives a brief description of the goods.

7 This shows whether freight is pre-paid, or whether it is payable at destination.

8 The exporter or his agent signs here to confirm the certification shown above.

9 This shows the date on which the airline took custody of the goods.

10 This is the signature on behalf of the carrier.

10.8 Other Transport Documents

When goods are sent by rail or road haulage, the transport documents will be rail or road consignment notes, or truck/carrier receipts. These are not documents of title, and goods are released to the consignee (importer) on application and identification.

When goods are sent by post, the document evidencing postage is a parcel post receipt.

All forms of waybill/consignment note/parcel post receipt fulfil two of the functions of a bill of lading. They act as a receipt for the goods by the carrier, and give some evidence of the contract of carriage. However, these documents are not negotiable and are not documents of title. Usually the words **not negotiable** will appear on these documents to indicate that they are not documents of title, but that goods will be released to the named consignee.

133

SPECIMEN

Shippers Name and Address	Not negotiable
Speirs and Wadley Ltd. Adderley Road Hackney London E8 1XY England ①	**Air Waybill*** (Air Consignment note) Issued by **ORIENT AIR** ①

Copies 1, 2 and 3 of this Air Waybill are originals and have the same validity

Consignee's Name and Address	Consignee's account Number
Philmen Int. Longtown, California. ①	

It is agreed that the goods described herein are accepted in apparent good order and condition (except as noted) for carriage SUBJECT TO THE CONDITIONS OF CONTRACT ON THE REVERSE HEREOF THE SHIPPER'S ATTENTION IS DRAWN TO THE NOTICE CONCERNING CARRIER'S LIMITATION OF LIABILITY Shipper may increase such limitation of liability by declaring a higher value for carriage and paying a supplement charge if required Carrier is not liable for the goods until they are received at its town terminal or airport office

Issuing Carrier's Agent Name and City	Accounting Information
Brunswick Air London Airport, Gatwick	

Agent's IATA Code	Account No
93-5-2221	SW 123456

Airport of Departure (Addr of first Carrier) and requested Routing
Gatwick ②

to	By first Carrier	Routing and Destination	to	by	to	by	Currency	WT/VAL PPD COLL	Other PPD COLL	Declared Value for Carriage	Declared Value for Customs
							US$			N.V.D	N.V.D ③

Airport of Destination	Flight Date	Flight Date	Amount of insurance
LONGTOWN ②	1-8-1997		$8135

INSURANCE If shipper requests insurance in accordance with conditions on reverse hereof, indicate amount to be insured in figures in box marked amount of insurance

Handling Information 5 cases
WL ④
124
LONGTOWN

No of Pieces RCP	Gross Weight	kg lb	Rate Class Commodity Item No	Chargeable Weight	Rate / Charge	Total	Nature and Quantity of Goods (incl. Dimensions or Volume) ⑥
5	950	K	4401	1000kg	0.80c ⑤	800.00	5 Wooden Cases containing 400 ELECTRIC POWER DRILLS Model LM 425 2 Speed (900RPM/2400RPM) 425 Watt high-torque motor 2 chucks – 12.5mm and 8mm supplied with each drill
5	950						

Prepaid	Weight Charge	Collect	Other Charges
800.00 ⑦			

Valuation Charge

Tax

Total other Charges Due Agent	Shipper certifies that the particulars on the face hereof are correct and that insofar as any part of the consignment contains restricted articles, such part is properly described by name and is in proper condition for carriage by air according to the International Air Transport Association's Restricted Articles Regulations
0.75	

Total other Charges Due Carrier	
2.00	*M.J. Elley* P.P. Brunswick Air ⑧ Signature of Shipper or his Agent

Total prepaid	Total collect		
802.75		1-8-1997 LGW ⑨	*M.J. Elley* ⑩ p.p. Brunswick Air

Currency Conversion Rates	cc charges in Dest Currency	Executed on (Date)	Signature of Issuing Carrier or its Agent

For Carriers Use only at Destination	Charges at Destination	Total collect Charges

ORIGINAL 3 (FOR SHIPPER)

Figure 2: Specimen Air Waybill

10.9 Self-assessment Questions

Question 1
What is meant by open account terms of payment?

Question 2
Who is normally the person named as **shipper** on a bill of lading or on an air waybill?

Question 3
What formality is necessary to ensure that a bill of lading, which shows the consignee as 'to order' can be transferred by delivery?

Question 4
A consignment of goods is in the process of being shipped abroad. Why is it necessary for the importer to have possession of a complete set of bills of lading, properly endorsed, to be sure of being able to obtain the goods on arrival at the overseas port?

Question 5
An exporter despatches goods by sea and is offered a choice of bills of lading or sea waybills by the carrier. Which transport documents should he choose if he sells on open account terms?

Question 6
What is meant by the term **clean** bill of lading?

Question 7
Which of the following is a document of title?

 a) Air consignment note;

 b) Parcel post receipt;

 c) Liner waybill;

 d) Bill of lading.

Question 8
What is the significance of the words **negotiable** and **not negotiable** on transport documents?

Question 9
An importer is named as consignee on an air waybill. The goods have now arrived at the importer's local airport, but the air waybill has gone astray. Is this a problem for the importer?

Question 10
List the basic functions of a bill of lading, and indicate which of those functions also apply to sea waybills or to air waybills.

(Answers given in Appendix VI)

Unit 11

Documents Other than Transport Documents

Objectives

On completion of this unit the student should be able to:

- **appreciate the important features of invoices;**

- **describe the various types of invoice which can be required in international trade;**

- **appreciate the open cover method of insurance of goods and understand the significance of the insurance certificate in this respect;**

- **understand the significance of the standard clauses of the Institute of London Underwriters;**

- **appreciate the importance of certificates of origin;**

- **be aware of other documents which may be encountered in overseas trade.**

11.1 Specimen Commercial Invoice

A commercial invoice gives details of the goods, details of the payment and delivery terms, and a detailed breakdown of the monetary amount due. Invoices are prepared by the seller.

If we study the specimen document (Figure 1), we can see the main details which appear on invoices. The numbers correspond to those on the document:

1 Name and address of the exporter.

2 Name and address of the importer.

3 Reference number, tax point and place and date of issue.

4 Terms of delivery (sometimes called Incoterms, sometimes called shipment terms). These terms are discussed fully in Unit 12.

5 Shipping marks. Note how these tie up with the marks on the specimen bill of lading and on the specimen air waybill.

SPECIMEN

INVOICE FACTURE RECHNUNG
FACTURA FACTUUR

Seller (Name, Address, VAT Reg No)	C.C.C.N No
Speirs and Wadley Ltd ❶ Adderley Road Hackney London E8 1XY England	8505

Invoice No. and Date (Tax Point)	Seller's Reference
247 11 Aug 19 ❸	Job No. 5678

Buyer's Reference
124

Consignee	Buyer (if not Consignee)
Woldal Ltd New Road Kowloon Hong Kong ❷	

Country of Origin of Goods	Country of Destination
EEC United Kingdom	Hong Kong

Terms of Delivery and Payment
CIP Kowloon Hong Kong ❹

Vessel/Aircraft etc	Port of Loading
Cardigan Bay	London

Port of Discharge
Hong Kong

Marks and Numbers, Numbers and Kind of Packages, Description of Goods	Quantity	@	Amount (State Currency)
WL ❺ 124 HONG KONG 1/5	❻ 5 Wooden Cases containing 400 ELECTRIC POWER DRILLS ❼ Model LM 425 2 Speed (900RPM/2400RPM) 425 Watt high-torque motor 2 chucks - 12.5mm and 8mm supplied with each drill	400 ❾	£10.27	£4108

❿ TOTAL
£4108.00 Stg

Gross Weight (kg)	Cube (m³)
950	2.376

Freight £96.00 ❽
Insurance £12.00

VAT Reg No. 241 8235 77

It is hereby certified that this invoice shows the actual price of the goods described, that no other invoice has been or will be issued, and that all particulars are true and correct

Name of Signatory
J McDonald Chief Clerk

Place and Date of Issue
London 11 Aug 19 ❸

Signature
⓫

380-1

©SITPRO OVERLAYS 1981 V1

Figure 1: Specimen Commercial Invoice

6 & 7   Description of goods.

8   Breakdown of the cost of freight and insurance. It is not always necessary for the seller to supply this information.

9   Quantity of goods, in this case 400 electric power drills.

10   Total amount payable by the importer.

11   Signature of the exporter, although signature is not strictly essential.

Note

For exports to other EU countries, the invoice must show the VAT number of the buyer to enable the exporter's goods to qualify for zero rating as regards VAT. This formality is unnecessary for exports outside the EU.

11.2   Other Types of Invoice

a)   Pro Forma Invoice

A pro forma invoice is very similar to a commercial invoice, except that it will not include any shipping marks, and it will be clearly stamped **pro forma**.

A commercial invoice is a claim for payment in connection with goods already shipped, whereas a pro forma invoice is an invitation to buy which is sent to a potential buyer. Once a definite order has been placed and once the goods have been shipped, an ordinary commercial invoice will be issued.

In some overseas countries there are exchange controls which restrict the remittance of funds abroad unless the Central Bank has given approval. Often a pro forma invoice is required by the Central Bank before approval can be given to pay for imports.

b)   Consular Invoice

This is required by some importing countries for customs purposes. The forms can be obtained from the embassy or the consulate of the importer's country. The exporter completes the details on the form and the document is then authenticated by the consulate of the importer. This consulate will be located in the exporter's country.

The purpose of consular invoices is to certify that the exporter is not **dumping** goods at artificially low prices. Their other function is to provide information which forms the basis of the import duty to be paid on the goods.

Not all importing countries require production of consular invoices. However, those countries which do require such invoices almost always charge a fee for certification. When a consular invoice is not available, the consulate will authenticate the exporter's own invoice. This is known as a 'legalised invoice'.

11.3   Insurance of Goods

It is a matter for negotiation between the exporter and the importer as to who is responsible for insuring the goods during their journey from the exporter's premises to the importer's premises. In some transactions, it may be agreed that the seller will insure the whole journey and in others the onus may be on the buyer. It is also possible for the agreement to say that the seller must cover part of the journey, and the buyer must arrange cover for the rest. (The precise details of who does what are set out in **Incoterms** which are covered in Unit 12 of this book.)

For the moment, let us consider the position of an exporter who is responsible for insurance of goods.

When an exporter sells goods on a regular basis, he will normally arrange an open policy of insurance to cover all his exports during a specific period. This provides insurance cover at all times within agreed terms and conditions. Each time a shipment is made, the exporter will declare the details and pay a premium to the insurer. A certificate of insurance is then issued by the exporter, who sends one copy to the insurance company for their records.

The benefit of the open cover system is that it avoids the need to negotiate insurance terms each time a shipment is made, and it avoids the necessity of issuing a separate policy for each individual shipment.

If an exporter sells goods on a one-off basis, then he will negotiate terms with the insurers and an insurance policy will be issued.

In the UK and in many other countries, an insured person must have a policy before he can take legal action against an insurer. A certificate alone is insufficient evidence on which to base a legal action. This legal problem is only important if the buyer needs to go to court because the insurance company has challenged a claim.

11.4 The Risks Covered by an Insurance Policy

The insurance cover is often based on the standard clauses of the Institute of London Underwriters. A detailed knowledge of these standard clauses is not required for this syllabus. However, questions sometimes mention the standard clauses in connection with risks.

There are three main standard clauses of the Institute of London Underwriters which refer to risk. Clause A begins:

> *This clause covers all risk of loss or damage to the subject matter below except as provided in clauses 4, 5, 6 and 7 below.*

Clause A provides the fullest available cover against risks, and students should not be misled into believing that the **except** clause is detrimental. Buyers and sellers are generally satisfied that Institute clause A is perfectly acceptable cover against all risks.

Institute cargo clauses B and C also cover risks, but the extent of cover they provide is less than that provided by clause A.

11.5 Specimen Insurance Certificate

This insurance document (Figure 2) has been issued in connection with the Speirs and Wadley transaction (see 10.3). We have already examined various transport and invoice documents in connection with this sale.

Insurance documents usually show the following details, the numbers of which correspond to those on the document:

1   The name and signature of the insurer.

2   The name of the exporter (Speirs and Wadley, in this case).

3   The risks covered. As you can see, this information consists merely of a list of standard clauses which apply.

4   The sum insured. Normally this is expressed in the same currency as that of the invoice, and is normally for the invoice value plus 10%. The 10% is to cover an element of profit which the importer would have made and any associated costs.

5   The description of the goods.

6   The place where claims are payable together with the details of the agent to whom claims are to be directed.

7   The signature of the exporter which is required to validate the certificate. (The certificate forms are usually pre-signed by the insurer. The exporter must complete the details and then sign.)

8   The date of issue. This date should be the same as, or earlier than, the date on the transport document. If the date on the insurance document is later, indications are that the goods have been uninsured for a time.

11.6 Certificate of Origin

Some countries insist on certificates of origin before they will allow goods into the country. The exporter inserts the relevant details, and the form has then to be authenticated by an independent body, such as a Chamber of Commerce. The shipping marks on the certificate of origin should tie up with those on other documents such as the invoice or bill of lading.

11.7 Other Documents Which are Found in International Trade

Black list certificate
A black list certificate will certify that the goods have no connection with certain countries, such as Israel. Many countries in the Middle East will insist on such a document before allowing goods to be imported. Recent political developments could reduce the use of such black list certificates.

ORIGINAL

⑥ Lloyd's Agent at Hong Kong
is authorised to adjust and settle on behalf
of the Underwriters and to purchase on
behalf of the Corporation of Lloyd's in
accordance with Lloyd's Standing
Regulations for the Settlement of Claims
Abroad any claim which may arise on this
Certificate

① **LLOYD'S**

Exporters
Reference

**THIS CERTIFICATE
REQUIRES ENDORSEMENT**

Job No. 5678

SPECIMEN

Certificate of Insurance No. C 8700/100051

This is to Certify that there has been deposited with the Committee of Lloyd's an Open Cover effected by *Barclays Insurance Brokers International Limited* of Lloyd's, acting on behalf of *Speirs and Wadley Limited* with Underwriters at Lloyd's, dated the *First* day of *January,* 19 . . ., and that the said Underwriters have undertaken to issue to *Barclays Insurance Brokers International Limited* Policy/Policies of Marine Insurance at Lloyd's to cover, up to £*100,000* in all by any one steamer *or sending by air and/or road and/or rail and/or conveyance Power Drills, other Interest held covered.* to be shipped on or before the *Thirty-first* day of *December* 19 . . ., from any port or ports, place or places in *the United Kingdom* to any port or ports, place or places in *the World. other voyages held covered* and that *Speirs and Wadley Limited* are entitled to declare against the said Open Cover the shipments attaching thereto. ②

① for the Committee of Lloyd's

Conveyance	From	
Cardigan Bay	**London**	
Via/to	**To**	**INSURED VALUE/Currency**
Hong Kong	**Kowloon, H. K.**	**£4520 Stg.** ④

Marks and Number

WL
124
HONG KONG
1/5

Interest

5 Wooden Cases
containing
400 ELECTRIC
POWER DRILLS ⑤
Model LM 425
2 Speed (900RPM/2400RPM)
425 Watt high-torque motor
2 chucks – 12.5mm and
8mm supplied with each drill

③ We hereby declare for Insurance under the said Cover interest as specified above so valued subject to the terms of the Standard Form of Lloyd's Marine Policy providing for the settlement of claims abroad and to the special conditions stated below and on the back hereof

Institute Cargo Clauses (A) (1 1 82) or Institute Cargo Clauses (Air) excluding sendings by post) (1 1 82) as applicable
Institute War Clauses (Cargo) (1 1 82) or Institute War Clauses (Air Cargo) (excluding sending by Post) (1 1 82) or Institute War Clauses (sendings by Post) (1 1 82) as applicable
Institute Strikes Clauses (Cargo) (1 1 82) or Institute Strikes Clauses (Air Cargo) (1 1 82) as applicable
General Average and Salvage Contribution payable in full irrespective of insured or contributing values

Underwriters agree losses, if any, shall be payable to the order of Speirs and Wadley Limited on surrender of this Certificate.

⑥ **In the event of loss or damage which may result in a claim under this Insurance, immediate notice should be given to the Lloyd's Agent at the port or place where the loss or damage is discovered in order that he may examine the goods and issue a survey report.**

(Survey fee is customarily paid by claimant and included in valid claim against Underwriters.)

This Certificate not valid unless the Declaration is signed by

SPEIRS AND WADLEY LIMITED
②

Dated at London   1 Aug 19 ⑧
p p *Speirs and Wadley Limited*

Signed W. H. Mewis ⑦

Brokers Barclays Insurance Brokers International Limited
India House 81/84 Leadenhall Street London EC3A 3DJ

14478/9

Figure 2: Specimen Insurance Certificate

Third-party inspection certificate

This is a certificate, issued by an independent third party resident in the exporter's country, stating that the goods conform to a certain standard. Sometimes the term 'clean report of findings' may be used.

Sometimes the buyer will insist that such a document is issued and this stipulation can form part of the terms of the sale contract.

Packing list/weight list

This gives details of the goods which have been packed and may also list the weight of individual items, together with a total weight.

Transport international routier (TIR) carnets

When goods travel overland across different frontiers outside the EU, a TIR carnet is necessary. This document certifies that the vehicle or container has been sealed by the customs authorities in the seller's country and ensures that no duty is payable in intermediate countries. When goods travel solely within the EU, the TIR carnet is unnecessary. TIR carnets usually accompany the goods on their journey. Bankers will not often see these documents and a detailed knowledge of their issue and procedures is unnecessary.

11.8 Automated Preparation of Shipping Documents

Efforts are constantly being made on a national and international basis to introduce methods of standardising and simplifying export documentation procedures. In the UK, SITPRO (the Simpler Trade Procedures Board) is charged with carrying out this task.

The basic methods of simplification all have one common factor: all documents in a set will be prepared on the basis of one single input of information.

SITPRO has produced an aligned series of export documents whereby the whole set of documents (from invoice, bill of lading to insurance document) are produced by the single input of relevant data onto a master document. The relevant information from the master document is then transferred onto the individual documents, using overlays and masks. For example, if the SITPRO master had been used in connection with the invoice and certificate of insurance shown on the preceding pages, then the details of the quantity, unit price and amount would have been transferred from the master to the commercial invoice, but these details would not have been transferred onto the insurance certificate. other details, such as the shipping marks, would have been transferred from the master onto both of the other documents.

An alternative method, using similar principles to those with the master document, is to use 'exportsets', which are 'self-carboned' paper formsets, which include a form for every document.

With the onset of computer technology, a single input of data into a computer can be used to provide the basic information for every document in a set. This technology can be used in EDI - see Appendix II.

Finally, SITPRO can provide a computerised system for preparing both the shipping documents and the relevant bank forms. For example, the SITPRO SPEX system can be used by exporters to prepare both shipping documents and documentary collection orders. (Documentary collections are covered in Unit 15.)

11.9 Self-assessment Questions

Question 1
Why are there no shipping marks on a pro forma invoice?

Question 2
A buyer and seller agree that the seller will insure the goods against all risks. The insurance document contains the standard Institute of London Underwriters clause A. This clause states that all risks are covered except certain risks specified in named clauses in the text below. Has the seller fulfilled his obligation?

Question 3
What insurance document will be issued as evidence of cover when an exporter sells goods insured under an open cover agreement?

Question 4
What is a black list certificate?

Question 5
Why is it important for a TIR carnet to accompany goods which are sent by road to countries outside the EC?

Question 6
A UK manufacturer makes an unexpected sale to a country where previously he had made no sales at all. The UK manufacturer is required to insure the goods. Would you expect a policy or a certificate to be issued?

Question 7
An exporter has made a number of different shipments of goods to different countries. Unfortunately, all the invoices, bills of lading and insurance certificates have become mixed up. What is the quickest way to decide whether a particular invoice, bill of lading and insurance certificate relate to the same shipment?

Question 8
What is the name of the document which can make a buyer feel confident that goods are of a certain standard?

Question 9
In what currency is the sum assured on an insurance document usually expressed?

Question 10
An importer and exporter agree that the exporter will insure the goods. The insurance document is dated two days after the transport document.

Why has the exporter failed to honour his obligation?

(Answers given in Appendix VI)

Unit 12

Incoterms

Objectives

On completion of this unit the student should be able to:

● understand the purpose of Incoterms;

● describe the obligations which the various Incoterms impose;

● understand how Incoterms affect the documents which an exporter must produce;

● assess the cost implication of Incoterms.

12.1 The Purpose of Incoterms

In international trade there are likely to be three separate contracts of transport for the goods:

a) From seller's premises to a transport operator within the seller's country;

b) From the transport operator's premises in the seller's country to a named point in the buyer's country (e.g. a port, airport, or container depot);

c) From the port, etc., in the buyer's country to the buyer's own premises.

It is vital to establish a clearly defined cut-off point to show where the exporter's responsibility ends and where the importer's begins. This cut-off point refers, in the main, to payment of freight and to insurance of the goods while in transit. Unless the demarcation of responsibility is clearly understood, it will be difficult for an exporter to price his goods accurately and for an importer accurately to calculate the full cost of the importation.

The problem in international trade is that different countries have different interpretations of the same contract wording, and this problem can only be solved by creating a set of internationally agreed terms.

The purpose of Incoterms is to provide such a set of standardised terms which mean exactly the same to both parties and which will be interpreted in exactly the same way by courts in every country.

Incoterms were drafted by the International Chamber of Commerce (ICC) and full details can be found in their brochure number 460, or in brochure number 461/90 (*Guide to Incoterms*).

Incoterms are not incorporated into national or international law, but they can be made binding on both buyer and seller, provided the sales contract specifies that a particular Incoterm will apply.

Note

In the context of the examination, the words *shipment terms* or *terms of delivery* could be substituted for the word *Incoterms*. For exam purposes, all these words and phrases are synonymous.

12.2 The 13 Incoterms

There are 13 different Incoterms, and each term sets out the obligations of the seller/ exporter. It is not necessary to memorise the 13 terms, but it is necessary to be able to work out their implications, should such a term appear in an exam question.

Generally speaking, Incoterms set out the obligations of the seller. Hence, by a process of elimination, any obligation which does not appear in a particular Incoterm must be the responsibility of the buyer

In Units 10 and 11, we examined various documents relating to a sale by Speirs and Wadley Ltd of Adderley Road, Hackney, to Woldal Ltd of New Road, Kowloon. Table 1 explains the implications where appropriate for both parties of the different Incoterms which could be applied to such a sale. The various Incoterms are set out in a logical order, starting with the one which imposes least obligation on Speirs and Wadley and ending with the one which imposes most obligations.

Table 1

Incoterm	Standard ICC Abbreviations	Obligations of Speirs and Wadley Ltd (Exporter)	Responsibilities of Woldal Ltd (Importer)
1 Ex Works (named place)	EXW	Make the goods available for collection from Adderley Road, Hackney by Woldal Ltd. Once collected by Woldal, all responsibility of Spiers and Wadley is ended. A commercial invoice or equivalent electronic message will be provided for Woldal and the goods will be suitably packaged for the type of transport being used.	Take delivery from Adderley Road. Make all arrangements at own cost and risk to take goods to own premises. Woldal should arrange appropriate insurance to cover this journey. The obtaining of relevant export and/or import licences is also the responsibility of Woldal.

Table 1 (Continued)

Incoterm	Standard ICC Abbreviations	Obligations of Speirs and Wadley Ltd (Exporter)	Responsibilities of Woldal Ltd (Importer)
2 Free Carrier (named place, e.g. FCA Hackney Container Depot)	FCA	Deliver the goods to Hackney Containers at their Inland Container Depot. Complete export and customs documentation including obtaining export licence where necessary. Pay any costs relating to these including export duties or taxes. Supply buyer with commercial invoice or an equivalent electronic message together with proof of delivery to Hackney Containers, e.g. container bill of lading or multimodal transport document.	Make all arrangements at their own cost and risk to cover transport of goods to their own premises from Hackney Containers Inland Container Depot. It is advisable to arrange appropriate insurance. Woldal should obtain an import licence if needed and should pay any import taxes or duties.
3 Free Alongside Ship (named port of shipment, e.g. London)	FAS	Deliver goods to the quayside of a nominated shipping line at the Port of London. Advise Woldal of delivery and supply a commercial invoice or its equivalent electronic message together with proof of delivery, e.g. dock receipt or equivalent electronic message. Speirs and Wadley's liability basically ceases once it has delivered the goods at the quayside.	Make arrangements with a shipping company for transport of goods by sea to Hong Kong. Notify Speirs and Wadley of the day and time delivery is required at the Port of London, and of the name of the nominated shipping line. Arrange relevant export and/or import licences if required. Pay all costs including taxes and duties. Woldal is responsible for all risks from the quayside in London to the delivery of the goods to their ultimate destination. It is therefore advisable to arrange appropriate insurance.

Table 1 (Continued)

Incoterm	Standard ICC Abbreviations	Obligations of Speirs and Wadley Ltd (Exporter)	Responsibilities of Woldal Ltd (Importer)
4 Free On Board (named port of shipment, e.g. London)	FOB	As for FAS, but Speirs and Wadley's delivery liability does not cease until the goods have crossed the ship's rail and have been loaded on board a named ship at London. They must also arrange any export licence and complete any customs formalities including the payment of costs, duties and taxes. Port loading costs must also be borne if not included in carriage charge.	As for FAS, with the exceptions of not having to arrange an export licence and not being responsible for the goods until they have crossed the ship's rail in the Port of London.
5 Cost and Freight (named port of destination, e.g. Hong Kong)	CFR	Arrange and pay for transport of goods to Hong Kong port. Loading and unloading costs should be met where they form part of the charge for carriage. Arrange issue of export licence where necessary and complete export customs formalities, including payment of costs, duties and taxes. Advise Woldal of details of voyage and supply commercial invoice or its electronic equivalent together with the relevant transport document, e.g. bill of lading. Speirs and Wadley are free of liability (for insurance purposes) once the goods have crossed the ship's rail in the UK port.	Arrange issue of import licence and pay any duties or taxes. Arrange and pay for insurance of goods from when they cross ship's rail in the UK port. If unloading costs are not covered by charge for carriage, Woldal must also pay these.
6 Cost, Insurance and Freight (named port of destination, e.g. Hong Kong)	CIF	As for CFR, but in addition Speirs and Wadley must insure the goods as far as the port of Hong Kong and supply the buyer with evidence of this, e.g. the insurance policy.	As for CFR, but insurance risk only falls on Woldal once the goods have crossed the ship's rail at Hong Kong.

Table 1 (Continued)

Incoterm	Standard ICC Abbreviations	Obligations of Speirs and Wadley Ltd (Exporter)	Responsibilities of Woldal Ltd (Importer)
7 Carriage Paid To (named place of destination)	CPT	Similar to CFR except that Speirs and Wadley must arrange and pay for transport to the named place of destination, which could be an inland container depot in Hong Kong as opposed to a port. They must advise Woldal of the name and address of the UK carrier into whose custody the goods have been given, so Woldal can arrange insurance. Arrange issue of export licence where necessary and complete export customs formalities including payment of costs, duties and taxes. Supply commercial invoice or its electronic equivalent together with a relevant transport document to Woldal.	Arrange issue of import licence and pay any duties or taxes. Insure goods from the moment they are delivered into the custody of the carrier in the UK. Pay all costs of transport from Kowloon Freight Yard to their own premises.
8 Carriage and Insurance Paid To (named place of destination)	CIP	Similar to CPT except that Speirs and Wadley must pay insurance charges during the carriage. The relevant insurance policy or document must be supplied to Woldal.	Similar to CPT except that Woldal does not have to arrange and pay insurance charges which are met by Speirs and Wadley.
9 Delivered at Frontier (named place)	DAF	Arrange and pay for transport and insurance of goods to a named point on the frontier of the buyer's country. This term usually applies when goods go overland across a continent. Supply commercial invoice or its electronic equivalent together with a relevant transport document or delivery order to Woldal. Arrange issue of export licence where necessary and complete export customs formalities including payment of costs, duties and taxes.	Arrange issue of import licence and pay any duties or taxes. All costs and risks from the frontier point are the buyer's responsibility.

Table 1 (Continued)

Incoterm	Standard ICC Abbre-viations	Obligations of Speirs and Wadley Ltd (Exporter)	Responsibilities of Woldal Ltd (Importer)
10 Delivered Ex Ship (named port of destination)	DES	Similar to CIF except that exporter's liability does not cease until the goods have been placed at the disposal of the buyer on board a vessel at the named port of destination. Theoretically the exporter need not insure the goods, but in practice the exporter would be wise to do so.	Similar to CIF. Importer's liability exists from the time when goods are placed at its disposal in the named port of destination.
11 Delivered Ex Goods Quay (Duty Paid) (named port of destination)	DEQ	Deliver the goods on the quay or wharf at the named port of destination and pay unloading costs. Supply Woldal with commercial invoice or its electronic equivalent and transport document or delivery order. Arrange import and/or export licences where necessary and complete export and import customs formalities including payment of costs, duties and taxes. Arrange and pay for contract of carriage to the named port of destination. This term can be amended to exclude any particular duties or taxes, e.g. 'DEQ VAT unpaid'. Theoretically, the exporter need not insure the goods on their voyage. However, in view of the exporter's liability for the goods, such action would be unwise.	Accept delivery of goods at named port of destination. Importer liable for goods from the time they are placed at its disposal on the quay or wharf.

Table 1 (Continued)

Incoterm	Standard ICC Abbreviations	Obligations of Speirs and Wadley Ltd (Exporter)	Responsibilities of Woldal Ltd (Importer)
12 Delivered Duty Unpaid (named place of destination)	DDU	Exporter must deliver the goods to the named place in the importing country. Must bear costs and risks involved in carrying the goods to the named place of destination including carrying out customs formalities. Exporter is not responsible for payment of import charges, duties or taxes unless they are specifically mentioned, e.g. 'DDU, VAT paid, named place of destination'. Supply importer with a commercial invoice or its electronic equivalent together with a relevant transport document or delivery order.	Importer must arrange issue of import licence and payment of import costs, duties and taxes. Importer must take delivery of goods at named place of destination and is liable for all risks from then on.
13 Delivered Duty Paid (named place of destination)	DDP	Similar to DDU except that the exporter is responsible for all import formalities and payments in addition. It is possible for this Incoterm to be amended to exclude certain taxes, e.g. 'DDP, VAT unpaid, named place of destination'.	Similar to DDU, except that the importer is not responsible for all import formalities and payments.

12.3 How Incoterms Affect the Documents which Exporters must Produce

One function of all documents in overseas trade is to act as proof that an exporter has fulfilled his obligations under a commercial sales contract. Since the Incoterm in the sales contract will determine where the exporter's obligations end, then proof of fulfilment of the commercial obligations of the exporter will depend on whether the documents conform to the relevant Incoterm.

Examples of the documents which meet the requirements of the major Incoterms are set out in Table 2. Specific examples from the Speirs Wadley/Woldal sale will be given.

Table 2

Incoterm	Relevant transport document to be produced by the exporter, Speirs and Wadley Ltd	Relevant insurance document to be produced by Speirs and Wadley covering overseas part of the journey
Ex Works, (named place)	None. All that is required is a receipt from Woldal or their agents for the goods.	None
Free Carrier (named place, e.g. FCA Hackney Container Depot)	Receipt from Hackney Container Depot for the goods. Normally this would be a container bill of lading or a through bill of lading marked 'freight payable at destination'.	None
Free Carrier (named place, e.g. FCA Gatwick Airport)	Air waybill showing Woldal as consignee, marked 'freight payable at destination'. The details of the flight must conform to those specified by Woldal. (If goods are sent by rail or road, a rail consignment note or an international consignment note may be used showing the goods consigned to Woldal, marked 'freight payable at destination'.)	None
Free Alongside Ship (named port of shipment, e.g. FAS London)	Clean bill of lading marked 'received for shipment' and 'freight payable at destination'. Details of the shipping line to conform to those stipulated by the buyer, and the port to be shown as London.	None
Free on Board (named port of shipment, e.g. FOB London)	Clean bill of lading marked 'shipped on board' and 'freight payable at destination'. Details of the ship or shipping line to conform to the details stipulated by Woldal (e.g. the port must be shown as London).	None
Cost and Freight (named port of destination, e.g. CFR Hong Kong)	Clean bill of lading marked 'shipped on board' and 'freight paid'. The destination of the ship must be Hong Kong.	None

Table 2

Incoterm	Relevant transport document to be produced by the exporter, Speirs and Wadley Ltd	Relevant insurance document to be produced by Speirs and Wadley covering overseas part of the journey
Cost, Insurance and Freight (named port of destination, e.g. CIF Hong King)	Same as for CFR.	Insurance policy or certificate covering journey from UK port to Hong Kong port. The date of the insurance document must be before the date of the bill of lading.
Carriage Paid To (named place of destination, e.g. CPT Kowloon Freight Yard)	Clean container bill of lading marked 'freight paid', covering the journey to Kowloon Freight Yard.	None
Carriage and Insurance Paid To (named place of destination, e.g. CIP Kowloon Freight Yard)	Same as for CPT	Insurance policy or certificate covering the journey from the exporter's country (UK) to Kowloon Freight Yard. The date of the document must be on or before the date of the bill of lading.
Delivered Ex Ship (named port of destination, e.g. DES Hong Kong)	Clean bill of lading marked 'shipped on board' and 'freight paid'. The destination of the ship must be Hong Kong.	None. However, the exporter will normally arrange insurance. The exporter is responsible for the goods up until the time they have been placed at the disposal of the buyer on board the vessel at the named port of destination.
Delivered Ex Quay (Duty Paid) (named port of destination, e.g. DEQ Hong Kong)	Clean bill of lading marked 'freight paid'. The destination of the ship must be Hong Kong.	None. However, the exporter will normally arrange insurance for the voyage. The exporter is responsible for the goods until they are placed at the disposal of the buyer on the quay or wharf of the named port of destination.
Delivered Duty Unpaid (named place of destination, e.g. DDU, New Road, Kowloon, Hong Kong)	Clean combined transport document marked 'freight paid' and showing the destination as New Road, Kowloon, Hong Kong.	None. However, the exporter will normally arrange insurance of the goods for the whole journey to the named place of destination. The exporter is responsible for them up to that point.
Delivered Duty Paid (named place of destination, e.g. DDP, New Road, Kowloon, Hong Kong)	Clean, combined transport document marked 'freight paid' and showing the destination as New Road, Kowloon, Hong Kong.	None. However, the exporter will normally arrange insurance of the goods for the whole journey to the named place of destination. The exporter is responsible for them up to that point.

Notes

a) Incoterms enable documents to be transmitted electronically using EDI. Both seller and buyer must agree to such a method being used.

b) Usually, it is assumed that transport of goods from the exporter's factory to his local port or airport, or container depot, is covered by his general insurance. Hence, it would be unusual for an exporter to be asked for proof of insurance for the *domestic* part of the journey. For example, in the CIF Hong Kong contract, Speirs and Wadley would not normally be expected to produce documentary evidence of insurance of the goods from Adderley Road to the port of London. They would be expected to produce documentary evidence of insurance for the journey from the time the goods were taken by the shipping company (i.e. the date of the bill of lading), and this insurance should cover the goods on their journey from London to Hong Kong.

c) Obviously the transport documents and the insurance document must describe the goods in the same way as they are described in the sales contract. Generally speaking, a brief general description, which is not inconsistent with the sales contract, will suffice.

d) When bills of lading are used, the exporter must endorse them in blank if the consignee is shown as *order.*

e) When waybills are used, the consignee must be the importer, or an agent of the importer who is specified in the sale contract. When bills of lading are used, the exporter must provide a full set of clean bills of lading, made out to order and blank endorsed.

f) When an insurance policy is required, it must be endorsed in blank by the exporter.

12.4   Why is Insurance for the Goods Necessary?

If goods are damaged in transit, the normal reaction would be to claim from the carrier. However, most transport contracts contain widely drawn clauses which, to a great extent, exclude liability on the part of the carrier unless damage is caused by the carrier's gross negligence. It is therefore necessary for either the buyer or the seller to take out insurance to cover the relevant parts of the journey.

One special form of insurance which an exporter can take out under a CIF contract is transit insurance, or seller's interest insurance. While the buyer is responsible for arranging insurance for the sea voyage under an FOB or CFR contract, the exporter can, for a much reduced fee, take out his own seller's interest cover. This insures the exporter against loss or damage to the goods on the sea voyage when the importer has failed to fulfil his insurance responsibility. Naturally, the existence of such insurance is not disclosed to the buyer.

12.5 The Cost Implications of Incoterms for Exporters

Both exporters and importers need to know the precise financial implications of Incoterms so as to be able to set sensible prices and calculate costs.

It is unnecessary to set out the full implications of all 13 Incoterms, since the application of logic will provide the required information. A few examples from the most commonly used Incoterms will suffice. The examples refer to sales by UK-based exporters.

a)   FAS Southampton
The exporter must take account of the following extra costs when setting his prices:

   i)   Insurance of the goods from the UK factory to Southampton;

   ii)   The cost of transport to Southampton.

b)   FOB Southampton
In addition to the costs shown in the FAS example, the exporter must bear in mind the cost of loading the goods on board the ship.

c)   FOB UK Port
The pricing implications of this term can be difficult to assess. The importer could specify any UK port as the port of loading. If the specified port were situated in a remote part of the country, the cost of transport and insurance could be very high.

12.6 The Cost Implications of Incoterm for Importers

The implications are the mirror image of those for exporters, and can be deduced by logical thought. The following examples, which relate to UK-based importers, will suffice.

a)   FOB Antwerp
In addition to the sale contract price, the importer will have to pay all transport costs from Antwerp to his premises in the UK. The importer must pay the insurance for this journey, since any damage to the goods while in transit will be the importer's responsibility.

b)   CIF London
In addition to the sale contract price, the importer will have to pay the cost of unloading the goods from the ship at London, and all freight costs from the port of London to his premises. The importer must also pay for insurance of the goods from the time they cross the ship's rail in London to his own premises, since any damage on this part of the journey will be the importer's responsibility.

12.7 Self-assessment Questions

Question 1
Briefly define the purpose of Incoterms.

Question 2
A UK exporter's factory is situated in Sheffield and he has entered into a sale contract with a buyer whose premises are located in Frankfurt, Germany. The Incoterm in the contract is CIF Hamburg.

    a) For what part of the journey from Sheffield to Hamburg will the exporter have to pay transport costs?

    b) Where will the exporter's responsibility as regards insurance of goods end?

Question 3
An exporter sells on FOB terms, but he cannot trust the importer to insure the goods for the overseas voyage.

    a) Name the form of insurance which the exporter could arrange to cover any failure on the importer's part to insure the goods.

    b) Why would the exporter not advise the importer that he had taken out the insurance referred to in (a) above?

Question 4
Why is FOB Southampton a more favourable Incoterm than FOB UK port, from the point of view of a UK exporter?

Question 5
Express the following Incoterms in full:

    a) CFR New York;

    b) CIF Hamburg.

Question 6
What transport and insurance documents should a UK exporter produce to prove fulfilment of the following Incoterms?

    a) FCA Heathrow Airport;

    b) CIF New Orleans.

Question 7
Apart from the normal requirements, what particular details would you look for on a bill of lading to ensure that the contract terms had been met by a UK exporter who sold on the following terms:

    a) FAS Liverpool;

    b) FOB Liverpool;

    c) CIF Oslo.

Question 8

What type of bill of lading would you expect a UK exporter to produce as proof of fulfilment of a contract with the term, 'DDP Buyer's premises in Chicago'?

Question 9

A UK importer buys on FOB Hamburg terms. What additional costs will he incur over and above the basic FOB price of the goods?

Question 10

An exporter is asked to quote two prices for a shipment of goods to a buyer in Germany. They are:

a) CIF Hamburg;

b) CFR Hamburg.

For which term will the exporter quote the higher price?

(Answers given in Appendix VI)

12.8 Specimen Exam Question

Held & Sons are steel stockholders in London whose account is operated on an overdraft basis. Hitherto, they have obtained their stocks in the UK, but they are now forced to look elsewhere for supplies of a specialised steel, for which they have received the following quotations:

Country		Price per ton	Terms for payment
a)	Belgium	BEF ll,030 FOB Antwerp	Open account - settlement one month after shipment
b)	Spain	ESB 26,500 CFR London	Documentary collection payment due two months after shipment (collection charges for buyer)
c)	France	FRF 1,697 CIF London	Irrevocable documentary credit payment three months after shipment

Using the additional information set out below, show by calculating the cost of 100 tons of the steel which of quotations a), b) and c) would be cheapest for your customer:

Freight charges from any Western European Port	£5 per ton
Insurance (to be effected on 100% of CFR value or equivalent)	1% payable in sterling
Collection charges (total for both banks)	0.25%
Documentary credit charges (including acceptance commission)	0.75%
Overdraft interest (one month may be considered as one twelfth of a year)	15% p.a.

Ignore all other possible charges.

It is to be assumed that your customers would have covered any exchange risk on day of shipment, in accordance with rates quoted below, and that all payments and charges relative to any particular quotation are debited on the same day.

		1 month	2 months	3 months
Belgium	64.00-64.10	15-5c pm	26-16 pm	38-28 pm
Spain	145.45-145.55	100-150c disc	220-290 disc	335-435 disc
France	9.32-9.33	2-lc pm	3-2 pm	4-3 pm

Note

Collections and documentary credits are covered in Units 15 and 16. For the purposes of answering this question, all you need know is that under the Spanish purchase, the importer will pay bank collection charges of 0.25% of the CFR cost, and for the French purchase the importer will pay bank documentary credit charges of 0.75%, of the CIF cost. For the purposes of the question, there are no bank charges to be calculated for the Belgium payment.

(Specimen Answer given in Appendix VI)

Unit 13

An Overview of Terms of Payment

Objectives

On completion of this unit the student should be able to:

- **understand what is meant by terms of payment;**

- **distinguish between the four basic terms of payment;**

- **appreciate which terms of payment are more secure for the exporter and which terms are more favourable to the importer;**

- **understand the significance of the words 'terms of payment' in an examination context.**

13.1 The Meaning of 'Terms of Payment'

Terms of payment reflect the extent to which the seller requires a guarantee of payment before he loses control of the goods. The more trustworthy and creditworthy the importer, the less will the exporter need to have payment guaranteed before he loses control of the goods.

There are four different terms of payment, which are:

a) Open account;

b) Documentary collection;

c) Documentary credit;

d) Payment in advance.

13.2 An Overview of the Four Terms of Payment

It is necessary for the exporter and importer to agree the terms of payment and incorporate the details in the contract of sale.

A detailed analysis of open account, documentary collection and documentary credit will appear in the remaining units of this part of the book. This unit contains a brief overview of these three terms, with full coverage of payment in advance.

a) Open Account

A brief description of this term has already been given at the beginning of this part of the book (see 10.1). However, to recap, open account terms mean that the exporter despatches his goods to the importer and invoices for payment. If there are any documents of title to the goods, these documents are sent directly to the importer.

The exporter loses all control of the goods, at the time he despatches them, trusting the importer to pay.

Terms such as net cash on receipt of goods are sometimes used and they are synonymous with open account.

b) Documentary Collection

The exporter despatches the goods, but instead of sending the documents of title directly to the importer, he uses the banking system.

The documents of title are usually sent via the following route:

a) The exporter ships goods and obtains documents of title;

b) The exporter sends documents of title to his bank with appropriate instructions;

c) The exporter's bank sends documents of title to the importer's bank with the instruction that the documents can only be released:

   i) On payment; or

   ii) On acceptance of a bill of exchange (which for the moment we shall simply consider as being a legally binding undertaking to pay the exporter on a set or determinable future date);

d) On payment or acceptance of the bill of exchange, the importer's bank releases the documents of title so that the importer can obtain the goods on their arrival in his country.

It can be seen that the exporter retains control over the goods under this method until either payment is made, or a legally binding undertaking to pay is given.

A full explanation of this method, including the procedures adopted when the transport documents are not documents of title, is given in Unit 15.

c) Documentary Credit

Briefly, a documentary credit is a guarantee of payment by the importer's bank, provided the exporter presents specified documents within a stipulated period and conforms to the terms of the letter of credit.

If a documentary credit has been arranged, the exporter can despatch his goods in the knowledge that he is relying, not on the importer's integrity and creditworthiness, but on the reputation and creditworthiness of the importer's bank. Obviously, the exporter must fulfil the terms of credit if the guarantee is to be relied upon.

The procedure in brief is:

a) The exporter and importer agree on payment by documentary credit and incorporate the details in their sale contract;

b) The importer authorises his bank to issue the documentary credit;

c) The importer's bank passes on the details to a bank in the exporter's country which then advises the exporter of the existence of the credit;

d) The exporter ships his goods, obtains the documents required under the credit, presents these documents via the banking system, and is paid.

d)   Payment in Advance

'Payment in advance' means exactly what it says. The importer will pay the exporter at some agreed stage prior to despatch of the goods.

Although full payment in advance is obviously most desirable for the exporter, he will only be able to obtain such terms when there is a seller's market, or occasionally when such terms are customary in that particular trade.

It is quite common for a sale contract to require partial payments in advance; for example the contract could stipulate, say, 20% payable on the signing of the contract with the remaining 80% payable after despatch of the goods under one of the other terms of payment.

13.3   The Order in which the Terms of Payment are Attractive to the Parties to a Sale

A moment's thought will show that from the exporter's point of view the order is:

most secure	-	payment in advance
then	-	documentary credit
then	-	documentary collection
least secure	-	open account.

The mirror image applies for importers:

most favourable	-	open account
then	-	documentary collection
then	-	documentary credit
least favourable	-	payment in advance.

13.4   Illustrative Examples

As this brief unit serves merely to give an overview, it is not necessary for you to attempt the usual self-assessment questions. Instead we shall look at two illustrative examples which explain the significance of terms of payment in an examination context. A brief comment will follow immediately after each of the two questions.

Example 1

Your exporter customer has completed a sale contract with an overseas buyer, and it contains the following details:

CIF Charleston. Payment in US $ by MT on terms. Net cash one month after receipt of goods.

Explain the possible risks to your customer in accepting the terms of payment which appear in this contract.

Comment

In this question you should describe the risks to an exporter under open account terms. You should **not** comment on MT as this is a method of settlement or a method of transfer of funds, and you should **not** comment on the exchange risk if the question simply refers to the terms of payment. The exchange risk would also apply if documentary collection or documentary credits had been selected as terms of payment.

Example 2

John Brown's Body Ltd are funeral directors. They have developed a business providing complete funeral services, including coffins, to British and American expatriates based in continental Europe, who wish to ensure that their deceased loved ones are returned to the UK or the USA for burial or cremation.

The company, which is sterling-based, has recently received orders for coffins from army units based in Germany. The terms of shipment will be either on a CIF Hamburg basis for shipments by sea, or on a CFR Frankfurt basis for air consignments. The cost of repatriation to the UK or the USA will be borne by the army groups outside the terms of the new orders.

As the customer has usually sold on an ex-works basis, a director asks you for an explanation of these terms of shipment and how they would affect the company.

You are informed that payments will be received in Deutschmarks, and that the company has no other foreign currency receipts or outgoings.

Required

Your explanation of:

i) The terms of shipment mentioned, including the responsibilities of the contracting parties under these terms

ii) Any risks, other than the credit risks, which the company will incur by agreeing to accept the payments as indicated in the question.

Comment

i) An explanation of the Incoterms ex works, CIF Hamburg and CFR Frankfurt is required, including the responsibilities of the parties;

ii) An explanation of the exchange risk is required.

Note

Terms of payment refers to the credit risk which is specifically excluded from this question, whereas the word **payment** refers to the fact that the sale is denominated in Deutschmarks.

In addition, the danger of damage to the goods on the journey to Germany could be mentioned along with the need to insure. Finally under CFR or CIF terms, the customer will need to ascertain the cost of transport to Germany.

Unit 14

Open Account Terms

Objectives

On completion of this unit the student should be able to:

- **appreciate the major risks which apply to exporters who sell on open account terms;**

- **appreciate how an exporter can reduce the risks inherent in open account terms;**

- **acquire an overview of the role of ECGD and NCM as insurers against bad debts on export sales.**

14.1 Introduction

So far the book has covered matters from the point of view of both the exporter and the importer. Up to and including Unit 20 of the book, we shall now concentrate on the subject matter **from the point of view of a UK exporter and of his bank**. Other providers of services to exporters will also be introduced where appropriate.

The position of importers and their banks as regards terms of payment will be covered from Unit 21 onwards.

Remember then that for these remaining three units we are looking at matters from a UK exporter's point of view.

14.2 The Major Risks which Apply to Exports on Open Account Terms

These risks can be classified under three main headings:

a)   Buyer Risk

This is also known as the 'credit risk' and it covers the danger that the buyer may not pay for the goods because of insolvency or wilful default.

Remember that the exporter lost control of the goods at the moment he despatched them.

b)   Country Risk

The importer may be perfectly willing and able to pay, but the importer's government may introduce laws, often called exchange controls, which prevent payment from being made.

The reason for the imposition of exchange controls can be political. Alternatively, exchange controls can simply result from financial pressures, such as the Third World debt problem, which mean that the importer's country cannot afford to pay for imports.

c)   Transit Risk

Goods travel much further in international trade than they do in a domestic deal, and therefore there is more danger of loss or damage to goods on their journey from seller to buyer.

Note

The exchange risk also applies if the exporter invoices in foreign currency, but the exchange risk will always apply in these cases, irrespective of the terms of payment between the two parties.

14.3   How an Exporter can Reduce the Risks under Open Account Terms

a)   Reduction of Buyer Risk

The exporter can obtain a status report on the buyer, and such reports should be updated at regular intervals. Alternatively, organisations such as the Department of Trade and Industry can supply more detailed reports on potential buyers. A favourable status report does not guarantee that the importer will pay his debts, but it does serve as a useful indication of his creditworthiness and integrity.

In addition, the exporter can insure against non-payment by the importer. See 14.4.

b)   Reduction of Country Risk

Most UK banks provide political and economic reports which comment on the situation in various overseas countries. These reports can give full details of current exchange control regulations in the overseas country, and can help the exporter assess whether any additional restrictions are likely.

In addition, insurance can be taken out to cover loss because of newly imposed exchange controls.

c)   Reduction of Transit Risk

The obvious remedy is for appropriate insurance cover to be taken. If an Incoterm has been specified in the sale contract, then it will be quite clear where the exporter's obligation ends and where the importer's obligation begins. In addition, the exporter can take out seller's interest insurance to cover himself against damage to goods if the importer has failed to insure under terms such as CFR.

Freight forwarders are firms which specialise in organising overseas transport. Most freight forwarders are capable of arranging appropriate transport, insurance and documentation, if they are given a copy of the sale contract.

The exporter's bank can recommend suitable freight forwarders, and the bank can arrange appropriate insurance of the goods, if required.

14.4 Credit Insurance

Historically, credit insurance has been provided by the Export Credits Guarantee Department (ECGD) which is a government department. However, in 1991 the short-term credit insurance business arm (i.e. credit insurance for up to two years) was sold off to the Netherlands-based NCM Group, which is one of the largest providers of credit insurance in the world.

This has resulted in NCM Credit Insurance Ltd being the main provider of short-tern credit insurance in the UK, although there are other notable providers, in particular, Trade Indemnity. Trade Indemnity is owned by a number of major insurance companies and provides cover against non-payment within the UK and also overseas. Insurers may be more interested in covering exports if the UK seller has a wide spread of domestic business which is also offered for cover.

ECGD still provides cover for terms in excess of two years. However, fiercer competition in the credit insurance market is expected with the arrival of the single European market, which will enable such credit insurers as HERMES from Germany and COFACE from France to increase their market base. There is also additional impact being made by other overseas companies, e.g. AIG of the USA who have opened offices in the UK.

14.5 NCM International Policy

The target market is exporters who deal in cash or on credit terms of up to 180 days. In order to avail themselves of the lowest possible premiums, exporters should spread the risks over as many contracts as possible. Hence, NCM are looking for exporters to cover all or most of their export turnover for at least one year and preferably for a longer period.

a)   Risks covered

- Buyer insolvency.

- The buyer's failure to pay within six months of the due date for goods accepted.

- Non-acceptance of the goods by the buyer, provided the goods conform to the contract.

- Country risks including:

    - Foreign government action which delays or prevents completion of the contract;

    - Political, economic, legislative or administrative action outside the UK, which delays or prevents payment transfers;

- Delays in money transfer from the buyer's country;

- War, civil unrest or similar actions outside the UK which prevents completion of the contract (war between the five major powers is specifically excluded).

- Export restrictions imposed after the date of the contract.

- Non-renewal or cancellation of an export licence.

- Where an importer is recognised by NCM as a public buyer, e.g. local or regional government. The exporter will be covered if the buyer fails to complete the contract.

b)   Additional Available Cover

- The policy normally covers the exporter from the date when the goods are sent to the buyer. By payment of an additional premium, cover can be provided from the date of the contract. This is known as covering pre-credit risk. It is of particular benefit to exporters who manufacture specialist one-off items which would have no other market if the underlying contract should fail.

- Payment of royalties under franchising or licensing agreements.

- Goods traded outside the UK, i.e. external trade.

- Sales through overseas subsidiaries.

- Services provided for foreign customers, e.g. maintenance contracts or professional services.

- Sales carried out through overseas subsidiaries.

- Sale of goods held overseas, including those exhibited at trade markets or exhibitions.

- Goods invoiced in foreign currencies. NCM will also accept claims, within certain parameters, for any additional losses incurred in meeting forward exchange contract commitments (e.g. close-outs).

- Where goods are sold on credit terms of more than 180 days but less than two years, or where their manufacture takes in excess of 12 months, an Extended Risk Endorsement can be added to the guarantee.

- Insurance against unfair calling of bonds may be available. This aspect is covered in Unit 20.

c)   Costs of Cover

Premiums are negotiable and tend to depend upon the spread of risks, the width of markets and the amount of cover involved. Obviously, if an exporter is negotiating business deals in a high-risk area of the world, premiums are likely to be higher than in other, more stable areas.

Costs will normally include the following:

- Payment of an annual fee set according to the exporter's turnover.

● Payment of a monthly flat rate fee established according to the amount of business which is declared.

d)   Amount of Cover Available

Risk Covered	Maximum % covered by NCM
Buyer insolvency	90
Buyer default	90
Non-acceptance of the goods by the buyer (provided goods conform to contract)	72*
Country risk	95

*In respect of non-acceptance of the goods by the buyer, the exporter must meet the initial 20% of the loss and NCM will meet 90% of the remaining balance, i.e. 90% of 80% = 72%.

e)   Pay-out of Claims

● Buyer insolvency: immediately, provided that evidence of insolvency is furnished.

● Payment default by the buyer on goods accepted: six months after due payment date.

● Non-acceptance of the goods by the buyer: one month after resale of the goods.

● For the majority of the remainder of losses: four months after the due date.

NCM will assist the exporter in attempting to recover the debt and may be prepared to defray legal expenses incurred in the recovery action.

14.6 NCM Compact Policy

The NCM Compact policy is designed for expanding businesses with an annual turnover of £3m or less. It can cover both UK and overseas sales and has a fixed annual fee.

a)   Risks covered

● Buyer insolvency.

● Buyer default on payment.

● Foreign government action which delays or prevents completion of a contract.

● Foreign government action which delays or prevents payment.

● Political action which delays money transfer from the buyer's country.

● Legal statutes in the buyer's country which can release the buyer from a large proportion of his contractual payment obligations.

● War or natural disasters which prevent completion of the contract.

- Where an importer is recognised by NCM as a public (government-owned) buyer and fails to complete the contract.

This policy is marketed as being easy to use and enables smaller businesses to access credit assessment facilities from a database of around 6m buyers, in addition to providing peace of mind.

14.7 ECGD Supplier Insurance Policy

For large-scale projects and sales of capital goods, credit terms often exceed two years and as such require credit insurance which has to be agreed on an individual basis. This insurance can be provided by ECGD's Supplier Insurance Policy (SIP). However, it must be remembered that SIP is only available in conjunction with ECGD's Supplier Credit Financing Facility and is not a free-standing insurance policy (see Unit 18).

The SIP covers the following risks:

a) Occurrences Outside the UK

- Buyer or guarantor insolvency.

- Default by the buyer or guarantor regarding payment within six months of its due date.

- Default by the buyer or guarantor to meet a final judgment or award within six months of its date.

- Where ECGD acknowledges that the buyer is a public buyer, default in payment or default in performance of the contract which prevents the supplier from carrying out his part of the contract.

- Statutes introduced in the buyer's country which discharge the debt if it is paid in other than the currency of the contract.

- Political or economic moves which prevent the transfer of contractual payments. This would include a general moratorium on debt repayment enforced by the buyer's government.

- Any action by a foreign government which prevents the performance of the contract.

- Any natural disasters, wars or civil strife which prevent the performance of the contract.

b) Occurrences within the UK

- Non-renewal or cancellation of a supplier's export licence.

- Measures introduced after the contract date which hamper the performance of the contract.

- Withdrawal of finance by ECGD where ECGD has withdrawn cover on the buyer's country.

Additional cover is provided under the SIP for bonds risk. See Unit 20.

The SIP provides cover for 90% of the insured risk, with the exporter bearing the remaining 10%.

14.8 Additional ECGD Insurance Facilities

Tender to Contract Scheme

a) Target market

Exporters who tender for contracts in foreign currency. These contracts must have a UK content of £5m or more.

b) Risks covered

Losses incurred due to adverse exchange rate movements between the date of tender and the date of contract.

c) Amount of cover

Cover will normally be limited to between 1% and 25% of the contract price.

Should exchange rates move in the exporter's favour during the period covered, any gain must be paid to ECGD.

Cover can be arranged for tendering periods of up to nine months.

An additional facility to the normal tender to contract scheme is the Forward Exchange Supplement. It is designed for exporters who believe that they may have problems in arranging forward contracts for large sums over long-time periods. If these forward contracts provide less sterling than expected, ECGD will make up the balance within the limits mentioned previously. This Forward Exchange Supplement can also be set up as a free-standing facility.

Project Participants' Insolvency Cover

a) Target market

Members of UK consortia involved in overseas contracts valued at £20m or more.

b) Risks covered

Where losses arise from the repercussions of the insolvency of a member of the consortium or a sub-contractor, they can be covered by this scheme. Cover can be extended to consortia, which include overseas consortia members or sub-contractors.

Overseas Investments Insurance Scheme

a) Aim of the scheme

To encourage British investment overseas.

b) Risks covered

Political risks for 3-15 years, including:

● Expropriation, e.g. nationalisation or other overseas government action to the detriment of the investor.

- War or revolution.

- Restrictions on remittance. This is to help investors overcome the potential problems which might arise if the transfer or return of funds to the UK is restrained or delayed.

c) *Target market*

Companies carrying on business in the UK and their overseas subsidiaries. Insurance is available for new investments of equity capital in the form of cash, plant or knowledge; for loans to overseas entities where the repayment period is at least three years from the date of payment; and for some guarantees of loans which have been arranged outside the UK. The investor must apply for cover before committing himself to any investment. Cover may be arranged in some cases where there are some existing investments but this will be based on each individual case.

d) *Amounts available under the scheme*

- Equity investments: amount of investment plus retained profits up to a maximum of double the amount of the original investment.

- Loan investments: the principal loan amount plus accrued interest.

e) *Payment of claim*

- Expropriation: one year following the commencement of the relevant action.

- War: evidence of damage to physical assets; OR where the overseas entity has been unable to operate for one year; OR where the overseas entity has been operating, its inability to make profits for three consecutive years.

- Restriction on remittance: inability for six successive months to repatriate currency. With regard to loan investment, six months must have passed since the due date for an unpaid amount of capital or interest.

Any recoveries or compensation will be divided between the ECGD and the investor on the same basis as the loss was suffered.

14.9 ECGD Fixed-rate Finance Scheme (FRF)

In order to attract business, exporters sometimes have to be able to offer favourable interest rates to overseas buyers. ECGD supports this through its FRF scheme, which provides reimbursement to banks which are supplying funds at fixed rates where the actual cost of funds is greater than the fixed rate.

Commercial Interest Reference Rates (CIRRs) form the basis for this system of minimum fixed-interest rates. They are reviewed monthly. The advantage of the FRF scheme to exporters is that they can quote a firm fixed-interest rate to a potential buyer which can be maintained for up to four months pending the satisfactory completion of preliminary talks culminating in a signed agreement or contract.

14.10 Self-assessment Questions

Question 1
Name two techniques which reduce the buyer risk to the exporter on open account terms.

Question 2
Name two techniques which reduce the country risk to the exporter on open account terms.

Question 3
What two basic risks are covered by the NCM International Policy and what is the usual percentage of cover for such risks?

Question 4
At what stage of a transaction does credit insurance cover usually commence? What is the difference if pre-credit cover is held?

Question 5
In what circumstances should an exporter take out **pre-credit** cover for open account sales?

Question 6
Is the ECGD Supplier Insurance Policy a free-standing insurance policy?

Question 7
What is the percentage cover available under the ECGD Supplier Insurance Policy?

Question 8
Briefly state what is meant by the NCM International Policy

Question 9
To whom does the ECGD Fixed-rate Finance Scheme offer cover?

(Answers given in Appendix VI)

14.11   Specimen Question

Your customers, ABC Ltd, are negotiating with a buyer in the USA for a large export order. The buyer has stipulated that payment should be in US dollars, and the goods delivered CIF New Orleans. Payment terms are net cash one month after arrival of goods.

 a) Explain these payment terms to the customer.

 b) What credit risks are there in the method of payment suggested?

 c) How can the customer guard against the exchange risk?

(Specimen Answer given in Appendix VI)

Unit 15

Documentary Collections

Objectives

On completion of this unit the student should be able to:

● understand what is meant by bills of exchange;

● appreciate the difference between sight drafts and term drafts;

● describe the detailed operation of documentary collections;

● appreciate the difference when air waybills make up the transport documents;

● appreciate the significance of the various clauses on a collection instruction;

● understand the meaning and purpose of Uniform Rules for Collections;

● describe the checks which a remitting bank makes before it sends the documents abroad;

● appreciate the difference between theory and practice as regards the timing of payments;

● understand the risks to an exporter with documentary collections and how these risks can be reduced;

● appreciate the difference in security between D/P and D/A.

15.1 Introduction

This introduction serves to remind you of the point made at the beginning of Unit 14. The following unit will consider documentary collections from the point of view of the exporter and his bank.

15.2 Definition of 'Bills of Exchange'

The definition of a bill of exchange can be found in the Bills of Exchange Act 1882. There are nine major aspects, which are as follows:

1 a bill of exchange is an unconditional order in writing;

2 addressed by one person (the drawer);

3   to another (the drawee);

4   signed by the drawer;

5   requiring the person to whom it is addressed (the drawee);

6   to pay;

7   on demand or at a fixed or determinable future date;

8   a certain sum in money;

9   to, or to the order of, a specified person (the payee) or to bearer. In the case of the specimen bills of exchange which follow, the drawer and payee are identical. The words our order indicate the order of Speirs and Wadley.

For convenience the above phrases are numbered to correspond to the reference numbers which appear on the specimen bills of exchange shown in Figures 1 and 2.

These specimen bills of exchange relate to an export sale by Speirs and Wadley to Woldal. As the exporter is the person who requires payment from the importer, we can see that, in documentary collections, the exporter is the drawer and the importer is the drawee.

Please note that the word 'draft' is often substituted for 'bill of exchange'. The words are synonymous for our purposes.

15.3   Sight Drafts and Term Drafts

As you will have seen, the two specimen bills of exchange are identical, apart from item seven which relates to the due time for payment.

The bill which requires payment **at sight** is a sight draft or an on demand draft. The drawee, Woldal, should pay the bill as soon as it is presented, if the bill is to be honoured. Woldal will not need to sign the bill in any way. All that is required is for them to authorise payment via the banking system.

On the other draft, payment is due 90 days after sight. When the bill of exchange is presented to the drawee, the drawee should **accept** it if he wishes the bill to be honoured. Thus, Woldal would sign the bill of exchange on the front and insert the date of acceptance. Woldal would be legally bound to pay 90 days after the date of acceptance shown on the bill of exchange.

Drafts which are payable at a future date are called **term drafts**. other descriptions which are synonymous are **tenor draft** and **usance draft**. When a term bill specifies the future date (e.g. if the specimen term draft had said on 1 January 1998...pay) then there is no need for the drawee to accept the bill (although from the exporter's point of view it is better to have it accepted). However, when the words specify payment on a fixed period after sight, then the drawee must accept the bill and insert the date of acceptance, otherwise it would be impossible to calculate the due date of payment.

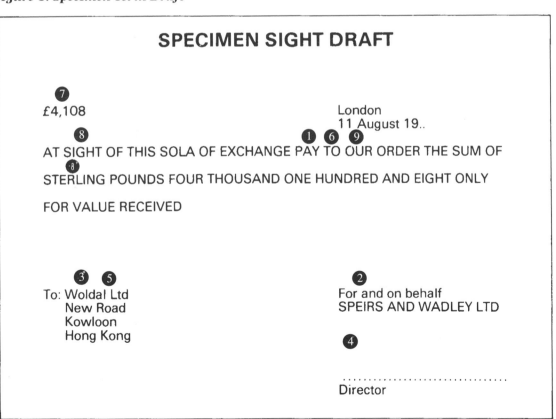

SPECIMEN TERM DRAFT

⑧
£4,108　　　　　　　　　　　　　London
⑦　　　　　　　　　　　　　　　11 August 19..

AT 90 DAYS AFTER DATE OF THIS FIRST OF EXCHANGE (SECOND OF THE

① ⑥ ⑨
SAME TENOR AND DATE BEING UNPAID) PLEASE PAY TO OUR ORDER THE
⑧
SUM OF STERLING POUNDS FOUR THOUSAND ONE HUNDRED AND EIGHT

ONLY FOR VALUE RECEIVED

③　⑤　　　　　　　　　　　②
To: Woldal Ltd　　　　　　　　For and on behalf of
　　New Road　　　　　　　　SPEIRS AND WADLEY LTD
　　Kowloon
　　Hong Kong　　　　　　　　④

　　　　　　　　　　　　　　　. . . . .
　　　　　　　　　　　　　　　Director

Figure 1: Specimen Term Draft

SPECIMEN SIGHT DRAFT

⑦
£4,108　　　　　　　　　　　　London
　⑧　　　　　　　　　　　　　11 August 19..
　　　　　　　　　　　　① ⑥ ⑨
AT SIGHT OF THIS SOLA OF EXCHANGE PAY TO OUR ORDER THE SUM OF
⑧
STERLING POUNDS FOUR THOUSAND ONE HUNDRED AND EIGHT ONLY

FOR VALUE RECEIVED

③　⑤　　　　　　　　　　②
To: Woldal Ltd　　　　　　　For and on behalf
　　New Road　　　　　　　SPEIRS AND WADLEY LTD
　　Kowloon
　　Hong Kong　　　　　　　④

　　　　　　　　　　　　　　. . . . .
　　　　　　　　　　　　　　Director

Figure 2: Specimen Sight Draft

15.4 Operation of a Documentary Collection

(**Note** This example involves goods being transported by sea.)

a) The exporter ships goods and obtains documents of title from the shipping line.

b) The exporter, who is known as the principal, hands in the following documents to his bank (the remitting bank):

   i) bill of exchange drawn on the importer;

   ii) documents of title (i.e. a complete set of clean, shipped on board bills of lading, made out to order and blank endorsed), and other relevant documents (insurance policy or certificate if CIF);

   iii) a collection instruction which contains the exporter's instructions to the remitting bank.

c) The remitting bank completes its own collection instruction addressed to the importer's bank. This collection instruction will contain the same instructions as the exporter's original collection order. This collection order is then sent to the importer's bank, along with the other documents.

d) If the instructions are D/P (documents against payment), the importer's bank will release the documents to the importer only against payment.

   If the instructions are D/A (documents against acceptance), the importer's bank will release the documents against acceptance of the bill of exchange by the importer.

e) If and when the bill of exchange is paid, the importer's bank sends the funds to the remitting bank for credit to the principal's account.

   The importer will require a bill of lading in order to obtain the goods from the overseas port. The bill of lading can only be obtained by payment of the bill of exchange (D/P), or by acceptance (D/A). Therefore, the importer cannot obtain the goods without paying or accepting the bill of exchange, and conversely an exporter retains control of the goods until payment or acceptance of the bill of exchange.

   When goods are sent by air freight, the airway bill could show the importer's bank as consignee. Once again, the importer must pay or accept a bill of exchange to be able to obtain the goods. Once the importer has paid or accepted the bill of exchange, the importer's bank will issue a delivery order. The delivery order is an authority, signed on behalf of the bank, authorising the airport to release the goods to the named importer. An exporter should obtain the prior agreement of the importer and the importer's bank before he consigns goods to that bank. In practice, the importer's bank will not often agree to be named as consignee, unless its own customer is of major importance.

Notes

i)   When D/P terms are used, it is unnecessary to include a bill of exchange, since the overseas bank can release documents on payment of the invoice amount. However, sight drafts are usually included.

ii) In some overseas countries, there are heavy stamp duties on bills of exchange. In such situations it may be possible to use the banker's receipt instead of a bill of exchange to avoid these duties. The banker's receipt is used extensively in Italy and is known as a 'ricevuta bancaria'.

iii) Variations on traditional remittance methods for documentary collections

a)   Accelerated Bills Service Provided by UK Remitting Banks

The UK exporter completes a collection instruction, quoting from a pre-arranged series of reference numbers, but instead of submitting the collection to the remitting UK bank, the collection is sent by the exporter directly to the collecting bank abroad. A copy of the collection instruction is sent to the exporter's UK bank, or alternatively the exporter advises his UK bank by electronic means.

All subsequent correspondence is dealt with by the UK bank, and the UK bank maintains records of the position of all bills collected in this way. If the exporter is linked to his bank via a computer terminal network, then the bank can advise the exporter of the position via this network.

The benefits to the exporter are:

- reduced bank charges;

- reduced processing time which should mean quicker payment.

This method is useful when the exporter submits many collections to the same buyers over a period of time, because the UK bank can then preselect an appropriate collecting bank.

b)   Direct Collections

In some cases, exporters may simply send their collections directly to the overseas collecting bank, without involving their own UK bank in any way. The overseas bank would act as agent of the UK exporter in obtaining the proceeds. The benefits from the exporter's point of view are saving in time and saving of UK bank charges.

The drawbacks from the exporter's point of view are:

- all correspondence, including that for any follow-up action in the event of default, is made directly with the overseas bank;

- the exporter may find it difficult to trace payment of the bill proceeds without the benefit of a UK bank's reference number;

- the documents are not checked by the UK bank before being sent abroad.

15.5 The Collection Instruction

The specimen collection instruction (Figure 3) is a standard form of authority which enables the exporter to include specific instructions to his bank regarding the documentary collection.

The top third of the form is largely self-explanatory. Perhaps it should be stated that if the goods were sent by air, with the air waybill showing the overseas bank as consignee, then the overseas bank would be shown as consignee with the importer as drawee.

You will see that specific instructions are required on the following points:

a) Release documents to the importer against payment (D/P) or against acceptance (D/A). Normally D/P will apply with sight drafts and D/A will apply with term drafts. It is, however, possible to arrange for D/P instructions to be given with term drafts and this can often arise in trade with the Far East.

b) If documents are not taken up on arrival of goods, instructions are required on whether to warehouse and insure the goods. This clause is known as a store and insure clause.

   If the importer does not pay or accept the bill of exchange, he cannot obtain the goods. However, the goods will be at the docks or airport, or container depot, in the overseas country. If this clause is adopted, the overseas bank will be instructed to warehouse and insure the goods if documents are not taken up. The cost of this operation will be claimed from the exporter's bank, who will debit their customer, the principal. If the goods are warehoused and insured, then they are protected, giving the exporter time to find an alternative buyer or to ship the goods back to the UK.

   If waybills showing the importer as consignee are used, the **store and insure** clause will be superfluous.

c) The collection instruction will state whether bank and other charges have to be collected in addition to the face value of the bill of exchange. The exporter should complete the clause in accordance with the details agreed in the sale contract.

d) Specific instructions are required on whether or not to protest in the event of dishonour by either non-payment or non-acceptance.

   If a bill of exchange is protested, a lawyer in the overseas country will undertake formal procedures whereby he asks the drawee the reason for dishonour and makes appropriate notes.

   Again, it will be the overseas bank which instructs the lawyer to protest. The overseas bank will have to be reimbursed by the exporter's bank who will then debit their customer.

   In some countries, the law requires a dishonoured bill of exchange to be protested within one working day, otherwise the drawer cannot sue on the bill.

e) Advice of dishonour, with reasons, should be given by airmail or cable. Cable is most desirable, but again the cost will ultimately be borne by the exporter.

f) When goods are transported by sea and documents go by air, it is quite common for the collection to be presented to the drawee before the arrival of the goods. If this clause is adopted, the overseas bank will be authorised to await the arrival of the goods before pressing the drawee for payment or acceptance.

g) The **case of need** referred to on the collection instruction is an agent of the exporter who is resident in the importer's country. The case of need can act in an advisory capacity or have **full powers**. The latter will allow the **case of need** to overrule the instructions contained in the collection schedule. If a case of need is named, the overseas bank will refer to him in the event of dishonour for guidance or instruction.

h) Finally, instructions as to the method of settlement are required. obviously urgent SWIFT would be best from the exporter's point of view, but this is a more costly method than MT.

15.6 Uniform Rules for Collections (URC)

The URC form an internationally accepted code of practice covering documentary collections. (The Rules are reproduced in Appendix III.) URC are not incorporated in national or international law, but become binding on all parties because all bank authorities (especially the collection instruction) will state that the collection is subject to URC. URC will apply unless the collection instruction states otherwise or the laws in one of the countries concerned specifically contradict them. The rules do not extend to transactions which use EDI. The working party, which drew up the new rules, felt that there were too many legal problems for international rules to be drafted at that time. (See Appendix 2 for latest developments.) You must have a good knowledge of URC. Matters solely affecting the overseas bank and drawee are covered later.

15.7 Summary of the Provisions of URC

a) **Article 1** states that banks do not have to deal with collections but must advise the party, from whom they receive the collection, of their decision as soon as possible.

b) **Article 2** defines and differentiates between various terms:

i) Financial documents are the instruments used for the purpose of obtaining payment, e.g. cheques.

ii) Commercial documents relate to the goods themselves, e.g. invoices, waybills.

iii) Clean collections comprise of financial documents which are not accompanied by commercial documents.

iv) Documentary collections are commercial documents which may or may not be accompanied by financial documents.

c) **Article 3** identifies the main parties to a collection:

    i) The principal, i.e. the exporter.

    ii) The remitting bank. This is the bank to which the principal entrusts the collection, normally the exporter's own bank.

    iii) The collecting bank. This is any bank, other than the remitting bank, which is involved with the collection. Usually, this will be a bank in the importer's country.

    iv) The presenting bank. This is the collecting bank which notifies the drawee of the arrival of the collection and which requests payment or acceptance.

    v) The drawee. This will normally be the importer to whom presentation will be made in accordance with the collection instruction.

The example given below will clarify the relevant positions of these parties in respect of a documentary collection:

An exporter (principal) hands in a documentary collection to his bank (Barclays - the remitting bank), drawn on an importer (drawee) in New York, USA. If the principal does not specify which collecting bank to use, Barclays will choose their New York office (collecting and presenting bank). However, if the importer banks at Chemical Bank, Barclays, New York may request Chemical Bank to attend to the actual presentation. In this latter case, Chemical Bank will be the presenting bank and Barclays the collecting bank.

d) **Article 4** mainly covers the constituent parts of a collection instruction. Additionally, it states that banks need not examine documents to ascertain instructions and can ignore any instructions from other than the party from whom the collection was received, unless the collection instruction states otherwise.

e) **Articles 5, 6, 7** and **8** discuss procedures relating to the presentation, release and creation of documents.

f) **Article 9** states that banks will act in good faith and exercise reasonable care.

g) **Article 10** excludes banks from responsibility or liability when goods are despatched direct to the address of a bank or consigned to a bank where prior permission has not been granted. Banks, in such circumstances, need not accept delivery of the goods.

h) **Article 12** obliges bank recipients of a collection instruction to advise the sender of this instruction of any documents, which are not as listed or are not received, without delay.

i) **Articles 16** to **19** cover payment procedures. An important point to note here concerns partial payments. In respect of clean collections, such payments can be accepted, provided that such an action is considered lawful in the place where payment is made. However, with regard to documentary collections, partial payments are only permissible where the collection instruction expressly allows them.

j) **Articles 20** and **21** relates to action to be taken by banks where payment of interest, charges and expenses is refused by the drawee.

k) **Article 24** states that a bank need not protest in the event of non-payment or non-acceptance unless expressly authorised to do so in the collection instruction.

l) **Article 25** indicates that a case of need (i.e. an agent of the exporter who is resident in the importer's country) must have his powers expressly stated in the collection instruction. In the absence of this, banks will not accept any instructions from the case of need.

m) **Article 26** imposes upon the collecting bank the duty of advising fate of a collection without delay to the bank from which the collection instruction was received.

Readers should note that this section of the unit is merely a summary of the contents of URC. Full details of URC are contained in Appendix III of this book.

PLEASE COLLECT THE UNDERMENTIONED FOREIGN BILL AND/OR DOCUMENTS   A

Full Name and Address of Drawer/Exporter			For Bank Use Only	Date	I.S.B. Collection No.	
			Drawers reference (to be quoted in all correspondence)			
			For Bank Use Only	Due Date	Correspondents Reference	
Consignee - Full Name and Address			Drawee (if not Consignee) - Full Name and Address			
			For Bank Use Only	Fate Dates		
TO Barclays Bank PLC			Drawers Bankers Barclays Bank		Sorting Code No. 20-	Ref. No.
S.W.I.F.T. ADDRESS BARC GB22			Account No.			

PLEASE FORWARD DOCUMENTS ENUMERATED BELOW BY AIRMAIL. FOLLOW SPECIAL INSTRUCTIONS AND THOSE MARKED X

Bill of Exchange	Comm'l. Invoice	Cert'd./Cons. Inv.	Cert. of Origin	Ins'ce Pol./Cert.	Bill of Lading	Parcel Post Rec'pt	Air Waybill

Combined Transport Doc.	Other Documents and whereabouts of any missing Original Bill of Lading

RELEASE DOCUMENTS ON	ACCEPTANCE	PAYMENT	If unaccepted		Protest	Do Not Protest
If documents are not taken up on arrival of goods	Warehouse Goods	Do Not Warehouse	and advise reason by		Cable	Airmail
	Insure Against Fire	Do Not Insure	If unpaid		Protest	Do Not Protest
Collect ALL Charges	Yes	No	and advise reason by		Cable	Airmail
Collect Correspondent's Charges ONLY	Yes	No	Acceptance/Payment may be deferred until arrival of goods		Yes	No
Goods and carrying vessel.			After final-payment remit proceeds by		Cable	Airmail

For Bank Use Only

In case of need refer to	For Guidance	Accept their Instructions

SPECIAL INSTRUCTIONS 1. Represent on arrival of goods if not honoured on first presentation

Date of Bill of Exchange	Tenor	Amount of Collection

Bill of Exchange claused		
	Please apply proceeds of this collection as indicated with an 'X'	Credit us in Sterling	
		Credit our Foreign Currency Account No.	
		Apply to Forward Contract No.	
	I/We agree that you shall not be liable for any loss, damage, or delay however caused which is not directly due to the negligence of your own officers and servants. Any charges and expenses not recovered from the drawees, including any costs of protecting the merchandise, may be charged to us		
For Bank use Only	Date & Signature		

371 (OC206) 1/85

Figure 3: Specimen Collection Instruction

15.8 The Legal and Practical Positions Regarding the Duties of the Remitting Bank

Question

An exporter customer hands you a documentary collection. What is your bank's liability regarding examination of the documents and what other points would the bank check in practice?

Answer

The bank's legal liability is set out in the Uniform Rules for Collections. Banks must check that they appear to have received the documents specified in the collection instruction, but they have no liability to examine the documents in more detail.

However, in practice the remitting bank will make the following additional checks before it sends the documents abroad:

a) Make sure the bill of exchange is correctly drawn, signed and endorsed.

b) Ensure that the amount of the bill of exchange agrees with the invoice (and collection order if applicable).

c) If the bill of lading is made out to order, it must be endorsed in blank by the shipper (who is usually the exporter).

d) If bills of lading are used, a full set would normally be required. If any are missing, an explanation should be obtained and the collecting bank must be advised accordingly. (See Figure 3, Specimen Collection Instruction, other documents and whereabouts of any missing bills of lading.)

e) Ensure that the shipping marks tie up on all documents.

f) If the invoice shows which Incoterms apply, check that the documents conform to it, e.g. with CIF, the bill of lading must be marked 'freight paid' and an insurance document should be present.

g) Make sure that the instructions on the collection order are logical, e.g. release documents on payment with a sight draft.

h) Check the bank's reference book to see if there are any special documentary requirements in the importer's country.

i) Ensure that the customer signs the collection instruction.

Note

If the remitting bank does not make a thorough check of the documents, disaster can quickly result. For instance, there may be some special requirement in the importer's country. Failure to fulfil the documentary requirements could mean that the goods are physically present in the importer's country, but the importer cannot obtain possession. In this case, the exporter has lost physical possession of the goods but will not be paid for them. This problem will have been caused by the UK bank's failure to check that the documents are in the proper form.

If a remitting bank fails to take proper care, then the exporter will soon transfer his account to one which does.

15.9 Payment under the Documentary Collection System: The Theory

The exporter should be able to make an accurate assessment of when payment can be expected. With sight drafts, the payment should be made as soon as the documents reach the presenting bank. The only additional delay will be if a **payment may be deferred pending arrival of goods** clause applies. There may be some delay whilst the importer is contacted by the presenting bank, but usually the importer will be eager to obtain the documents, and hence the goods, as quickly as possible.

The same timing considerations apply with term bills except that the period allowed after sight must be added.

15.10 Timing of Payments: The Practice

Some banks publish a list of countries with the average length of time which can be expected to elapse from:

a) remittance of the collection from the United Kingdom when it is a sight draft;

b) number of days after due date when it is a term draft.

Obviously, the time taken will depend on the method of remittance of proceeds (MT, SWIFT or TT).

A previous Chief Examiner has stated "Most experienced exporting companies appreciate that when they sell goods in a foreign country, a sight bill means, in effect, giving 20-30 days' credit, and similarly 20-30 days can be 'added on' to the due date of any usance bill. This is simply due to the delay in receiving funds."

15.11 Acceptance Pour Aval

This is an alternative to straightforward D/A. If the collection order states **release documents against acceptance pour aval**, it means that the bill of exchange must be accepted by the drawee and then guaranteed for payment at maturity by the drawee's bankers. Only then may the documents be released. The benefit to the exporter is that:

a) the drawee's bank is liable on the bill, thus eliminating risk of non-payment if the bank is sound;

b) funds will be remitted on the due date, thus reducing the 20-30 days' delay normally met.

The prior permission of the importers and their banks should be obtained before submitting such a collection.

15.12 Risks to Exporters Who Sell on Documentary Collection Terms

The risks are the same as for open account, i.e. buyer risk, country risk, and transit risk. As with all of the terms of payment, the exchange risk applies if the exporter invoices in foreign currency.

a)   Ways to Minimise the Risks

The country risk, exchange risk and transit risk are reduced by the same methods as those applying to open account (see 12.3).

The buyer risk can also be reduced by taking status enquiries and by insurance against bad debts.

b)   How to Further Reduce the Buyer Risk with D/P Collections

Provided that documents of title are used, the buyer cannot obtain the goods without paying the bill of exchange (or, where a bill of exchange is not included, paying the amount specified on invoice/collection instruction).

However, where a buyer refuses to pay, the physical goods are at the overseas port, in danger of being damaged or stolen and possibly incurring demurrage (demurrage means charges levied by port authorities for goods which are not collected).

To overcome this problem a **store and insure** clause should be incorporated on the collection schedule. The exporter knows the goods will then be protected until an alternative buyer can be found.

If the exporter has a reliable agent, he can insert details of a **case of need** on the collection instruction. If the agent is reliable, the collection instruction will give him full authority to sell the goods on behalf of the exporter.

With air freight, the airway bill could show that the goods are consigned to the presenting bank. The bank's prior permission is required, however, and this will not often be forthcoming.

c)   How to Reduce the Risk with D/A Collections

The additional risk with a D/A collection is that the documents, and therefore the goods, are released on acceptance, with no guarantee that the payment will be forthcoming at maturity.

Once the bill of exchange has been accepted, the exporter is in no better position than under open account terms, except that there is an accepted bill of exchange on which he can sue the buyer if it is dishonoured at maturity.

However, if the exporter, importer and importer's bank agree beforehand, the collection order could stipulate **release documents against acceptance pour aval**. This means the importer's bank will accept the bill of exchange and hence guarantee payment.

15.13 Self-assessment Questions

Question 1

An exporter and importer agree to deal on documentary collection terms. Whose name would you expect to appear as the drawer of the draft and whose name would you expect as drawee?

Question 2

An exporter hands in a bill of exchange drawn at sight, together with a collection instruction form. What instruction would you expect to see as regards release of documents?

Question 3

Suppose that Speirs and Wadley, who bank at Barclays, agree to sell on documentary collection terms to Woldal Ltd who bank at Downtown Trust Company, Hong Kong.

Who would be: the principal, the remitting bank, the collecting bank and the presenting bank? Assume that Speirs and Wadley do not know where Woldal bank, and that Barclays send the documents to Hong Kong and Shanghai Bank.

Question 4

What are the Uniform Rules for Collections?

Question 5

Give one example of a financial document, and two examples of commercial documents, as defined in URC.

Question 6

An exporter hands in a set of documents which only include two bills of lading. You notice that there are three originals required to make a complete set. Why is it usual to insert an explanation on the collection instruction concerning the missing bill of lading?

Question 7

An exporter hands in a set of documents, together with a collection instruction. What is the quickest way to check if the documents all tie up with one another?

Question 8

An exporter hands in a set of documents with a collection instruction. The invoice quotes FOB terms. Would you expect to see an insurance document amongst the documents?

Question 9

Which is the more secure from an exporter's point of view, D/P or D/A?

Question 10

What form of acceptance can overcome the basic problem of D/A collections, and what prior formalities are necessary if this form of acceptance is to be requested on the collection instruction?

(Answers given in Appendix VI)

15.14 Specimen Question

Your exporter customer has previously sold goods on open account terms, but he now requires more secure terms of payment.

His overseas buyer has suggested the following terms:

FCA Gatwick

Documentary collection sight drafts D/P.

What particular formalities would you suggest to ensure that the new payment terms are really more secure than open account?

(Specimen Answer given in Appendix VI)

15.16 A Set of Shipping Documents Being Sent for Collection

The illustrated examples which follow constitute a set of shipping documents presented by the drawer to his bank for collection. An examination of the documents will establish that they appear to be in order. Points to note are:

i)   The drawee will be able to obtain delivery of the goods.

ii)   He may claim from the insurers in the case of loss.

iii)   The invoice and bill amount agree.

iv)   The bill of exchange is properly drawn.

v)   Bills of lading are marked 'freight paid' (CIF invoices).

vi)   The insurance cover is at least the amount of the invoice.

vii)   According to the reference books, no additional documentary requirements are necessary to satisfy the importing authorities.

viii) The instructions on the collection instruction form have been completed and are not contradictory.

FOREIGN BILL AND/OR DOCUMENTS FOR COLLECTION

Drawer/Exporter	Drawer's/Exporter's Reference(s) (to be quoted by Bank in all correspondence)
Power Woollen Company Limited P O Box 799 Bradford West Yorkshire BD1 1AA	34/81 18-5-8 34/8

Consignee	Drawee (if not Consignee)
Tulla AS HC Andersens Boulevard 18 Copenhagen Denmark	

To (Bank)	For Bank use only

FORWARD DOCUMENTS ENUMERATED BELOW BY AIRMAIL. FOLLOW SPECIAL INSTRUCTIONS AND THOSE MARKED X

Bill of Exchange	Comm'l. Invoice	Cert'd./Cons. Inv.	Cert. of Origin	Ins'ce Pol./Cert.	Bill of Lading	Parcel Post Rec'pt.	Air Waybill
1	3			1	2/2		

Combined Transport Doc.	Other Documents and whereabouts of any missing Original Bill of Lading

RELEASE DOCUMENTS ON	ACCEPTANCE	PAYMENT X	If unaccepted ——→	Protest	Do Not Protest
If documents are not taken up on arrival of goods	Warehouse Goods	Do Not Warehouse	and advise reason by	Cable	Airmail
	Insure Against Fire	Do Not Insure	If unpaid ——→	Protest	Do Not Protest X
Collect ALL Charges		X	and advise reason by	Cable X	Airmail
Collect Correspondent's Charges ONLY			Advise acceptance and due date by	Cable	Airmail
Return Accepted Bill by Airmail			Remit Proceeds by	Cable	Airmail X
In case of need refer to				For Guidance	Accept their Instructions

SPECIAL INSTRUCTIONS: 1. Represent on arrival of goods if not honoured on first presentation.

Date of Bill of Exchange 18 May 19	Bill of Exchange Value/Amount of Collection GBP 683.75
Tenor of Bill of Exchange SIGHT	
Bill of Exchange Claused:—	Please collect the above mentioned Bill and/or Documents subject to the Uniform Rules for Collections 1996 Revision ICC publication No 522 I/We agree that you shall not be liable for any loss, damage, or delay however caused which is not directly due to the negligence of your own officers or servants.
	Date and Signature Bradford 18 May 19

Exhibit 1: Collection Instruction

| INCORPORATING BILL OF EXCHANGE | ADDITIONAL COPY FOREIGN BILL AND/OR DOCUMENTS FOR COLLECTION |

Drawer/Exporter

Power Woollen Company Limited
P O Box 799
Bradford
West Yorkshire   BD1 1AA

Drawer's/Exporter's Reference(s) (to be quoted by Bank in all correspondence)

34/81   18-5-81   34/81

Consignee

Tulla AS
HC Andersens Boulevard 18
Copenhagen
Denmark

Drawee (if not Consignee)

To (Bank)

English Banking Ltd
Mill Street
Bradford   BD1 1AA

For Bank use only

FORWARD DOCUMENTS ENUMERATED BELOW BY AIRMAIL. FOLLOW SPECIAL INSTRUCTIONS AND THOSE MARKED X

Bill of Exchange	Comm'l Invoice	Cert'd/Cons. Inv.	Cert. of Origin	Ins'ce Pol/Cert.	Bill of Lading	Parcel Post Rec'pt	Air Waybill
1	3			1	2/2		

| Combined Transport Doc | Other Documents and whereabouts of any missing Original Bill of Lading |

	ACCEPTANCE	PAYMENT			Protest	Do Not Protest
RELEASE DOCUMENTS ON		X	If unaccepted →			
If documents are not taken up on arrival of goods	Warehouse Goods	Do Not Warehouse	and advise reason by		Cable	Airmail
	Insure Against Fire	Do Not Insure	If unpaid →		Protest	Do Not Protest X
Collect ALL Charges		X	and advise reason by		Cable X	Airmail
Collect Correspondent's Charges ONLY			Advise acceptance and due date by		Cable	Airmail X
Return Accepted Bill by Airmail			Remit Proceeds by		Cable	Airmail
In case of need refer to					For Guidance	Accept their Instructions

SPECIAL INSTRUCTIONS   1   Represent on arrival of goods if not honoured on first presentation

447/490
Tear

SITPRO OVERLAYS 1979

Date of Bill of Exchange

BILL of EXCHANGE for   GBP 683.75

At   Sight   Pay against this sole of exchange to our order the sum of   Six hundred and eighty three pounds 75.

Tulla AS
HC Andersens Boulevard 18
Copenhagen
Denmark

Power Woollen Co Ltd
0274 45336

Richard King

DRAWEE

FOR VALUE RECEIVED
Bradford 18 May 1981

Signature

Exhibit 2: Collection Instruction and Bill of exchange

INVOICE	FACTURE FACTURA	RECHNUNG FACTUUR		

Seller (Name, Address, VAT Reg No.)
Power Woollen Company Limited
P O Box 799
Bradford
West Yorkshire BD1 1AA

C C C N No. C003

Invoice No. and Date (Tax Point) 34/ 18-5-?

Seller's Reference 34/.

Buyer's Reference 345

Consignee
Tulla AS
HC Andersens Boulevard 18
Copenhagen
Denmark

Buyer (if not Consignee)

Country of Origin of Goods
United Kingdom

Terms of Delivery and Payment
FOB UK port. Plus freight and
insurance. Cash against documents
through English Banking Ltd.,
Mill St.. Bradford.

Vessel/Aircraft etc. Charlotte

Port of Loading London

Port of Discharge Copenhagen

Marks and Numbers, Number and Kind of Packages, Description of Goods		Quantity	@ £	Amount (State Currency)
TUL 345 COPENHAGN 1/1	1 Carton - 1000 pairs woollen knee length stockings assorted colours Type 92	1000	.65 each	£650.00
	Freight			£30.00
	Insurance			£ 3.75

TOTAL GBP 683.75

Gross Weight(kg) 60kg **Cube (m³)** 1.25m3

Name of Signatory
Richard King

Place and Date of Issue
Bradford 18 May 19?

Signature

It is hereby certified that this invoice shows the actual price of the goods described,
that no other invoice has been or will be issued, and that all particulars are true and
correct

Exhibit 3: Invoice (Three copies required for Collection)

Exporter's Reference   34/.

Norwich Union Fire Insurance Society Ltd.
Maritime Insurance Company Ltd.

NORWICH HOUSE, WATER STREET, LIVERPOOL L2 8UP.

INSURANCE CERTIFICATE No. A.R. /   CODE No. 66/KK/

This is to Certify that
have been issued with an Open Policy and this certificate conveys all rights of the policy (for the purpose of collecting any loss or claim) as fully as if the property were covered by a special policy direct to the holder of this certificate but if the destination of the goods is outside of the United Kingdom this certificate may require to be stamped within a given period in order to comply with the Laws of the country of destination. Notwithstanding the description of the voyage stated herein, provided the goods are at the risk of the Assured this insurance shall attach from the time of leaving the warehouse, premises or place of storage in the interior.

Conveyance	From	
Charlotte	London	
Via/To	To	Insured Value / Currency
Copenhagen		GBP 750 so valued

Marks and Numbers	Interest
TUL 345 COPENHAGN 1/1	1 Carton - 1000 pairs woollen knee length stockings assorted colours Type 92

SPECIMEN

CONDITIONS - ALL RISKS as per current Institute Cargo Clauses. (All Risks)
Subject to Institute Replacement Clause. (as applicable)
Including War, Strikes, Riots and Civil Commotions as per current Institute Clauses.
Refer to Clauses as over.

SURVEY CLAUSE :- In the event of loss or damage which may give rise to a claim under this certificate, notice must be given immediately to to the undernoted agent/s so that he/they may appoint a Surveyor if he/they so desire.

Agents at .... are ....

CLAIMS In the event of a claim arising under this Certificate it is agreed that it shall be settled in accordance with English Law and Custom
and shall be so settled in Liverpool or at ....
by ....

G. W. Umson
Liverpool Marine Underwriter

Dated
Bradford 18 May 19

This Certificate Requires Endorsement.   Signed

The original Certificate must be produced when claim is made and must be surrendered on payment.

Exhibit 4: Insurance Certificate (front)

IMPORTANT

PROCEDURE IN THE EVENT OF LOSS OR DAMAGE FOR WHICH UNDERWRITERS MAY BE LIABLE

LIABILITY OF CARRIERS, BAILEES OR OTHER THIRD PARTIES

It is the duty of the Assured and their Agents, in all cases, to take such measures as may be reasonable for the purpose of averting or minimising a loss and to ensure that all rights against Carriers, Bailees or other third parties are properly preserved and exercised. In particular, the Assured or their Agents are required:—

1. To claim immediately on the Carriers, Port Authorities or other Bailees for any missing packages.

2. In no circumstances, except under written protest, to give clean receipts where goods are in doubtful condition.

3. When delivery is made by Container, to ensure that the Container and its seals are examined immediately by their responsible official.

   If the Container is delivered damaged or with seals broken or missing or with seals other than as stated in the shipping documents, to clause the delivery receipt accordingly and retain all defective or irregular seals for subsequent identification.

4. To apply immediately for survey by Carriers' or other Bailees' Representatives if any loss or damage be apparent and claim on the Carriers or other Bailees for any actual loss or damage found at such survey.

5. To give notice in writing to the Carriers or other Bailees within three days of delivery if the loss or damage was not apparent at the time of taking delivery.

NOTE.—The Consignees or their Agents are recommended to make themselves familiar with the Regulations of the port Authorities at the port of discharge.

SURVEY AND CLAIM SETTLEMENT

In the event of loss or damage which may involve a claim under this insurance, immediate notice of such loss or damage should be given to and a Survey Report obtained from the Office or Agent nominated herein.

In the event of any claim arising under this insurance, request for settlement should be made to the Office or Agent nominated herein.

DOCUMENTATION OF CLAIMS

To enable claims to be dealt with promptly, the Assured or their Agents are advised to submit all available supporting documents without delay, including when applicable:—

1. Original policy or certificate of insurance.

2. Original or copy shipping invoices, together with shipping specification and/or weight notes.

3. Original Bill of Lading and/or other contract of carriage.

4. Survey report or other documentary evidence to show the extent of the loss or damage.

5. Landing account and weight notes at final destination.

6. Correspondence exchanged with the Carriers and other Parties regarding their liability for the loss or damage.

The Institute clauses stated herein are those current at the date of printing of this certificate but where such clauses are revised the Institute clauses current at the time of commencement of the risk hereunder are deemed to apply.

Exhibit 5: Insurance Certificate (back)

© GCBS 1979

Shipper		COMMON	UK Customs Assigned No.	B/L No.
Power Woollen Company Limited		SHORT FORM BILL OF LADING	6003	67
			Shipper's Reference 34/	
			F/Agent's Reference	

Consignee (if "Order" state Notify Party and Address)

Tulla AS

Name of Carrier

P. Bork Shipping Limited

Notify Party and Address (leave blank if stated above)

The contract evidenced by this Short Form Bill of Lading is subject to the exceptions limitations conditions and liberties (including those relating to pre carriage and on carriage) set out in the Carrier's Standard Conditions applicable to the voyage covered by this Short Form Bill of Lading and operative on its date of issue
If the carriage is one where the provisions of the Hague Rules contained in the International Convention for unification of certain rules relating to Bills of Lading dated Brussels on 25th August 1924 as amended by the Protocol signed at Brussels on 23rd February 1968 (the Hague Visby Rules) are compulsorily applicable under Article X the said Standard Conditions contain or shall be deemed to contain a Clause giving effect to the Hague Visby Rules Otherwise except as provided below the said Standard Conditions contain or shall be deemed to contain a Clause giving effect to the provisions of the Hague Rules
The Carrier hereby agrees that to the extent of any inconsistency the said Clause shall prevail over the exceptions limitations conditions and liberties set out in the Standard Conditions in respect of any period to which the Hague Rules or the Hague Visby Rules by their terms apply. Unless the Standard Conditions expressly provide otherwise neither the Hague Rules nor the Hague Visby Rules shall apply to this contract where the goods carried hereunder consist of live animals or cargo which by this contract is stated as being carried on deck and is so carried
Notwithstanding anything contained in the said Standard Conditions the term Carrier in this Short Form Bill of Lading shall mean the Carrier named on the front thereof
A copy of the Carrier's said Standard Conditions applicable hereto may be inspected or will be supplied on request at the office of the Carrier or the Carrier's Principal Agents

Pre-Carriage by*	Place of Receipt by Pre-Carrier*
	Bradford
Vessel	Port of Loading
CHARLOTTE	LONDON
Port of Discharge	Place of Delivery by On-Carrier*
COPENHAGEN	Copenhagen

Marks and Nos. Container No.	Number and kind of packages; Description of Goods	Gross Weight	Measurement
TUL 345 COPENHAGN 1/1	1 Carton stockings	60Kgs	1.25m3

Freight Details; Charges etc.

RECEIVED FOR CARRIAGE as above in apparent good order and condition, unless otherwise stated hereon, the goods described in the above particulars.

IN WITNESS whereof the number of original Bills of Lading stated below have been signed, all of this tenor and date, one of which being accomplished the others to stand void.

GCBS CSF BL 1979

710

Ocean Freight Payable at	Place and Date of Issue
Prepaid	London 16.5.19
Number of Original Bs/L	Signature for Carrier; Carrier's Principal Place of Business
Two	P. Bork Shipping Ltd London

Authorised and Licensed by the
General Council of British Shipping © 1979

*Applicable only when document used as a Through Bill of Lading

Particulars declared by Shipper

Exhibit 6: Bill of Lading (full set of originals required for Collection)

Unit 16

Documentary Credits

Objectives

On completion of this unit the student should be able to:

- give a clear and accurate definition of a 'documentary credit';

- explain briefly who the parties to a credit are, and describe their main responsibilities;

- understand the meaning of revocable/irrevocable and unconfirmed/confirmed;

- acquire an overview of how a documentary credit operates;

- understand the meaning of 'payment', 'acceptance', 'negotiation', and 'deferred payment';

- understand the meaning and purpose of Uniform Customs and Practice for Documentary Credits;

- understand the meaning and purpose of Uniform Rules for Bank-to-Bank Reimbursements under Documentary Credits;

- understand the benefits and drawbacks of documentary credits for exporters;

- appreciate the reasons behind the creation of Documentary Credit Dispute Expertise System.

16.1 Definition of and Parties to a Documentary Credit

A **documentary credit** can be simply defined as a conditional guarantee of payment made by a bank to a named beneficiary, guaranteeing that payment will be made, provided that the terms of the credit are met. These terms will state that the beneficiary must submit specified documents, usually to a stated bank and by a certain date.

However, before considering how documentary credits operate and the responsibilities of the various parties involved, it is important that students become familiar with the more detailed definition taken from the Uniform Customs and Practice:

Applicant
This is the buyer/importer who asks his bank, the issuing bank, to issue credit. The applicant is sometimes called the 'opener' or the 'accreditor'.

Issuing bank
The applicant is a customer of the issuing bank, and it is the issuing bank which gives the conditional guarantee in favour of the beneficiary.

Advising bank

This is a bank, usually domiciled in the beneficiary's country, which is requested by the issuing bank to advise the beneficiary on the terms and conditions of the credit. If the advising bank agrees to advise the credit, it must take reasonable care to check the apparent authenticity of that credit. If the advising bank elects not to advise the credit, it must inform the issuing bank without delay. If the advising bank is not able to establish the apparent authenticity of the credit, it must inform without delay the bank from which the instructions appear to have been received. In addition, the advising bank may, if it wishes, advise the unauthenticated credit, but at the same time must inform the beneficiary that it has not been able to establish the authenticity of that credit.

There is no liability on the part of the advising bank to honour the credit.

Beneficiary

This is the seller or exporter in whose favour the guarantee operates. Note that UK banks can issue letters of credit on behalf of UK clients in favour of UK beneficiaries, who may themselves be importing the goods.

Confirming bank

The 'confirming bank' is a bank which, at the request of, or with the permission of, the issuing bank, adds its own irrevocable undertaking to honour the credit if the issuing bank should default. Banks will only confirm irrevocable credits.

This undertaking is in addition to, and not in substitution for, that already given by the issuing bank. In effect, the beneficiary has the benefit of two bank guarantors. First recourse is to the issuing bank, and then to the confirming bank in the event of default. Naturally, there is no liability on the part of the confirming bank if the beneficiary has failed to comply with the terms of the credit.

Normally the advising and confirming bank are one and the same.

Obviously, a confirmed irrevocable documentary credit is the safest form of credit from the exporter's point of view, but it will be more costly than an unconfirmed credit because of the extra bank being involved.

Under Uniform Customs and Practice (see 16.4), branches of the same bank in different countries are considered to be different banks. Hence, for example, National Westminster Bank in London could be asked to confirm a credit issued by one of its own overseas branches.

Revocable/irrevocable

All credits should state whether they are revocable or irrevocable and in the absence of any such indication, the credit will be deemed to be irrevocable. An irrevocable credit cannot be amended without the consent of all parties, whereas a revocable one can be amended or cancelled without the exporter's knowledge. For obvious reasons most credits are irrevocable.

16.2 Example of How a Documentary Credit Operates

Let us return to our old friends, Speirs and Wadley and Woldal Ltd. Let us now assume that these two companies have agreed that payment terms will be by way of an irrevocable, confirmed documentary credit.

The procedures which now occur are as follows:

a) Woldal ask their bankers, Downtown Bank and Trust Co., to issue an irrevocable credit and to request confirmation by Barclays Bank. Let us assume that Downtown Bank agree.

b) Downtown Bank, the issuing bank, request Barclays to advise the beneficiary, Speirs and Wadley Ltd, of the details. Barclays are asked to confirm the credit, and we shall assume that they agree to this.

c) Barclays, as advising bank, now write to Speirs and Wadley, along the lines indicated in the specimen document (Figure 1).

Notes on the specimen advice letter

(These notes correspond with the numbers in the example.)

1   The type of credit (revocable or irrevocable);

2   The name and address of the exporter (beneficiary);

3   The name and address of the importer (accreditor);

4   The amount of the credit, in sterling or a foreign currency;

5   The name of the party on whom the bills of exchange are to be drawn, and whether they are to be at sight or of a particular tenor;

6   The Incoterm in the underlying sales contract;

7   Precise instructions as to the documents against which payment is to be made;

8   A brief description of the goods covered by the credit (too much detail should be avoided as it may give rise to errors which can cause delay);

9   Shipping details, including whether transhipments are allowed. Also recorded should be the latest date for shipment and the names of the ports of shipment and discharge. (It may be in the best interests of the exporter for shipment to be allowed *from any UK port* so that he has a choice if, for example, some ports are affected by strikes. The same applies for the port of discharge.);

10 Whether the credit is available for one or several shipments;

11 The expiry date and place for presentation of documents;

12 The credit is confirmed, as evidenced by the final sentence in the letter.

d) Speirs and Wadley should immediately check that they will be able to produce the required documents at the appropriate time.

e) Speirs and Wadley ship the goods, and obtain the necessary documents which are presented to Barclays Bank along with the bill of exchange.

As sight drafts are called for, and as Barclays are the drawee, Speirs and Wadley will receive immediate payment, provided they have complied strictly with the terms and conditions of the credit.

f) Barclays send the documents to Downtown Bank and Trust Co., and claim reimbursement of the sterling funds paid to Speirs and Wadley from the vostro account in the name of Downtown.

g) Provided Woldal have the funds. Downtown debit their account with the Hong Kong dollar equivalent of £4,108, and release the documents. (Even if Woldal do not have funds, Downtown are bound by the terms of the credit to honour the presentation.)

h) The goods are delivered by the transport operator to Woldal's premises, and Woldal will be required to surrender an original combined transport document in exchange.

16.3 Types of Credit

Unless the credit states that it is available only with the issuing bank, all credits must nominate the bank which is authorised to pay, to incur a deferred payment undertaking, to accept or to negotiate.

If you examine the specimen advice letter from Barclays Bank to Speirs and Wadley (Figure 1), you can see that, while the drafts under this particular credit were to be presented to Barclays for payment, the alternatives of negotiation or acceptance or of deferred payment could also have been applicable.

The four terms apply as follows:

Payment
The meaning of the term 'payment' is self-evident. The nominated bank will pay the beneficiary on receipt of the specified documents and on fulfilment of all the terms of the credit.

Sometimes the issuing bank nominates itself as paying bank, in which case payment will be made on receipt of the correct documents at their counters abroad. On other occasions, usually with confirmed credits expressed in sterling, the issuing bank will nominate the UK advising bank to pay. This is the position with our specimen documentary credit (Figure 1).

The term 'payment' only applies to sight drafts.

Negotiation
Sometimes the issuing bank will nominate the advising bank to negotiate a credit, or it may even make the credit freely negotiable, in which case any bank is a nominated bank.

BARCLAYS

Barclays Bank PLC
1 Union Court, London EC2P 2HP.

DOCUMENTARY CREDITS DEPARTMENT

date   20th July 19

SPECIMEN

(1)
IRREVOCABLE CREDIT No:- UTDC 65432
To be quoted on all drafts and correspondence

Beneficiary(ies) (2)	Advised through
Speirs and Wadley Ltd. Adderley Road Hackney, London E8 1XY	

Accreditor (3)	To be completed only if applicable
Woldal Ltd. New Road Kowloon, Hong Kong	Our cable of Advised through Refers

Dear Sir(s)

In accordance with instructions received from The Downtown Bank & Trust Co.
we hereby issue in your favour a Documentary Credit for £4108
(say) Four thousand, one hundred and eight pounds sterling (4)   available by your drafts
drawn on us (5)

at sight
for the 100% c.i.f. (6)   invoice value, accompanied by the following documents:-

1. Signed Invoice in triplicate.
(7)   2. Full set of clean Combined Transport Bills of Lading made out to
order and blank endorsed, marked 'Freight Paid' and 'Notify Woldal
Ltd., New Road, Kowloon Hong Kong'.
3. Insurance Policy or Certificate in duplicate, covering Marine and
War Risks up to buyer's warehouse, for invoice value of the goods
plus 10%.

Covering the following goods:-
(8)
400 Electric Power Drills

(9)   (6)
To be shipped from   London   to   Hong Kong c.i.f.

not later than (10)   10th August 19

Partshipment not permitted   Transhipment   permitted
(11)
The credit is available for   presentation to us   until   31st August 19

Documents to be presented within 21 days of shipment but within credit
validity.

Drafts drawn hereunder must be marked "Drawn under Barclays Bank PLC 1 Union Court,
London   branch, Credit number   UTDC 65432   "
We undertake that drafts and documents drawn under and in strict conformity with the terms of this credit will
honoured upon presentation.

Yours faithfully,   *R E Daw*

Co-signed (Signature No. 9847   )   Signed (Signature No. 10247   )

CRF 202 (replacing CRE 83, 606 series)   PLEASE SEE REVERSE

Subject to Uniform Customs and Practice for Documentary Credits 1993 Revision ICC Publication No. 500

Figure 1: Specimen Document

If a bank negotiates a credit, it will advance money to the beneficiary on presentation of the required documents and will charge interest on the advance from the date of the advance until such time as it receives reimbursement from the issuing bank.

Such negotiation advances are said to be **with recourse**, so that if payment is not ultimately forthcoming from the issuing bank, the negotiating bank will be able to claim repayment from the beneficiary of the advance, plus interest. However, the negotiating bank will only be able to obtain recourse from the beneficiary if the issuing bank is unable to reimburse because of insolvency or government restriction. If the negotiating bank has missed a discrepancy in the documents after examination, then there is no recourse to the beneficiary. It is the banks' loss!

One final point: if the negotiating bank has confirmed the credit, then the advance will be on a 'without recourse' basis, provided the terms of the credit have been complied with.

Acceptance

The term 'acceptance' can only apply when the credit calls for usance bills (term bills), i.e. bills of exchange payable at a specified time after acceptance by the drawee.

The acceptance credit is also referred to as a 'term credit' or 'usance credit', which means that the seller draws a draft on the nominated bank demanding payment at some determinable future date, e.g. **at 30 days' sight** instead of **at sight**, as shown in the specimen credit (Figure 1).

In practice, this means that instead of receiving immediate payment on presentation of the documents (at sight), the seller's draft is returned to him endorsed on the face with the nominated bank's acceptance. This acceptance represents an undertaking by the bank to honour payment of the draft on the due date.

Deferred payment credits

Normally the terms of a documentary credit will include an instruction to the beneficiary to draw bills of exchange, and the issuing bank will guarantee that such bills will be honoured, provided all the other terms of the credit are met.

However, in deferred payment credits, there is no need for the exporter to draw a bill of exchange. The issuing bank simply guarantees that payment will be made on a fixed or determinable future date, provided the other conditions have been fulfilled.

Although the exporter does not draw a bill of exchange, in all other respects these credits are identical to other documentary credits. Although bills of exchange are not drawn, in practice some banks will negotiate the documents providing they are entirely satisfied with the standing of the issuing bank.

One benefit of deferred credits is that they avoid the need for payment of stamp duty on bills of exchange. In some countries stamp duty is set at a low rate, or there may not be any stamp duty at all, whereas in other countries stamp duties can be much higher.

Currently, at least one major UK bank is seeking to end the use of drafts in documentary credits.

Wording of the credit as regards payment, acceptance, negotiation or deferred credit

All credits must clearly indicate whether they are available by sight payment, by deferred payment, by acceptance or by negotiation. All credits must nominate a bank (the 'nominated bank'), which is authorised to pay, incur a deferred payment undertaking, to accept drafts or to negotiate. When the nominated bank is a bank other than the issuing bank, then unless it is the confirming bank, nomination by the issuing bank does not constitute any undertaking by the nominated bank to honour the credit. However, if the nominated bank does honour the credit, then provided the credit terms have been fulfilled, the nominated bank is entitled to claim reimbursement from the issuing bank.

Thus, where the nominated bank is neither the issuing bank nor the confirming bank, the beneficiary must bear in mind that the nominated bank is not obliged to honour the credit unless that nominated bank has expressly agreed with the beneficiary that it will be liable.

16.4 Uniform Customs and Practice for Documentary Credits (1993 Revision)

The Uniform Customs and Practice for Documentary Credits (UCP) is a set of internationally accepted rules and definitions which cover the liabilities and duties of all parties to documentary credits. (The relevant provisions are reproduced in Appendix IV.) All bank authorities and advices of documentary credits will state that the credit is subject to UCP 1993. Where the terms of the credit contradict UCP, the terms of the credit will prevail and where national laws conflict with UCP, national laws will prevail.

The main provisions of UCP 1993, as they affect exporters and their banks, are as follows:

Article 3
Banks are concerned only with the documents presented under the credit. Even when the underlying sales contract is mentioned in the credit (e.g. where invoice stipulates the Incoterm), the bank's decision to pay depends solely on whether the documents presented conform to the credit.

Comment
The issuing bank should ensure that a credit is logical and workable when it is set up (e.g. if the sales contract is FOB, do not call for an insurance document) and beneficiaries should ensure that the credit meets their requirements as soon as it is advised to them.

However, once the credit has been set up, the bank's decision to pay or not depends solely upon whether the documents presented conform to the credit. The only way payment can be made against the wrong documents is if the applicant agrees to accept the documents despite the discrepancies and authorises the issuing bank to debit the account.

Article 4
Banks are only concerned with documents, not goods nor the performance of the underlying contract.

Article 6
Credits should clearly indicate whether they are revocable or irrevocable. In the absence of any such indication, the credits are deemed irrevocable.

Article 7
The advising bank must take reasonable care to check that the credit is genuine, if it elects to advise the credit. If the advising bank cannot establish authenticity, it must inform the bank from which the instructions appear to have been received without delay. The advising bank may advise an unauthenticated credit but if it does so it must inform the beneficiary that authenticity has not been established. In all cases, there is no obligation on the part of the advising bank to advise a credit, but if it elects not to do so, it must inform the issuing bank without delay.

Comment
If a credit is received by the beneficiary directly from the issuing bank, the beneficiary should ask his own bank to check its authenticity.

Articles 13 and 15
Banks must examine all documents with reasonable care to ensure that on the face of it they appear to be in order. Documents which on the face of it appear to be inconsistent with one another will be considered as not appearing to comply with the credit terms. Any documents which are not called for by the credit will not be examined by banks.

Banks shall have a reasonable time, not to exceed seven banking days following the day of receipt of documents, to examine the documents and determine whether to take up or refuse the documents and to inform the party from which the documents were received of the decision.

If the credit contains terms and conditions without stating the document(s) to be presented in compliance with such conditions, then banks will disregard the conditions.

Banks assume no liability for the genuineness of documents.

Article 20
Unless otherwise stipulated in the credit, banks will accept as an original document a document produced or appearing to have been produced by photocopier, carbon systems or computer, provided such a document is marked as original, and where necessary, appears to have been signed.

Any symbol executed or adopted by a party with the intention to authenticate should be accepted as a signature. one example of such a signature is the traditional chop mark used in Asia which is a legal and valid signature.

Unless otherwise stipulated in the credit, a condition calling for a document to be authenticated or certified will be satisfied by any signature, mark, stamp or label which appears to satisfy such conditions.

Articles 21 and 22
When documents other than transport documents, invoices and insurance documents are called for, the credit should stipulate by whom the documents are to be issued, and the required wording or data content.

If no such instructions are received, banks will accept such documents as tendered.

Banks will accept a document bearing a date of issue prior to that of the credit, subject to such a document being presented within the time limits set out in the credit and in other parts of UCP.

Article 23 - Marine/Ocean Bill of Lading

i) When a credit calls for a bill of lading covering port-to-port shipment, banks will accept the following unless otherwise stipulated in the credit:

- a bill of lading which indicates the name of the carrier and which has been signed or otherwise authenticated by the carrier, a named agent of the carrier, the ship's master or a named agent of the ship's master (the agents must indicate in what capacity they sign);

and which

- indicates that the goods have been loaded on board or shipped on a named vessel.

ii) The loading on board may be indicated by preprinted wording, in which case the date of loading on board will be deemed to be the date of issue of the bill of lading. Where the loading on board is evidenced by a notation on the bill, the date of shipment will be deemed to be the date of loading on board.

iii) If the credit calls for any signatures or initials to authorise the on-board notation, banks will have no duty to check the genuineness of such signatures or initials.

iv) A full set of bills of lading would be required unless the credit stipulates otherwise. Nowadays, some carriers issue only one original bill of lading in set, and in such cases that single bill would constitute a full set.

v) Transport documents which are subject to a charter party, for example charter party bills of lading, will be rejected unless specifically authorised by the credit.

vi) When a bill of lading indicates that transhipment will take place (that is the unloading and reloading from one vessel to another during the course of ocean carriage) then such a transhipment bill of lading will be accepted unless prohibited by the credit.

Even if transhipment is prohibited by the credit, so long as the bill of lading indicates that the cargo is shipped in containers, trailers and/or LASH barges, then transhipment is acceptable so long as the same bill of lading covers the entire ocean voyage.

vii) If the credit prohibits transhipment, a bill of lading which indicates that the carrier reserves the right to tranship is still acceptable.

Article 24 - Non Negotiable Sea Waybill

This article contains similar provisions to those in Article 23 on marine/ocean bill of lading. The stipulations concerning transhipment, charter party bills and authentication are identical.

Article 26 - Multimodal Transport Document

i)   When a credit calls for a transport document which covers at least two modes of transport, banks will accept a document which indicates the name of the carrier or multimodal transport operator, provided this is authenticated or signed by the carrier, multimodal transport operator or master or any named agent of these parties who must indicate in what capacity he signs.

ii) The document must indicate that the goods have been despatched, taken in charge or loaded on board. If this indication is pre-printed, then the date of issuance is deemed to be the date of despatch.

If the indication is by means of a stamp or some other additional notation, the date of despatch, taking in charge or loading is deemed to be the date of shipment.

iii) The position regarding transhipment and charter party is the same as that for marine/ocean bills of lading.

iv) Documents which bear names such as combined transport bills of lading or similar titles will be accepted.

Article 27 - Air Transport Documents

Banks may accept, unless stated otherwise in the credit, a document which indicates the name of the carrier and which has been signed or otherwise authenticated by the carrier or by a named agent of the carrier.

Article 30 - Transport Documents Issued by Freight Forwarders

Unless otherwise authorised in the credit, banks will only accept a transport document issued by a freight forwarder which:

● indicates the name of the freight forwarder as a carrier or multimodal transport operator and which appears to have been signed or otherwise authenticated by the freight forwarder as carrier or multimodal transport operator; or

● has been signed or otherwise authenticated by the freight forwarder as agent for a named carrier or multimodal transport operator.

Article 32 - Clean Transport Documents

A clean transport document is one which bears no clause or other indication which declares that the goods or the packing are defective. Where such clauses exist, banks must reject the documents, unless the credit specifically authorises such clauses or notations.

Article 33 - Freight Payable/Pre-paid Transport Documents

Unless otherwise stipulated in the credit, banks will accept transport documents which state that freight or transport charges have still to be paid.

If the credit calls for transport documents which show freight paid, banks will accept a document clearly indicating that the charges have been paid even if such indication is simply by way of a stamp or other notation.

Articles 34 and 36

Insurance documents They must be expressed in the same currency as the credit, must cover CIF or CIP value plus 10%, must show cover effective from date of shipment (e.g. date on the bill of lading), must be issued by underwriters or their agents, and any certificates must be signed or authenticated by the shipper. Insurance certificates or declarations under an open cover policy, pre-signed by the insurers, are acceptable unless prohibited by the credit.

Brokers' cover notes are not acceptable unless specifically authorised.

Note

Where CIF or CIP value cannot be calculated, the bank will accept as a minimum amount 110% of the amount of the credit or 110% of the amount of the invoice, whichever is the greater.

Where the credit calls for an all-risks policy, any form of words covering all risks on the policy is acceptable, including the standard London Underwriters Cargo Insurance, **'all risks except...'**

Article 37

Invoices need not be signed.

The description of the goods in the commercial invoice must correspond exactly with the description in the credit.

In all other documents the goods may be described in general terms not inconsistent with the credit.

The invoice must appear to have been issued by the beneficiary and must be made out in the name of the applicant (except in the case of transferable credits which come under Article 48 and are covered in Part Four of this book).

Articles 39 and 40

The word **circa** or **about** or **approximately** indicates that a difference of 10% either way can be allowed.

Where the goods are described by volume or weight, a 5% tolerance in the amounts actually shipped is allowed, provided the monetary amount claimed is adjusted accordingly. Part shipments are allowed, unless the credit states otherwise.

Article 42

All credits must stipulate an expiry date and a place for presentation of documents for payment. Where a credit is freely negotiable, the implication is that the documents can be presented to any bank.

Article 43

Banks will reject any transport document presented more than 21 days after its date. Such documents are considered **stale**.

Article 44

When the expiry date of a credit falls on a non-business day, banks will accept presentation on the following business day. However, the transport document must be dated on or before the expiry date of the credit, or on or before the last date of shipment if the credit stipulates such a date.

16.5 Uniform Rules for Bank-to-bank Reimbursements under Documentary Credit

Documentary credit operations have increased and become more refined over the years. As already seen in 14.4, Uniform Customs and Practice for Documentary Credits (1993 Revision) is the main set of rules to which parties to documentary credits adhere and these have been regularly updated. Article 19 of these rules covers bank-to-bank reimbursements. However, it was felt that Article 19 did not cover the procedures in sufficient depth and that bank-to-bank reimbursement required its own set of rules to complement this article.

Inter-bank reimbursement procedures have to a great extent materialised out of practices considered acceptable at a local level in the major financial centres. The one exception to this has been in the USA, where rules have been specifically designed. In order to standardise international bank-to-bank reimbursement practices, a working party was set up in 1993 out of which has evolved ICC Publication No 525, Uniform Rules for Bank-to-bank Reimbursements under Documentary Credits (URBBR). It became operational in July 1996 and consists of 17 articles. Full details of these are contained in Appendix V and students and practitioners should ensure that they read these in order to appreciate their full implications.

16.6 The Importance of Documents in Documentary Credits

As can be seen from Article 4 of UCP, banks are concerned only with the documents in documentary credits. If the documents do not conform, the issuing bank is freed from liability under its guarantee. If the documents do conform, then the bank must pay.

A common occurrence, which causes a problem for the beneficiary, arises when the buyer contacts the seller direct and requests a change in transport arrangements. If the transport document which is subsequently presented does not conform to the credit, then presentation will be rejected by the banks. The fact that the buyer and seller have agreed to the change is immaterial, unless the buyer agrees to authorise the issuing bank to amend the credit.

16.7 Documentary Credits: Advantages and Problems

With a documentary collection, exporters retain a measure of control over the goods, either until they are paid or until the importer accepts a bill of exchange. Where D/P collections are used, importers can refuse to have anything to do with the collection, thus leaving the exporter with the problem of arranging an alternative sale while needing to pay the costs of storing and insuring the goods. With D/A collections, importers may not pay the accepted bill of exchange on the due date, thus leaving the exporter unpaid and without any control of the goods.

However, with a documentary credit, exporters know that they have a bank guarantee of payment provided they comply with the terms and conditions of the credit. Thus, on receipt of an advice of a documentary credit, exporters can confidently begin to assemble and ship the goods knowing that they hold a bank guarantee of payment.

The buyer risk is virtually eliminated, since an unknown buyer's agreement to pay is replaced by a conditional bank guarantee.

The transit risk does not really apply, provided the exporter produces the insurance document, if any, specified in the credit. Banks are concerned only with the documents, not the goods, and payment will be forthcoming against correctly tendered documents, irrespective of any damage which may have arisen to the goods themselves.

Problems Which Can Arise for the Beneficiary

The country risk can still occur since the importer's government may prevent the issuing bank from making payment. In addition, there are certain areas of the world where banks are not as sound as they might be, and the issuing bank could possibly fail.

Finally, two problems which exporters often overlook are:

a) If the credit advice is received direct from an unknown bank, there is a danger that it may be forged.

b) The exporter may not be able to fulfil the terms of the credit, because it calls for documents which he cannot provide.

16.8   How the Exporter Can Minimise the Problems

The actions which the exporter can take are as follows:

a) If the credit is received directly from an unknown bank, the exporter should ask his own bank to check the validity of the credit.

b) If there is any doubt about the standing of the issuing bank, the credit should be confirmed by a bank in his, the exporter's, own country. Confirmation will also overcome country risk.

c) Immediately on receipt of the advice, the exporter should check that he will be able to produce the required documents. If not, he should ask the importer to arrange for the issuing bank to amend the credit.

Note

UK banks must take care not to advise or confirm fraudulent credits sent by mail directly to UK exporters.

16.9 Alternative Course of Action When an Exporter has Presented Documents which do not Conform to the Credit

By far the best course of action is to have the documents corrected/amended locally, but it is not always possible to do this before the expiry date of the credit. When this amendment is not possible, the alternatives are:

a) The exporter could present the documents to the advising bank and ask that they be treated as a simple documentary collection.

   Where the exporter is sure of the creditworthiness and integrity of the importer, this is a reasonable step to take, but he must bear in mind that the issuing bank (and the confirming bank, if any) are freed from their guarantee.

b) Where the advising bank is nominated to pay or negotiate documents drawn under a credit, the exporter could request that bank to negotiate or pay despite the discrepancies. In these circumstances the advising bank would not be prepared to negotiate if there were discrepancies but would pay under reserve for their own customer or against a bank indemnity from the beneficiary's bankers.

   The advising bank would require the exporter to join in a suitable indemnity whereby the exporter undertook to reimburse the advising bank if payment were later refused by the issuing bank on account of the discrepancies.

   When the exporter is a customer of the nominated bank, the bank will consider creditworthiness before agreeing to pay under reserve against an indemnity. Where the exporter is a non-customer, the exporter's bankers will be required to join in the indemnity.

c) The bank could cable the issuing bank for permission to pay despite the discrepancies. The issuing bank will require the authority of the applicant before such permission can be granted. The cost of the cable will be charged to the beneficiary.

16.10 Documentary Credit Dispute Expertise System (DOCDEX)

Most documentary credits are found to have discrepancies on their first presentation. Many of these can be easily corrected. However, there have been a growing number of disputes between parties to documentary credits which have been difficult to resolve within the operative time period of the credits concerned.

Consequently, the ICC has set up DOCDEX, which is designed to expedite resolution of disputes by providing impartial and expert recommended solutions. The ICC's International Centre for Expertise oversees the operation of DOCDEX.

16.11 Self-assessment Questions

Question 1
Define a documentary credit.

Question 2
Which type of credit overcomes the country risk for the beneficiary?

Question 3
Give the correct names for the following parties to a documentary credit (assume no other banks are involved).

a) Importer;

b) Importer's bank;

c) Exporter's bank;

d) Exporter.

Question 4
How will an exporter know that a documentary credit has been issued in his favour?

Question 5
In what way is the buyer risk reduced by a documentary credit?

Question 6
What must an exporter do to obtain payment under a documentary credit?

Question 7
What is the function of UCP 1993?

Question 8
A documentary credit, which calls for bills of lading, has been issued.

Just prior to despatch of goods, the exporter receives a written request from the buyer to send the goods by air freight instead of by sea. The exporter agrees. The exporter now presents an air waybill to the paying bank and requests payment.

What is the position?

Question 9
A documentary credit is issued which does not call for any insurance document. Unfortunately, the goods are damaged on the sea voyage, and it transpires that no insurance was arranged.

The exporter now presents the documents called for under the credit. If the documents conform to the credit, is the exporter entitled to payment?

Question 10
An exporter is the beneficiary of a confirmed, irrevocable documentary credit. Would you advise him to take out credit insurance?

Question 11

Under URBBR reference is made to 'claiming banks'.

What is a claiming bank?

Question 12

Under URBBR, reimbursing banks are given a reasonable time period in which to process claims.

What is the extent of this time period?

Question 13

Q Bank issues a documentary credit. It provides the relevant reimbursement authorisation to P Bank, which will act as the reimbursing bank.

Does P Bank need to take note of the terms of the documentary credit in its role as reimbursing bank?

Question 14

If an issuing bank wishes to amend a reimbursement authorisation, what form should this take?

Question 15

Is an expiry date necessary for a reimbursement authorisation?

(Answers given in Appendix VI)

16.12 Specimen Question

Your bank has been nominated as paying bank under a documentary credit where your customer is the beneficiary.

The credit calls for the following documents:

a) A multimodal transport document evidencing transport of goods from London to Hamburg;

b) An insurance policy covering all risks.

Other details are:

i) Expiry date and last date for taking in charge by carrier is 24 February (Sunday);

ii) Description of goods: 500 tonnes of Grade 1 foil priced at £10 per ton;

iii) Amount: Not to exceed £5,250;

iv) Transhipment: Not allowed.

When the documents are received, you note the following:

1) The combined transport document describes the goods as 525 tons of foil, and shows the destination as Hamburg. The document indicates that transhipment may take place.

2) The invoice is for £5,250, and describes the goods as 525 tons of foil.

3) The insurance document consists of a broker's cover note containing reference to the Institute of London Underwriters Cargo Insurance Clauses. These clauses state **all risks** are covered but then indicate certain risks which are excluded.

4) The documents are presented on Monday, 25 February.

Required

a) Are these documents acceptable and can you pay?

b) If not, what action can you take?

(Specimen Answer given in Appendix VI)

Revision Questions 2

You are advised to attempt the following questions before you proceed to Part Four of this book.

CIB Multiple-choice Test

Exam Question 1

Exam Question 2

Exam Question 3

CIB Multiple-choice Test

(Please tick correct answer)

Question 1
Which of the following is the most secure payment term from an exporter's point of view?

a) Net cash on receipt of goods.

b) Cash with order.

c) Documentary collection D/P.

d) Confirmed irrevocable documentary credit.

Question 2
Which of the following is the most favourable Incoterm from a UK exporter's point of view?

a) FOB Southampton.

b) CIF Hamburg.

c) FCA Hackney Container Depot.

d) CFR Hamburg

Q

Question 3

An exporter wishes to retain control of his goods until payment. Which of the following terms of payment will achieve this objective?

a) Documentary collection D/P.

   -   transport documents

       air waybills with importer as consignee.

b) Net cash on receipt of goods.

c) Documentary collection D/P

   -   transport documents

       air waybills with the presenting bank as consignee.

d) Open account.

Question 4

Which of the following terms of payment will entirely eliminate country risk?

a) Revocable documentary credits.

b) Documentary collection D/P (with NCM insurance).

c) Confirmed irrevocable documentary credits.

d) Documentary collection D/A, with acceptance pour aval.

Question 5

Which of the following payment terms eliminates the exchange risk, assuming the exporter invoices in foreign currency?

a) Confirmed irrevocable documentary credit.

b) Open account.

c) Documentary collection D/A.

d) None of these.

Question 6

If an exam question asks for a definition of a **traditional** method of eliminating the exchange risk, which item would you define?

a) Currency borrowing.

b) Currency accounts.

c) Currency options.

d) Forward contracts.

Question 7

For which of the following Incoterms would seller's interest insurance **not** be applicable for a UK exporter?

a) CIF Hamburg.

b) FOB Southampton.

c) FCA Hackney Container Depot.

d) CFR Hamburg.

Question 8

An exporter sends his goods from London via Southampton to Hamburg. Where does the exporter's responsibility end regarding insurance of goods under CFR Hamburg terms?

a) London.

b) Southampton - as soon as the goods reach the docks.

c) Hamburg.

d) Southampton - as soon as the goods cross the ship's rail.

Question 9

Your bank is nominated as the paying bank of a documentary credit in favour of your customer. The credit describes the goods as 1,000 litres of fruit juice. Which of the following bills of lading would be an acceptable document for this credit if it described the goods as follows:

a) 1,100 litres of fruit juice.

b) 960 litres of fruit juice.

c) 900 litres of fruit juice.

d) 1,060 litres of fruit juice.

Which of the following is a document of title?

Question 10

a) Sea waybill.

b) Liner waybill.

c) Charter party bill of lading.

d) Bill of lading (Liner).

(Answers given in Appendix VII)

Exam Question 1

Your customer, Super Steaks Ltd, is a successful meat-marketing organisation. It sells high-quality meat products to many outlets in the UK and Europe. You learn that your customer is considering a contract to supply lamb to the Middle East. Payment would be by confirmed irrevocable letter of credit, payable at sight at your counters. Your bank would confirm the letter of credit, which would show your bank as the bank nominated to pay.

The following events take place:

i)   The contract is awarded to your customer, Super Steaks Ltd, and is signed in March.

ii) Before the end of March, your bank receives, confirms and advises an irrevocable letter of credit for French francs 1,500,000, calling for shipments in three equal lots, during the months of April, May and June. The expiry date of the letter of credit is 30 June.

iii) On 1 April, your customer asks you to establish forward contracts for each of its potential currency receipts.

iv) The first shipment takes place on 6 April, when payment is claimed, and made.

v)   The second shipment takes place on 12 May. During that day, and before you have made payment for this second shipment, you receive a telex *from the issuing bank* informing you that, owing to a French Customs authorities dispute, delivery of the goods will be delayed. They request you to arrange to cancel the presentation of documents in respect of the May shipment. You advise your customer of the receipt of the telex and seek their instructions; but the directors of Super Steaks Ltd insist upon receiving payment immediately.

vi) On 1 June, you receive a further telex from the issuing bank, requesting you to amend the letter of credit as follows:

The third shipment to be effected during July.

The expiry date of the letter of credit to be extended to 31 July.

Your customer agrees to these amendments, provided the forward contract in respect of the third shipment can be amended.

Note

For the purposes of this question, you should assume that all documents are presented strictly in accordance with the terms of the letter of **credit** *on the date of each shipment.*

The rates of exchange for French francs/sterling are:

1 April

Spot 9.2950		9.3055
1 Month	1.75 cpm	1.40 cpm
2 Months	3.90 cpm	3.25 cpm
3 Months	5.50 cpm	4.70 cpm

1 June

Spot 9.3100		9.3175
1 Month	1.15 cpm	0.90 cpm
2 Months	2.95 cpm	2.40 cpm
3 Months	4.75 cpm	4.10 cpm

Required

a) Detailed calculations of the forward rates you would quote on 1 April, and the expected sterling proceeds which your customer should receive upon presentation of the documents during the months of April, May and June.

[6]

b) The replies you would give to your customer and the issuing bank, concerning payment or otherwise of the documents presented in respect of the May shipment, giving reasons for your replies.

[3]

c) Calculations of the sterling amount, if any, which will be passed to your customer's account as a result of the extension to the forward contract relating to the third shipment.

[3]

d) Detailed calculations of the new forward rate which you would quote to cover the third shipment, which, as a result of the telex, is to be effected during July.

[4]

e) A method that you would suggest to your customer which would protect your customer from foreign exchange risks, and at the same time avoid possible losses when forward contracts have to be cancelled or amended. Your answer should include a brief definition of the method and should explain to the customer how this method operates.

[4]

[Total marks for question - 20]

Note All charges and commissions are to be ignored

(Specimen Answer given in Appendix VII)

Exam Question 2

You are a branch manager and. as a member of the local Export Club, you agree to join a panel of speakers in an open forum discussion of local exporters' problems. The following question is posed by a member of the audience:

"We have recently been approached by a US company to arrange to supply them with deck-fittings for racing yachts. The terms quoted are 90 days after shipment D/A. As it is a buyers' market, and we are unable to vary the terms of shipment. What risks are there in the company accepting this quotation and can you indicate any remedies?"

Required

In brief note form, cover the points which you would make, outlining:

    (i)   the risks to the company;   [13]

    (ii) your recommendations to help the company to overcome some of the difficulties.   [7]

[Total marks for Question - 20]

(Specimen Answer given in Appendix VII)

Exam Question 3

The directors of Flower Power Ltd, your customer, ask you to visit them regarding a possible contract they are discussing with Dutch purchasers. Your customer has 'bred' a range of plants, and full ownership and rights to the plants are retained by them. However, the actual plants are being grown on their behalf by a UK horticultural factory unit, producing the plants by means of a cloning system. A well-known international carrier, who is used to handling produce of this nature, will collect the goods and deliver them to Holland.

Your customer has agreed to pay the growers 70 Dutch cents per plant. The Dutch purchasers have agreed to pay 1.40 Dutch guilders per plant, but have asked for 30 days' credit against accepted bills of exchange. You understand that the terms of shipment will be 'horticultural unit'. The first series of orders for 10,000 plants a month has been received.

The directors ask you to explain to them the banking methods by which the company can claim payments from Holland. They also ask you if there is a simple way in which they can protect themselves against any exchange risk.

Required

    a)   A description of the banking method by which you would suggest that claims for payment should be presented to the Dutch purchasers, together with reference to the internationally accepted procedures involved.   [6]

    b)   A specific instruction that should be included amongst those given by your customer to the banks involved, which would give further protection to Flower Power Ltd in this particular transaction. [3]

c) An explanation of the difference between the terms 30 days D/P and 30 days D/A, indicating whether your customer would obtain any additional protection if D/P terms were used, bearing in mind the method/terms of shipment proposed for this particular transaction. [7]

d) An explanation of the simple banking arrangement which would enable your customer to obtain protection against the exchange risk. [4]

[Total marks for question - 20]

(Specimen Answer given in Appendix VII)

Part Four

Introduction

In the earlier part of the book, we examined foreign exchange, methods of settlement between banks, documents, Incoterms, and methods of payment.

Now that we have a sound understanding of the mechanics of foreign trade, we can proceed to study the remaining bank services for exporters. These services can be divided into financial and non-financial categories, and we shall see that in many cases there is a link between the terms of payment and the relevant service.

The syllabus for the examination, quite rightly, requires an understanding of the services which are offered by non-bank competitors, and it is in this part of the book where this aspect is of most relevance.

Finally, please remember that this part of the book is in no way connected with importers. The services which banks and others provide for importers are covered in Part Five.

Unit 17

Short-term Finance for Exports

Objectives

At the end of this unit the student should be able to:

- understand what is meant by 'short-term finance';
- distinguish between 'pre-shipment' and 'post-shipment' finance for exporters;
- appreciate the significance of 'with recourse' and 'without recourse' finance;
- describe the various forms of short-term finance which clearing banks and their group affiliates can provide.

17.1 The Definition of 'Short-term Finance'

No legal definition of 'short-term finance' exists, but for our purposes we shall consider any facility which would normally be repaid within two years to be of a 'short-term' nature.

Facilities which cover a two-to-five year period are usually classed as 'medium-term' facilities and any period in excess of five years is normally classed as 'long-term'.

Usually, exporters of consumer goods require short-term finance because importers do not expect long periods of credit. Exports of capital goods are often sold on medium- or long-term credit.

17.2 The Difference Between Post-shipment and Pre-shipment Finance

Post-shipment finance is money required to finance the exporter between despatch of goods and receipt of payment. Usually this period is longer for exporters than for businesses which sell purely in the domestic market, and special schemes have been developed to meet the needs of exporters.

Pre-shipment finance is the money required to finance the business between the commencement of the manufacturing process and the despatch of goods. This period will be identical for the exporter and the non-exporter.

17.3 With Recourse and Without Recourse Finance

If finance is provided with recourse then the exporter is legally responsible for repayment of that money.

17.4 An Overview of the Short-term Facilities Available to Exporters from Banks and their Group Affiliates

Table 1

Name of facility	Exporter/importer payment terms which are appropriate	Credit period	With or without recourse	Special facilities
Loan or Overdraft.	Open account or documentary collection.	Up to two years.	With recourse.	-
Loan or over-draft secured by an assignment of the exporter's credit insurance policy.	Open account or documentary collection.	Up to two years.	With recourse.	-
Banks' special export finance schemes.	Open account or documentary collection.	Up to two years.	With recourse.	-
Negotiation of collections.	Documentary collection.	Usually short-term, say, maximum six months.	With recourse.	-
Bill advance.	Documentary collection.	Usually short-term, say, maximum six months.	With recourse.	-
Acceptance credit.	Usually documentary collection.	Six months is the usual maximum.	With recourse.	Minimum transaction usually £100,000.

Table 1 (Continued)

Name of facility	Exporter/importer payment terms which are appropriate	Credit period	With or without recourse	Special facilities
Negotiation of bills drawn under documentary credits.	Documentary credit.	Usually short-term, say, maximum six months, but longer periods can apply.	With recourse if the credit is unconfirmed. Without recourse if it is confirmed.	-
Assignment of proceeds of documentary credit.	Documentary credit.	Provides pre-shipment credit.	See detail in section 17.7.	-
Red clause documentary credit.	Documentary credit.	Provides pre-shipment finance.	With recourse to the issuing bank only.	-
Export factoring invoice discounting.	Open account (or sometimes documentary collection).	Usually six months maximum.	Usually without recourse.	-

Note

Hire purchase, leasing, forfaiting and export house type facilities may be for both short- and medium-term credit periods. For convenience, these facilities are covered in Unit 18.

If finance is provided **without recourse**, it means that the lender has agreed to look to someone other than the exporter for repayment.

With recourse finance must be shown on the customer's balance sheet as a liability, whereas, subject to the agreement of the company auditors, **without recourse** will not appear there.

17.5 Loans, Overdrafts, Use of Credit Insurance Policies as Security and Specialised Bank Exporter Schemes

a)   Loan or Overdraft to be Repaid from the Export Sale Proceeds
These facilities can be secured or unsecured, and the bank's considerations are the ones which apply to any lending proposition. (Lending criteria are examined in one of the specialised option papers and a detailed knowledge of credit assessment is not required for this examination.)

The customer benefits of an overdraft facility are its simplicity and flexibility. Interest is charged only on the debit balances actually outstanding on a day-to-day basis.

Loan accounts and overdrafts for export or import finance are completely exempt from the Consumer Credit Act 1974.

b)   Loan or Overdraft Secured by an Assignment of a Credit Insurance Policy

This is a traditional type of facility which has formed the basis of many of the specialist schemes covered in c) below.

The exporter signs a standard assignment form which instructs the insurance company to allow the lending bank to take over the exporter's rights to:

i)   any claim against the policy; or

ii)   any claim against a particular buyer; or

iii) any claim against any buyer from a particular country.

This assignment is useful backing to the bank if an exporter cannot repay because a particular buyer has defaulted. The bank will be able to stand in the shoes of the exporter, and eventually will be able to receive the proceeds (if any!) of the claim from the insurance company.

Some students mistakenly believe that this form of security is absolutely safe, but this is not the case. The bank's rights are no better than the exporter's. Thus, if the exporter's claim is refused by the insurance company, then the bank's assignment will be worthless.

An exporter's claim under his credit insurance could fail because:

i)   The exporter did not fulfil the commercial contract;

ii)   The exporter did not declare the shipment and pay the premium;

iii) The amount outstanding from the buyer who defaulted exceeded the credit insurance limit for that buyer.

In addition, the maximum percentage of risk covered by the policy is 95%.

Nevertheless, for a commercially reliable exporter, such an assignment is a very useful security for a lending bank, and some banks would charge a slightly lower rate of interest than would apply to an ordinary unsecured overdraft.

c)   Individual Banks' Short-Term Export Finance Schemes

Major banks over the years have provided off-the-shelf schemes for exporters where the latter have acceptable credit insurance (either their own policy or under the umbrella of the banks' policy).

However, in recent times, the banks have suffered losses in respect of these schemes. These have arisen for a number of reasons. The first has been the inability of exporters to meet the conditions laid down in the relevant insurance policies, either deliberately or by accident. Another has been the provision of funds for one-off export situations which naturally have a higher risk factor. There has also been a growth in fraudulent activity in respect of the presentation of documentation.

Consequently, the banks are nervous about the provision of short-term export finance schemes. Students should, therefore, ascertain what schemes are currently being offered by their banks and make a note of their salient points.

In general, banks have had two main schemes on offer. The smaller exports scheme is aimed at businesses with annual export turnover of under £1m. The finance for exports scheme has a target market of businesses with an annual export turnover of more than £1m.

Both these schemes are marketed as 'without recourse' facilities, which is not technically true. If the exporter has failed to fulfil the terms of the credit insurance policy, or the terms of the underlying commercial contract, or has reneged on the payment of the credit insurance premiums, the schemes are considered to be 'with recourse' to the exporter. However, in respect of non-payment of premiums and contravention of credit insurance conditions, some banks have agreed with the credit insurers that the latter will cover such risk.

i)   *Smaller exports scheme*
The smaller exports scheme provides post-shipment finance for up to 100% of the invoice value for up to 180 days' credit.

The customer's exports are covered under a banks' own credit insurance policy. This will normally cover up to 95% of the invoice amount with the remaining 5% of risk being stood by the bank itself. Facilities are only offered subject to status.

The scheme is appropriate for exporters who trade on open account or who use promissory notes or bills of exchange.

The scheme operates as follows:

- The exporter will furnish the bank with a copy of the buyer's order, relevant invoice and evidence of despatch/shipment, e.g. bill of lading together with the appropriate lodgement form.

- In respect of open account trade, details of the payment terms must be given to the bank, together with confirmation that such payments will be forwarded direct to the bank. With regard to bills and notes, the relevant bill and note will be given to the bank.

- The exporter's bank then sends the relevant documents to the buyer's bank on a collection basis via its Bills Department.

- Payment will then be forwarded by the buyer's bank on the due date through the banking system to the exporter's bank.

- As stated above, in the event of buyer payment default, the bank will seek restitution under its credit insurance policy for up to 95% of the invoice amount, with the remaining 5% of risk being stood by the bank itself.

ii) *Finance for exports scheme*

The main differences with this scheme, as opposed to the smaller exports scheme (apart from the difference in annual export turnover), are as follows:

- Credit periods can be for up to two years;

- Finance is normally only available for up to 90% of the invoice amount;

- Exporters participating in this scheme can hold their own credit insurance, although if they do not do so, the exporter and the bank can become joint policyholders on an appropriation policy, subject to the credit insurer accepting the exporter (and bank) as such.

17.6 Negotiations of Documentary Collections, Bill Advances and Acceptance Credits

a) Negotiation of Documentary Collections

When a customer sells on documentary collection terms, he may be able to arrange a negotiation facility with his bank. A negotiation facility is a lending facility, and normal lending criteria apply.

The facility works as follows:

i) The exporter submits the normal documentary collection items to his bank, but instead of signing a collection order, he signs a **negotiation request**, which is very similar to the collection order. This form requests a negotiation facility and gives the exporter's bank the right to deal with the documents in any way it thinks fit, to ensure repayment. By negotiating, the bank is in fact buying the bill of exchange and documents from the exporter and therefore collects the proceeds in its own name. The advance is therefore for 100% of the bill amount.

ii) If the bank agrees to the facility the procedure is as follows:

- If the bill of exchange is drawn in sterling, the bank immediately credits the customer's current account with the full face value. If the bill is drawn in currency, the bank credits the current account with the sterling equivalent at the bank's spot buying rate, assuming the customer does not maintain an account with the bank denominated in that currency.

- The bank debits a negotiation account with the face value of the bill of exchange. If the bill is drawn in sterling, then there is a sterling amount debited to the negotiation account, and if the bill is drawn in foreign currency, then a foreign currency account is debited.

iii) The exporter's bank then sends the collection to the collecting/presenting bank in the usual way. The standard customer authority gives the exporter's bank the right to vary the customer's instructions on the collection order, should it so wish. Generally speaking, the collecting bank will wish to include **protest** instructions, even if the customer prefers not to do so. As far as the collecting/presenting bank is concerned, the collection is received and dealt with in the same way as any other documentary collection. The exporter's bank completes its own standard collection order, so the collecting/ presenting bank will not know of the negotiation facility.

iv) On receipt of the proceeds, the negotiation account is cleared. Interest is calculated, and then debited to the current account.

If the negotiation account is denominated in currency, then the interest is calculated in currency and the customer's current account is debited with the sterling equivalent at the bank's spot selling rate. Naturally, the rate of interest will be based on the inter-bank rates for the relevant currency.

v) If the bill of exchange is dishonoured, the exporter's bank has rights against:

- the exporter, since this finance is with recourse;

- the drawee, provided he has accepted the bill of exchange;

- the goods, provided they have not been released to the importer. Under a D/P collection, goods will not have been released, but under D/A terms, the goods will have been released to the importer on acceptance.

vi) The bank's basic considerations when asked to grant a negotiation facility are:

- creditworthiness of exporter;

- creditworthiness of importer;

- existence of exchange control regulations in importer's country;

- saleability of goods if D/P terms;

- whether the terms are D/P or D/A, D/P being much more secure;

- whether credit insurance is held, and if so whether it is assigned to the bank;

- whether there is an agreement for **acceptance pour aval** on D/A terms;

- whether the documents give full control of the goods.

b)   Bill Advance

This method works in exactly the same way as the negotiation facility, except that the bank advances only a percentage of the amount of the bill, instead of lending the full face value. The bank then collects the proceeds on behalf of the exporter.

Bill advances will apply:

i) When the exporter does not need to borrow the full face value; or

ii) When the bank does not feel justified in lending the full face value; or

iii) When the bank is not entirely satisfied with the status of the importer or his country.

Note

With a negotiation, the bank has recourse only in the event of dishonour, whereas with a bill advance the bank can recall the advance at any time.

c)   Acceptance Credit

These facilities are only available for transactions of £100,000 minimum, and thus only large, established customers can use them.

The exporter's bank allows the exporter to draw a bill of exchange on the bank itself, and the bank accepts that bill of exchange. Since this bill is a bank bill the exporter can discount it in the discount market at a fine rate, which may be below base rate.

As security, the exporter's bank usually obtains authority to take over all rights to a documentary collection, which it submits on the exporter's behalf. For undoubted customers, the bank may agree to grant an acceptance credit facility when the exporter sells on open account terms.

Traditionally, acceptance credits have only been made available by merchant banks, but nowadays clearing banks are active in this market.

17.7   The Special Facilities Available in Connection with Documentary Credits

a)   Negotiation of Bills of Exchange Drawn under Documentary Credits

This facility operates in the same way as the negotiation facility described at 17.6 a) except that the bill of exchange is always drawn on the issuing bank. Provided the issuing bank is sound and the credit terms have been fulfilled, the bill will be accepted by the issuing bank and honoured at maturity. Thus the exporter's bank will look upon such facilities as being risk-free.

Such finance is with recourse, unless the lending bank has confirmed the credit. When the credit is unconfirmed, recourse can only be effected if the issuing bank fails to accept or honour the bill for reasons other than discrepancies being found in the documents.

If the negotiating bank failed to spot errors in the documents before negotiating, there is no recourse to the exporter.

b)   Discounting of Bills of Exchange Drawn under Documentary Letters of Credit

Bills of exchange which have been drawn on and accepted by banks and are drawn for a period of 180 days' sight or less are called **eligible bills**. The rates of discount are much lower on eligible bills. The term **fine rate of interest** is used to indicate that a bill is an eligible one which qualifies for lower rates.

When the credit calls for sterling bills at a tenor of below 180 days, the UK bank will be nominated as the accepting bank. Hence, such bills will automatically become eligible bills once the UK bank has accepted them.

Finally, exporters should remember that it may be possible to persuade the importer to pay the costs of negotiating/discounting bills of exchange drawn under documentary credits. If such an agreement is made, the details should be incorporated in the credit at the time of issue.

c)   Assignment of the Proceeds of a Documentary Credit

This is a means of obtaining pre-shipment credit with the co-operation of the exporter's bank. The exporter's bank, acting on its customer's authority, issues a letter of comfort to the exporter's local suppliers indicating:

i)   That the exporter is the beneficiary of a documentary credit;

ii)   That the bank is authorised to pay over, direct to the supplier, a certain sum from the proceeds (if any!) of the credit when received.

This letter of comfort may persuade the exporter's local suppliers to grant pre-shipment, and post-shipment credit to the exporter.

d)   Red Clause Documentary Credits as a Form of Pre-Shipment Finance

A red clause documentary credit contains an instruction from the issuing bank for the advising bank to make an advance to the beneficiary prior to shipment. When the exporter subsequently presents the documents, the amount of the advance, and interest, will be deducted from the full amount of the credit.

The advance can be in two forms:

i)   Conditional, whereby the beneficiary must sign an undertaking to use the money to help him assemble the goods referred to in the credit. In some cases the beneficiary may have to produce receipts for specified goods/raw materials before the advance can be made;

ii)   Unconditional, whereby the beneficiary merely signs a receipt for the money.

In either case, the issuing bank will be responsible for reimbursing the advising bank if the exporter should subsequently fail to present the documents called for under the credit. (The issuing bank will then seek reimbursement from its customer, the applicant.)

17.8 Export Factoring and Invoice Discounting Compared

1 The bank's customer sends his invoices to the factor (most factoring companies offer invoice discounting services).	1 The bank's customer sends his copy invoices to the factor.
2 For approved debts, the factor will advance up to 80% of the invoice at once. The factor then collects the debt himself.	2 The factor will advance up to 80% of the invoice value. The customer collects the debt himself.
3 The debtor receives an invoice from the factor and sends his remittance to the factor.	3 The client's debtor pays the client in the usual way.
4 The factor then pays over the balance to the exporter, less interest and charges.	4 The client settles with the factor when the debtor's remittance is received.
5 The factor takes over the sales ledger administration of the exporter.	5 The exporter is responsible for sales ledger administration.
6 Factoring is disclosed to the debtor.	6 Invoice discounting is not disclosed to the importer.
7 Charges are between 1% and 3% of turnover, plus interest on any advances.	7 Interest is charged on amounts advanced. The administration fee is relatively small, because the factor is not involved in any sales ledger administration.
8 The factor will deal with every invoice of the exporter. In other words, the factor takes over the sales ledger administration.	8 With invoice discounting the factor only deals with invoices against which an advance is required.
9 Factoring would be applicable if the exporter does not have the personnel to handle sales ledger administration.	9 Invoice discounting is applicable when the customer wishes to continue to handle sales ledger administration himself.
10 Usually bad debt insurance is included as part of the package, and the facility is without recourse.	10 Usually bad debt insurance is included as part of the package, and the facility is without recourse.

Conditions Which Would Apply

1 Both facilities are applicable to fast-growing companies with good-quality debtors. The minimum annual turnover varies between factoring companies.

2 The terms of trade must be simple, with no complex documentary requirements. With factoring, normally only open account terms will apply, although documentary collection would be appropriate for invoice discounting.

3   The factor must approve the debtors. Debtors should be well spread, and the factor may be more keen to cover the export business if the UK exporter has a good spread of domestic business which is offered as well.

Customer Benefits of Factoring

1   Sales ledger administration. (With overseas debtors the factor can handle correspondence in the language and even in the dialect of the overseas debtor.)

2   Protection against bad debts is available for an extra fee.

3   The client has the benefit of the factor's computerised credit reference system.

4   Cash flow is more predictable because the client knows that he can claim up to 80% as an immediate advance against his invoices.

5   Debtors settle more quickly because the factor is more efficient at collecting the debt. Some clients use the factor purely for this reason and do not utilise the right to advances against the invoice.

6   Saving in management time. All overdue debts are 'chased' by the factor.

7   Advice on trading terms in export markets.

8   Local collections and assistance with the resolution of disputes.

9   Protection against exchange risk when invoicing in foreign currency.

10 Swifter transfer of funds to the UK.

11 Expert local knowledge of overseas buyers' creditworthiness.

12 Financial facilities available in sterling or major currencies.

Note
UK factors will provide factoring facilities to overseas exporters who sell to UK buyers. The overseas exporter sends his invoices to the UK factor.

Customer Benefits of Invoice Discounting

1   As for factoring, except that the client must run his own sales ledger administration.

2   Invoice discounting is not disclosed to the debtors of the factor's client.

3   Useful if the client has an efficient sales ledger team of his own.

4   This is a very fast-growing service for exporters.

Conclusion Regarding Export Factoring and Invoice Discounting
Using these export services means that the exporter can spend more time developing a positive sales relationship with export customers. He can adopt a more aggressive approach to his marketing in the knowledge that collection problems and bad debts will be taken care of.

Export factoring/invoice discounting is particularly suitable for exports to the USA or to the EU. These facilities are not always appropriate for exports to Third World countries.

17.9 Self-assessment Questions

Question 1

A bank lends to an exporter against an assignment of his credit insurance policy. Is this security completely reliable in all circumstances?

Question 2

Many banks offer specialist export finance schemes. Are these facilities with or without recourse?

Question 3

A bank negotiates a bill of exchange drawn in US $, and the customer's current account is credited with the sterling equivalent on the day of negotiation.

    a)   Is the rate of interest based on sterling or on dollar rates?

    b)   When the bank converts the dollars to sterling, will it use its buying or selling rate?

Question 4

A bank negotiates a bill of exchange drawn in connection with a documentary collection.

    a)   When the collection is received by the presenting bank, will that bank know about the negotiation aspect?

    b)   The exporter instructs the bank **not to protest** on the collection order. Can the negotiating bank legally amend the collection order to indicate **protest**?

Question 5

A sole trader has just commenced business and he has received his first export order, valued at £5,000. Would you recommend export factoring?

Question 6

State which of the following forms of export finance would be disclosed to the buyer:

    a) Overdraft;

    b) Export factoring;

    c) Invoice discounting.

Question 7

Name a facility which can provide pre-shipment finance to the exporter in connection with documentary credits.

Question 8

A UK exporter manufactures steel pipes and he has just obtained a sale abroad on confirmed irrevocable documentary credit terms. The credit has been issued, confirmed and advised to the exporter. The exporter needs to obtain supplies of steel locally and requires credit. How could the exporter use the documentary credit to help persuade his local steel supplier that payment for the steel would be forthcoming?

Question 9

Name three forms of short-term export finance which can be non-recourse.

Question 10

A UK bank negotiates its customer's documentary collection on condition that the documents will give the bank control of the goods until payment. What is the bank's position if the exporter submits liner waybills?

Question 11

Why is a D/P collection more secure than D/A from the point of view of a negotiating bank?

(Answers given in Appendix VI)

17.10 Specimen Question

Bitter Beers Ltd sells canned drinks to many parts of the world. The company has in the past insisted on **irrevocable letters of credit** payable at your bank.

Recently, the company has been invited to quote for business in the USA, but the potential buyers will agree to a contract only if they can make payment on **open account terms**. As **cash flow** considerations are causing concern to the company directors, they feel that it is vital they should explore a method by which they can **obtain finance immediately** following **despatch of the goods**. If immediate finance were available to them, Bitter Beers Ltd would be willing to ship all of their exports on open account terms with payment to be made 30 days after the invoice date, provided that they were able to obtain protection from the credit risk.

Bitter Beers Ltd is seeking a funding method which will provide around 70% of the invoice values.

A satisfactory status report has been obtained on the potential US buyers. However, regular reports have not been obtained on other established buyers, because irrevocable letters of credit have in the past been issued in favour of Bitter Beers Ltd and therefore status reports were felt to be unnecessary.

Bitter Beers Ltd do not have any credit insurance, nor do they wish to use any credit insurer's services.

Required
A concise explanation of a scheme which is outside normal banking activities but which would enable Bitter Beers Ltd to obtain the immediate cash injection it is seeking and also protect its credit risk.

(Specimen Answer given in Appendix VI)

Unit 18

Medium- and Long-term Finance for Exports

Objectives

On completion of this unit the student should be able to:

- distinguish between supplier and buyer credit;

- understand the role of ECGD guarantees in the provision of medium- and long-term finance;

- know how forfaiting operates and appreciate its customer benefits;

- understand the various ways in which hire purchase and leasing can provide finance for exports;

- appreciate the services offered by members of the British Exporters' Association.

18.1 Introduction

There are several specialist forms of longer-term export finance available. It is vital that the student can distinguish between these different facilities, since the examiner often sets practical problems to which only one of the various types of finance is applicable. If the student chooses an inappropriate facility, he will receive no marks, since, in the real world, this would be of no help whatsoever to the customer.

18.2 Supplier Credit and Buyer Credit

In Unit 17, we considered the terms 'pre-shipment finance' and 'post-shipment finance'; in this unit our two major definitions are 'supplier credit' and 'buyer credit'.

Supplier credit involves the exporter's bank in the lending of money to the exporter, to provide post-shipment finance. The onus is on the exporter to repay the bank.

Buyer credit facilities involve a loan from a UK bank to enable the buyer to pay the full cash price of the export on shipment. (The loan can be made directly to the overseas buyer, or via an intermediary organisation in the importer's country.) There is no recourse to the exporter if the buyer defaults, since it is the buyer who has borrowed the money, not the exporter. Buyer credit facilities turn the export sale into a cash on shipment sale from the exporter's point of view.

18.3 ECGD Supplier Credit Financing Facility

The ECGD Supplier Credit Financing facility (SCF) enables exporters to obtain credit for between two and five years usually, although this upper time limit can be extended where the surrounding circumstances warrant it. The SCF is principally used by those exporters dealing in semi-capital or capital goods. The minimum value of contracts under this scheme is £25,000. There is no obligation on the exporter to cover all his export business, as cover under the facility can be provided on a contract-by-contract basis. It also has the added benefit to the exporter of being on a 'without recourse' basis for the most part. It is only in a relatively few cases that ECGD will insist upon the exporter having a recourse responsibility, such as where there are complicated or substantial contract obligations. Such a recourse responsibility would normally be limited in value to a maximum of 15% of ECGD's total liability under the contract. Finance under the facility is not purely limited to sterling and is available in a range of currencies for up to 85% of the contract price.

Operation of the SCF Facility

Banks offering finance under the scheme will have joined in a Master Guarantee Agreement (MGA) with ECGD. This details the terms and conditions under which the banks can provide the finance and the SCF facility. The exporter can approach any bank in the scheme and must obtain approval for the transaction to be covered by ECGD. Initially, however, the exporter will require to know the likely premium for the facility and the interest rate. It is possible to obtain a commitment from ECGD on the credit terms, and interest factor for up to four months prior to the signing of the commercial contract. This is of great help to the exporter when concluding negotiations with the overseas buyer.

Interest rates will normally be at Commercial Interest Reference Rates (see Unit 14).

If the exporter wishes to go ahead under the scheme, an application must be made via the bank. It is at this time that the exporter must apply for pre-finance insurance cover under the ECGD Supplier Insurance Policy, if required (see Unit 14 for details).

ECGD will then make an offer of finance and of a Supplier Insurance Policy (if requested). This will be accepted by the exporter and the bank who will complete declaration and acceptance forms and forward the required premium.

The exporter will then receive an ECGD 'Certificate of Approval', a copy of which will be forwarded to the bank. (The exporter will also receive an ECGD Supplier Insurance Policy, if it has been requested.)

Once the exporter has carried out his obligations under the commercial contract, the 'Certificate of Approval' should be presented to the bank together with the following:

- Bills of exchange or promissory notes, which have been guaranteed/avalised, normally by financial institutions.

- Documentary evidence of delivery of the underlying goods or of performance of the services contracted for.

- A confirmation warranting that the terms agreed between the relevant parties have been met.

● Any other documents which may have been stipulated by the bank.

The bank will ensure that the documents are in order and will then purchase the bills or notes from the exporter for their full value. If the buyer were to default, the bank is not at risk. It would initially seek restitution from the avaliser/guarantor and if payment was not forthcoming, the bank would then look to ECGD for repayment.

Under the SCF, bond insurance is an additional facility which is available (see Unit 20. 6 a)).

Note:
It is necessary to arrange for a third party (bank or government) to avalise or guarantee payment of the bills of exchange before the UK bank can advance the funds.

18.4 ECGD Buyer Credit Facility

a) Operation and Availability
The ECGD buyer credit facility is usually available where the contract value is for a minimum of £5m. The exporter and his bank should contact the ECGD before commercial negotiations begin, to see if the facility will be available. Certainly the exporter should be aware of the ECGD's attitude and likely conditions before he submits any tender or quotation to the overseas buyer.

Normally the overseas purchaser makes a down payment of about 15% of the contract value, and the UK bank lends the buyer the remaining 85% so that he can pay cash for the exports.

b) Position if the Buyer Defaults
The loan from the UK bank to the buyer is guaranteed in full by the ECGD. There is no right of recourse by the ECGD if the buyer defaults on the loan, unless the exporter is in default on the commercial contract. Hence, two particular advantages of buyer credit facilities for the exporter are:

i) **No contingent** liabilities need appear in his balance sheet because there is no right of recourse;

ii) There is no need to take out any form of ECGD insurance as, from the exporter's point of view, the sale is on cash terms.

c) Other Advantages to the Exporter from Buyer Credit Facilities

i) The exporter does not have to pay interest on the loan, since the loan is made to the buyer.

ii) The interest rate, payable by the buyer, is fixed. Consensus rates and Commercial Interest Reference Rates apply in exactly the same way as for the ECGD SCF facility.

iii) ECGD may be prepared to grant bond support. This aspect is covered in Unit 20, 20.6 a).

d) **The Disadvantages of Buyer Credit Facilities**

i) There is usually a minimum contract value of £5m.

ii) Complex documentation, which takes a long time to finalise.

iii) The buyer may object to having a loan from a UK bank and paying interest and charges to a UK bank. (This is usually for political reasons.)

e) **Procedure**

i) The exporter, importer, UK bank and ECGD agree in principle that buyer credit guarantees are suitable.

ii) Four agreements are made simultaneously:

- Supply contract - the commercial contract of sale.

- Loan agreement - UK bank to overseas buyer.

- Guarantee ECGD - the UK bank.

- Premium agreement - exporter - ECGD.

iii) The money covered by the ECGD buyer credit facility is paid directly to the exporter by the lending bank, against presentation of documents specified in the loan agreement and in the supply contract. Legally, this transaction amounts to a transfer of loaned funds on the buyer's instructions, and the buyer becomes liable to repay.

18.5 ECGD Lines of Credit

a) **Common Principles which Apply to all Types of Lines of Credit**
From the UK exporter's point of view, lines of credit operate in a similar way to buyer credit. The lines of credit cover loans to buyers to enable them to pay on cash terms for UK exports of capital, semi-capital goods and associated services.

Common factors which apply to both buyer credits and to lines of credit are:

i) Commercial Interest Reference Rates apply in exactly the same way as for the other two facilities already described.

ii) The buyer must pay a percentage of the contract value from his own resources.

iii) Being a buyer credit facility, there are no contingent liability problems.

iv) As there is no recourse to the exporter, he does not require any ECGD insurance of the debt, but must contribute towards the overall cost of the ECGD cover given to the lending bank.

v) Details of all lines of credit are available from the specialist export finance departments of the banks, or from the ECGD.

How then does a line of credit differ from buyer credit? The basic difference is as follows: from the individual exporter's point of view, the minimum amount, although varying with different lines of credit, can be as low as US $25,000, as opposed to the usual £5m minimum contract value of a buyer credit.

b)   Project Lines of Credit

This facility is useful for major projects where a number of UK suppliers are nominated by the overseas buyer to provide goods and services in connection with a single project.

The ECGD will guarantee a loan from the UK bank to the overseas buyer or procurement agent. The buyer can split up the loan using it to pay various UK suppliers on individual contracts which may be as low as US $25,000 each. The total amount lent to the overseas buyer will normally exceed £3m, but, as already shown, this sum can be divided to cover individual contracts of US $25,000 minimum, with credit periods of two to five years.

c)   General Purpose Lines of Credit

In this case the UK bank lends a sum normally in excess of £3m to an overseas financial institution, as opposed to the overseas buyer. The overseas financial institution can use this money for loans to the individual overseas buyers to enable them to pay on cash terms for approved UK exports.

The UK exporter and overseas buyer can negotiate a commercial contract knowing that up to 85% of the contract price can be loaned to the buyer. Again, individual contracts for as low as £15,000 can be financed in this way, with credit periods of two to five years.

d)   Lines of Credit to Overseas Banks

From the UK exporter's point of view, the differences between these lines of credit and general-purpose lines of credit are merely academic.

From the point of view of the ECGD, the difference is that the ECGD is concerned solely with the repayment of the loan to the UK bank by the overseas financial institution. If the individual overseas buyer defaults on the loan from the overseas institution, the ECGD is in no way liable. Thus, the ECGD can set up these facilities very quickly, since it does not need to see the individual commercial contracts.

18.6 Forfaiting

The forfaiting service provides finance to exporters who grant credit periods of between 180 days and seven years. Usually the total minimum value of a forfaiting deal is £50,000 or the equivalent in currency. Forfaiting deals, however, tend to be flexible and credit periods of ten years are seen.

a)   How Forfaiting Operates

i)   The importer finds a bank or other first-class institution which is willing to guarantee his liabilities. The institution is not resident in the exporter's country (and in fact would normally be resident in the importer's country). However when the buyer is resident in a Third World country, the guarantor institution may well be a European bank.

247

ii) The method of guarantee can take the following forms:

- An aval, whereby the guarantor endorses bills of exchange drawn on the importer, thus becoming liable on them.

- A separate form of guarantee of the importer's liabilities. This usually applies when promissory notes are signed by the importer, as opposed to bills of exchange being used.

- When the guarantor is a bank from the USA, the guarantee takes the form of a stand-by letter of credit whereby the American bank undertakes to honour bills of exchange drawn in the prescribed way.

iii) The form of the guarantee is unimportant, provided the guarantee is legally binding. What matters is the status of the guarantor institution.

iv) Provided the guarantor is undoubted, the exporter's bank, known as the forfaitist, will discount the bills or promissory notes, i.e. will pay the exporter the face value less the discount charge. If the importer is undoubted, then the forfait facility could be provided without the need of a guarantee from another institution. It is rumoured that a UK football club was able to obtain forfait finance for the transfer of a UK soccer star to Italy. The forfaitist did not require a guarantee because the Italian club was probably more creditworthy than its bank.

b)   Benefits of Forfaiting to the Exporter

i)   The facility is flexible. The documentation can be set up in a matter of hours, whereas ECGD buyer credit facilities can take up to three months to arrange. In suitable cases. the forfait facility can cover the full amount of the contract price.

ii) The rate of discount applied by the forfaitist is fixed, and subsequent changes in the general level of interest rates do not affect the discount.

iii) The finance is without recourse, so there is no need for any contingent liability on the exporter's balance sheet. Forfaiting does not affect any other facilities, e.g. overdraft.

iv) All exchange risks, buyer risks, and country risks are removed.

v)   The exporter receives cash in full at the outset.

vi) The finance costs can be passed on to the buyer if the exporter is in a strong bargaining position.

vii) Administration and collection problems are eliminated.

c)   Disadvantages of Forfaiting

i)   Costs can be high, and there is no interest rate subsidy.

ii) It may be difficult to find an institution which will be prepared to guarantee the importer's liabilities. Sometimes the guarantor institution may charge a high commitment fee if the buyer is not considered undoubted.

18.7 Leasing and Hire Purchase

Leasing of goods which are exported, operates in much the same way as the leasing of goods traded within the domestic market. The leasing company (the lessor) buys the goods outright from the supplier and then leases them to the ultimate buyer, who has the use of the goods for an agreed period, subject to payment of the agreed rent to the lessor. There are various taxation complexities in connection with leasing, but these are not in our syllabus.

The system can work in one of two ways:

a) by arranging for a lessor in the exporter's country to buy the goods and to lease them to the overseas buyer. This is known as **cross-border leasing**; or

b) by arranging for a lessor in the buyer's country to act.

UK commercial banks all have subsidiary or associate leasing companies which can provide cross-border leasing facilities. These companies are also able to arrange for overseas lessors to act, where appropriate.

The benefit to the UK exporter is that the sale is in effect a cash sale and that there is no recourse unless he has defaulted on the commercial contracts.

Most forms of plant and machinery, vehicles or office equipment can be leased. Hire purchase performs a similar function to leasing, but the buyer may be required to pay a deposit from his own resources. Once again the legal differences between leasing and hire purchase are outside the scope of the syllabus.

18.8 The Traditional Role of Members of the British Exporters' Association

These organisations are well-known firms in the City of London who specialise in providing four main forms of service:

a) Export Merchants

An export merchant buys goods from a UK manufacturer and then sells them abroad. As far as the UK manufacturer is concerned, the sale is a domestic sale. All normal export risks are eliminated, since the manufacturer receives sterling payment from an undoubted UK organisation in accordance with the terms agreed. The disadvantage is that the UK manufacturer can tend to become out of touch with his market. In addition the export merchant will pay a lower price than would be received if the manufacturer sold to the overseas buyer directly.

b) Manufacturers' Export Agents

In this case, a UK manufacturer employs the organisation to act as an agent for the purpose of obtaining overseas orders. A period of credit is agreed for the overseas buyer. The manufacturer then ships the goods, and the export agent pays as soon as the goods have been despatched. The overseas buyer then pays the manufacturer's export agent in accordance with the agreed credit terms.

The finance is in effect without recourse, post-shipment finance. Although the sale contract is between the UK manufacturer and the importer, the manufacturer's export agent stands the credit risk.

c) Confirming Houses

They act in exactly the same way as manufacturers' export agents, but it is the buyer who employs them. Hence a confirming house's fees are paid by the buyer whereas a manufacturers' export agent's fees are paid by the exporter.

d) Export Finance Houses

Export finance houses provide finance for semi-capital or capital goods on a non-recourse basis. This will be supplied over the total period of credit granted to the importer for up to 100% of the total amount due.

Export finance houses tend to be flexible in their outlook. Although their primary objective is to supply finance for large capital projects, they will also finance smaller deals. They will also arrange finance for bank consortia where huge projects and joint ventures are being contemplated. Finance can be provided on a one-off basis or to cover a number of orders, or even through a line of credit arranged with an overseas bank in the importer's country.

Major UK banks have established subsidiaries which have infiltrated the traditional market of the export houses. New innovative services are being continually marketed by these companies. Students should therefore make enquiries as to how subsidiaries of their own banks have broken into this market and what services they currently offer.

18.9 Pre-shipment Finance

The foregoing sections have all covered what is essentially post-shipment finance. Pre-shipment finance can be available from a number of sources:

- Assignment of documentary credit (see 17.7). Red clause documentary credit (see 17.7).

- ECGD buyer credits generally provide post-shipment finance, but can be structured to include stage payments prior to actual physical export of goods, where the exporter's contract allows such payments.

- Buyers may agree to avalise bills of exchange prior to shipment and these bills could then be discounted.

- Forfaiting of avalised bills which the buyer has made available prior to shipment, probably for part only of the contract value.

- Overdraft or loan, possibly secured by a debenture.

- Bridgeover facility, whereby the bank provides pre-shipment finance, which will be cleared from, say, post-shipment buyer credit or forfaiting. Much depends on the standing of the exporter, the ultimate buyer and the terms of the sale contract. Documentary credits can also be used by the exporter to persuade the bank to grant pre-shipment finance on a bridgeover basis.

18.10 Self-assessment Questions

Question 1
When may the ECGD SCF facility be **with recourse** to the exporter?

Question 2
Which ECGD facilities normally provide **without recourse** finance to exporters?

Question 3
What is the minimum contract amount for finance under the ECGD SCF facility?

Question 4
An exporter has arranged ECGD buyer credit facilities, and the facility has been drawn upon. The overseas buyer has now gone into liquidation and the money owing to the UK bank will not be repaid by the buyer. Against whom can the UK bank claim?

Question 5
What facility, traditionally provided by members of the British Exporters' Association, turns exports into domestic sales from the point of view of the UK manufacturer?

Question 6
List the advantages of forfaiting for exporters.

Question 7
An exporter requires a source of without recourse finance which can be arranged very quickly. Which facility would you suggest?

a) ECGD buyer credit facility;

b) Forfaiting.

Question 8
From the exporter's point of view, what is the main difference between an ECGD line of credit and an ECGD buyer credit facility?

(Answers given in Appendix VI)

18.11 Specimen Question

Contractors plc has found a potential buyer in Eastern Europe for a sale of capital equipment. The contract value is around £800,000. The buyer requires a period of credit in excess of three years.

Required
Identify an appropriate scheme which will provide post-shipment finance to Contractors plc, and will provide insurance cover against non-payment.

(Specimen Answer given in Appendix VI)

Unit 19

Non-financial Services for Exporters

19.1 Introduction

This unit will cover all the non-financial services which are available to exporters, except for countertrade, bonds and standby letters of credit which are covered in Unit 20.

19.2 Travel Facilities

'Travel facilities' constitute a service which can be used by export salesmen when they visit overseas countries on sales tours. For convenience, the travel facilities which apply to holidaymakers are also covered in this unit, since in many cases the needs and requirements of both export salesmen and holidaymakers are very similar.

The main forms of travel facilities, together with their advantages and disadvantages, are described below. These comments relate to travellers who are leaving the UK to travel abroad.

a)   Sterling Notes

There are no government restrictions on how much cash is taken out of the UK, but only relatively small amounts should be taken, to cover:

i)   Sundry payments on board planes, ships or ferries and at UK airports;

ii) Payment of taxi fares and expenses for the homeward journey from the UK port or airport to home.

The disadvantages of relying entirely on sterling notes are:

i)   Danger of loss or theft;

ii) Inconvenient because of bulk;

iii) Poor rates of exchange may be given for sterling notes;

iv) The traveller runs the exchange risk if he converts his sterling notes into local currency;

v)   There may be restrictions imposed by the overseas exchange controls on the amount of sterling notes allowed into or, more vital still, out of the country.

b)   Foreign Currency Notes

It is a good idea to take a small number of foreign currency notes to meet initial expenses on arrival in the overseas country.

Once the traveller has acquired the notes, he has eliminated the exchange risk, unless he has surplus cash on his return which has to be reconverted to sterling. The disadvantages which apply if the traveller relies entirely upon taking foreign currency notes are:

i)   Danger of loss or theft;

ii) Inconvenience because of bulk;

iii) The overseas government may impose exchange controls limiting the amount of cash which a traveller can take into or out of the country;

iv) At the end of the holiday, any surplus foreign coins cannot normally be converted into sterling;

v)   Exchange risk applies to any surplus notes which are reconverted to sterling at the end of the holiday.

c)   Sterling Traveller's Cheques

Sterling traveller's cheques are purchased and paid for before the traveller leaves the UK, and they can be cashed at most banks throughout the world, or can be used to pay bills in certain hotels, shops or restaurants.

The UK bank makes a charge when the traveller's cheque is first issued, and a charge may be made by the organisation which cashes the cheque abroad.

Advantages of sterling traveller's cheques:

i)   There is a refund service available if the traveller's cheques are lost or stolen;

ii) Traveller's cheques can be purchased in high denominations (e.g. £100), and hence may be less bulky than sterling or currency notes;

iii) The purchaser does not have to have an account to buy traveller's cheques from a bank. Payment can be made in cash if necessary;

iv) Traveller's cheques issued by well-known banks can be used to make purchases in a variety of establishments, such as restaurants, shops, hotels.

Disadvantages of sterling traveller's cheques:

i) The travellers run the same exchange risk as with sterling notes;

ii) Sterling traveller's cheques are not always readily encashable abroad (for example travellers should always take dollar traveller's cheques to the USA).

d) Foreign Currency Traveller's cheques

Most UK banks offer traveller's cheques denominated in various currencies, including the European Currency Unit (ECU).

Foreign currency traveller's cheques have all the advantages of sterling traveller's cheques, and in addition the exchange risk is eliminated if the traveller's cheque is cashed in the country of the currency in which it is denominated. The traveller usually obtains a better rate of exchange if he buys his traveller's cheques in the United Kingdom.

The only disadvantage is that the traveller runs the same exchange risk as applies to foreign currency notes, i.e. any unused cheques will be reconverted to sterling at the end of the holiday at the rate of exchange ruling on that date.

e) Eurocheque Scheme

Most banks now offer a special eurocheque card and a pack of special uniform eurocheques. The eurocheques can be used at any outlet at home or abroad where the **EC** symbol is displayed.

In most countries the traveller will write out his eurocheque in local currency, and each cheque is guaranteed up to the equivalent of approximately £100 when used in conjunction with the eurocheque card. If the amount required exceeds the sterling equivalent of £100, two or more eurocheques can be used.

Eurocheques are issued at the discretion of the branch manager, the criteria being similar to the conditions for the issue of a domestic UK cheque card. There is a fee for the issue of the eurocheque card itself, and usually the eurocheques are issued free of charge.

The advantages of eurocheques are as follows:

i) They do not require any initial cash outlay (apart from the fee mentioned above) as opposed to the facilities previously mentioned which are paid for in full before the journey begins. Thus the traveller saves on interest and the bank loses the 'float time' which applies to traveller's cheques.

ii) They are flexible, and this is particularly useful for travellers who are country hopping around Europe or the Mediterranean.

iii) Employers can arrange for eurocheques to be purchased on the firm's account to cover the business expenses of employees.

iv) Eurocheques can be cashed at more than 250,000 bank branches. (This figure will increase as time goes by.)

v) Eurocheques can be used to make purchases at four million retail outlets such as shops, garages and hotels in over 40 countries, including the USA. (This figure will probably increase as time goes by.)

vi) With some banks the eurocheque card performs a double function. As well as being a cheque guarantee card, it can act as a cash card to obtain money from cash dispensers located overseas.

vii) Eurocheques avoid the need to carry large amounts in notes or traveller's cheques.

viii) Eurocheques can be used to pay motorway tolls on the continent.

The disadvantages of eurocheque cards are that:

i) There are a limited number of cheques in each eurocheque book.

ii) Cheques are written in local currency, and are usually converted to sterling at the spot rate ruling on the date of presentation to the United Kingdom. There is thus an exchange rate risk of a few days' duration.

iii) The eurocheque card or eurocheques could be stolen. Cases of loss or theft must be reported to the issuing bank at once.

f) Credit Cards

The credit cards operate abroad in much the same way as they operate domestically, and the traveller can use them at any outlet displaying the appropriate symbol. Advantages and disadvantages are much the same for the eurocheque scheme, apart from the following additional benefits:

i) Credit cards, as the name implies, give the holder the opportunity of enjoying a period of up to eight weeks' credit before paying off the amount owing on the card. (Eurocheques are debited to the customer's account as soon as they are presented for payment.)

ii) There is much greater flexibility than with the eurocheque system since there is no need to take sufficient eurocheques. A single plastic card will cover any number of transactions, provided the traveller keeps within his credit limit.

iii) Credit cards usage can help the holder to benefit from incentive schemes such as air miles or free travel assurance.

g) Debit Cards or Charge Cards (Travel and Entertainment Cards, e.g. Diners Card)

Such cards operate in a similar way to credit cards except that:

i) there is usually an annual subscription;

ii) there is no period of credit allowed beyond the date of the account settlement, which must be made in full, usually by cheque, or by the favoured direct debit.

Bank publications quote that their charge cards and credit cards are accepted in more than nine million shops, hotels and restaurants all over the world.

h)   Open Credit

Open credit involves a similar arrangement to a domestic UK open credit facility. The traveller's bank sends a specimen of the traveller's signature to a nominated bank branch abroad, and the overseas bank branch is instructed to cash the traveller's own personal cheques up to a stated amount.

Advantages of open credits are:

i)   no risk of loss or theft;

ii)   cash can be drawn as required. No loss of interest as applies to traveller's cheques and float time.

The disadvantage is that encashment is restricted to a named bank branch.

i)   Company Credit Card

Company credit cards are suitable for business customers who are limited companies, partnerships, associations, sole traders and other groups of particular individuals. The company is given an overall limit by the credit card company, and it then issues company credit cards to individual employees who travel abroad. Each individual's card can have an individual limit programmed on it.

Advantages to the company are:

i)   The credit cards can be used throughout the world. Most airlines, restaurants and hotels accept payment by credit card.

ii)   The company card scheme enables a company to simplify its expense accounting system yet still maintain a complete record of all transactions. Cash flow is improved, since expenses are debited once a month, instead of being debited at unpredictable times.

iii) The company receives a detailed statement for each executive together with a summary statement and payment invoice. Overseas transactions are converted and shown in sterling on the statements.

Advantages to the employee are:

i)   The fact that he has a company credit card can give him status in the eyes of his overseas counterparts.

ii)   The employee is not required to use his own funds to meet company expenses, nor does he have the problem of claiming reimbursement from the company.

j)   Emergency Cash

If a traveller finds himself without cash, money can easily be provided from his own bank, provided there are sufficient funds available. Many banks now have dedicated help lines or fax numbers to help in emergencies, especially when these are caused by the loss or theft of a credit card or traveller's cheques.

i)   Full name.

ii)   Full address of where the traveller is currently residing.

iii) The amount of money required.

iv) If possible, the name and address of a local bank to which the funds should be remitted. Generally speaking the funds will then be made available against passport identification.

19.3   Should a Business Enter the Export Market?

A business must bear in mind the following considerations when deciding whether or not to enter the export market:

a)   Is there a market for the product?

b)   If there is a potential market, what selling price could be set?

c)   What additional costs must be incurred, for example in packaging, shipping and insurance?

d)   Is it possible to deliver the product overseas? Are there any import tariffs or quotas, or any onerous customs problems to solve? (Please refer to Unit 1 for details of how GATT, WTO and SMP have reduced these problems).

e)   How is the exporter to sell the goods? Does he require an agent or will the exporter sell direct to a distributor?

f)   The exporter will almost certainly need to visit the potential buyers, to ascertain whether there is any prospect of firm orders.

g)   The potential exporter must decide in the light of the above, whether it would be profitable to export his product.

h)   Buyer and country risk.

i)   Exchange controls.

j)   Competition.

19.4   How the Bank Can Help New Exporters

The following list of services will help exporters to answer the questions posed in 19.3.

a)   **Status reports** on potential buyers and agents abroad.

b)   **Political and economic reports** on various overseas countries to help the exporter decide upon the economic prospects and on the likelihood of country default.

c)   **Trade development departments** which give advice on technical problems affecting the export marketability of products. Some departments also offer a service which involves obtaining several contacts for an exporter in a particular market.

d)   Details of any **trade fairs** being held overseas, where the customer could benefit from renting a stand. The bank may have its own representative present at such events and he can help arrange on-the-spot introductions to the exporter.

e) **Letters of introduction** to overseas banks who may have detailed knowledge of the market and who could arrange introductions with buyers and agents. The UK bank could arrange for copies of the exporter's brochures and price lists to be forwarded.

f) **Registers of potential buyers** for the customer's product.

g) Recording the details of the exporter's' product on **registers** which are made available to potential overseas buyers.

h) **Travel facilities** for export salesmen on their travels abroad.

i) Advice on matters in general which affect the exporter, e.g.

    i) Overseas documentary requirements, overseas tariffs, quotas and import requirements.

    ii) Information on any exchange control restrictions on payments by overseas governments.

    iii) Advice on the meaning and significance of Incoterms. Arrangement of appropriate insurance for terms such as CIF.

    iv) Advice on the significance of the various methods of payment for exports (open account, documentary collection, documentary credit, payment in advance), with an explanation of the risks and means of reduction of such risks. In areas such as the USA and the EU, open account trading is the usual method of payment.

    v) Advice on the exchange risk, together with appropriate methods of reducing the risk (forward contracts, currency borrowing, currency options and foreign currency accounts if there are receipts and payments in the same currency. Bear in mind that currency options may not be appropriate for **new** exporters).

    vi) The bank can recommend, without responsibility, a freight forwarder who would normally be a member of the British International Freight Association

    vii) Introduction to other providers of export services such as the Chamber of Commerce.

    viii) The bank can provide information on trade missions which are supported by the Overseas Trade Services see 19.5 below) .

Note
Normally new exporters will be too small to become involved in the bank's confirming house operations.

19.5 Services Available from Non-bank Sources

a) The Overseas Trade Services

Overseas Trade Services (OTS) is the UK Government's central trade promotion organisation. Commercially focused people at the DTI and at the Foreign Colonial Office and posts around the world work alongside the Scottish Office, Welsh Office and Northern Ireland Office. The aim is to allow all companies access to the information and experience needed to make a rational commercial decision about selling abroad. The British Overseas Trade Board provides guidance to OTS, supported by a series of specialist committees: Area Advisory Groups for each geographical region; the Small Firms Committee; the Oil, Gas and Petrochemicals Supplies Office Board and the Overseas Projects Board.

The support provided by OTS falls into four broad categories:

- Dedicated market support in the UK including advice and information services for initial market research (such as the Export Market Information Centre in London).

- Help with meeting the language and cultural requirements of target markets.

- Help with marketing UK products overseas including bringing key contacts to the UK and grants for visiting the market, carrying out marketing research and exhibiting at trade fairs. Support too for companies pursuing major projects.

- Services to provide research tailored to specific company needs produced by the overseas posts. Posts can provide on-the-ground help when you visit the market, as well as business briefings and local promotional support. Posts also report specific sale leads which can be accessed through OTS.

  Each of the UK's top 80 export markets now has an individual market menu which contains a comprehensive description of all of the services and literature that are available to help exporters targeting a particular market. The text of all 80 market menus together with that of the *Winning Through Exporting* Overseas Trade Services booklet and additional market and sector information, is available on CD-ROM and the Internet (on http://www.dti.gov.uk/ots).

  The initial point of contact for the Overseas Trade Services in England is the local Business Link. Business Links provide a single point of access for business support services - a national network of local partnerships between Training and Enterprise Councils (TECs), chambers of commerce, enterprise agencies, local authorities, DTI and other providers of business support.

Specialist advice on various fields is available through Business Links. Many International Trade Teams now have Export Development Councillors. These export specialists use their years of experience in export markets to provide advice and guidance for those new to overseas trade.

b) Libraries

The business section of most libraries can answer most queries, varying from 'What is the rate of inflation in Germany now and what have the rates been over the last five years?' to details of the total annual sales of a particular product in a particular overseas market over the last five years.

c)   Chambers of Commerce

Chambers of Commerce usually specialise in the products of the local area. The Chambers often advise on the technical requirements of local products exported to particular markets and in appropriate circumstances, the Chamber of Commerce can issue **third-party inspection certificates** showing that the exporter's goods meet the specifications of the importing country.

19.6   Bank Assistance for UK Manufacturers who Wish to Set up Joint Ventures with Overseas Distributors

a)   What is a Joint Venture?

Sometimes high import duties make the exporter's product uncompetitive in the overseas country. One means of avoiding such duties is to set up a joint venture with the local distributor. Such an operation can overcome import quotas as well.

The UK exporter will usually take a small cash stake in the joint venture, and will provide the expertise, and possibly some specialised plant and machinery, to help set up the manufacturing operation. Once the operation is on stream, the UK manufacturer will provide some of the specialised components, but the joint venture company will assemble the product locally.

The product will then be sold in the overseas country, and the UK exporter will be entitled to payment in accordance with agreed financial arrangements.

Joint ventures can be seen in reverse if we look at Japanese car operations in the UK.

b)   How Can a UK Bank Assist in a Joint Venture?

i)   The bank can provide travel facilities for executives who visit the overseas country. (Small amounts of local currency, traveller's cheques for short stays, and credit cards for longer journeys.) Company credit cards can also be arranged.

ii)   The bank, through the expertise of its international division, can advise:

- Whether an equity stake or a loan capital injection is better. Some overseas countries tax interest more favourably than dividends, and vice versa.

- Whether there are any overseas exchange controls which could affect remittance of dividends or capital back to the UK.

- What is the likelihood of expropriation or country default. (Bank political and economic reports.)

iii) If this information is not available at the international division, the division could obtain the details from the local office of the bank, if there is one in the area. Otherwise a correspondent (agent) bank will be asked to assist.

iv) The bank will provide letters of introduction to:

- a reputable local lawyer;

- a reputable local accountant.

v) All financial arrangements and other agreements should be drawn up, if possible, subject to English law.

c)   Help with Local Banking Arrangements when the Joint Venture Begins

i) The UK bank can open an account at the local branch of the bank if one exists. Failing that, it could provide a letter of introduction to a local correspondent bank.

ii) If there is a local branch office, the UK bank can arrange overdraft facilities.

iii) If a correspondent bank is used, the UK bank could agree to guarantee the joint venture's overdraft with them.

19.7 International Licensing and International Franchising

a)   What is International Licensing and International Franchising?
International licensing is an arrangement whereby an exporter who is the owner of exclusive rights gives permission for someone overseas to use the rights. The **exclusive rights** could be a brand name, product, process or service.

The exporter, who is known as the **master licensor**, will grant the overseas business, the **master licensee**, the right to use the product or service in a specified territory for a given period. The master licensee must pay a licence fee or royalty or both.

International franchising is similar to licensing, but the overseas business, the franchisee, is subject to much stricter controls in the use of the product or service. The franchisee becomes, in effect, a controlled outlet of the franchisor. Financial arrangements vary, but usually the franchisee pays a lump sum up front and then pays a royalty on subsequent sales.

b)   Examples of Products and Countries which would be Suitable for Licensing or Franchising
Any uniquely British products would be suitable, for example:

i) specialist quality clothing;

ii) food and drink;

iii) specialist cosmetics (e.g. Body Shop);

Countries with a similar cultural background are most suitable, for example, Commonwealth countries, Western Europe and North America. (Examples of franchising in reverse are MacDonald and Wimpey. Here the franchisor is American and the franchisee is in the United Kingdom.)

c)   **Advantages of Franchising or Licensing from the Point of View of a UK Exporter**

 i) Greater commitment on the part of licensees than is found among traditional agents or distributors.

 ii) Greater control over presentation and pricing of products.

 iii) Lower start-up costs compared with joint ventures or traditional selling techniques.

 iv) Closer involvement with the overseas market place.

d)   **Bank Assistance to UK Exporters**

Some banks already have specialist departments, and others are about to follow. The bank can advise on:

 i) Market research to test suitability.

 ii) Financial projections to cover cost of setting up the arrangements and the potential revenue.

 iii) Legal matters to ensure the licensee is committed to payment of fees and proper treatment of the product.

 iv) Exchange controls in overseas countries.

 v) Promotions to find potential licensees and franchisees.

 vi) Advice on differences between the home market and the overseas market.

Note

Licensing only applies to well-established products or services. Do not suggest licensing or joint ventures for small firms just starting.

Joint ventures apply more to capital goods, whereas licensing/franchisi   pplicable mainly to consumer goods or services.

19.8 Problems Relating to Agents Because Regulations

a)   **The Difference between Distributors and Agents**

The exporter appoints a distributor who is usually based in th
The exporter sells goods to the distributor who then sells the
account.

When an exporter appoints an agent, that agent may enter i
buyer on the exporter's behalf, or the agent may introduce t

264

b)   Sole Agents and Exclusive Agents

Sole agents

The exporter cannot appoint another agent in the sole agent's agreed territory. However, the exporter may obtain orders directly from buyers in the agreed territory without having to pay commission.

Exclusive agents

Not only is the exporter barred from appointing another agent in the agreed territory, but the exporter is also barred from obtaining orders directly from that territory or, if such orders are obtained, then commission must be paid to the exclusive agent.

c)   Effect of the EU's Commercial Agent Directive 1986

From 1 January 1994, this directive applies to UK exporters. Mercifully, it does not apply to agents for the supply of services, but it does apply in the supply of goods.

UK exporters should beware of the following pitfalls which can apply in the case of an agency for goods:

i)   The exporter must inform the agent, within a reasonable period, of any unexpected downturn in the volume of business or of non-execution, for whatever reason, of orders arranged through the agent.

ii)   An agent may claim compensation for any loss he may suffer as a result of the termination of an agency agreement, up to one year after the termination, even if the termination occurred in a proper, legal manner.

EXPORTERS SHOULD TAKE SPECIALIST LEGAL ADVICE BEFORE APPOINTING AGENTS!

19.9 Self-assessment Questions

Question 1

Name one major country in which sterling traveller's cheques definitely would be unsuitable.

Question 2

A company sends several salesmen abroad at any one time. The finance directors have difficulty in keeping control of the book-keeping of the expenses of these salesmen, while the salesmen complain that they are out-of-pocket because of the time-lag between payment and reimbursement.

Name the bank service which could overcome these problems.

Question 3

What considerations should a business bear in mind when deciding whether or not to export?

Question 4

A UK exporter of capital goods is finding that sales are proving more and more difficult because of tariffs, quotas and import duties. Name the method by which these problems could be overcome by way of a transfer of technology.

Question 5

A UK-based business has a unique fashion design which is widely acclaimed, and it now wishes to sell the design abroad.

The business does not wish to become involved in building factories abroad, nor does it wish to set up an export shipping department.

Name one method which will enable the business to generate overseas revenue with the minimum of capital outlay.

Question 6

A business is considering a joint venture. What particular point must be borne in mind regarding the way the legal agreements are drawn up?

Question 7

Name three non-bank organisations which can help exporters.

Question 8

How can a UK bank help new exporters?

Question 9

State the disadvantages involved if a traveller takes foreign currency notes abroad, and does not take any other travel facility.

(Answers given in Appendix VI)

19.10 Specimen Questions

Question 1
SPECIAL OPTICS LTD

Your UK customer, Special optics Ltd, has a turnover of between £1 to £2 million achieved with a skilled workforce of six people. The company produces quality products for which there is a good demand from leading industrial companies in the UK.
Few large companies around the world compete in this market because of the specialist expertise and equipment needed.

Up until now, Special optics has received occasional export orders from:

1. One-off approaches from other UK companies for goods to be on-sold abroad.

2. Overseas companies visiting Special optics' stand at leading industrial exhibitions in the UK.

3. Responses from abroad to news reports on new products covered in UK trade magazines.

Export orders have tended to be expressed in sterling in the £5 to £50,000 range, and Special optics has required either payment in advance or, more usually, irrevocable documentary credits (some of which have been confirmed), payable at sight.

When appropriate, Special optics has employed an export management company to raise the necessary documentation to present under the documentary credit.

The managing director of Special optics Ltd, Mr J. Glass, is looking for a significant increase in exports.

Following a trade promotion activity, Special optics Ltd has achieved an early breakthrough in France. It has identified a distributor in Paris through whom it could export, rather than exporting direct to a number of buyers throughout France.

In view of the extent of the potential market, it will be necessary for Mr Glass to make regular visits to Paris, staying overnight.

It has been suggested that Special optics should operate a collection account with a French bank in Paris to which export proceeds could be paid.

Required:

a) What would be the main advantages and disadvantages to Special optics of employing a distributor rather than exporting direct to buyers?

b) Describe specific travel services offered by **UK** banks that would assist Mr Glass during his trips to Paris.

c) List and explain the advantages and disadvantages if Special optics opens a collection account as suggested.

(Specimen Answer given in Appendix VI)

Question 2

TELECOM EXPORTS LTD

Telecom Exports Ltd is the UK subsidiary of a large UK corporate customer of your bank. It specialises in providing telecommunications equipment and software on a worldwide basis to major corporates and institutions like banks which have a network of offices.

Telecom Exports Ltd has a subsidiary in the USA to handle sales in North America and another in Singapore to cover sales in the Far East. The UK company looks after the rest of the world, for which they are willing to provide a full service including installation and training.

The office is capably organised by the export manager, Mrs Erin Daws.

The company has been active in its existing markets for a number of years. However, as yet, it has not been successful in breaking into Eastern Europe.

Telecom Exports is shortly to launch a new product and its parent company wants to use this as a springboard to develop new markets.

Mrs Daws is to conduct desk research before the group devises a market strategy. She is to see an export advisor from the British Overseas Trade Board shortly and asks for your help in drawing up a list of questions to ask and points to raise.

Required:

a) Name and describe appropriate trade promotion services offered by the Overseas Trade Services and the British Overseas Trade Board that Mrs Daws should be considering.

b) In view of the group's inexperience in Eastern Europe, briefly explain in what ways they might develop new business in this market area.

(Specimen Answer given in Appendix VI)

Unit 20

Bonds, Stand-by Letters of Credit and Countertrade

Objectives

On completion of this unit the student should be able to:

- **understand the role of bonds in international trade;**
- **describe the various types of bonds;**
- **appreciate the function of a stand-by letter of credit;**
- **distinguish between *on demand* and *conditional* bonds;**
- **describe the procedures for issuing bonds;**
- **appreciate the problems which bonds cause for exporters;**
- **understand how these problems can be reduced;**
- **describe the various forms of countertrade;**
- **appreciate the role of banks and others in promoting countertrade.**

20.1   The Role of Bonds in International Trade

A bond is issued by a guarantor, usually a bank or an insurance company, on behalf of an exporter. It is a guarantee to the buyer that the exporter will fulfil his contractual obligations. If these obligations are not fulfilled, the guarantor undertakes to pay a sum of money to the buyer in compensation. This sum of money can be anything from 1% to 100% of the contract value.

If the bond is issued by a bank, then the exporter is asked to sign a counter-indemnity which authorises the bank to debit his account with any money paid out under the bond.

Bonds are usually required in connection with overseas contracts, or with the supply of capital goods and services. When there is a buyer's market, the provision of a bond can be made an essential condition for the granting of the contract. Bonds are commonly required by Middle Eastern countries, but nowadays many other countries also require them. Most international aid agencies, such as the World Bank or the European Development Fund, and most government purchasing organisations in the developing world, plus major purchasers of goods and services in the North Sea oil sector now require bonds from sellers.

20.2 Types of Bond

The various types of bond are set out below:

a)   Tender or Bid Bonds

A tender or bid bond is usually for between 2% and 5% of the contract value, and will guarantee that the exporter will take up the contract if it is awarded. Failure to take up the contract results in a penalty for the amount of the bond. In addition, the tender bond usually commits the exporter and his bank to joining in a performance bond if the contract is awarded. Tender bonds serve to prevent the submission of frivolous tenders.

b)   Performance Bonds

Performance bonds guarantee that the goods or services will be of the required standard and a stated penalty is payable if they are not. The amount payable will be a stated percentage of the contract price; often 10% but sometimes more.

c)   Advance Payment Bonds

Advance payment bonds undertake to refund any advance payments if the goods or services are unsatisfactory.

d)   Warranty or Maintenance Bonds

Warranty or maintenance bonds undertake that the exporter will maintain the equipment for a period of time.

e)   Retention Bonds

Retention bonds enable retention monies, which would otherwise be held by the buyer beyond the completion of the contract, to be released early. These bonds guarantee the return to the buyer of these retention monies in the event of non-performance of post-completion obligations by the exporter.

f)   Recourse Bonds

Recourse bonds are sometimes demanded by the ECGD to cover the potential recourse by the ECGD under buyer credits.

g)   Stand-by Letter of Credit

An alternative to the bond is a stand-by letter of credit issued by the UK bank in favour of the importer, promising to pay a given amount against specified documents, usually a formal default claim. From the UK bank's point of view, a stand-by letter of credit is better than a bond because it will be subject to UCP for documentary credits instead of being subject to complex legalities. In addition, a stand-by letter of credit will always have a definite expiry date.

20.3 'On Demand' Bonds and Conditional Bonds

a)   'On Demand' Bonds

These bonds, sometimes known as 'unconditional bonds', can be called at the sole discretion of the buyer. The bank must pay if called upon to do so, even in circumstances where it may be clear to the exporter that the claim is wholly unjustified. UK courts have often ruled that the bank must honour claims under on demand bonds.

If the bank has to pay under the bond, it will debit the customer's account under the authority of the counter-indemnity. The exporter will then be left with the unenviable task of claiming reimbursement in the courts of the buyer's country.

It must be stressed that banks never become involved in contractual disputes. If payment is called for which conforms to the terms of the bond, the bank must pay.

b)   Conditional Bonds

Conditional bonds can be divided into two types:

   i)   conditional bonds requiring documentary evidence;

   ii)   conditional bonds which do not require documentary evidence.

Conditional bonds requiring documentary evidence give maximum protection to the exporter. Payment can only be called for by the buyer against production of a specified document, such as a certificate of award by an independent arbitrator. Unfortunately, this type of conditional bond is often unacceptable, particularly in the case of Middle East buyers.

On the other hand, conditional bonds which do not require documentary evidence are little better than on demand bonds from the exporter's point of view. Such bonds often specify that payment must be made **in the event of default or failure on the part of the contractor to perform his obligations under the above-mentioned contract**. This terminology is so vague that banks are often obliged to pay a simple on demand claim if one is received.

20.4   The Procedure for Issuing Bonds

If the UK bank is satisfied that joining in a bond is justified, it would prefer to issue its own bond direct to the importer. However, in certain countries, notably in the Middle East, local laws or customs prevent importers from accepting bonds issued directly by UK banks. In these circumstances, the UK bank will instruct a bank domiciled in the buyer's locality to issue a bond against the UK bank's own indemnity.

At the same time as the bond is issued, the exporter will complete the counter-indemnity to authorise the bank to debit the account with the cost of any payments under the bond. The bank will make a suitable charge for the service, usually a stated annual percentage of the bond's value. This percentage usually varies between 0.5% and 1.5% a year, payable quarterly in advance. In addition, if a local bank is involved, it will charge between 2% and 3% per annum.

20.5   The Problems which Bonds Cause for Exporters

a)   The Effect of Bonds on the Credit Rating of the Exporter

Banks treat the issue of bonds in exactly the same way as they would treat any lending facility. If payment is called for within the terms of the bond, the bank must pay, irrespective of whether its customer has funds to honour the counter-indemnity. Hence, banks would normally wish to reduce a customer's maximum borrowing facilities pound for pound by the same amount as the bond.

Tender bonds involve the worst problems. The average success rate is often said to be one in eight for tenders, so the average contractor may at any one time have eight tenders outstanding. If each of these tenders involves a tender bond of, say, 2%, then the exporter's total potential borrowing facilities are reduced by 16% of his overall tender volume.

b) Unauthorised Extension of Bonds
Some countries, such as Syria, have laws which prevent the local bank from cancelling the bond without the importer's specific authority. This prohibition applies even if the bond contains an expiry date.

Sometimes the local bank will threaten to call for payment unless the bond is formally extended. The usual result is that the local bank is able to persuade the UK bank to extend the bond, and that the annual bank charges continue to be levied by both banks.

Sometimes tender bonds are not cancelled, even when the contract has been awarded and a performance bond has been issued.

c) Unfair Calling of Bonds
The buyer may call for payment, even when such a call is unjustified. If the call conforms to the terms of the bond, the bank must pay and will debit the exporter's account under the terms of its counter-indemnity. The exporter can be left with the task of claiming reimbursement from the buyer via the overseas courts.

There is also a danger that advance payment or retention bonds could be called, even though the advance payment or retention monies have never been paid over to the exporter in the first place.

20.6 How an Exporter can Overcome or Reduce the Problems of Bonds

a) Effect of the Bond on the Exporter's Credit Rating
Insurance may be available against unfair calling of bonds through the ECGD's Bond Support Scheme.

ECGD will consider each case on its merits and the scheme usually has the following conditions:

i)   The contract must be covered by ECGD SCF facility, buyer credit facility, or an ECGD line of credit;

ii) The buyer will normally be a public sector borrower if the bond is on demand;

iii) The credit period must exceed two years for the financing of the contract.

The ECGD is willing to transfer the bond support from the exporter to the bank which issues the guarantee. This means that from the bank's point of view the issue of the bond is risk-free since, in the event of a claim, the bank will pay out and be reimbursed by the insurer. The insurer will only claim against the exporter if the bond has been called with justification, and there will be no recourse if the bond has been called unfairly. However, whatever the justification for the claim, the bank will be reimbursed for the full amount by the insurer.

Naturally, the issue of bonds which are covered by insurers' indemnities will not affect the bank's credit assessment, since the facility will be risk-free for the bank.

b)   Unauthorised Extension of Bonds

i)   If the bond can be issued directly by the UK bank, then standard wording can be incorporated to ensure that the bond has an expiry date and that the bond will be governed in accordance with English law. In such cases, the bond cannot be extended without the exporter's agreement.

ii)   Finally, if i) above is not possible, the UK bank may agree to insert a clause in the counter-indemnity which specifies that the exporter's liability is limited to the period stated in the bond, and that any extension must be approved by the exporter.

Obviously, this concession transfers the risk of an unauthorised extension from the exporter onto his bank, and the bank will only agree to this for important customers. If the ECGD or private-sector indemnity covers the bank in the event of unauthorised extension, then the bank will obviously be happy to amend its counter-indemnity.

iii) When a tender bond stipulates that a performance bond must be issued if the contract is awarded, the performance bond should be worded so that it is only effective when the tender bond has been returned to the UK bank for cancellation.

c)   Unfair Calling of Bonds

In addition to the protection which may be available from the ECGD bond support scheme, there is a facility which may be available as additional cover under the NCM International Policy (see 14.5).

NCM will consider covering unfair calling of performance bonds, advance payment bonds or retention bonds, but not tender bonds. The buyer must be a government principal and the exporter must also hold pre-shipment insurance through NCM (see 14.5(b)). There are no specific minimum amounts and bonds as low as £5,000 have been covered in suitable instances.

While such insurance may provide some comfort to the bank issuing the bond, it must be remembered that NCM will pay out only when such calling can be classed as 'unfair'. There is no automatic pay-out.

d)   Unfair Calling of Advance Payment Guarantees and Retention Money Guarantee

Ensure that the bond incorporates a reduction clause. This should state that the guaranteed value can be reduced in line with performance of the contract. An operative clause should also be included. This will ensure that the bond is only effective on receipt by the exporter of the advanced payment.

20.7 Other Precautions which an Exporter can Take when He is Required to Provide Bonds

In addition to the suggestions made in 20.6, the exporter can take the following precautions:

a) Information

The exporter should obtain the most detailed commercial and financial information on the prospective buyer and the market. Banks can assist in this matter, along with the DTI or the Chamber of Commerce.

b) Agent

He should consider employing a good local agent in markets where there are many contracts which require bonds. An agent can be particularly useful in obtaining the return of an expired bond so that formal cancellation can be effected. Many foreign banks continue to charge commission on bonds which have been issued against an indemnity from a UK bank, even though the expiry date has passed. Only on formal return and cancellation do they cease to charge. In addition, the UK bank must consider the contingent liability to continue to apply on such bonds, pending formal return of the document.

c) Build Cost into Price

The cost of bonding can be built into the contract price. When tender bonds are required, a price escalation clause in the commercial contract could avoid situations where the contract has become uneconomic due to delayed adjudication. If this arises, the exporter has the unenviable choice of completing an uneconomic contract or declining the contract and being made to pay under the tender bond.

d) Sub-contractors

Ensure that if the exporter acts purely as a sub-contractor, any bond only relates to the part of the work for which he is sub-contracted.

e) Insurance

The exporter should also consider ECGD or private sector insurance against unfair calling of the bond, where available.

20.8 Countertrade

a) What is Countertrade?

There is no one accepted definition of countertrade and the term is used by different specialists to describe different operations. Nevertheless, most participants would find the following definition acceptable:

Countertrade is an international trading transaction where export sales to a particular market are made conditional upon undertakings to accept imports from that market.

It is thus a form of bilateral trade which has continued to grow despite its condemnation by some international agencies because of its limiting effect on free trade and therefore multilateral trade.

There are two basic reasons for the development of countertrade:

i)   Some countries do not have the cash or credit facilities to pay for imports, so countertrade has become their only means of arranging deals;

ii)   Some developing countries wish to build up their manufacturing exports. Brazil, for example, one of the leading exponents of countertrade outside Europe, countertrades manufactured goods rather than raw materials such as coffee or iron ore. The objective is not to help dispose of the basic commodities, which can be sold on the world market (albeit for a low price) but rather to build up exports of manufactures.

In addition, it is common for restrictions to be placed on the markets in which the manufactured goods can be sold so as to achieve **additionality** of exports, rather than having the manufactures disposed of in markets where cash buyers could be found independently of any countertrade deal.

b)   Forms of Countertrade

i)   **Counter-purchase** (also known as **link purchase**). This is the most common form of countertrade, especially with Eastern European countries and with developing countries such as Indonesia.

The exporter agrees, as a condition of obtaining the order, to arrange for purchase of goods or services from the importer's country.

The sequence of events is as follows:

1)   The exporter obtains an order subject to arranging for the disposal of goods or services from the importing country.

2)   Two parallel, but separate contracts are set up, one for the sale of goods to the importing country, and one for the counter-purchase of goods from the importing country.

The organisation directly responsible for the counter-purchase will not necessarily be the exporter himself, but could be some other trading house or trader. There is normally recourse to the original exporter if the counter-purchase obligations are not fulfilled.

ii)   **Barter**. Barter involves a single contract for the simultaneous exchange of goods for goods between two parties. An example would be British exports of machinery to Zambia, paid for by a simultaneous shipment of wood or bitumen. Straightforward barter is popular with some African and Latin American countries, especially those with a shortage of hard currency, but pure barter deals are rare.

iii) **Compensation or buyback deals**. Buyback is a form of barter which is favoured by some Eastern European countries. Suppliers of capital goods agree to be paid by the future output of the factory which they are supplying. For example, ICI could sell a chemical processing plant and take part of the plant's future output of chemicals as payment.

iv)   **Barter by means of trust accounts**. A typical example would be the sale of trucks by a UK manufacturer to an African country, such as Kenya, with payment to come from the sale proceeds of local produce, say coffee.

The sequence of events is as follows:

1) The coffee is shipped to the UK and the payment is retained in a UK bank in a trust account, also called an escrow account.

2) The Kenyans arrange a documentary credit in favour of the UK truck manufacturer. The credit will be confirmed by the UK bank which maintains the escrow account, once there are sufficient funds from the sale of the coffee to cover the credit.

3) The credit is then advised to the UK manufacturer who ships his goods and then presents the required documents to obtain payment.

v) **Offset**. Offset is widely used in high-technology products. Export orders are given for items such as aircraft on condition that the exporter incorporates components or sub-assemblies manufactured in the importing country.

vi) **Switch trading**. This is best described by way of example. Colombia could sell coffee to Hungary and instead of being paid builds up a credit balance. If Colombia then wishes to import coal from Poland, arrangements can be made to use the credit balance from the coffee sales to pay for the coal. Hungary would thus settle with Poland.

A market is becoming established for dealing with such credit balances, presumably along the lines of the secondary market which is now developing in Third World loans.

vii) **Evidence accounts**. Companies with a significant level of continuing business in certain markets may be required to arrange for counter-purchase of goods from that market. For example, a multinational company with a subsidiary in a Third World country may be required to counter-purchase goods from the Third World country to match the value of the subsidiary's import of raw materials. It may not be practical to balance this kind of trade item by item so the company may maintain an **evidence account** of all transactions. Usually this account must be kept in balance on a year-by-year basis.

Countertrade is becoming more innovative as it adapts to the changing international market-place. In addition to the above, new forms of financial countertrade are emerging, such as debt/equity swaps which have been pioneered by certain Latin American countries. Also, many countries are adopting official countertrade policies, e.g. Thailand. This all seems a far cry from the predictions of a steep decline in countertrade operations following the break-up of the Soviet Union. Particularly, in reality, where this occurrence only served to increase countertrade deals and their international popularity.

c) **Pitfalls of Countertrade for the Exporter**
The main problems which can arise are:

i) Contractual commitments to purchase large quantities of unmarketable goods without any means of selling them.

ii) Penalty payments because the party to whom the counter-purchase has been committed has not honoured his obligations.

iii) Loss of profits on the sale of the principal goods because the costs of arranging the counter-purchase have not been considered.

iv) The discount between the face value of the goods taken in countertrade and the actual sale proceeds available.

When the counter-purchase goods are raw materials or commodities such as soya beans, a discount of 2% may be sufficient to cover the exporter. However, in the case of manufactured goods, a discount of 40%-50% can sometimes arise.

As a general rule, the nearer the counter-purchase goods are to commodities, the better.

v) The costs involved in marketing counter-purchased goods is continually rising. Exporters are therefore seeking alternative methods of meeting their countertrade obligations, e.g. training the importer's employees.

d) Sources of Help for the Countertrade Exporter

i) **Bank**. Banks have many advantages which make them highly suitable for countertrade operations:

- A massive computer database which is already used to match potential buyers and sellers.

- A huge customer base.

- Expertise gained already from experience in arranging ECGD buyer credit facilities.

- Ability to innovate and arrange an imaginative deal in the circumstances which apply. In particular, banks can advise the exporter on the premium to be included in the export price to offset the discount on counter-purchase goods.

- Ability to provide guarantees or bonds to cover the exporter's liability under a counter-purchase agreement.

- Some banks have representative offices in cities such as Moscow, Hong Kong or Singapore.

ii) **ECGD**. The ECGD will provide insurance and financial guarantees for countertrade deals, but only in limited circumstances.

The most important proviso is that the payment obligation of the buyer (or borrower in the case of buyer credit guarantees) must be totally independent of the provisions of the counter-purchase agreement. In other words, for ECGD support to be available, the covered transaction must have all the characteristics and effect of a transaction to which no countertrade arrangements are related.

The ECGD is not prepared to involve itself in deals where payment for the export sale depends on fulfilment of the counter-purchase obligation, largely because the risks are unquantifiable. In addition, the ECGD does not wish to be seen to contravene EU or Berne Union agreements.

The ECGD will never become involved in insuring successful disposal of counter-purchase goods, although such insurance is available from specialist brokers or from countertrade specialists known as trading houses.

iii) The Projects and Export Policy Division of the DTI has information on countertrade opportunities and may be able to supply details of specialist brokers who may be able to assist in setting up deals.

20.9 Self-assessment Questions

Question 1

Which bank will be ultimately responsible for meeting a valid claim under a bond? (Ignore any bond support schemes and choose between the exporter's bank and the importer's bank.)

Question 2

What is the usual name for the authority which enables the seller's bank to debit its customer in connection with payments under a bond?

Question 3

Why do banks treat on demand bonds issued without any form of bond support as a real liability?

Question 4

Why is a stand-by letter of credit less onerous than a bond, from the point of view of the exporter's bank?

Question 5

A stand-by letter of credit is issued in connection with a contract for a UK manufacturer to supply goods to the USA.

Name the applicant, issuing bank, advising bank and beneficiary of the stand-by letter of credit.

Question 6

Why should an exporter be concerned if a bond is extended without his agreement?

Question 7

How can the risks to an exporter be reduced under an advance payment bond?

Question 8

A UK bank is asked to issue a tender bond for 2% of the full contract value. What are the possible financial implications for the bank over and above the 2% of the contract value?

(Answers given in Appendix VI)

20.10 Specimen Question

Your customers, major suppliers of power-generating equipment, are negotiating large contracts on near-cash terms in the US and Middle East which will involve them in erection and commissioning on site.

a) What support, other than direct financial support, can your bank give in connection with this type of business?

b) Is there any UK government-backed support also available?

Tabulate your answers in brief note form.

(Specimen Answer given in Appendix VI)

Exhibit 7 Tender Guarantee

OUR GUARANTEE (GUARANTEE NUMBER)

We do understand that (APPLICANT'S NAME) ('the Applicant') (APPLICANT'S ADDRESS) are tendering for the (DESCRIPTION OF GOODS) under your invitation to Tender (TENDER/CONTRACT NUMBER ETC.) and that a Bank Guarantee is required for (AGREED PERCENTAGE OF CONTRACT)% of the amount of their tender.

We, BANK PLC, overseas Branch, London HEREBY GUARANTEE the payment to you on demand of up to (AMOUNT IN FIGURES) (say, (AMOUNT IN WORDS)) in the event of your awarding the relative contract to the Applicant and of its failing to sign the Contract in the terms of its tender, or in the event of the Applicant withdrawing its tender before expiry of this guarantee without your consent.

This guarantee shall come into force on (COMMENCEMENT DATE) being the closing date for tenders, and will expire at close of banking hours at this office on (EXPIRY DATE) ('EXPIRY').

Our liability is limited to the sum of (AMOUNT IN FIGURES) and your claim hereunder must be received in writing at this office before Expiry accompanied by your signed statement that the Applicant has been awarded the relative contract and has failed to sign the contract awarded in the terms of its tender or has withdrawn its tender before Expiry without your consent, and such claim and statement shall be accepted as conclusive evidence that the amount claimed is due to you under this guarantee.

Claims and statements as aforesaid must bear the confirmation of your Bankers that the signatories thereon are authorised so to sign.

Upon Expiry this guarantee shall become null and void, whether returned to us for cancellation or not and any claim or statement received after expiry shall be ineffective.

This guarantee is personal to yourselves and is not transferable or assignable.

This guarantee shall be governed by and construed in accordance with the Laws of England.

Exhibit 8 Performance Bond

OUR GUARANTEE(GUARANTEE NUMBER)

We understand that you have entered into a Contract (TENDER/CONTRACT NUMBER ETC.) (the Contract) with (APPLICANT'S NAME) (APPLICANT'S ADDRESS)(the Applicant) for the (DESCRIPTION OF GOODS) and that under such Contract the Applicant must provide a Bank Performance Guarantee for an amount of (AMOUNT IN FIGURES) being (AGREED PERCENTAGE OF CONTRACT)% of the value of the contract.

We, BANK PLC, overseas Branch, London, HEREBY GUARANTEE payment to you on demand of up to (AMOUNT IN FIGURES) (say, (AMOUNT IN WORDS)) in the event of the Applicant failing to fulfil the said Contract, provided that your claim hereunder is received in writing at this office accompanied by your signed statement that the Applicant has failed to fulfil the Contract. Such claim and statement shall be accepted as conclusive evidence that the amount claimed is due to you under this guarantee.

Claims and statements as aforesaid must bear the confirmation of your Bankers that the signatories thereon are authorised so to sign.

This guarantee shall expire at close of banking hours at this office on (EXPIRY DATE) ('EXPIRY') and any claim and statement hereunder must be received at this office before Expiry and after Expiry this guarantee shall become null and void whether returned to us for cancellation or not and any claim or statement received after Expiry shall be ineffective.

This guarantee is personal to yourselves and is not transferable or assignable.

This guarantee shall be governed by and construed in accordance with the Laws of England.

Exhibit 9 Advance Payment Guarantee

OUR GUARANTEE (GUARANTEE NUMBER)

We understand that you have entered into a Contrast (TENDER/CONTRACT NUMBER ETC.) with (APPLICANT'S NAME) (the Applicant (APPLICANT'S ADDRESS) for the (DESCRIPTION OF GOODS) and that under the Contract the sum of (AMOUNT IN FIGURES) being (AGREED PERCENTAGE OF CONTRACT)% of the total contract value is payable in advance against a Bank Guarantee.

In consideration of your making an Advance Payment of (AMOUNT IN FIGURES) (the Advance Payment) to the Applicant we, BANK PLC, overseas Branch, London, HEREBY GUARANTEE to refund to you on demand up to (AMOUNT IN FIGURES) (say, (AMOUNT IN WORDS)) in the event of the Applicant failing to fulfil the Contract.

Our maximum liability hereunder shall automatically reduce by (REDUCTION PERCENTAGE) of the value of (SERVICE/GOODS TO EFFECT REDUCTIon) as evidenced by presentation to us by (PRESENTER FOR REDUCTION) of (DOCUMENTS FOR REDUCTION) showing the (EVIDENCE PRESENTED BY DOCUMENTS) which we shall be entitled to accept as conclusive evidence that the (CONCLUSIVE EVIDENCE OF) has been effected.

This guarantee shall remain valid until reduced to nil in accordance with the foregoing procedure or until close of banking hours at this office on (EXPIRY DATE) ('EXPIRY') whichever shall first occur. Any claim hereunder must be received in writing at this office before Expiry accompanied by your signed statement that the Applicant has failed to fulfil the Contract, and such claim and statement shall be accepted as conclusive evidence that the amount claimed is due to you under this guarantee.

Claims and statements as aforesaid must bear the confirmation of your Bankers that the signatories thereon are authorised so to sign.

This guarantee shall become operative upon issue of our amendment making it effective, which will be issued upon receipt by us of written confirmation from the Applicant that the latter has received the Advance Payment.

Upon Expiry, this guarantee shall become null and void, whether returned to us for cancellation or not and any claim or statement received after expiry shall be ineffective.

This guarantee is personal to yourselves and is not transferable or assignable.

This guarantee shall be governed by and construed in accordance with the Laws of England.

* ALTERNATIVE

*This guarantee shall become operative automatically on receipt of the Advance of Payment of (AMOUNT IN FIGURES) on the account of (APPLICANT'S NAME) at our (BRANCH) Branch.

Exhibit 10 Progress Payment Guarantee

OUR GUARANTEE (GUARANTEE NUMBER)

We understand that you have entered into a Contract (the Contract) (TENDER/ CONTRACT NUMBER ETC.) with (APPLICANT'S NAME) (the Applicant) (APPLICANT'S ADDRESS) for the (DESCRIPTION OF GOODS) and that under the Contract a Progress Payment of (AMOUNT IN FIGURES) the Progress Payment being (AGREED PERCENTAGE OF CONTRACT)% of the total contract value is payable to the Applicant against a Bank Guarantee.

In consideration of your making a Progress Payment of (AMOUNT IN FIGURES) (the Progress Payment) to the Applicant we, BANK PLC, overseas Branch, London, HEREBY GUARANTEE to refund to you to demand up to (AMOUNT IN FIGURES) (say, (AMOUNT IN WORDS)) in the event of the Applicant failing to fulfil the Contract.

Our maximum liability hereunder shall automatically reduce by (REDUCTION PERCENTAGE)% of the value of (SERVICE/GOODS TO EFFECT REDUCTION) as evidenced by presentation to us by (PRESENTER FOR REDUCTION) of DOCUMENTS FOR REDUCTION) showing the (EVIDENCE PRESENTED BY DOCUMENTS) which we shall be entitled to accept as conclusive evidence that the (CONCLUSIVE EVIDENCE OF) has been effected.

This guarantee shall remain valid until reduced to nil in accordance with the foregoing procedure or until the close of banking hours at this office on (EXPIRY DATE) ('EXPIRY'), whichever shall first occur. Any claim hereunder must be received in writing at this office before Expiry accompanied by your signed statement that the Applicant has failed to fulfil the Contract, and such claim and statement shall be accepted as conclusive evidence that the amount claimed is due to you under this guarantee.

Claims and statements as aforesaid must bear the confirmation of your Bankers that the signatories thereon are authorised so to sign.

This guarantee shall become operative upon issue of our amendment making it effective, which will be issued upon receipt by us of written confirmation from the Applicant that the latter has received the Progress Payment.

Upon Expiry this guarantee shall become null and void, whether returned to us for cancellation or not and any claim or statement received after Expiry shall be ineffective.

This guarantee is personal to yourselves and is not transferable or assignable.

This guarantee shall be governed by and construed in accordance with the Laws of England.

* ALTERNATIVE

*This guarantee shall become operative automatically on receipt of the Progress Payment of (AMOUNT IN FIGURES) on the account of (APPLICANT'S NAME) at our (BRANCH) Branch.

Exhibit 11 Retention Monies Bond

OUR GUARANTEE (GUARANTEE NUMBER)

We understand that under the terms of your Contract (TENDER/CONTRACT NUMBER ETC.) with (APPLICANT'S NAME) (the Applicant) (APPLICANT'S ADDRESS) for the (DESCRIPTION OF GOODS) you are retaining the sum of (AMOUNT IN FIGURES) being (AGREED PERCENTAGE OF CONTRACT)% of the Contract value by way of retention monies (the Retention Monies) and that you are prepared to release the said retention monies against a Bank Guarantee.

In consideration of your releasing the sum of (AMOUNT IN FIGURES) to the Applicant we, BANK PLC, overseas Branch, London HEREBY GUARANTEE repayment to you on demand of up to (AMOUNT IN FIGURES) (say, (AMOUNT IN WORDS)) in the event of the Applicant failing to fulfil the Contract.

This guarantee shall remain valid until close of banking hours at this office on (EXPIRY DATE) ('EXPIRY'). Any claim hereunder must be received in writing at this office before Expiry accompanied by your signed statement that the Applicant has failed to fulfil the Contract, and such claim and statement shall be accepted as conclusive evidence that the amount claimed is due to you under this guarantee.

Claims and statements as aforesaid must bear the confirmation of your Bankers that the signatories thereon are authorised so as to sign.

*This guarantee shall become operative upon issue of our amendment making it effective, which will be issued upon receipt by us of written confirmation from the Applicant that the latter has received the Retention Monies.

Upon Expiry, this guarantee shall become null and void, whether returned to us for cancellation or not any claim or statement received after Expiry shall be ineffective.

This guarantee is personal to yourselves and is not transferable or assignable.

This guarantee shall be governed by and construed in accordance with the Laws of England.

* ALTERNATIVE

*This guarantee shall become operative automatically on receipt of the Retention Monies of (AMOUNT IN FIGURES) on the account of (APPLICANT'S NAME) at our (BRANCH) Branch.

Exhibit 12 Overdraft Guarantee

OUR GUARANTEE (GUARANTEE NUMBER)

In consideration of your granting advances by way of (TYPE OF BORROWING) on the account of (BORROWER) we hereby guarantee on demand being made to us in writing the due repayment of such advances in the event of (BORROWER) failing to repay such advances when required to do so by yourselves provided that the amount for which we shall be liable under his guarantee shall not exceed the sum of (AMOUNT IN FIGURES) (say, (AMOUNT IN WORDS)) *inclusive of interest and Bank charges.

Unless previously renewed by us, this guarantee is to be determined on (EXPIRY DATE) ('EXPIRY') subject to your right to cancel the facility prior to that date if you should think fit so to do, and to our right to determine our liability hereunder by giving notice in writing and upon receipt of such notice by you no further advances are to be made with recourse to us.

Claims under this guarantee must incorporate your declaration that the amount claimed represents outstanding advances by way of (TYPE OF BORROWING) on the account of (BORROWER) as aforesaid, *inclusive of interest and Bank charges, which have not been repaid by (BORROWER) as requested by you, and must be received by us at this office in writing or by authenticated telex/cable not later than 30 days after the above-mentioned expiry date, or not more than 40 days after the date of our prior notice of determination of liability, after which time this guarantee shall become null and void, whether returned to us for cancellation or not, and our liability hereunder shall terminate.

This guarantee is personal to yourselves and is not transferable or assignable.

This guarantee shall be governed by and construed in accordance with the Laws of England.

* ALTERNATIVE

* and in addition interest and Bank charges for a period not exceeding six months.

Exhibit 13 Warranty Bond

OUR GUARANTEE (GUARANTEE NUMBER)

We understand that you have entered into a Contract (the Contract) (TENDER/CONTRACT NUMBER ETC.) with (APPLICANT'S NAME) (the Applicant) (APPLICANT'S ADDRESS) for the (DESCRIPTION OF GOODS) and that under the Contract the Applicant must provide a Bank Warranty Bond for an amount of (AMOUNT IN FIGURES) being (AGREED PERCENTAGE OF CONTRACT)% of the value of the Contract.

We, BANK PLC, overseas Branch, London, HEREBY GUARANTEE payment to you on demand of up to (AMOUNT IN FIGURES) (say, (AMOUNT IN WORDS)) in the event of the Applicant failing to fulfil the terms of the Warranty obligations under the Contract. Any claim hereunder must be received in writing at this office before expiry accompanied by your signed statement that the Applicant has failed to fulfil the Warranty obligations under the Contract and such statement and claim shall be conclusive evidence that the amount claimed is due to you under the warranty.

Claims and statements as aforesaid must bear the confirmation of your Bankers that the signatories thereon are authorised so to sign.

This guarantee shall remain valid until close of banking hours at this office on (EXPIRY DATE) ('EXPIRY'). After Expiry this guarantee shall become null and void whether returned to us for cancellation or not and any claim or statement received after Expiry shall be ineffective.

This guarantee is personal to yourselves and is not transferable or assignable.

This guarantee shall be governed by and construed in accordance with the Laws of England.

Revision Questions 3

Short-answer Test

Question 1
A question on export finance concerns a customer who requires a borrowing facility of £10,000. Why is the acceptance credit facility **not** the correct answer?

Question 2
A UK bank negotiates an exporter's bill of exchange which is denominated in US $. Which rate will the bank use (its buy or its sell rate) to convert the dollars to sterling in the initial credit to the exporter's current account?

Question 3
You are asked to suggest an appropriate facility, which would be provided by a bank subsidiary rather than by the branch bank, for the following exporter, who:

    a)   Sells on open account to a large number of buyers on short-term credit.

    b)   Has an export turnover of £1m p.a.

    c)   Has an experienced sales ledger team within his own organisation.

    d)   Requires immediate post-shipment finance without recourse.

Which facility would you recommend?

Question 4
Why is forfaiting not an appropriate answer for Question 3?

Question 5
Is there any ECGD guarantee which allows a UK bank to lend at fixed and subsidised interest rates for exports to Japan and the USA?

Question 6

An exporter with a competent sales ledger staff requires finance to bridge the gap between shipment and payment. He sells consumer goods to a wide range of overseas buyers on open account terms. If asked to choose between factoring and invoice discounting, which facility would appear appropriate?

Question 7

Why does an ECGD single buyer credit guarantee provide without recourse finance?

(Answers given in Appendix VII)

Exam Question 1

Farmers Friends Ltd manufacture a range of agricultural equipment and have been successfully selling this in Western Europe for many years. They have recently had discussions with an official from the People's Republic of China but unfortunately it appears that the company's products. allowing for transportation costs etc.. would not be competitively priced in the Chinese market. However, it might be possible for the company to sell technical expertise, if they cannot sell their manufactured equipment.

The Managing Director and Sales Director call to see you to discuss a forthcoming business trip to China and they ask you for help and advice on how they should approach the matter. They know that your bank has a representative office in China (Beijing) and a large office in Hong Kong and they understand that a line of credit is being arranged which might be of assistance to a company selling technical expertise to the Chinese as an alternative to manufactured goods. They have been given to understand that, if a contract is successfully negotiated, their company will be expected to purchase raw materials from the People's Republic of China as part of the same contract.

They propose that Farmers Friends Ltd should take part in a British Exhibition which is being organised through the Overseas Trade Service in Beijing.

Required

a) Details of any help. other than financial and travel facilities, which you can give to Farmers Friends Ltd in connection with the proposed visit.

[4]

b) A brief description of what is meant by a line of credit and how it operates.

[11]

c) Is there any way in which your bank can assist Farmers Friends Ltd if they are required, as part of the same contract, to purchase from the People's Republic of China raw materials which cannot be used in the company's business?

[5]
[Total marks for question - 20]

(Specimen Answer given in Appendix VII)

Two Revision Questions

Question 1: Canadian Exports

Your customer exports capital goods to Canada and has found a buyer for a machine costing £25,000. The buyer requires a long period of credit at fixed-interest rates.

Describe the ECGD facility which will meet the problem without affecting the exporter's balance sheet contingency liability position.

Question 2: Capital Contracts Ltd

One of your customers, Capital Contracts Ltd, manufactures large items of capital plant and has obtained an order from a Third World country. The company understands that guaranteed payment will be available from a European bank and it asks to discuss with you the various ways in which this method of finance is provided. ECGD cover is not involved and it will take up to five years for payment to be effected.

Required
A brief description of:

    a)   the salient features of the method of finance involved;

    b)   the advantages of the method;

    c)   the disadvantages.

(Specimen Answers given in Appendix VII)

XYZ Question

XYZ Ltd, an export company customer of your bank, has sold goods to a buyer in the USA for $100,000, to be paid for in exactly three months' time against an accepted bill of exchange. The Finance Director of the company wishes to know which of the following methods of financing the transaction would be the more profitable for the company (which normally operates on overdraft):

a) Borrow $100,000 now, immediately convert the dollars into sterling to provide working capital, and repay the borrowing from the dollar proceeds of the bill of exchange when it falls due.

b) Borrow sterling at 1.5% over base rate under the bank's specialist export finance scheme, and repay from the proceeds of the bill of exchange which is to be covered forward fixed.

Required

Using the additional information given below, show by calculation which would be the more profitable method for your customer.

	Spot	Three months forward
i) US dollar rates	$1.8950-1.9150	2.47-254c disc

ii) US dollar three months' LIBOR rate is 17% and for this important customer you would apply a margin of 0.75%.

iii) UK base rate is 11% for the whole period.

iv) Three months can be regarded as exactly one quarter of a year.

v) Interest in (a) is to be converted at the **middle** rate today of 1.905. (The correct rate would not be known at the time when the transaction was discussed with the customer, and this middle rate is used to give the customer an indication of the amount of interest to be charged when effecting transactions of this nature.)

(Specimen Answer given in Appendix VII)

Exam Question 2

Ancient Mariners Ltd offers a wide range of services to the shipping world, including the provision of officers and crew on standard ship delivery contracts. These contracts entail the provisioning, crewing and delivery of vessels to the owners or their agents at named ports. The company has a long, satisfactory banking relationship with your branch.

The directors are discussing a potential contract with Neptune Inc. of the USA, the new owners of a vessel, to provision, crew, and deliver this vessel to Neptune Inc. in Savannah, Georgia, USA.

The terms being considered are:

- 30% payable to Ancient Mariners on signing of the contract;

- 35% payable, at the latest, 10 days after the vessel has sailed for the USA;

- the balance of 35% payable, at the latest, 10 days after delivery of the vessel to Neptune Inc.

Mr David Jones, Managing Director of Ancient Mariners Ltd, calls to see you to discuss this contract. He wishes to ensure that secure methods of payment are used so that, provided the company fulfils the contract terms, payments will be obtained. However, he is aware that Neptune Inc. will require some form of undertaking in respect of the 30% advance payment.

Required

a) A brief description of:

  i) a banking instrument which could be issued on behalf of Neptune Inc. and would give Ancient Mariners Ltd the security it is seeking in respect of all the payments;

[3]

  ii) a banking instrument, issued in conjunction with (i) above, which would satisfy the requirements of Neptune Inc. in connection with the advance payment.

[3]

b) An explanation of how Ancient Mariners Ltd, using these instruments, could claim and obtain access to all the payments mentioned in the question.

[6]

c) A brief explanation of the liability which your bank and your customer will enter into under (a)(ii) above, and any conditions which could be included in the instrument to minimise this liability.

[8]

[Total marks for question - 20]

(Specimen Answer given in Appendix VII)

Exam Question 3

Icy Products plc, a UK company, manufactures, installs and maintains food-processing plants. It has been negotiating with a major UK contractor to build and install food-processing and freezing equipment in several Eastern European countries. Firm proposals have been put forward and, subject to government-backed finance, Icy Products is hoping to establish contracts with at least two of the more creditworthy countries.

You are asked to discuss the financing of these two projects, which you understand will each have contract values of about £900,000. During your meeting with Icy Products, the Export Sales Director, Mr Icicle, says that his company has been asked to grant credit **over three years**, but he has been unable to identify any scheme which would be appropriate for Icy Products and would provide it with cover and finance.

Required

a) Identify the appropriate scheme which would allay the fears of Mr Icicle.

[2]

b) Briefly explain the key features of the scheme and the normal steps/procedures necessary to obtain cover.

[18]

[Total marks for question - 20]

(Specimen Answer given in Appendix VII)

Part Five

Introduction

This fifth and final part of the book is concerned with two major aspects of the syllabus:

a) Bank services for importers. including all relevant aspects of documentary collections and documentary credits;

b) Transferable and back-to-back credits.

Note
The Uniform Rules for Collections, Uniform Customs and Practice for Documentary Credits and Uniform Rules for Bank-to-Bank Reimbursements under Documentary Credits are set out in full in Appendices III, IV and V to this book. In addition. there are appendices covering correspondent banking and electronic commerce.

Unit 21

Inward Documentary Collections

Objectives

On completion of this unit the student should be able to:

- **explain the difference between a clean and a documentary collection;**

- **understand and explain the responsibilities of all parties to a collection as stated in the Uniform Rules for Collection (URC);**

- **explain the process of presenting a bill of exchange for payment or acceptance;**

- **explain what action must be taken when a bill of exchange is dishonoured;**

- **explain the procedure for dealing with goods consigned to the collecting bank;**

- **explain how offers of partial payment are handled under URC and UK banking practice;**

- **appreciate the significance of 'avalisation' of inward bills for collection;**

- **explain how banks can help importers when bills of lading have gone missing;**

- **explain how the produce loan procedure can be used to provide finance to importers who buy on documents against payment terms.**

21.1   Introduction to Importing

Every vessel or aircraft arriving in the UK from a foreign departure point must report its arrival to the UK Customs authorities, and all goods must be **entered** into Customs on the prescribed form. There may be various levies such as VAT and excise duties to pay. Finally, it may be necessary to obtain an import licence for certain categories of goods, such as arms, drugs and livestock. However, most goods imported into the UK fall under the category of **open general licence**, which means that no licensing formalities are required.

Importers must conform to the Customs procedures, otherwise they cannot obtain possession of the goods. However, a detailed knowledge of Customs regulations is not required by the International Trade Finance syllabus, and questions on these matters do not appear on the exam papers.

Once Customs formalities have been completed, the importer will present an original bill of lading (made out to order and blank endorsed) to the carrier who will authorise the Docks Superintendent to release the goods. If waybills apply, the importer will present the waybill to the carrier, who will authorise the Docks Superintendent to release the goods, provided the importer is named as consignee.

Similar procedures apply when the goods come by air, but in this case the transport document will be an air waybill.

21.2 General Rules for the Handling of Inward Collections

The handling of inward collections received by UK banks from their overseas correspondents (banks) is considered to be a very important service which, if not taken seriously, can result in monetary loss and also damage a banking relationship.

A collection can be:

Clean - a bill of exchange or cheque unsupported by documents; or

Documentary - documents supported (or unsupported) by a bill of exchange.

All documents sent for collection must be accompanied by a collection instruction giving complete and precise instructions. Banks are only permitted to act upon the instructions given in such collection instructions and in accordance with these rules. Any deviation from these instructions at the request of the drawee will be at the responsibility of the collecting bank.

The instructions of the remitting bank override the banking relationship, if any, between drawee and collecting bank.
Banks will act in good faith and exercise reasonable care and must verify that the documents received appear to be as listed in the collection instruction and must immediately advise the party from whom the collection instruction was received of any documents missing. Banks have no further obligation to examine the documents.

All UK banks will act in accordance with URC unless UK law or the collection instruction prevents this.
In the case of documents payable at sight, the presenting bank must make presentation for payment without delay and, in the case of documents payable at a tenor other than sight, the presenting bank must, where acceptance is called for, make presentation for acceptance without delay and where payment is called for, make presentation for payment not later than the appropriate maturity date.

In respect of a documentary collection including a bill of exchange payable at a future date, the collection instruction should state whether the commercial documents are to be released to the drawee against acceptance (D/A) or against payment (D/P). In the absence of such statement, the commercial documents will be released only against payment.

21.3 Procedure for Obtaining Acceptance of a Bill of Exchange

Acceptance of a bill of exchange is an unconditional undertaking to pay the bill on maturity. The drawee should not, therefore, when accepting the bill, impose any conditions on payment. Acceptances citing for instance:

a) lesser amount

b) payable at a different date

are referred to as 'qualified acceptances' and would not be acceptable to the remitting bank.

The bill may be accepted payable at a place other than the acceptor's address, normally at his bank, viz. 'Accepted payable at Barclays Bank plc...' This practice should be encouraged as the procedure for obtaining payment at maturity is greatly simplified; the bill needs only to be presented at the bank counters for payment.

The presenting bank is responsible for seeing that the form of the acceptance of a bill of exchange appears to be complete and correct, but is not responsible for the genuineness of any signature or for the authority of any signatory to sign the acceptance.

However, when the drawee is a customer, good banking practice dictates that the signature must be checked against the mandate.

Strict control must be maintained over an accepted bill which must not be presented for payment at maturity through the post.

21.4 Action to be Taken in the Event of Dishonour

A bill of exchange is dishonoured when a sight draft is unpaid on presentation or when a tenor draft is unaccepted on presentation or unpaid at maturity.

When an inward collection is dishonoured, the presenting bank must examine the collection order to see whether the bill is to be protested. Protesting a bill provides legal evidence of dishonour acceptable to a court of law.

If protest is to be carried out, a Notary Public will personally call upon the drawee/acceptor and demand payment or acceptance. If the payment/acceptance is not forthcoming, the Notary Public will draw up a **deed of Protest** which will give the reasons stated for dishonour. A bill should be protested within one working day of dishonour, otherwise, under the Bills of Exchange Act 1882 (S51), all signatories are freed from liability on that bill.

a)   Noting
Protesting is expensive and must be done within one working day of dishonour. To save money, it is possible to ask the Notary Public to note the dishonour. At maturity of an accepted bill, the Notary will present the bill either at the drawee's address or at the bank if payable there. If a bill is noted, the right to protest at a later date remains without any time limit.

b)   Householder's Protest

When a Notary Public is not available, a member of the bank staff can make a formal protest. Two ratepayers resident in the area of the drawee must witness the formal document. This is a valid form of Protest.

SPECIMEN FORM OF HOUSEHOLDER'S PROTEST

Date:...................................

Know all persons that
I..

householder of... in the County
of...........................
in the United Kingdom, at the request of Midland Bank plc, there being no Notary Public available, did on the ....   day of...........19
at..
demand...........................*Payment/Acceptance of the Bill of Exchange hereunder written
from..

to which demand answer was
made...
Wherefore I now in the presence
of...
and...do protest the said Bill of Exchange.
*Delete as appropriate

        Signature:...
....   )
Name..   )
....   )
Address.)
....   )
....   ) Two Witnesses
....   )
Name..   )
....   )
Address.)
....   )
....   )
....   )

Copy of the Bill of Exchange

c)   UK Practice

UK practice with inward documentary collections which are dishonoured is to note them if the collection order does not give any instructions regarding protest. This will retain the liability of all parties. This practice overrules Article 24 of URC which states that in the absence of specific instructions there is no need to note or protest a dishonoured bill of exchange. It is important that the remitting bank is kept fully informed of the situation in accordance with their instructions. If applicable, the **case of need** should also be advised, depending on his powers (Article 25).

21.5   Protection of Goods

Banks have no obligation to take any action in respect of the goods to which a documentary collection relates. Nevertheless, in the case that banks take action for the protection of the goods, whether instructed or not, they assume no liability or responsibility with regard to the fate and/or condition of the goods and/or for any acts and/or omissions on the part of any third parties entrusted with the custody and/or protection of the goods. However, collecting bank(s) must immediately advise the bank from which the collection order was received of any such action taken.

Any charges and/or expenses incurred by banks in connection with any action for the protection of the goods will be for the account of the principal.

In practice however, the collecting bank will take reasonable care when entrusting the goods to a warehouse agent.

21.6   Goods Consigned to the Collecting Bank

Goods should not be despatched direct to the address of a bank or consigned to a bank without prior agreement on the part of that bank.

In the event of goods being despatched direct to the address of a bank or consigned to a bank for delivery to a drawee against payment or acceptance or upon other terms without prior agreement on the part of that bank, the bank has no obligation to take delivery of the goods, which remain at the risk and responsibility of the party despatching the goods (Article 10).

In practice, great care is required when goods are consigned to the bank as large losses have resulted from incorrect procedures being followed.

Quite often, goods consigned to the bank will arrive by air before the supporting documents have been received. At this stage we will have little indication of the value of the collection other than the declared value of the goods for Customs purposes. It is, therefore, important that a letter of release is only handed to the drawee who is undoubted and is prepared to sign an irrevocable undertaking to honour the documents upon presentation **regardless of the terms of those documents.**

Decisions of this nature will need to be made by a member of management.

21.7 Procedure for Dealing with Offers of Partial Payment

In respect of clean collections, partial payments may be accepted if and to the extent to which and on the conditions on which partial payments are authorised by the law in force in the place of payment. The documents will only be released to the drawee when full payment thereof has been received.

In respect of documentary collections, partial payments will only be accepted if specifically authorised in the collection order. However, unless otherwise instructed, the presenting bank will only release the documents to the drawee after full payment has been received.

Where a customer offers a part payment after accepting a bill of exchange and taking control of the goods, it is **UK banking practice** to accept the payment (even though the collection order may state that part payments are not allowed), note/protest **the bill** for dishonour, and hold the part payment on a suspense account, pending further instructions from the remitting bank.

Note
The bill is protested, not the **balance of the bill**, as it is the bill which is dishonoured and not a part of the bill.

21.8 Charges

Banks may deliver documents against payment or acceptance without collecting charges unless the collection instruction specifically states that the documents must not be released unless charges are paid. Where no specific instructions are given, the bank is in order to release the documents without collecting charges which are for account of the remitting bank.

21.9 Settlement

Settlement of an inward collection must be carried out strictly in accordance with the instructions contained in the collection instruction. Students must be familiar with the requirements laid down in URC.

Some overseas countries have specific exchange control laws which insist on all payments first of all being paid in local currency and then being subject to an application to that country's Central Bank for conversion and remittance abroad. Where such laws exist, they will prevail over URC, but there are no such rules in the UK.

21.10 Avalisation of Inward Collections

Let us briefly recall the parties to an inward collection in connection with imports to the UK.

They are:

Principal - the overseas exporter;

Remitting bank - the exporter's bank;

Collecting/presenting bank - the importer's bank;

Drawee - the importer.

From the point of view of inward collections, avalisation can be defined as 'the addition of the presenting bank's name to a bill of exchange with the intention of guaranteeing payment at maturity'. It will usually take the form of the following words being placed on the reverse of the bill of exchange:

Endorsed by way of aval (for the acceptor) for and on behalf of
.... Bank plc (i.e. UK presenting bank)
.... Authorised Signature

While the practice of avalisation is not recognised within the UK Bills of Exchange Act, nevertheless when a UK bank avalises a bill of exchange, that bank in practice guarantees payment.

Avalisation involves a contingent liability, and a bank will consider the granting of such a facility in the same way as it considers any lending facility. In other words, the bank will consider the creditworthiness of its importer customer. If the bank avalises a bill of exchange, it will require the customer to complete an authority whereby the bank is irrevocably authorised to debit the customer's account upon presentation of the bill at maturity.

A brief comparison of avalisation and documentary credit facilities appears in Unit 22.

Note
Large losses have resulted from the failure to recognise the words **aval**, **pour aval** and **avalisation** appearing on inward collection schedules received from banks abroad - the documents being released to the drawee merely against his acceptance and without the bank's agreement to **avalise** the accepted bill of exchange.

21.11 How Banks Can Help Importers When Bills of Lading Have Gone Missing

Any failure by the importer to remove his goods from the dockside within a specified time will result in demurrage charges. Demurrage is a storage charge made by dock authorities on importers who fail to remove their goods.

One of the most common causes of a demurrage charge is the arrival of goods before the relevant bills of lading have reached the importer. A typical situation is set out at 21.12, which shows how a bank indemnity can solve the problem.

21.12 Use of a Bank Indemnity when Bills of Lading are Missing

A typical question could be set on the following lines:

Your customer telephones to say that a machine which he is importing has arrived in this country. However, he is unable to take delivery because the bills of lading have not arrived.

The machine is incurring demurrage charges. How can the bank help the customer to obtain the machine and what precautions are involved?

An answer along the following lines is required:

a) The bank could join in an indemnity to the freight company (carrier) requesting the release of the machine without the bills of lading, and promising to reimburse the carrier if he suffered any loss.

b) The customer must sign a counter-indemnity authorising the bank to pay any claims and debit the customer's account in reimbursement.

c) The counter-indemnity will also promise that the importer will immediately send the missing bills of lading to the bank, should they come to hand.

d) The bank will also ascertain whether the customer has paid for the machine, and, if not, what terms of payment have been agreed. If payment is by documentary collection, the customer must sign an irrevocable authority to honour the terms of the collection when presented. The bank could ask for the customer to place money on a suspense account earmarked to pay the collection, if the terms are D/P. Whether the bank insists on this will depend on the integrity and creditworthiness of the customer.

e) The bank will issue the indemnity, provided the customer is creditworthy and trustworthy. The amount of the indemnity will be similar to the value of the goods. The indemnity must be in standard form so as not to impose any unreasonable obligations on the bank. The bank will consider the same principles as apply to consideration of the issue of bonds on behalf of a customer (see Unit 20).

f) The bank will make a charge for the indemnity, and can justify that charge by pointing out the saving on demurrage.

g) If the missing bills of lading do subsequently come to hand, the bank will give them up to the carrier in exchange for cancellation of the indemnity.

h) Indemnities such as these represent a contingent liability on the part of the importer, since at some future date there could be a claim from the carrier. However, most banks would regard the real risk as being very low or non-existent.

   In practice, the bills of lading usually turn up and are surrendered in exchange for the cancelled indemnity.

21.13 Produce Loan Procedure

Sometimes importers buy goods on D/P collection terms for resale to a third party in the same country. It can happen that the importer requires finance to bridge the gap between payment of the sight draft, and receipt of funds from the ultimate buyer.

In such cases a produce loan facility can enable the importer's bank to advance funds against the security of goods and/or their sale proceeds. The procedure is as follows:

a) Take a letter of pledge from the customer. This will state that the documents and/or goods are pledged as security to the bank.

b) Pay the bill of exchange in accordance with the instructions on the collection order.

c) Debit a produce loan and credit the customer's current account with the agreed amount of the advance.

d) The documents will be retained by the bank. The bank will arrange with its agents to have the goods warehoused in the **bank's** name.

e) The goods must be insured at the customer's expense.

f) A status enquiry will be made on the supplier of goods to ensure that the goods should be of sound quality and on the ultimate buyer to ensure that he should be able to pay for the goods.

g) The goods remain in the warehouse until the time comes for delivery to the ultimate buyer. When that time comes, the customer must sign a trust receipt. The bank will then issue a delivery order to enable the customer to obtain the goods and take them to the ultimate buyer. The trust receipt states that the customer holds the goods as trustee for the bank.

The bank has now lost physical control of the goods and relies on the customer to deliver them to the ultimate buyer.

h) The ultimate buyer pays directly to the bank and the proceeds are used to clear the produce loan, including interest and charges.

21.14 Special Forms of Finance for Imports

Apart from produce loans, which have just been described, the main specialist forms of finance are:

a)   Factoring or Invoice Discounting
This applies when the goods are to be on-sold to other business organisations usually, but not necessarily always, located in the same country as the importer.

Note
UK factors will also provide finance to overseas exporters who have a good spread of UK debtors. The overseas exporter sends the invoices to the UK factor.

The principles are the same as those described in Part Two of this book.

b)   Acceptance Credit Facilities
Again, these facilities apply when the goods are to be on-sold.

Normally the bank would lend unsecured, but it could conceivably require the security of the goods under a produce loan type facility.

The procedure is similar to that already described for exporters in Part Two of the book. The importer draws a bill of exchange (minimum £100,000) on the bank, the bank accepts the bill, and the importer discounts it. Provided the tenor of the bill is below 180 days, it will be classed as a bank bill and thus can be discounted at fine rates.

c)   Documentary Credits Payable after Sight but which Contain a Negotiation Clause
When the seller is in a strong enough bargaining position to insist on documentary credits, there can be a problem if the seller requires payment immediately on presentation of documents and the buyer requires credit terms.

One possible solution is a documentary credit which calls for term drafts, but which contains an authority for the advising bank to negotiate against correct presentation of documents. Provided that the applicant has agreed to be responsible for all discount costs, then this credit will meet the requirements of the beneficiary.

From the importer's point of view, this facility is more generous than open account terms or documentary collection terms with overdraft/loan or factoring or acceptance credit facilities to allow for payment to the supplier on shipment.

d)   VAT deferment
In the absence of any arrangement to the contrary, importers will have to pay VAT on goods as they are cleared through Customs. However, it is possible for importers to arrange to open an account with the VAT authorities so that VAT is settled on a monthly basis. Usually all VAT incurred in January would be settled on 15 February, and all VAT incurred in February would be settled on 15 March and so on.

The importer would require a bank indemnity in favour of HM Customs to cover any non-payment of VAT incurred on the monthly settlement. The bank would apply normal credit criteria when deciding whether to grant the indemnity, would require a counter-indemnity from the importer and would charge a fee. These considerations will follow the principles described in Unit 20, concerning the issue of bonds on behalf of customers.

The importer must decide whether the cash-flow gains, interest savings and convenience outweigh the bank's fee for the indemnity. The earlier in the month the goods clear Customs, the greater the cash flow and interest benefits.

An additional means of legally avoiding VAT is available in connection with goods which are being brought into the UK from abroad, and temporarily warehoused in the UK pending re-export. Such goods should be kept in a customs or bonded warehouse whilst in the UK. This will legally avoid the need to pay VAT, so long as the goods remain there until subsequent re-export. A variation of this method is the 'E' type warehouse, which can be located at the importer's own premises. Provided computerised stock control methods, backed up by periodic spot checks, show that the goods are accounted for separately, then there will be no VAT to pay so long as the goods are exported when they leave the control of the importer.

21.15 Revision Question on Importers

Question

Your customer, X Ltd, is negotiating for the first time with sellers abroad for the supply of raw materials. The terms of payment are 90 days' sight draft, documents against acceptance through a UK bank, subject to URC.

The terms of shipment are CFR UK port.

a) Explain these terms of shipment and payment and state what instructions you would expect to see on a collection order accompanying the documentary collection.

b) What particular points would you expect to see on the bills of lading as regards this transaction?

Suggested Solution

a)   ***CFR UK port***

'Cost and Freight'. This is an Incoterm. The seller will be responsible for all freight costs as far as the UK port. X Ltd will be responsible for the marine insurance of the sea voyage and for all costs after arrival of goods at the UK port.

90 Days Sight Draft D/A

The seller will submit a documentary collection. X's bankers will be authorised to release documents against acceptance of the bill on X Ltd. The bill of exchange will be payable 90 days after acceptance by X Ltd. X Ltd will have possession of goods once it accepts the B/E. It will not need to pay for 90 days. Therefore X Ltd is receiving 90 days' credit.

Uniform Rules for Collections

An internationally accepted set of rules governing documentary collections. All aspects of the collection will be governed by these rules unless the collection order stipulates anything to the contrary, or unless the rules contradict the laws of the land.

Instructions on Collection Instruction

i)   Release documents against acceptance.

ii)   Whether to protest if unaccepted/unpaid.

iii) Remit proceeds by airmail/cable.

iv) Case of need and powers.

v)   Whether to store and insure if bill of exchange is not accepted.

vi) Can acceptance be delayed pending arrival of goods?

vii) Charges - can they be waived?

viii)Advise non-payment by airmail or by cable.

b)   i)   There should be a complete set of bills of lading(B/L),

or an explanation if any are missing.

ii)   The B/Ls should be clean, shipped on board and blank endorsed by the shipper (i.e. exporter).

iii)   The B/Ls should show a UK port as destination.

iv)   The B/Ls should be marked 'freight paid'.

21.16 Specimen Questions on Dishonoured Inward Collections
Question 1

Question

You have received from a bank in Germany documents for collection consisting of:

a)   sight draft £5,000 drawn on your customer Imports Ltd;

b)   invoice showing value of goods as £5,000 CIF London;

c)   insurance certificate;

d)   full set of bills of lading evidencing shipment of goods from Hamburg to London.

The instructions from the German bank are to release the documents against payment of the sight draft. on presentation your customers offer £2,500 cash plus a post-dated cheque for one month ahead for the balance when they have received the sales proceeds from the ultimate buyers in this country. What action should you take in response to this offer and why?

Suggested Answer

The UK presenting bank is acting as agent of the German remitting bank. The duty of care is owed to the German bank.

The collection instruction will stipulate that it is subject to Uniform Rules for Collections, unless any clauses in the collection instruction contradict these rules. If the Rules contravene UK law, UK law will prevail.

Proceed as follows:

a)   Do not release the documents as URC will only allow release of documents against full payment. Treat the bill as being dishonoured.

b)   Advise the German bank of the offer and ask for their instructions.

c)   Examine the collection instruction for:

    i)   Whether to protest;

    ii) The method of advice of dishonour to the German bank (cable or airmail);

    iii) Whether there is a case of need;

    iv) Whether to store and insure the goods.

Follow the instructions of the German bank when they reply. Any expenses incurred by the UK bank will be claimed from the German bank, as they are our principal and we are their agent.

21.17 Specimen Questions on Dishonoured Inward Collections: Question 2

Question

You have, as a branch of XYZ Bank Ltd, received during the last year a number of documentary collections from a bank in Finland, accompanied by bills of exchange drawn on your customers, Timber Ltd, at 60 days sight D/A. Hitherto these bills of exchange have been paid promptly on the due date but your customer has now declined to pay the latest accepted bill of exchange for £15,000.

  a) What action should you take on dishonour?

  b) Would your answer to (a) be any different if your customer explained that the reason for non-payment was a dispute over the quality of the goods shipped?

  c) What action should you take if the customer offers a part payment of £10,000?

Suggested Solution

    a) The collection will be subject to URC. Examine the collection instruction for:

        i)   whether to protest;

        ii) the method of advice of non-payment;

        iii) whether there is a case of need.

(**Note** The documents will have been released to the customer on acceptance, thus there is no question of storing and insuring of the goods.)

    b) The UK bank is acting as agent for the Finnish bank and its duty is to act for that bank's interest. The UK bank would proceed as above. The reason for non-payment is irrelevant.

    c) The UK bank should accept the part payment and remit it to Finland in accordance with the instructions on the collection instruction.

        The Finnish bank must be advised of the position.

        The UK bank will endorse a receipt for £10,000 on the bill of exchange.

        If the collection instruction asks for protest, it will be protested for the full amount of the bill.

21.18 Self-assessment Questions

Question 1
A collecting bank is employed by which of the following?

a) The principal;

b) The remitting bank;

c) The drawee, who is its customer.

Question 2
An inward collection is dishonoured by the drawee and the presenting bank protests the bill in accordance with the collection instruction. From whom will the presenting bank claim reimbursement.

Question 3
Why would the presenting bank examine the collection instruction for a **store and insure clause** on a dishonoured D/P collection, but not on a dishonoured D/A collection when the accepted bill had been presented at maturity?

Question 4
An inward collection is dishonoured and there are no instructions at all on the collection instruction as regards protest. What will the presenting bank do?

Question 5
A D/P collection is dishonoured, and there is no **store and insure clause** on the collection instruction. Will the presenting bank arrange insurance?

Question 6
What is the practical position regarding an inward collection which has been avalised by the UK presenting bank?

Question 7
A UK importer has previously accepted a D/A collection for £15,000. At maturity he offers to pay £5,000 only. What should the presenting bank do?

Question 8
In what circumstances will a UK bank carry out a householder's protest?

Question 9
Why is noting cheaper than protesting?

Question 10
A UK importer has asked his bank to avalise an inward collection and the bank has completed the necessary formalities. The maturity date of the bill is in one week's time.

The UK importer now wishes to countermand payment of the bill of exchange. What is the position?

Question 11

An importer buys on open account terms the goods to be transported by sea. What document must he produce to obtain possession of the goods on their arrival at the home port:

a) When the carrier has issued bills of lading?

b) When the carrier has issued ship's waybills?

Question 12

What document can a bank provide to enable an importer customer to obtain his goods when bills of lading have gone astray?

Question 13

What name commonly describes the authority which the customer signs in connection with the document in Question 12 above?

Question 14

What are the bank's main considerations if asked to issue an indemnity in connection with missing bills of lading?

Question 15

In what circumstances can an importer's bank become involved in problems of missing air waybills?

(Answers given in Appendix VI)

DELIVERY ORDER

No. 107   4th July   19

To The Superintendent of London Warehouses Ltd.

PLEASE DELIVER TO Alexander Productions   or Order

the undermentioned Goods,

ex Ship Mustansir   Rotation No.   6640L

Charges to be paid by consignee

Marks and Numbers	Quantity	Description
M M M M M M	One case	Photographic spools

S P E C I M E N

Per pro
NATIONAL WESTMINSTER BANK LIMITED

Chesil Beach

Office or Branch

Manager

430-1-9 69

Exhibit 14: Delivery order

SIVEWRIGHT TRANSPORT & STORAGE LIMITED

SPECIMEN ONLY OF   ADVICE OF GOODS RECEIVED

R 8067
R 8067

Into....Morpeth Tongue....................WAREHOUSE, BIRKENHEAD.

On (date)....25th June, 19'..................   I. No........12554........

Sender or Ex....ex. 'TOKIO EXPRESS'....................   M/C No....................................

A/c....Messrs. Black & Sons Ltd.,....................

Senders Ref.	Marks and or Numbers	Quantity of Packages	WEIGHTS, Descriptions or other particulars (provided by senders)					Remarks
			Tons	Cwts.	Qts.	Lbs.		
1231	BLACK/BLUE	4		400 Kilos			Pallets Empty Glass Ink Bottles. A number of bottles broken. UNEXAMINED	
	TOTALS	(-4-) FOUR						

OBSERVATIONS.   E. & O. E., and subject to our Conditions of Storage.

For SIVEWRIGHT TRANSPORT & STORAGE LTD.

Exhibit 15: Warehouse receipt

NWB1044 Trust Certificate

To Rimmer Glendz & Co
9, Trottingham Park
London E. 1.

3rd May ....19___

The Customer

Dear Sir,

We hand you herewith the undermentioned documents of title to the undermentioned goods (now in pledge to us as security for advances) on the following terms and conditions:—

You undertake to hold the documents of Title and the said goods when received (and the proceeds thereof when sold) as trustees for NATIONAL WESTMINSTER BANK LIMITED (the Bank).

(a) (b) (c)
one or more of
these to be deleted.

(a) As you require the said documents in order to obtain delivery of the said goods you undertake to warehouse them in the name of the Bank and to hand us the Warrants forthwith; also to insure the goods against all risks to their full insurable value and to hold the policies on our behalf and in case of loss to pay the Insurance moneys to us in the same manner as proceeds of sales.

(b) As you require the said goods in order to despatch the same to your agents for the purpose of sale or for processing printing or for the further preparation of the said goods in any manner whatsoever for immediate or eventual sale you undertake to hand us the receipts of your agents for the said goods and at all times to keep the goods fully insured against all risks however caused and to hold the policies on our behalf and in case of loss to pay the Insurance money to us in the same manner as proceeds of sales.

Insert number
of days

(c) As you require the said goods in order to deliver the goods to the Buyers you undertake to pay us the proceeds of sales without deduction of any expenses and immediately upon the receipt thereof or of each portion thereof, as the case may be within 15 days days from the date hereof and to give us on request full authority to receive from any person or persons the purchase moneys of such goods or any of them and in the meantime to hold the goods in trust for us.

You undertake also to keep this transaction separate from all other transactions.

We authorise you to take delivery of the goods on our behalf and to act as our trustees in the custody and realisation of the same and we request you to pay the proceeds of all sales to us immediately and specifically as received by you and to act on the above terms.

Yours faithfully,

NATIONAL WESTMINSTER BANK LIMITED

PRINCES STREET OFFICE ____ Branch

____ Manager

Exhibit 16: Trust receipt (front)

The Schedule of Documents and Goods

Description of Documents	Description of Goods	Vessel	Name of Buyer	Invoice Price
3/3 B/Ls Insurance Pol. Invoice in trip	Tinned peaches	Flemmington	Andrew Sprite & Son	£2,400

7th May _____ 19 __

To The Manager,

National Westminster Bank Limited
PRINCES STREET OFFICE
1, PRINCES STREET, E.C.2. _____ Branch

Dear Sir,

I/We acknowledge receipt of the above-mentioned documents relating to the above-mentioned goods of the Bank which I/we receive and/or will deal with upon the above terms and conditions giving as I/we do hereby all the undertakings mentioned above.

(*)to be deleted if (c) above is deleted

(*) I/We hereby declare that I am/ we are not indebted to the Buyers of the goods.

Yours faithfully,

For & on behalf of
Rimmer Glends & Co.

Secretary

Exhibit 17: Trust receipt (back)

Unit 22

Documentary Credits for Imports

Objectives

On completion of this unit the student should be able to:

- appreciate the risks which a bank undertakes when issuing a documentary credit on behalf of an importer;

- explain how some of these risks can be reduced;

- understand and explain the technicalities which must be resolved to ensure that the documentary credit is logical and workable;

- understand and explain the effects of Uniform Customs and Practice for Documentary Credits on the issuing of the credit and the responsibilities of the applicant and issuing bank.

22.1 The Risks which a Bank Runs when it Issues a Documentary Credit

When a bank issues a documentary credit, it guarantees payment if the correct documents are presented in conformity with all the terms and conditions of the credit. Normally, the issuing bank would obtain reimbursement by debiting the customer's account in accordance with the authority (please see item (a) in the terms and conditions of the specimen authority at Figure 1).

However, the issuing bank must honour the credit, provided its terms have been fulfilled, irrespective of whether the applicant has funds in his account. As a result, the issuing bank treats the documentary credit in much the same way as any other lending facility, and a limit will be marked on the account.

22.2 How the Issuing Bank can Reduce its Risks under Documentary Credits

As with any lending facility, the bank's prime considerations are the creditworthiness and integrity of its customer. However, an additional consideration is that the underlying goods can be used as security, provided the correct formalities are observed.

Thus, the considerations apart from general creditworthiness and integrity are:

a)   The nature of the goods. Are they easily saleable if the bank has to sell them to cover its liability in the event of the applicant's default?

b)   Should the credit call for a third-party inspection certificate? If such a document is called for and is produced, then the goods should be of the required standard. If the document is not produced, then the issuing bank is free of liability and will refuse payment because of a discrepancy in the presentation of documents.

c)   The beneficiary should be well known, or a good status report should be held regarding his commercial reliability and integrity.

d)   The bank could insist on a measure of cash cover from the applicant. Please see clause (f) on the terms and conditions of the specimen application form (Figure 1).

e)   The goods must be insured. If the credit calls for an insurance document, which would be the case if the underlying sale contract were CIF, then all is well. If the credit does not call for an insurance document, as would be the case with an FOB sale contract, then the bank must satisfy itself that the applicant is to effect the necessary insurance.

f)   If air waybills are called for, the issuing bank must decide whether it wants to be named as consignee. If the bank feels it is necessary to retain control of the goods, then the credit must stipulate that the air waybill shows the bank as consignee.

g)   If the goods come by sea, then it is in the interests of both bank and customer for the credit to call for a complete set of clean, shipped on board, bills of lading, made out to order and blank endorsed.

22.3   The Authority which the Applicant Completes

Once an importer and exporter have agreed to deal on documentary credit terms, then the importer must request his bank to arrange the credit. You will recall from Part Three of the course that the importer is the applicant and his bank is the issuing bank.

From the specimen application form reproduced at Figure 1, you will see that the main details which are required are:

1   Full name and address of beneficiary.

2   Whether the credit is revocable or irrevocable (Article 6). (On the Barclays authority, only irrevocable credits can be issued.)

3   Whether the details are to be passed to the advising bank by mail or teletransmission. If mail is to be used, check that there is adequate time before the expiry date (Article 11).

4   The amount of the credit. If the word 'about' is used, then a 10% deviation either way will be allowed (Article 39).

5   The documents called for. These must be logical. For instance, if the goods are coming by air, it would be illogical to call for bills of lading.

PLEASE COMPLETE THIS BY TYPEWRITER OR IN BLOCK CAPITALS USING BALL POINT PEN | *FOR BANK USE ONLY*

| DOCUMENTARY CREDIT APPLICATION **BARCLAYS** | Branch Ref. | ISB Ref. |

To
BARCLAYS BANK PLC _____ Branch | Date

| Customer/Applicant: | Name and address of beneficiary |

Address:

Customer's Reference:

Please open an *IRREVOCABLE* Letter of Credit by *(see note 1)*

☐ Mail Only   ☐ Mail with brief details Teletransmitted   ☐ Full details Teletransmitted with no mail confirmation

Advising Bank:
(Bank use only)

Amount (see note 1)
(in words and figures)
(specify currency)
☐ Up to
☐ About

Available by drafts on Barclays Bank PLC or its correspondents at *(see note 1)*

☐ sight   ☐ ___ days sight   ☐ ___ days after ___

for ___ per cent of the ___ invoice value, accompanied by the following documents:
(see note 2)

Invoice *(see note 3)*

Full set of clean on board blank endorsed BILLS OF LADING *(see note 4)* marked notify:

INSURANCE policy or certificate *(in duplicate)* endorsed in blank for the invoice value of the goods plus ___ per cent, covering:
(see note 5)

Any Other Documents:

Brief description of goods:
(see note 6)

Shipment from:
to
At latest by:

	Partshipments	Transhipments
	☐ Allowed	☐ Allowed
	☐ Prohibited	☐ Prohibited
		See note 1

Documents to be presented within ___ days of shipment but in any event within the validity of the credit.

Credit to expire on ___ in the beneficiary's country.

Additional Information *(see note 7)*

375/4/85/CBF201

Figure 1: Specimen authority

▼ IF APPLICABLE PLEASE INDICATE

☐ Forward Contract No. _____ Maturity _____ Rate _____

☐ CFC Account No.

TERMS AND CONDITIONS
In consideration of your issuing this Letter of Credit:

a) We authorise you to debit our account with all your commissions/charges and expenses together with those of your correspondents where applicable as and when they become due and with drawings either (i) on presentation if drafts are drawn at sight or where no drafts are involved, or, (ii) at maturity in respect of accepted drafts in which case we hereby undertake to provide you with funds not later than 3 days before maturity, unless you have been previously provided with funds for this purpose.

b) Where drafts are drawn in a currency other than Sterling, your demand for reimbursement from us will be calculated, unless previously agreed to the contrary, at your selling rate of exchange for the currency concerned, for the day you effect payment, or receive advice from your branch or correspondent that payment has been made. Interest where applicable is payable by us from the date of payment by your branch/correspondent until the reimbursement currency is available to you, and any exchange risks are for our account.

c) Where the beneficiary is not required to provide an insurance document, we undertake to arrange such insurance and deliver the relative policies/certificates to you on request. If the insurance is not arranged to your satisfaction you are authorised to arrange such insurance at our expense.

d) The relative shipping documents, as and when received by you, are to be delivered to us provided all costs, expenses and interest have been paid. If we fail to pay, you are authorised to sell the goods, and we undertake to pay on demand the amount of any deficiency on such sale.

e) It is agreed that this credit is subject to Uniform Customs and Practice for Documentary Credits 1993 Revision) I.C.C. Publication No. 500.

Clause (f) below should only be completed when full or part cash cover is being provided

f) To provide you with security you are authorised immediately to

(i) debit our account with _____ (say _____

_____)

(ii) buy the sum of _____ (say _____

_____)

on our behalf and debit our account with the Sterling equivalent.

Such sums to be held by you until all claims regarding this Letter of Credit have been satisfied.

For and on behalf of _____
(Insert Company Name)

Capacity of Signatory(ies) _____

<u>NOTES</u>
ALL DELETIONS AND ALTERATIONS TO BE INITIALLED

1) Indicate instruction to be followed by placing a tick or cross in appropriate box. One item only is to be completed in each section.

2) Insert Term of Contract, C.I.F., F.O.B., etc.

3) Indicate if required in duplicate, triplicate etc.

4) If Bill of Lading not required delete and insert other transport document (e.g. Air Waybill, Forwarding Agents Receipts etc.) indicating name and address of consignee.

5) If the insurance is being arranged by the beneficiary, complete this clause and state risks to be covered, Marine/Air/War etc. If insurance is being arranged by applicant, see note (c) above.

6) Goods description may include reference to proforma invoices or contracts but such documents should not be attached.

7) Include any additional information such as whether beneficiary has agreed to pay bank charges outside the U.K. and beneficiary's bankers (if known).

FOR BANK USE ONLY	AUTHORISING BRANCH TO INDICATE BELOW BY PLACING TICK IN BOX IF FULLY CASH COVERED	
BRANCH AUTHORISATION		☐
	ISB USE ONLY	
		SIGNATURES VERIFIED

TO INTERNATIONAL SERVICES BRANCH

Figure 2 (continued): Specimen authority

FOLD ALONG THIS LINE

6   The description of the goods is important, since on presentation of documents the invoice must describe the goods in exactly the same way, whereas the transport document can describe the goods in general terms not inconsistent with this wording on the credit (Article 37).

7   The latest date of shipment and the expiry date. It is not necessary to show a latest date of shipment, but if one is shown it must be not later than the expiry date of the credit. If a latest date of shipment is shown and it is more than 21 days before the expiry date, then there is a danger that all documents would be stale (Article 43).

8   If the credit amount is expressed in foreign currency, both the bank and the customer must decide whether it is necessary to cover the exchange risk.

Note

The International Chamber of Commerce has produced a series of standardised documentary credit forms which will enable all types of form (e.g. application, advice to bank) to be produced from a single input of data.

22.4 Re-instatement Documentary Credits

Re-instatement documentary credits are best explained through an example. The 'Flotsam and Jetsam Ltd' question provides a good illustration of the use of such techniques in an examination context.

Question

Flotsam and Jetsam Ltd imports a range of consumer items from many overseas countries. The directors have recently asked you to arrange an irrevocable letter of credit in favour of an overseas supplier to cover the company's imports for the next 12 months. Bank facilities are fully utilised and you are reluctant to issue an irrevocable letter of credit covering shipments valued in excess of £50,000 in any one month for the next 12 months. You are, however, prepared to issue an irrevocable letter of credit covering up to three months' shipments for a maximum of £150,000 (or the foreign currency equivalent), but you are not prepared to go beyond that limit. Nevertheless, the supplier has insisted that a bank undertaking should be issued in its favour, otherwise the company's source of supply will dry up.

Required

a)   Specify the banking instruments which would satisfy the customer's needs utilising irrevocable letters of credit, but which would not extend the bank facilities beyond the limit you are prepared to sanction.   [2]

b)   Briefly describe how these banking instruments would operate.   [7]

c)   Make brief notes showing the explanation you would give to the directors describing the advantages and disadvantages to the company, and the beneficiary (its supplier), of each of the methods described in (a) and (b) above.   [11]

[Total marks for question - 20]

Introduction to Flotsam and Jetsam Question

A documentary credit is a real liability to the issuing bank, since the bank must pay if the correct documents are tendered at the correct time.

The overseas supplier requires a documentary credit for a total sum of £600,000 which will allow part shipment against pro rata drawings. The supplier then knows that payment of his full year's sales to Flotsam is guaranteed, provided he conforms to the terms of the credit.

However, our bank is only prepared to sanction a maximum liability of £150,000 on behalf of Flotsam.

The supplier is in a strong bargaining position, so if Flotsam is to obtain the supplies, a documentary credit will be required.

Basically, the question asks what compromise is available whereby the supplier obtains a documentary credit, but our bank's liability is restricted to £150,000 maximum.

Answer

a)   i)   A re-instatement letter of credit;

    or

      ii)   A stand-by letter of credit.

b)   i)   Operation of a re-instatement documentary credit.

      The terms of the credit would be as follows:

      1   Expiry date in 12 months' time.

      2   Maximum amount £150,000 (i.e. three months' shipments).

      3   The credit will call for a specific sum, say £50,000 in value, to be shipped each month.

      4   The credit will state that the value of any documents, drawn in accordance with the terms of the credit, will be **re-instated** provided that Flotsam agrees.

      5   The credit will state that if documents are presented which do not conform to the credit, then either the bank or Flotsam could refuse to re-instate and would allow no further drawings.

      6   The credit will state that Flotsam has the right to refuse re-instatement.

      ii)   Operation of stand-by letter of credit.

      1   Our bank is the issuing bank and Flotsam is the applicant.

      2   The credit would be for a maximum of £150,000.

      3   The credit could guarantee payment against presentation of an invoice and copy bill of lading, together with a signed certificate from the supplier certifying that payment had not been made. Alternatively, payment could be guaranteed against a dishonoured, protested, bill of exchange drawn on Flotsam.

4 The supplier would then trade on an open account basis, but he would be able to claim under the stand-by letter of credit if Flotsam did not pay. Alternatively, the supplier would trade on a documentary collection basis, and in the event of dishonour would then use the stand-by credit to obtain payment.

c)   i) *Advantages of Re-instatement Documentary Credit for Flotsam (Importer/ applicant)*

1) The bank regards this facility as a liability of £150,000, rather than £600,000.

   Hence borrowing facilities are a much lower amount and bank charges are reduced.

2) Flotsam has the right to refuse to authorise re-instatement of any amount drawn under the credit. Thus, Flotsam are only committed to three months' purchases and could cancel the facility if alternative supplies were available.

3) The credit is subject to UCP, and so payment can only be made against stipulated documents.

ii) *Disadvantage of Re-instatement Documentary Credit for Flotsam*
As with all documentary credits, payment is made against documents, not against goods. Hence, payment will be made against the correct documents even if the goods prove to be faulty.

iii) *Advantages of Re-instatement Documentary Credit to the Supplier/ Beneficiary*
As with all documentary credits, payment of the amount (£150,000) is guaranteed against presentation of documents.

iv) *Disadvantages of Re-instatement Credit for Supplier/Beneficiary*
Only three months' sales are guaranteed, not twelve, since Flotsam could refuse to re-instate drawings.

Note
Importers prefer to issue 'ordinary' credits, which can be extended by amendment.

Advantages of Stand-by Letter of Credit to Buyer/Applicant	*Disadvantages of Stand-by Letter of Credit to Applicant*
i) If Flotsam refuses, for whatever reason, to honour invoices on open account or bills under documentary collection, payment will be delayed until the supplier can assemble the documents to claim under the stand-by credit.	i) If bills of exchange are used, dishonour will result in protest. This will damage Flotsam's credit.

Advantages of Stand-by Credit to Beneficiary	*Disadvantages of Stand-by Credit to Bene-ficiary*
i) Good security up to £150,000.	i) In effect, only three months' sales are guaranteed. Thus, the seller cannot rely upon a guarantee of payment for a full 12 months' sales
ii) If the buyer does not honour the 'open account' or 'documentary collection' claim, this will act as a warning not to ship any further goods in excess of the £150,000 available under the limit.	

22.5 Specimen Question

Question

What are the disadvantages and advantages of irrevocable documentary credits for importers, and how can the disadvantages be reduced?

Suggested Answer

a) Disadvantages of an irrevocable letter of credit for importers:

   i) As banks deal in documents not in goods, correct documents will eventually be paid unless the beneficiary agrees to the cancellation of the credit (see Article 4).

   ii) Even if the documents presented are in accordance with the credit terms, this does not necessarily mean that the goods will be as ordered.

   iii) When giving an undertaking on behalf of the importer, the issuing bank will be giving an unalterable undertaking to effect payment, despite the condition of the goods.

   iv) The importer's credit/facilities with the bank may be restricted because of the liability the issuing bank accepts when establishing a credit. This may mean a restriction/curtailment in the borrowing powers or facilities of the customer/importer.

   v) The customer may have to pay for all costs and charges associated with establishing the letter of credit. This will depend upon the bargaining strength of the two parties.

b) Advantages of an irrevocable letter of credit:

   i) The importer can obtain help and advice from his bankers in calling for appropriate documents for the type of goods ordered and can stipulate latest dates for shipment and presentation of documents.

ii) Payment will only be made against documents specified by the importer and called for under the credit.

iii) Documents called for under the credit will not be paid until they are strictly in accordance with the terms and conditions of the credit. The letter of credit can also state that an indemnity is not acceptable for discrepancies in the documents (see below c) iv)).

iv) The importer may be able to obtain a longer credit period than otherwise if a letter of credit was not issued in favour of the supplier.

v) Depending upon the contract between buyer and seller it may be possible for the importer to be able to pass on all costs to the exporter. Again this will depend upon the bargaining strength of the two parties.

vi) Some protection may be offered by the fact that the letter of credit will be issued and be subject to Uniform Customs and Practice for Documentary Credits, Publication No. 500.

vii) If the importer can produce a documentary credit, it gives him status in the eyes of the seller.

c)   Protection (some of the disadvantages might be removed and the highest degree of protection can be obtained by the importer, by observing some or all of the following):

i) The importer should obtain appropriate status reports on suppliers, not only from the point of view of credit, but wherever possible from the point of view of their technical capability, etc.

ii) Irrevocable letters of credit should, wherever possible, be arranged through the correspondent or office of the importer's own bank. This gives some protection in that the advising bank should be reasonable and trustworthy, being chosen by the importer's own bank.

iii) It is possible to call for third-party documentation, i.e. an inspection certificate covering the quality, quantity, condition, etc. of the goods.

iv) To obtain the maximum protection, the credit should clearly state that the documents must be presented strictly in accordance with the terms of the credit and that a banker's indemnity is not allowed.

v) It is possible to restrict negotiation or payment of documents to an office/subsidiary of the issuing bank, which should protect the applicant to some extent.

vi) If short sea journeys are involved, or air freight is used, it is possible to diminish demurrage costs. This is done by asking for evidence to be presented as part of the documentation required by the letter of credit. Such a document should state that a negotiable shipping document or a document required for Customs clearance has been forwarded by registered mail.

Alternatively, it can state that such a document has been placed in the carrier's bag addressed to the importer or the importer's clearing agent.

vii) It might be possible, subject to the relative strength of the parties, to call for revocable letters of credit.

22.6 Comparison of Avalisation and Documentary Credit Facilities from the Point of View of the Importer's Bank

a) Similarities
Each facility involves the bank in guaranteeing the indebtedness of the customer. Therefore, the facilities are only available to good customers.

b) Differences

i) Avalisation is usually unsecured, in that the collection is clean, or documents are released on acceptance.

ii) The issuing bank can gain a measure of protection by calling for suitable documents under a documentary credit (e.g. third-party inspection certificate). Such protection is not available for avalisation.

iii) Documentary credits can be issued on any mutually agreed terms between the bank and the applicant. Avalisation is normally confined to bills of exchange of minimum amounts of £10,000.

iv) Avalisation facilities can be agreed quickly; documentary credits take more time to set up.

v) In the UK, there is no statutory recognition of avalisation. Thus, the UK bank will require a special indemnity from its customer to authorise reimbursement of any money paid by the bank to the presenter of the bill.

22.7 Self-assessment Questions

Question 1
Why will the granting of a documentary credit restrict an applicant's total borrowing facilities?

Question 2
A bank has issued a documentary credit which calls for a complete set of clean, shipped on board, bills of lading, blank endorsed. The credit calls for sight drafts. On presentation, the documents are in order, but the applicant is insolvent. Briefly explain what the issuing bank will do.

Question 3
A bank has issued a documentary credit calling for a complete set of clean bills of lading, blank endorsed. The credit calls for term drafts. On presentation, the documents are in order, but the issuing bank fears that the applicant will be insolvent by the due date.

Briefly explain what the issuing bank could do.

Question 4
The applicant is completing an application form for a transaction with CFR Incoterms. Should he call for an insurance document?

Question 5
What is meant by **cash cover** in connection with an applicant's contingent liability to the issuing bank?

Question 6
A documentary credit calls for air waybills which name the importer as consignee. Will the bank be able to look upon the goods as security for the contingent liability of the customer?

Question 7
A documentary credit application form requests the issuing bank to use airmail to pass on the details to the advising bank. To what other detail on the form should the issuing bank refer, before accepting this instruction?

Question 8
Name one type of organisation which could issue a third-party inspection certificate. In which country, exporter's or importer's, is the organisation situated?

Question 9
Documents are presented to the issuing bank under the terms of a documentary credit. What is the first act of the issuing bank if it sees a discrepancy in the documents?

Question 10
What particular information would an issuing bank request if it took a status enquiry on the beneficiary of a documentary credit?

(Answers given in Appendix VI)

Unit 23

Transferable Letters of Credit and Back-to-back Letters of Credit

Objectives

On completion of this unit the student should be able to:

● understand and explain the nature of transferable credits;

● differentiate between transferable and back-to-back credits;

● appreciate the differences between transferable credits, back-to-back credits, red clause credits and produce loans.

23.1 Description of a Transferable Credit and Situations when Transferable Credit can be Used

A transferable credit is defined in Article 48 of the Uniform Customs and Practice for Documentary Credits (UCP). Under UCP a credit is only transferable if it is expressly designated transferable by the issuing bank. Terms such as 'divisible', 'assignable', 'transmissible' and 'fractionable' do not render a credit transferable.

The transferable credit will be used when the supplier of goods sells them through a middleman and does not deal directly with the ultimate buyer. If the supplier is in a strong bargaining position, he may insist that a documentary credit be set up in his favour.

The middleman may not wish to arrange a documentary credit himself, and his bankers in any case may not be willing to issue a credit on his behalf. Thus the middleman will approach the ultimate buyer and ask him to arrange a transferable documentary credit in his (the middleman's) favour. The middleman is known as the first beneficiary of the credit.

The credit will be designated transferable, and will allow the first beneficiary to request the bank authorised to pay, incur a deferred payment undertaking, accept or negotiate, or in the case of a freely negotiable credit the bank specifically authorised as the transferring bank to make the credit available to one or more third parties who are known as 'second beneficiaries'. Thus the original supplier of the goods is known as the second beneficiary.

23.2 The Terms on which the First Beneficiary can Authorise Transfer of the Rights under the Credit to the Second Beneficiary

The transferring bank shall be under no obligation to transfer the credit, unless it agrees to do so. A transferable credit can be transferred only once, thus the second beneficiary or beneficiaries cannot transfer their rights to a third beneficiary.

The transfer will be in accordance with the terms of the original credit except for:

a) The name and address of the first beneficiary will be shown instead of that of the applicant.

b) The amount of the credit and unit price may be reduced to allow for the middleman's profit.

c) The expiry date (and last permissible date for shipment if one is stipulated) will be earlier than on the original credit.

d) The percentage for which insurance cover must be effected may be increased to provide the amount of cover stipulated in the original credit.

It is the transferring bank, acting on the instructions of the first beneficiary, who will advise the credit to the second beneficiary.

The first beneficiary must irrevocably instruct the transferring bank whether or not it may advise any subsequent amendments to the second beneficiary.

23.3 Operation of a Transferable Credit when the Second Beneficiary has Shipped his Goods and Presented his Documents

The second beneficiary will present his documents. usually via his own bankers, to the transferring bank. The invoice and bill of exchange will be for less than the amount advised to the first beneficiary. On receipt of the documents, the transferring bank will substitute the invoice of the first beneficiary and replace his bill of exchange with one for the full amount of the credit.

The transferring bank will then present the documents to the issuing bank and obtain payment. on receipt of the funds, the amount claimed by the second beneficiary will be paid to him, and the difference will be paid over to the middleman as his profit. If for any reason the first beneficiary fails to present his own invoices, the transferring bank may send to the issuing bank the documents it has received, including the second beneficiary's invoices without further responsibility to the first beneficiary.

23.4 Uniform Customs and Practice

Students should note the following points:

a) UCP cover all aspects except those expressly covered by the terms of the credit.

b) All authorities stipulate **subject to UCP 1993**.

c) Transferable credits are covered in Article 48.

d) A credit can only be transferred if it is expressly stated to be transferable.

e) The first beneficiary can only request the bank to transfer. The bank is not obliged to do so.

f) The first beneficiary must pay all charges and the bank need not effect the transfer until charges are paid.

g) The credit can be transferred only on the terms and conditions specified in the original credit, except for lower amount, lower price per unit, earlier expiry date/date of shipment. The first beneficiary can call for the second beneficiary to provide the full amount of insurance, based on the price paid by the applicant.

h) Under Article 49, the fact that a credit is not stated to be transferable shall not affect the beneficiary's right to assign any proceeds to which he may become entitled under the credit (see Unit 17, 17.7(c)).

23.5 Transferable Credits: Flow Charts

a) The Arrangements for Setting up the Credit

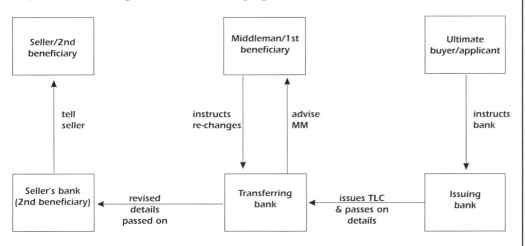

Changes in details when transferring bank pass on details:

a) 1st beneficiary's name substituted for applicant's;

b) Lower amount;

c) Earlier expiry date;

Note

Only credits which expressly say they are transferable can be transferred (Article 48 UCP).

b)   Presentation of Documents under TLC

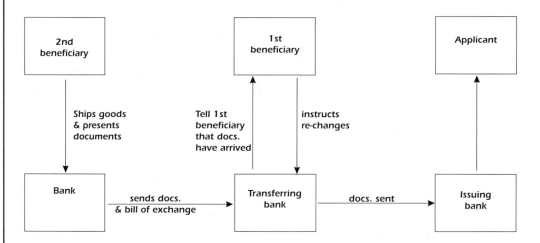

Changes in documents when transferring bank send them to issuing bank:

a)   Substitutes 1st beneficiary's invoices which will be for a higher amount;

b)   Substitutes a new bill of exchange for the full amount;

c)   Payment under TLC (Ignore complexities of nostro/vostro accounts).

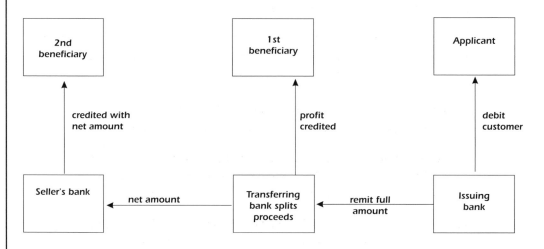

Note

Goods shipped direct from seller's country to ultimate buyer's country.

23.6 Back-to-back Credits

a)   Description or Back-to-back Credits and Situations When they Can Be Used

Back-to-back credits consist of two entirely separate documentary credits, but one credit may act as security for the other. They apply in transactions when original suppliers and ultimate buyers deal through a middleman. In fact, back-to-back credits are used in the same situations as transferable credits, but the rights and obligations of the parties differ with the two types of credit.

If the supplier insists on a documentary credit, the middleman may apply to his bankers for them to issue one on his behalf. If the middleman's bankers are satisfied as to his creditworthiness, they will issue the credit in the normal way and no other formalities will apply. However, the 'back-to-back' aspect comes into play if the middleman's bankers insist that the middleman obtains a documentary credit in his favour from the ultimate buyer as security for one which the middleman has applied for in favour of the seller.

Only the middleman and his banker need know of the back-to-back aspect, and only they are concerned with the back-to-back aspect. The other parties, that is the ultimate buyer, the original supplier and their bankers, are not affected in any way whatsoever by the back-to-back aspect.

b) Procedure for Arranging Back-to-Back Credits When the Middleman's Bankers Require a Documentary Credit as Security for a Credit They Are Asked to Issue

i) The middleman asks the ultimate buyer to arrange a documentary credit in his favour. This is known as the 'first credit'.

ii) The middleman then requests his bankers to issue a credit in favour of the supplier of the goods. This is known as the 'second credit' and the middleman is the applicant for the second credit. The second credit will not be issued until the first one has been advised.

iii) The second credit must call for the same documents as the first credit, apart from the invoices, and must have an earlier expiry date and be for a lower amount than the first credit.

c) Procedure When the Original Supplier Ships his Goods and Presents the Documents in Accordance with the Second Credit

i) The documents are presented via the supplier's advising bank to the issuing bank which is the bank of the middleman. This issuing bank pays the supplier, debiting the middleman by way of a separate loan.

ii) The middleman's bankers, who will be the advising bank of the first credit, substitute the middleman's invoices for those of the supplier. The bill of exchange will be for a higher amount and will agree with the amount on the new invoices.

iii) The middleman's bankers, then, as advising bank of the first credit, present the documents to the issuing bank.

iv) The issuing bank of the first credit pays in accordance with the terms, debiting the cost to the ultimate buyer.

v) On receipt of the proceeds of the first credit, the middleman's bankers clear the loan account in the name of the middleman and any surplus represents the middleman's profit.

d)   Liabilities of the Parties with Back-to-back Credits

The credits are entirely separate instruments, and thus the middleman and his bank are responsible for paying the second credit irrespective of whether payment is subsequently received under the first credit.

The second credit must have an earlier expiry date than the first, otherwise the documents required to procure payment under the first credit would not be available in time. It is a good precaution to make the second credit expire in the place of issue otherwise the issuing bank is in the hands of the postal authorities, and delayed receipt of documents could mean non-payment under the first credit.

23.7   Comparison of Difference between Transferable and Back-to-back Credits

a)   With transferable credits the ultimate buyer is aware that he is dealing with a middleman; with back-to-back credits he is not.

(b) With transferable credits the middleman and his bankers have no liability, but with back-to-back credits they are fully liable on the second credit.

23.8   Position when the First Credit Calls for an Insurance Document

a)   When the Second Credit Does Not Call for an Insurance Document

In this case the middleman's bankers must make sure that their customer has insured and can produce the appropriate document in time for presentation under the first credit.

b)   Where the Second Credit Calls for an Insurance Document

Care must be taken to stipulate that the amount of insurance evidenced by the document required by the second credit is sufficient to meet the amount of insurance required by the first credit.

This may seem self-evident, but it must be remembered that the amount of cover is generally based on the amount of the invoice. Since the invoice value of the second credit is less than that of the first credit, the second credit must specify a sufficiently high amount of cover.

Note

There are no special rules in UCP to deal with back-to-back credits. Each credit stands on its own merits.

23.9 'Cash Flow' from the Point of View of the Middleman

a)   Transferable Credits

There are no debits to the account at all. When the funds are paid over the middleman's bank credit him with the 'profit' and pay the balance to the second beneficiary. The only entry on the middleman's bank account will be a credit for the profit.

b)   Back-to-back Credits

The middleman is the applicant for the second credit and the beneficiary of the first credit. The second credit has the earlier expiry date, and so the middleman will be debited with the full amount of the second credit, and shortly afterwards will be credited with payment of the full amount of the first credit. There will be two separate entries on the account:

a)   debit for the amount of the second credit;

b)   a credit for the amount of the first credit.

23.10 Self-assessment Questions

Your customer, Dealer, has arranged for a shipment of widgets from Brazil to Australia, but the Brazilian seller requires a documentary credit (irrevocable) in his favour.

You are unwilling to become involved in hazardous liabilities on behalf of Dealer.

Question 1
In what way can this deal be completed and a documentary credit arranged in favour of the Brazilian?

Question 2
Who are the applicant(s)/beneficiaries under the credit(s)?

Question 3
The transaction consists of 1,000 tons at US $S per ton bought from Brazil, and sold to Australia at US $5.50. What amounts are advised to the various banks concerned? Assume for the purposes of this question that the credit specifically excludes any '5% tolerance' regarding amounts.

Question 4
After the credit(s) have been issued and advised, who will actually present the documents?

Question 5
What changes will our bank make on receipt of the documents?

Question 6
Payment under the credit is to be by TT reimbursement from the issuing bank. Assume documents show 1,000 tons shipped.

    a)   Which bank accounts will be used to carry out the transaction (i.e. nostro or vostro)?

    b)   How much will our bank receive and from whom?

    c)   How will our bank distribute the proceeds?

Question 7
If no forward contract has been arranged, at what rate will the proceeds be converted when they are credited to Dealer's sterling account? (Specify buying or selling.)

Question 8
For how many dollars would the forward contract be arranged if our customer decided to cover forward?

Question 9
What happens if there is a discrepancy in the documents presented by the second beneficiary?

    a)   Is our bank at risk?

    b)   Does our customer have to pay anything?

Question 10

The credit would call for bills of lading. The bills of lading would show movement of:

a) What goods?

b) From which port?

c) To which destination?

(Answers given in Appendix VI)

23.11 Question on Transferable and Back-to-back Credits

Question

Your customer, X Ltd, has recently received a contract for the sale of fertiliser to India for a contract price of £1 million.

X Ltd requires to import some phosphate from Australia. This phosphate is to be processed in X's factory as part of the fertiliser.

The Australian phosphate manufacturer requires a documentary credit for £0.5m.

Required

State whether back-to-back or transferable credits are appropriate here.

(Specimen Answer given in Appendix VI)

23.12 Revision Questions

Please attempt to answer the following three questions, and then compare your solution with the following answers.

Question 1: Held & Sons
Your customers, Held & Sons, decide to accept a quotation from France for the supply of special steel. The suppliers ask them to arrange, in accordance with Uniform Customs and Practice for Documentary Credits, an irrevocable documentary credit which is transferable and confirmed.

a) Describe precisely but briefly what it is that the seller requires.

b) Explain the seller's possible reason for the stipulation that the credit be transferable.

c) In view of the request that the credit be transferable, what factor should your customers consider before proceeding, and what particular document would they be wise to insist should be provided under the documentary credit?

Question 2: Junk Galore
Your customers, Junk Galore Ltd, are negotiating to purchase goods from overseas for the first time. They advise you that they wish to purchase electronic calculators and that their suppliers have asked for an irrevocable letter of credit to be established in their favour. Under the terms of the letter of credit, the bills of exchange will be drawn on a UK bank in sterling at 90 days sight. You are also advised that shipment will be effected by sea and that the price basis is CIF UK port. Junk Galore Ltd have a contract to supply a buyer in the south of England within one month of the goods being received in the UK. Your customers' facilities are fully extended but you would like to assist them in financing this import.

Required
Brief notes listing:

a) The points you must consider from the bank's point of view when establishing a letter of credit on behalf of your customer and the protection which may be available in the transaction itself.

b) The practical steps necessary to ensure that at all stages the bank is fully protected.

Question 3: Trees Cut and Sawn
Trees Cut and Sawn are your customers who are timber importers. They have had difficulty in obtaining supplies of timber from overseas. However, the company has now managed to contact a reputable Norwegian company which has offered, subject to receiving finance for each transaction, to buy timber from various suppliers in Norway and to ship the timber to the UK for Trees Cut and Sawn.

Required
Explain briefly any methods by which your customers might arrange for the finance of such transactions by using only documentary credits. In your answer give details of the various steps to be taken, and the part played by all the parties involved, indicating their respective responsibilities.

(Model Answers given in Appendix VI)

Revision Questions 4

The following questions are selected from various parts of the syllabus. You are advised to attempt written answers and then to compare your answers with those given in Appendix VII.

Multiple-choice Questions

(Please tick correct answer)

Question 1

Your bank is nominated as paying bank under a documentary credit which describes the goods as '5 tonnes of Chilean full fishmeal'.

Which of the following documents would you accept? (Assume that all other aspects of the credit have been complied with.)

   a)   An invoice describing the goods as '5 tonnes of Chilean fishmeal'.

   b)   A bill of lading describing the goods as '5.25 tonnes of Chilean full fishmeal'.

   c)   An invoice describing the goods as '5.5 tonnes of Chilean full fishmeal'.

   d)   A bill of lading describing the goods as '4.5 tonnes of Chilean full fishmeal'.

Question 2

The expiry date of a documentary credit is Sunday, 24 February, and documents have to be presented to you. Which of the following is an acceptable presentation? (Assume there is no latest stated date for shipment stipulated.)

   a)   Presentation to you on Monday, 25 February with the bill of lading dated 25 February.

   b)   Presentation on Tuesday, 26 February with the bill of lading dated Sunday, 24 February.

   c)   Presentation on Monday, 25 February with bill of lading dated Sunday, 24 February.

   d)   Presentation on Friday, 22 February with bill of lading dated 29 January.

Question 3

Your customer is a UK importer who has arranged to sell the goods to someone else in the UK. You have issued a documentary credit which undertakes to pay sight drafts, but the ultimate UK buyer is not due to pay until three months after the arrival of the goods in the UK. Which operation will minimise the bank's risks under the credit?

    a) Transferable credits;

    b) Red clause documentary credits;

    c) Back-to-back credits;

    d) Produce loan procedure.

Question 4

Your customer is a manufacturer who has arranged for shipment of phosphate from an Australian seller. The phosphate is to be used by the customer to manufacture fertiliser for sale to an Indian buyer.

A confirmed irrevocable credit has been set up in favour of your customer, and he is now required to set up a documentary credit in favour of the Australian. Which type of documentary credit is applicable?

    a) Transferable;

    b) Back-to-back;

    c) Revolving;

    d) None of these.

Question 5

Your customer, X Ltd, has arranged a deal whereby an Australian ships some bauxite to America. The Australian is selling to X Ltd for US $30,000, and the American has agreed to pay X Ltd US $35,000. A transferable credit is set up, and X Ltd covers the transaction forward. What forward contracts would be taken out?

    a) Bank to buy $5,000;

    b) Bank to sell $35,000 and buy $30,000;

    c) Bank to sell $30,000 and buy $35,000;

    d) Bank to sell $5,000.

Question 6

Who makes the first presentation of documents under a transferable credit?

    a) First beneficiary;

    b) Second beneficiary;

    c) Applicant;

    d) None of these.

Question 7

You are nominated as paying bank and the beneficiary has presented the documents to you. Which of the following circumstances would cause you to refuse payment?

a) You believe that the goods have been damaged.

b) You see that the insurance document contains a clause which covers 'all risks', but then goes on to indicate that certain risks are excluded. The credit stipulates 'insurance against all risks'.

c) The combined transport document is a document approved by the ICC, but issued by a freight forwarder.

d) The invoice description of the goods differs slightly from the description of the goods in the credit.

Question 8

How can the applicant reduce his risks under a documentary credit?

a) Take status enquiry on the beneficiary;

b) Call for a third-party inspection certificate;

c) See if the beneficiary will agree to, say, 80%, payment under a documentary credit and the remaining 20% by open account;

d) All of these.

Question 9

In what circumstances would the beneficiary of a confirmed documentary credit not receive payment?

a) Failure of the applicant;

b) Failure of the issuing bank;

c) Failure to fulfil the credit terms;

d) Failure to fulfil the commercial contract.

Question 10

Your customer is the applicant for a documentary credit. Which of the following points would appear to be illogical if they appeared on the application form?

a) Invoice price shown as FOB, bills of lading to be marked freight paid.

b) Last date for shipment one week before expiry date.

c) Invoice price shown as CFR, but no insurance document requested.

d) No mention of the latest date of shipment.

(Answers given in Appendix VII)

345

Scenario for Exam Questions 1, 2 and 3
UK Auto Mart Ltd

UK Auto Mart Ltd is a medium-sized corporate; it imports car components and spares on a world-wide basis. From humble beginnings, it has grown into a major wholesaler and distributor to the motor trade and also has a network of retail outlets in the UK.

The directors are very experienced and capable and are well regarded by your bank. The financial affairs are run prudently and there have been no problems in obtaining credit-control sanction for facilities.

The company has to date been trading on very favourable terms but the purchasing director, Mr A. Daily, advises you that contracts are at present being negotiated with existing suppliers and less attractive terms are being offered.

Exam Question 1

Please read the scenario above before attempting this question.

UK Auto Mart Ltd has found a new source of components in the USA. Samples have proved to be very good and the company would be able to secure good prices if it was able to provide irrevocable documentary credits payable at sight.

Mr Daily comes to see you and says that the company has been asked for one letter of credit for £400,000 covering shipments over six months.
He has a number of concerns:

1. issuing such a large letter of credit;

2. receiving a consistent quality of goods throughout the life of the contract;

3. experiencing fraud in transit, which he has heard is becoming prevalent in some trades.

Required

a) Your answer to Mr Daily as to whether the letter of credit may cancelled if the first delivery is not up to the standard of the samples already provided or if the company becomes aware of fraud.   [3]

b) Describe ways in which the letter of credit may be worded to cover shipments over a period of six months.   [3]

c) Name and explain documentary evidence that could be built into the letter of credit to minimise the risk of not receiving goods of the quality required. [6]

d) Outline ways in which the letter of credit requested could be reworded to provide a greater degree of protection to UK Auto Mart Ltd.   [8]

[Total marks for question - 20]

(Specimen Answer given in Appendix VII)

Exam Question 2

Please read the scenario opposite before attempting this question.

Most of the trading undertaken by UK Auto Mart Ltd over the years has been on an open account basis.

With the world-wide recession, they are finding that a number of their suppliers are no longer willing to grant the 60 days' credit terms they require, without more secure payment terms.

Whilst UK Auto Mart do not mind the additional costs in issuing letters of credit, Mr Daily is concerned at:

1   having to handle shipping documents;

2   encountering problems because of delays in the movement of this paperwork.

He books an appointment to discuss the possible alternatives.

Required

a)   Name and describe other payment terms that might be arranged by Mr Daily as an alternative to the current open account terms, apart from documentary credits.   [12]

b)   Which of the methods you have described in (a) above would provide secure payment terms?   [5]

c)   Which of the terms you have suggested in (a) above would overcome the problem of handling shipping documents and possible delays in the movement of paperwork?   [3]

[Total marks for question - 20]

(Specimen Answer given in Appendix VII)

Exam Question 3

Please read the scenario opposite before attempting this question.

In view of the vast range of components, it is not possible for UK Auto Mart Ltd to stock every line.

Instead, they have arrangements with a relatively small number of suppliers in the EU to provide hundreds of shipments of components on 'adjust in time' basis by air or road. Clean payments are required on receipt of goods.

The company has tended to settle by cheque in sterling or foreign currency, using the cheque book on their sterling account. The suppliers have been complaining about the time and cost in clearing these cheques.

UK Auto Mart are keen to keep their suppliers happy and Mr Daily writes to ask about ways of overcoming this problem.

Required

a) List the alternative methods of payment which will provide cleared funds more quickly.   [4]

b) Outline developments that have been taking place in Europe to streamline international payments.   [10]

c) Explain the potential benefits of these new services. [6]

[Total marks for question - 20]

(Specimen Answer given in Appendix VII)

Exam Question 4

Far East Crafts Ltd, your customer, imports goods from the Far East into the UK on a collection basis. Documents of title are accompanied by drafts drawn at 60 days' sight.

Problems have arisen in the past owing to:

i)   goods being consigned to your bank without your authority;

ii) collection orders containing no indication as to whether documents are to be released against payment (D/P) or acceptance (D/A);

iii) Far East Crafts Ltd accepting a bill of exchange, examining the goods and subsequently offering partial payment of the accepted bill of exchange;

iv) Far East Crafts Ltd refusing to pay bank charges claimed by remitting banks in their collection order.

You see your customer to discuss these problems, and you explain your bank's position under URC, as all collections have been presented to you under the protection of these international rules.

Required

a) Brief notes indicating the responsibilities of your bank under current URC regarding:

   i)   goods consigned to the bank without authority;   [4]

   ii) failure of the collection instruction to indicate the basis upon which documents are to be released: [4]

   iii) the offer of a partial payment to you by your customer after the company has obtained the underlying documents by accepting a bill of exchange;   [3]

   iv) the refusal of your customer to pay the charges claimed by the remitting bank.   [3]

b) Your explanation, with regard to a) iii) above, of how you would deal with an offer of partial payment in accordance with normal UK banking practice.[6]

[Total marks for question - 20]

(Specimen Answer given in Appendix VII)

Exam Question 5

Your customers, Scrap Metals Ltd, are scrap metal dealers exploiting the flourishing merchanting trade between the USA and the Far East. They buy scrap metal from the USA and sell it to buyers in the Republic of Korea, Republic of China (Taiwan) and Japan.

The American suppliers generally require secure methods of payment, and your customers have been able to arrange for the buyers in the Far East to establish in their favour (i.e. the first beneficiary - your customers) an irrevocable letter of credit. transferable in whole or in part, some of the terms of which are as follows:

Amount: about US $1m.
Expiry: 10 July in London (i.e. at your counters).
Covering: a shipment of non-ferrous metal scrap to be effected in one lot between 1 May and 30 June inclusive.
Shipment: from San Francisco to Kaohsiung.

On 1 April, you, as the advising bank, are asked to transfer 75% of the value of the letter of credit in favour of a second beneficiary - the US Scrap Company Incorporated, San Francisco. On the same day, your customers ask you to cover their potential earnings of US $250,000 forward, based upon the following rates:

1 April	Spot $1.7755	$1.7775
1 month forward	0.36 cents discount	0.41 cents discount
2 months forward	1.18 cents discount	1.23 cents discount
3 months forward	2.40 cents discount	2.45 cents discount
15 May	Spot 1.7950	1.8000

The documents are presented in order at your counters on 15 May. The documents cover a shipment valued at US $760,000 exactly. On that day, your customers substitute their invoices to allow claims for the full value of the scrap metal shipped. In effect, they are increasing the value of their invoices by one third of the value of the invoices presented by the second beneficiary. This claim brings it into line with the amount available under the letter of credit.

Note

For the purposes of this question, assume the entries win be passed on the day that the documents are presented, namely, 15 May. Ignore the proceeds which will be made available to the second beneficiary in the USA and any commissions which might be claimed in connection with documents presented under the credit.

Required

a) Your calculations showing the rates which would be applied. and a final figure of the sterling proceeds which will be credited to your customers' account.

[10]

b) BRIEF notes indicating any specific international rules which apply to this particular transaction.

[10]

[Total marks for question - 20]

(Specimen Answer given in Appendix VII)

Scenario for Exam Questions 6 and 7
Euro Multinational Co. Ltd

Euro Multinational Co. Ltd is the UK subsidiary of a US corporation, World-wide Machinery Inc. Euro Multinational has a sterling account with your bank and is an important customer.

You handle regular urgent transfers in US dollars to the parent company in settlement of goods imported. Euro Multinational issues such instructions after notification of the arrival of the goods in the UK.

Up until now, the company has used spot rates, but the new finance director, Mr Money, is keen to explore other ways of fixing exchange rates.

The following market report with closing rates appeared in the *Financial Times* on Tuesday, 26 January:

"The dollar fell nearly two pfennigs against the D-Mark in European trading yesterday. After closing in London at DEM l.5900 on Friday night, the US currency tumbled to a low of DEM1.5690 before closing at DEM1.5725.

Sterling consolidated against the D-Mark following last week's sharp fall. It closed at DEM2.4525, Up 1 3/4 pfennigs on the day, helped by a report from the Confederation of British Industry (CBI) on business confidence."

Pound spot - forward against the pound

	Close	
US dollars	1.5590- 1.5600	
One month	0.56 - 0.54 cpm	4.23% p.a.
Three months	1.46 - 1.43 cpm	3.71% p.a.
Eurocurrency interest rates		

	One Month	*Three months*
Sterling	71/16 - 75/l6	71/16 - 615/16
US dollars	33/16 - 31/16	35/16 - 33/16

Exam Question 6

Please read the scenario opposite before attempting this question.

The finance director of Euro Multinational Co. Ltd, Mr Money, visits you on 26 January to obtain information based on the FT market report.

Required

a) An indication of the costs in sterling of remitting US $250,000 value in two working days' time by SWIFT transfer to the US parent company.

   Calculate the cost to two places of decimals using the rates given in the FT market report. [2]

b) Mr Money asks approximately how many US $ Euro Multinational could have remitted to its parent company if it had received DEM2m and converted it to US $ on 25 January.

   Make your calculations using the closing rate from the FT report. [2]

c) Mr Money asks what details are agreed in a forward exchange contract and what the conditions of such a contract are.

   List the information he requires. [10]

d) The company has a payment of US $2m to make to its parent company in three months' time. Mr Money requests an approximate cost of covering the transaction forward.

   Calculate the cost in sterling to two places of decimals using the rates given in the FT market report. [2]

e) Mr Money want to know what is meant by '4.23% p.a.' quoted in the FT market report.

   Give an explanation and shown how the figure is calculated. [4]

[Total marks for question - 20]

(Specimen Answer given in Appendix VII)

Note
For the purposes of this question, one year should be expressed as 360 days and each month as 30 days. Ignore any bank charges or commissions.

Exam Question 7

Please read the scenario opposite before attempting this question.

a) Euro Multinational's finance director, Mr Money, telephones to say that he is pleased to read of the dollar's weakness.

   Mr Money notes that the market reacted favourably to the growth in UK business confidence. He asks what other factors might affect the sterling/dollar rate.

Required

i) Why should Mr Money be pleased at the dollar's weakness? [2]

ii) Name the main factors that affect exchange rates and explain how they might affect the sterling/US $ exchange rate. [8]

iii) Would your answer in ii) above be different if you were asked to give the factors that affect the sterling/DEM rate?

Give reasons for your answer. [4]

b) Euro Multinational is considering a contract to on-sell goods to a UK buyer, Regional Distribution plc, and payment is expected seven working days after delivery to the UK buyer.

Mr Money asks whether he could invoice Regional Distribution in US $ to avoid exchange risk.

Required

i) What banking arrangements could Euro Multinational make with your bank to ensure that there would be no exchange risk if it invoiced Regional Distribution in US $? [3]

ii) What procedures should Regional Distribution follow to pay Euro Multinational in US $? [3]

[Total marks for question - 20]

(Specimen Answer given in Appendix VII)

Exam Question 8

Special Optics has the opportunity to quote for a large export order to a major company in Germany. It normally trades in irrevocable documentary credit terms.

The Managing Director, Mr Glass, wishes to consider two ways of obtaining payment which he has heard about recently:

1. For Special Optics to draw a bill of exchange at 30 days' sight and send the bill directly to the German company's bankers, a leading German bank.

2. For the German company to send Special Optics a promissory note avalised by the German bank prior to shipment. Mr Glass would ask your bank to collect the proceeds of the promissory note at maturity as an outward bill for collection.

Required:

a) List and explain the advantages and disadvantages to Special Optics of the two options listed above in comparison with its usual requirement of irrevocable documentary credit terms. [10]

b) How would the procedures to obtain payment after shipment differ in 1 and 2 above? [4]

c) Describe the main features of the accelerated bills service provided by some UK banks as an alternative to the two systems mentioned above. [6]

[Total marks for question - 20]

(Specimen Answer given in Appendix VII)

Note

For the purposes of this question, ignore the possibility of stamp duty being payable abroad on either bills of exchange or promissory notes.

Exam Question 9

Builders Merchants Ltd, customers of your bank, supply the building construction industry with a wide range of building materials and products. Their Financial Director, Mr Kit Chendor, calls to see you to discuss a CIF contract, which has been signed, to supply a range of fittings and building materials to an overseas buyer.

During your conversation you discover that many of the goods will be bought from overseas as well as in the UK and that all the suppliers are insisting upon secure methods of payment. The Financial Director asks you to suggest a method by which his company can be fully protected, since cash-flow considerations are causing some concern at the present time. The overseas CIF contract is expressed in sterling but one supplier, based in Germany, is insisting upon being paid in Deutschmarks.

Required

a) A brief description of the basic instrument which would be appropriate in answering the needs of Builders Merchants Ltd. Indicate why your suggestion will cater for your customers by assisting them to overcome their cash-flow difficulties and why it will also give some comfort to their potential suppliers. [10]

b) State briefly whether the method described by you in a) is, or is not. appropriate to the contract with the German supplier. Give reasons for your answer. [4]

c) A compromise that you would consider arranging for Builders Merchants Ltd, which would assist them in complying with the request of the German supplier, bearing in mind that the German company requires security of payment. [6]

[Total marks for question - 20]

(Specimen Answer given in Appendix VII)

Q

Exam Question 10

Your customers, Northern Trading, are finding it difficult to obtain adequate sources of supply of raw materials for their operation in the UK. They have identified an Australian manufacturer who can meet their needs against secure methods of payment. You have been asked to establish an irrevocable letter of credit in favour of the Australian suppliers but the customers advise you that they do not understand the implications for the company.

They would like to know:

a) What is an irrevocable letter of credit?   [8]

b) The basic documents they should call for and the details which they would expect to find in those documents if the bank agreed to establish a letter of credit.   [6]

c) Any precautions that the buyers can take to ensure that they receive the goods they have contracted to buy, while at the same time satisfying the seller's needs.   [6]

State briefly, in note form, what you would tell your customer.

[Total marks for question - 20]

(Specimen Answer given in Appendix VII)

Exam Question 11

Bric-a-Brac Ltd have a number of outlets at holiday resorts in various parts of the UK. Traditionally, they have purchased fancy goods from local wholesalers but now find their prices are unattractive. Ceside Crafts of Manila have offered to supply them with a whole range of products but insist upon secure methods of payment at sight on a CIF UK port basis. To the benefit of their cash flow, your customers had in the past been able to obtain sufficient credit (90 days) from the wholesalers to enable them to sell the goods before having to pay for them.

Required

a) Brief notes describing a method of payment which would afford Ceside Crafts the protection they need and, at the same time, take account of the cash-flow requirements of Bric-a-Brac Ltd.   [10]

b) A brief description of the documents you would expect the sellers to provide for your customer.   [10]

[Total marks for question - 20]

(Specimen Answer given in Appendix VII)

Exam Question 12

Your customer, Thermapants Ltd, manufactures underwear and is finding ready markets in France and Germany. Sales have always been invoiced in sterling but your customer's cash-flow position has suffered because there has been some delay in receiving payment on the due dates.

The French buyer readily accepts bills of exchange drawn at 30 days' sight sent direct to him by Thermapants Ltd but the funds do not arrive until some six weeks after the bills fall due. As regards the German buyer, he usually forwards his own cheque drawn in sterling and this takes some time to clear, thus putting additional pressure on the company's cash-flow situation.

The company's financial director, Mr Lonjon, calls to see you to find out if there is any way in which you can assist the company in reducing the time before cleared funds are actually credited to the company's account. You understand that the French buyer is unwilling to arrange for documentary letters of credit, but nevertheless you are asked if there is any scheme under which the bank can assist in trying to cut down the delay before funds are received for the credit of your customer's account.

Required

a) A description of:

    i)   a basic method by which the bank can help the customer to obtain payment without unacceptable delays;   [4]

    ii)   a specific variation of the basic method which would be suitable for the needs of the French buyer, who obviously requires a period of credit before paying for the goods;   [5]

    iii)   a specific variation of the basic method which would be suitable for the German buyer, who is perfectly willing to pay as soon as he is requested to do so.   [5]

b) Explain how the method in ii) and iii) above will give some protection to Thermapants Ltd, and indicate reasons why the buyers in France and Germany could be expected to comply with any conditions regarding payment.   [6]

[Total marks for question - 20]

(Specimen Answer given in Appendix VII)

Exam Question 13

As manager of a branch of a bank in the UK, you learn that the London office of an overseas bank is complaining about the delay in effecting settlement of a documentary collection sent to your branch.

The collection instruction was accompanied by a 30 days' sight draft on D/A terms and a full set of bills of lading. Protest instructions were not given in the collection instruction but you were asked to contact the remitting bank if any difficulty arose. The documents, together with the bills of exchange for acceptance, were sent 'in trust' to your respected customer, XYZ Ltd. Although 45 days have passed since the customer received the documents and bills of exchange, you still have not received an acceptance.

You now discover that XYZ Ltd examined the goods and arranged for half to be delivered to a customer. The other half are at present being unloaded at the docks. XYZ Ltd is prepared to pay for half the value of the goods and to negotiate with the suppliers for the balance, since it claims that the goods were not in accordance with the agreed specification.

Required
In brief note form, a statement of:

    i)   your position under United Kingdom law and banking practice.   [12]

    ii)   the action which you should immediately take.   [8]

[Total marks for question - 20]

(Specimen Answer given in Appendix VII)

Exam Question 14

A. Clothier, senior director of your customers, Cover-up Ltd, is negotiating for the first time with suppliers abroad to purchase some outerwear garments, which are at present unobtainable in the UK. The terms of payment which the sellers have suggested are a 90 days' sight draft D/A with presentation through a UK bank. You understand that the presentation will be subject to Uniform Rules for Collections (and the shipping terms are to be CFR UK port). Your customer believes that he will have the opportunity of examining the goods when they are received in the UK and that, if they are not in accordance with specification, he can refuse the goods and will not be liable to pay the sellers, since all charges will be against the goods.

Required

    a)   Brief notes on the terms of payment mentioned above;   [4]

    b)   The instructions you would expect to see on the collection order;   [9]

    c)   What you would say to the suggestion by Mr Clothier that, if the goods were not in accordance with specification, the company could refuse to take them up and pay for them.   [7]

[Total marks for question - 20]

(Specimen Answer given in Appendix VII)

Exam Question 15

Angles and Saxons Ltd, a substantial customer of yours, imports a range of farming machinery from Germany.

The invoices are normally expressed in Deutschmarks, and are accompanied by a collection instruction and a bill of exchange, drawn and payable at 60 days after the date of the invoice. No documents of title are attached to the collection instruction. The German bank's instructions are to release documents against acceptance, but no protest instructions are given.

You have usually presented the bills of exchange to your customer for acceptance, but the company has not always been meticulous about returning the accepted bills to you. Difficulties have also arisen because your customer often attempts to delay payment of the bills of exchange and owing to the standing of the company you have not wished to apply any pressure with regard to these collections.

You have now received a claim from the remitting bank for your customer's account for one month's interest, which the German suppliers claim is payable because of the failure of your customer to pay the most recent bill of exchange on the specific maturity date.

Required
Your comments on:

a) your position under current ICC rules in connection with the most recent
    presentation.   [6]

b) your position under UK banking practice in connection with the presentation
    of a bill of exchange for acceptance in circumstances similar to those
    described above.   [6]

c) the position of your bank and your customer in connection with the claim for
    interest   [4]

d) the specific instruction that could be incorporated in future collection
    instructions and would be acceptable under International Rules and UK law
    which might encourage your customer to pay the bills promptly at maturity.
                                                                         [4]
                                          [Total marks for question - 20]

(Specimen Answer given in Appendix VII)

Exam Question 16

Your customer, Far East Traders Ltd, acts as a 'middleman', selling a range of engineering products to various countries in the Far East. One of the directors, a Mr Fixit, calls to see you to discuss a potential contract which the company is hoping to arrange to sell goods to a total value of £0.5m. The proposals are that the supplier of the goods would require a guarantee of payment, and that the eventual purchaser would arrange for some form of undertaking in favour of your customer. As your customer's balance sheet has insufficient strength to finance an operation of this nature, you are asked if you can suggest a banking instrument which would assist your customer.

You understand that the contract will be established in sterling and that the price basis is ex works. The supplier and buyer are aware of one another's existence, but both parties insist that their names are not disclosed to anyone, other than your own bank.

Required

a)   A description of a banking instrument which would cater for the needs of all parties, bearing in mind the customer's financial position. Give reasons for your answer. Include specific reference to the internationally agreed procedures applicable.   [9]

b)   The terms and conditions you would suggest that Mr Fixit insists should be incorporated into the banking instrument. Give your reasons.   [11]

[Total marks for question - 20]

(Specimen Answer given in Appendix VII)

Appendix I

Electronic Commerce

II.1   Background

With the advancement of modern technology international business is being conducted increasingly in a global market place. Business computerisation continues at a phenomenal pace. As a result, the use of paper-based systems is becoming outmoded and inefficient. The days of electronic commerce or 'paperless trading' are therefore upon us and will soon become the accepted norm.

II.2   Electronic Data Interchange (EDI)

EDI has existed in various forms for about thirty years. Because of the increase in trade, the amount of paperwork generated has slowed up the relevant processes and has added substantially to costs both in terms of financial and human resources. Consequently, interest in EDI has grown considerably.

EDI in the business world is the exchange of electronically generated trade related data, whether commercial or financial, between the computers of various parties. Such parties not only include buyers and sellers but also such organisations as freight forwarders, shipping companies, banks and credit insurers.

EDI is facilitated by using agreed message standards. These include EDIFACT (EDI for Administration, Commerce and Transport) and TRADACOMS (Trading Data Communication Standard)

II.3   Benefits of EDI

● Improvements in the time efficiency of trading processes. EDI negates the need to print details of a contract from one computer's file, which are then sent by post to a recipient who then inputs this information onto another computer file.

● Errors from repeated manual input of data are reduced.

● Cost reduction. It has been estimated that costs of processing paperwork in connection with orders can be reduced by up to 90%.

● Automation provides more accurate information on which to base key decisions e.g. cash flow needs, stock requirements.

● By improving business efficiency and cost effectiveness, organisations can increase competitive advantage and profitability.

II.4   Problems Related to Full EDI Implementation

● Initial cost of installing the relevant hardware and software for EDI to operate.

● Additional training costs in ensuring that staff can operate the new systems.

● Having alternative systems on hand in case of a technical breakdown.

● Possibility of fraud due to bogus trade orders or unauthorised payment instructions.

● All trading partners may not be operating EDI systems.

II.5   The Internet

The Internet is a global communications system which links together a wide variety of computer networks throughout the world. Its popularity with both private and commercial users is phenomenal. (The number of users is growing by in excess of 10% per month).

For exporters and importers, the Internet has two particular beneficial services. - electronic mail (known as e-mail) and the World Wide Web (WWW)

E-mail allows parties to send electronic equivalents of letters or memoranda to one another via computer. Linked to this, complete computer files can be sent via e-mail.

WWW provides traders with an electronic shop window for their goods which can be regularly updated. Such traders can have their own WWW.page which can display both graphics and text and can include all relevant information about their goods and services including prices, delivery costs and payment terms. At the present time, most of these are targeting the private consumer but it is only a matter of time before the WWW becomes the forum for global commercial trading.

II.6   Problems with Trading on the Internet

In order for any trade deal to be completed there must be absolute trust between the parties to such a deal. When you are negotiating the purchase of goods face to face, you can at least gain some impression of the person you are dealing with. To achieve a cyberspace impression is somewhat more difficult!

How do you know that the owner of a WWW page is authentic? How does the supplier of goods know that payment will be made? Coupled to these questions, would you be happy sending details of your credit card via the Internet? What would happen if such details were intercepted en route and became known by criminal elements?

In respect of the standing of suppliers or buyers, parties will still have to carry out status enquiries via their banks or credit reference agencies. However, a greater potential problem lies with the security of information supplied via the Internet.

A number of organisations have investigated this problem and in February 1996 Visa International and MasterCard announced a single technical standard known as Secure Electronic Transaction (SET) which would protect the use of payment cards over the Internet.

SET involves the use of digital certificates which authenticate the identity of cardholders making purchases. It therefore provides some security for all parties to such transactions.

Further research into secure electronic commerce procedures is ongoing and readers should try to keep abreast of developments in the financial press.

II.7   Current Electronic Commerce Initiatives

II 7.1 Project Bolero

Project Bolero has been designed to provide a central repository for computerised shipping documents. It monitors electronic bills of lading and identifies the current state of ownership of the goods to which they refer at any time during their transportation. The system indicates all relevant parties including freight forwarders and insurers. In addition to reducing ownership disputes, Project Bolero should seriously reduce delays in payment and clearance of goods through customs.

II. 7.2   International Chamber of Commerce (ICC)

The ICC has under its Project E - 100 looked into the development and promotion of electronic alternatives to paper based systems during the last few years. Under this project various working parties examined such areas as electronic credits; open account trading; electronic transport documents; legal and regulatory matters and how electronic commerce could interface with paper based/auxiliary systems.

From this work has evolved the Electronic Commerce Project (ECP). ECP's main activities will involve the creation/development of international guidelines and policies on electronic commerce and business services. By doing this, and working in partnership with other electronic commerce initiatives, its intention is to aid a more secure transaction environment.

In addition to a steering committee, ECP has three working groups dealing with E-Terms; Electronic Trade Practices and Information Security respectively.

The E-Terms working group is looking at the setting of a repository for electronic terms. The repository is to be designed so that it can be accessed globally and that all contracting parties will be bound by these terms. It is expected that these E-Terms will be either commercial or legal in context. In addition, the E-Terms Repository is likely to house 'Best Practice Rules' for electronic commerce and also relevant treaties, conventions and standards.

The Electronic Trade Practices working group is beginning the creation of electronic trade practice rules similar to the ones which ICC has published in respect of Uniform Rules for Collections.

The Information Security working group aims to have accepted internationally the Uniform International Authentication and Certification Practices publication. This provides details of guidelines relating to authentication procedures and digital signature certification.

The ICC is likely to continue to be a major player in the development of electronic commerce. It has already produced the ' ICC Guide to Electronic Commerce' and, no doubt, will be creating web sites on the Internet.

Appendix II

Correspondent Banking and Competition Between Banks

i)   What is Correspondent Banking?

Now that the whole of the services and facilities have been covered, the student needs to place correspondent banking in context.

In the 1980s, when capital was relatively cheap, many banks tried to expand their own operations abroad, by setting up new offices overseas, or by acquiring a ready-made banking network by means of a takeover. In many instances, these methods have proved to be too great a drain on capital and their operations in any event have not been too successful.

In today's more sober economic climate, some banks now provide an international service for their customers by means of correspondent banks. Correspondent banking simply means that the home country bank will aim to provide overseas services for its own customers by using an overseas, correspondent, bank as agent. Examples of the use of correspondent banks are:

- nostro/vostro accounts used in international settlement to facilitate international funds transfer;

- documentary credits advised via a correspondent bank, with a correspondent bank nominated to pay;

- special technology links (for example, National Westminster Bank and Société Générale), to enable the banks to provide low-cost cross-border funds transfer for their respective customers;

- the willingness to recommend the services of the correspondent bank to facilitate a deal. For example, a UK bank may not wish to agree with a request to provide export factoring services, but it may well investigate whether the importer's bank could offer import factoring to its own customer so that the UK exporter can be paid upfront in cash by the importer.

In international trade, with the onset of the single European market and technology links between banks and customers, the correspondent banks have become an important part of the customer base of any bank with customers who have cross-border business. Fees received by banks for the provision of correspondent banking services can prove to be a significant contribution to total bank profits.

One problem relating to the use of correspondent banks has been the need to ensure that the standard of service of these banks was satisfactory. One major UK bank is currently negotiating a series of 'performance benchmarks' with its overseas correspondent banks. This will provide specific remedies against the correspondent bank should its service be substandard in any way.

The maintenance of a first-class network of correspondent banks will help a bank gain a competitive edge and will generate a useful source of income from the services that the bank provides for its correspondents. Students should always be ready to suggest the use of a correspondent bank to deliver a customer service which our own bank cannot provide.

Management of the correspondent banking relationships is a very complex business. On the one hand, the correspondent is our bank's agent abroad helping our bank to deliver a complete service to our customers. On the other hand, that bank is a customer of ours (e.g. when our bank is collecting bank for an inward collection), and yet at the same time the correspondent is a potential competitor (e.g. our exporter customers may submit documentary collections directly to the overseas correspondent bank).

ii)   Competition between Banks within the EU
Under the EU's Second Banking Co-ordination Directive, there is a 'single banking licence', under which any bank which is authorised to act as such in a member state will also be allowed to set up branches or to supply cross-border services in other member states.

Some European banks have set up pan-European banking groups, offering a wide range of services. both retail and corporate. Now that the single European market is upon us, competition from banks of other member states for UK customer business is bound to increase. Examples already occur whereby banks in Germany encourage UK exporters to route their documentary collections directly to the German bank where the importer maintains his account.

UK banks will no doubt use different strategies to counter the competition, and they will establish a credibility in overseas markets by a mixture of correspondent banking relationships, branch networks acquired via takeovers, or by means of representative offices. It is vital to the UK that the banking system as a whole continues to operate in such a way as to maintain the pre-eminence of London as a major international financial centre.

Appendix III

Uniform Rules for Collections, ICC 522

A.   General Provisions and Definitions

Article 1

Application of URC 522

a) The Uniform Rules for Collections, 1995 Revision, ICC Publication No 522, shall apply to all collections as defined in Article 2 where such rules are incorporated into the text of the 'collection instruction' referred to in Article 4 and are binding on all parties thereto unless otherwise expressly agreed or contrary to the provisions of a national, state or local law and/or regulation which cannot be departed from.

b) Banks shall have no obligation to handle either a collection or any collection instruction or subsequent related instructions.

c) If a bank elects, for any reason, not to handle a collection or any related instructions received by it, it must advise the party from whom it received the collection or the instructions by telecommunication or, if that is not possible, by other expeditious means, without delay.

Article 2

Definition of Collection

For the purposes of these Articles:

a) 'Collection' means the handling by banks of documents as defined in sub-Article 2(b), in accordance with instructions received, in order to

    i)   obtain payment and/or acceptance,

    or

    ii)   deliver documents against payment and/or against acceptance,

    or

    iii)   deliver documents on other terms and conditions.

b) 'Documents' means financial documents and/or commercial documents:

    i)   'Financial documents' means bills of exchange, promissory notes, cheques, or other similar instruments used for obtaining the payment of money;

    ii)   'Commercial documents' means invoices, transport documents, documents of title or other similar documents, or any other documents whatsoever, not being financial documents.

c) 'Clean collection' means collection of financial documents not accompanied by commercial documents.

d) 'Documentary collection' means collection of:

   i)   Financial documents accompanied by commercial documents;

   ii) Commercial documents not accompanied by financial documents.

Article 3

Parties to a Collection

a) For the purposes of these Articles the 'parties thereto' are:

   i.   the 'principal' who is the party entrusting the handling of a collection to a bank;

   ii. the 'remitting bank' which is the bank to which the principal has entrusted the handling of a collection;

   iii) the 'collecting bank' which is any bank other than the remitting bank, involved in processing the collection;

   iv) the 'presenting bank' which is the collecting bank making presentation to the drawee.

b) The 'drawee' is the one to whom presentation is to be made in accordance with the collection instruction.

B.   Form and Structure of Collections

Article 4

Collection Instruction

a) i)   All documents sent tor collection must be accompanied by a collection instruction indicating that the collection is subject to URC 522 and giving complete and precise instructions. Banks are only permitted to act upon the instructions given in such collection instruction, and in accordance with these Rules.

   ii) Banks will not examine documents in order to obtain instructions.

   iii) Unless otherwise authorised in the collection instruction, banks will disregard any instructions from any party/bank other than the partyl/bank from whom they received the collection.

b) A collection instruction should contain the following items of information, as appropriate.

   i)   Details of the bank from which the collection was received including full name, postal and SWIFT addresses, telex, telephone, facsimile numbers and reference.

   ii) Details of the principal including full name, postal address, and if applicable telex, telephone and facsimile numbers.

   iii) Details of the drawee including full name, postal address, or the domicile at which presentation is to be made and if applicable telex, telephone and facsimile numbers.

   iv) Details of the presenting bank, if any, including full name, postal address, and if applicable telex, telephone and facsimile numbers.

   v)   Amount(s) and currency(ies) to be collected.

   vi) List of documents enclosed and the numerical count of each document.

      vii) a) Terms and conditions upon which payment and/or acceptance is to be obtained.

         b) Terms of delivery of documents against:

           1) payment and/or acceptance

           2) other terms and conditions

It is the responsibility of the party preparing the collection instruction to ensure that the terms for the delivery of documents are clearly and unambiguously stated, otherwise banks will not be responsible for any consequences arising therefrom.

    viii) Charges to be collected, indicating whether they may be waived or not.

    ix) Interest to be collected, if applicable, indicating whether it may be waived or not, including:

        a. rate of interest

        b. interest period

        c. basis of calculation (for example 360 or 365 days in a year) as applicable.

    x) Method of payment and form of payment advice.

    xi) Instructions in case of non-payment, non-acceptance and/or non-compliance with other insfructions.

c)   i) Collection instructions should bear the complete address of the drawee or of the domicile at which the presentation is to be made. If the address is incomplete or incorrect, the collecting bank may, without any liability and responsibility on its part, endeavour to ascertain the proper address.

      ii) The collecting bank will not be liable or responsible for any ensuing delay as a result of an incomplete/incorrect address being provided.

C.   Form of Presentation

Article 5

Presentation

a) For the purposes of these Articles, presentation is the procedure whereby the presenting bank makes the documents available to the drawee as instructed.

b) The collection instruction should state the exact period of time within which any acttion is to be taken by the drawee.

Expressions such as 'first', 'prompt', 'immediate' and the like should not be used in connection with presentation or with reference to any period of time within which documents have to be taken up or for any other action that is to be taken by the drawee. If such terms are used banks will disregard them.

c) Documents are to be presented to the drawee in the form in which they are received except that banks are authorised to affix any necessary stamps at the expense of the party from whom they received the collection unless otherwise instructed, and to make any necessary endorsements or place any rubber stamps or other identifying marks or symbols customary to or required for the collection operation.

367

d) For the purpose of giving effect to the instructions of the principal, the remitting bank will utilise the bank nominated by the principal as the collecting bank In the absence of such nomination, the remitting bank will utilise any bank of its own, or another bank's choice in the country of payment or acceptance or in the country where other terms and conditions have to be complied with.

e) The documents and collection instruction may be sent directly by the remitting bank to the collecting bank or through another bank as intermediary.

f) If the remitting bank does not nominate a specific presenting bank the collecting bank may utilise a presenting bank of its choice.

Article 6

Sight/Acceptance

In the case of documents payable at sight the presenting bank must make presentation for payment without delay.

In the case of documents payable at a tenor other than sight the presenting bank must, where acceptance is called tor, make presentation for acceptance without delay and where payment is called for, make presentation for payment not later than the appropriate maturity date.

Article 7

Release of Commercial Documents
Documents Against Acceptance (D/A) vs. Documents Against Payment (D/P)

a) Collections should not contain bills of exchange payable at a future date with instructions that commercial documents are to be delivered against payment.

b) If a collection contains a bill of exchange payable at a future date, the collection instruction should state whether the commercial documents are to be released to the drawee against acceptance (DIA) or against payment (DIP).

   In the absence of such statement commercial documents will be released only against payment and the collecting bank will not be responsible for any consequences arising out of any delay in the delivery of documents.

c) If a collection contains a bill of exchange payable at a future date and the collection instruction indicates that commercial documents are to be released against payment, documents will be released only against such payment and the collecting bank will not be responsible for any consequences arising out of any delay in the delivery of documents.

Article 8

Creation of Documents

Where the remitting bank instructs that either the collecting bank or the drawee is to create documents (bills of exchange, promissory notes, trust receipts, letters of undertaking or other documents) that were not included in the collection, the form and wording of such documents shall be provided by the remitting bank, otherwise the collecting bank shall not he liable or responsible for the form and wording of any such document provided by the collecting bank and/or the drawee.

D.   Liabilities and Responsibilities

Article 9

Good Faith and Reasonable Care

Banks will act in good faith and exercise reasonable care.

Article 10

Documents vs. Goods/Services/Performances

a) Goods should not be despatched directly to the address of a bank or consigned to or to the order of a bank without prior agreement on fhe part of that bank.

Nevertheless, in the event that goods are despatched directly to the address of a bank or consigned to or to the order of a bank for release to a drawee against payment or acceptance or upon other terms and conditions without prior agreement on the part of that bank, such bank shall have no obligation to take delivery of the goods, which remain at the risk and responsibility of the party despatching the goods.

b) Banks have no obligation to take any action in respect of the goods to which a documentary collection relates, including storage and insurance of the goods even when specific instructions are given to do so. Banks will only take such action if, when, and to the extent that they agree to do so in each case. Notwithstanding the provisions of sub-Article 1(c), this rule applies even in the absence of any specific advice to this effect by the collecting bank.

c) Nevertleless, in the case that banks take action for the protection of the goods, whether instructed or not, they assume no liability or responsibility with regard to the fate and/or condition of the goods and/or for any acts and/or omissions on the part of any third parties entrusted with the custody and/or protection of the goods. However, the collecting bank must advise without delay the bank from which the collection instruction was received of any such action taken.

d) Any charges and/or expenses incurred by banks in connection with any action taken to protect the goods will be for the account of the party from whom they received the collection.

e)   i) Notwithstanding the provisions of sub-Article 10(a), wtlere the goods are consigned to or to the order of the collecting barlk and the drawee has honoured the collection by payment, acceptance or other terms and conditions, and the collecting bank arranges for the release of the goods, the remitting bank shall be deemed to have authorised the collecting bank to do so.

ii) Where a collecting bank on the instructions of the remitting book or in terms of sub-Article 10(e)i arranges for the release of the goods, the remitting bank shall indemnify such collecting bank for all damages and expenses incurred.

Article 11

Disclaimer For Acts of an Instructed Party

a) Banks utilising the services of another bank or other banks for the purpose of giving effect to the instructions of the principal, do so for the account and at the risk of such principal.

b) Banks assume no liability or responsibility should the instructions they transmit not be carried out even if they have themselves taken the initiative in the choice of such other bank(s).

c) A party instructing another party to perform services shall be bound by and liable to indemnify the instructed party against all obligations and responsibilities imposed by foreign laws and usages.

Article 12

Disclaimer on Documents Received

a) Banks must determine that the documents received appear to be as listed in the collection instruction and must advise by telecommunication or, if that is not possible, by other expeditious means, without delay, the party from whom the collection instruction was received of any documents missing, or found to be other than listed.

Banks have no further obligation in this respect.

b) If the documents do not appear to be listed the remitting bank shall be precluded from disputing the type and number of documents received by the collecting bank.

c) Subject to sub-Article 5(c) and sub-Articles 12(a) and 12(b) above, banks will present documents as received without further examination.

Article 13

Disclaimer on Effectiveness of Documents

Banks assume no liability or responsibility for the form, sufficiency, accuracy, genuineness, falsification or legal effect of any document(s), or for the general and/or particular conditions stipulated in the document(s) or superimposed thereon; nor do they assume any liability or responsibility for the description, quantity, weight, quality, condition, packing, delivery, value or existence of the goods represented by any document(s), or for the good faith or acts and/or omissions, solvency, performance or standing of the consignors, the carriers, the forwarders, the consignees or the insurers of the goods, or any other person whomsoever.

Article 14

Disclaimer on Delays, Loss in Transit and Translation

a) Banks assume no liability or responsibility for the consequences arising out of delay and/or loss in transit of any message(s), letter(s) or document(s), or for delay, mutilation or other error(s) arising in transmission of any telecommunication or for error(s) in translation and/or interpretation of technical terms.

    b) Banks will not be liable or responsible for any delays resulting from the need to obtain clarification of any instructions received.

Article 15

Force Majeure

Banks assume no liability or responsibility for consequences arising out of the interruption of their business by Acts of God, riots, civil commotions, insurrections, wars, or any other causes beyond their control or by strikes or lockouts.

E.   Payment

Article 16

Payment Without Delay

    a) Amounts collected (less charges and/or disbursements and/or expenses where applicable) must be made available without delay to the party from whom the collection instruction was received in accordance with the terms and conditions of the collection instruction.

    b) Notwithstanding the provisions of sub-Article 1(c) and unless otherwise agreed, the collecting bank will effect payment of the amount collected in favour of the remitting bank only.

Article 17

Payment in Local Currency

In the case of documents payable in the currency of the country of payment (local currency), the presenting bank must, unless otherwise instructed in the collection instruction, release the documents to the drawee against payment in local currency only if such currency is immediately available for disposal in the manner specified in the collection instruction.

Article 18

Payment in Foreign Currency

In the case of documents payable in a currency other than that of the country of payment (foreign currency), the presenting bank must, unless otherwise instructed in the collection instruction, release the documents to the drawee against payment in the designated foreign currency only if such foreign currency can immediately be remitted in accordance with the instructions given in the collection instruction.

Article 19

Partial Payments

    a) In respect of clean collections, partial payments may be accepted if and to the extent to which and on the conditions on which partial payments are authorised by the law in force in the place of payment. The financial document(s) will be released to the drawee only when full payment thereof has been received.

b) In respect of documentary collections, partial payments will only be accepted if specifically authorised in the collection instruction. However, unless otherwise instructed, the presenting bank will release the documents to the drawee only after full payment has been received, and the presenting bank will not be responsible for any consequences arising out of any delay in the delivery of documents.

c) In all cases partial payments will be accepted only subject to compliance with the provisions of either Article 17 or Article 18 as appropriate.

Partial payment, if accepted, will be dealt with in accordance with the provisions of Article 16.

F.   Interest, Charges and Expenses

Article 20

Interest

a) If the collection instruction specifies that interest is to be collected and the drawee refuses to pay such interest, the presenting bank may deliver the document(s) against payment or acceptance or on other terms and conditions as the case may be, without collecting such interest, unless sub-Article 20(c) applies.

b) Where such interest is to be collected, the collection instruction must specify the rate of interest, interest period and basis of calculation.

c) Where the collection instruction expressly states that interest may not be waived and the drawee refuses to pay such interest the presenting bank will not deliver documents and will not be responsible for any consequences arising out of any delay in the delivery of document(s). When payment of interest has been refused, the presenting bank must inform by telecommunication or, if that is not possible, by other expeditious means without delay the bank from which the collection instruction was received.

Article 21

Charges and Expenses

a) If the collection instruction specifies that collection charges and/or expenses are to be for account of the drawee and the drawee refuses to pay them, the presenting bank may deliver the document(s) against payment or acceptance or on other terms and conditions as the case may be, without collecting charges and/or expenses, unless sub-Article 21(b) applies.

Whenever collection charges and/or expenses are so waived they will be for the account of the party from whom the collection was received and may be deducted from the proceeds.

b) Where the collection instruction expressly states that charges and/or expenses may not be waived and the drawee refuses to pay such charges and/or expenses, the presenting bank will not deliver documents and will not be responsible for any consequences arising out of any delay in the delivery of the document(s). When payment of collection charges and/or expenses has been refused the presenting bank must inform by telecommunication or, if that is not possible, by other expeditious means without delay the bank from which the collection instruction was received.

c) In all cases where in the express terms of a collection instruction or under these Rules, disbursements and/or expenses and/or collection charges are to be borne by the principal, the collecting bank(s) shall be entitled to recover promptly outlays in respect of disbursements, expenses and charges from the bank from which the collection instruction was received, and the remitting bank shall be entitled to recover promptly from the principal any amount so paid out by it, together with its own disbursements, expenses and charges, regardless of the fate of the collection.

d) Banks reserve the right to demand payment of charges/and expenses in advance from the party from whom the collection instruction was received, to cover costs in attempting to carry out any instructions, and pending receipt of such payment also reserve the right not to carry out such instructions.

G.   Other Provisions

Article 22

Acceptance

The presenting bank is responsible for seeing that the form of the acceptance of a bill of exchange appears to be complete and correct, but is not responsible for the genuineness of any signature or for the authority of any signatory to sign the acceptance.

Article 23

Promissory Notes and Other Instruments

The presenting bank is not responsible for the genuineness of any signature or for the authority of any signatory to sign a promissory note, receipt, or other instruments.

Article 24

Protest

The collection instruction should give specific instructions regarding protest (or other legal process in lieu thereof), in the event of non-payment or non-acceptance.

In the absence of such specific instructions, the banks concerned with the collection have no obligation to have the document(s) protested (or subjected to other legal process in lieu thereof) for non-payment or non-acceptance.

Any charges and/or expenses incurred by banks in connection with such protest, or other legal process, will be for the account of the party from whom the collection instruction was received.

Article 25

Case-of-Need

If the principal nominates a representative to act as case-of-need in the event of non-payment and/or non-acceptance the collection instruction should clearly and fully indicate the powers of such case-of-need. In the absence of such indication banks will not accept any instructions from the case-of-need.

Article 26

Advices

Collecting banks are to advise fate in accordance with the following rules:

a) **Form of Advice**

All advices or information from the collecting bank to the bank from which the collection instruction was received, must bear appropriate details including, in all cases, the latter bank's reference as stated in the collection instruction.

b) **Method of Advice**

It shall be the responsibility of the remitting bank to instruct the collecting bank regarding the method by which the advices detailed in (c)i, (c)ii and (c)iii are to be given. In the absence of such instructions, the collecting bank will send the relative advices by the method of its choice at the expense of the bank from which the collection instruction was received.

c)   i) ADVICE OF PAYMENT

The collecting bank must send without delay advice of payment to the bank from which the collection instruction was received, detailing the amount or amounts collected, charges and/ or disbursements and/or expenses deducted, where appropriate, and method of disposal of the funds.

   ii) ADVICE OF ACCEPTANCE

The collecting bank must send without delay advice of acceptance to the bank from which the collection instruction was received.

   iii) ADVICE OF NON-PAYMENT AND/OR NON-ACCEPTANCE

The presenting bank should endeavour to ascertain the reasons for non-payment and/or non-acceptance and advise accordingly, without delay, the bank from which it received the collection instruction.

The presenting bank must send without delay advice of non-payment and/or advice of non-acceptance to the bank from which it received the collection instruction.

On receipt of such advice the remitting bank must give appropriate instructions as to the further handling of the documents. If such instructions are not received by the presenting bank within 60 days after its advice of nonpayment and/or non-acceptance, the documents may be returned to the bank from which the collection instruction was received without any further responsibility on the part of the presenting bank.

Appendix IV

Uniform Customs and Practice for Documentary Credits

A. General Provisions and Definitions

Article 1

Application of UCP

The Uniform Customs and Practice for Documentary Credits, 1993 Revision, ICC Publication no. 500, shall apply to all Documentary Credits (including to the extent to which they may be applicable, Standby Letter(s) of Credit) where they are incorporated into the text of the Credit. They are binding on all parties thereto, unless otherwise expressly stipulated in the Credit.

Article 2

Meaning of Credit

For the purposes of these Articles, the expressions 'Documentary Credit(s)' and 'Standby Letter(s) of Credit' (hereinafter referred to as 'Credit(s)'), mean any arrangement, however named or described, whereby a bank (the 'Issuing Bank') acting at the request and on the instructions of a customer (the 'Applicant') or on its own behalf,

  i) is to make a payment to or to the order of a third party (the 'Beneficiary') or is to accept and pay bills of exchange (Draft(s)) drawn by the Beneficiary

  or

  ii) authorises another bank to effect such payment, or to accept and pay such bills of exchange (Draft(s)),

  or

  iii) authorises another bank to negotiate,

against stipulated document(s), provided that the terms and conditions of the Credit are complied with.

For the purposes of these Articles, branches of a bank in different countries are considered another bank.

Article 3

Credits v. Contracts

  a) Credits, by their nature, are separate transactions from the sales or other contract(s) on which they may be based and banks are in no way concerned with or bound by such contract(s), even if any reference whatsoever to such contract(s) is included in the Credit. Consequently, the undertaking of a bank to pay, accept and pay Draft(s) or negotiate and/or to fulfil any other obligation under the Credit, is not subject to claims or defences by the Applicant resulting from his relationships with the Issuing Bank or the Beneficiary.

b) A Beneficiary can in no case avail himself of the contractual relationships existing between the banks or between the Applicant and the Issuing Bank.

Article 4

Documents v. Goods/Services/Performances

In Credit operations all parties concerned deal with documents, and not with goods, services and/or other performances to which the documents may relate.

Article 5

Instructions to Issue/Amend Credits

a) Instructions for the issuance of a Credit, the Credit itself, instructions for an amendment thereto, and the amendment itself, must be complete and precise.

In order to guard against confusion and misunderstanding, banks should discourage any attempt:

 i) to include excessive detail in the Credit or in any amendment thereto;

 ii) to give instructions to issue, advise or confirm a Credit by reference to a Credit previously issued (similar Credit) where such previous Credit has been subject to accepted amendment(s), and/or unaccepted amendment(s).

b) All instructions for the issuance of a Credit and the Credit itself and, where applicable, all instructions for an amendment thereto and the amendment itself, must state precisely the document(s) against which payment, acceptance or negotiation is to be made

B.   Form and Notification of Credits

Article 6

Revocable v. Irrevocable Credits

a) A Credit may be either

 i) revocable,

 or

 ii) irrevocable

b) The Credit, therefore, should clearly indicate whether it is revocable or irrevocable.

c) In the absence of such indication the Credit shall be deemed to be irrevocable.

Article 7

Advising Bank's Liability

a) A Credit may be advised to a Beneficiary through another bank (the 'Advising Bank') without engagement on the part of the Advising Bank, but that bank, if it elects to advise the Credit, shall take reasonable care to check the apparent authenticity of the Credit which it advises. If the bank elects not to advise the Credit, it must so inform the Issuing Bank without delay.

b) If the Advising Bank cannot establish such apparent authenticity it must inform, without delay, the bank from which the instructions appear to have been received that it has been unable to establish the authenticity of the Credit and if it elects nonetheless to advise the Credit it must inform the Beneficiary that it has not been able to establish the authenticity of the Credit.

Article 8

Revocation of a Credit

a) A revocable Credit may be amended or cancelled by the Issuing Bank at any moment and without prior notice to the Beneficiary.

b) However, the Issuing Bank must:

   i) reimburse another bank with which a revocable Credit has been made available for sight payment, acceptance or negotiation - for any payment, acceptance or negotiation made by such bank - prior to receipt by it of notice of amendment or cancellation against documents which appear on their face to be in compliance with the terms and conditions of the Credit;

   ii) reimburse another bank with which a revocable Credit has been made available for deferred payment, if such a bank has, prior to receipt by it of notice of amendment or cancellation, taken up documents which appear on their face to be in compliance with the terms and conditions of the Credit..

Article 9

Liability of Issuing and Confirming Banks

a) An irrevocable Credit constitutes a definite undertaking of the Issuing Bank, provided that the stipulated documents are presented to the Nominated Bank or to the Issuing Bank and that the terms and conditions of the Credit are complied with:

   i) if the Credit provides for sight payment - to pay at sight;

   ii) if the Credit provides for deferred payment - to pay on the maturity date(s) determinable in accordance with the stipulations of the Credit;

   iii) if the Credit provides for acceptance:

   a. by the Issuing Bank - to accept Draft(s) drawn by the Beneficiary on the Issuing Bank and pay them at maturity,

   or

   b. by another drawee bank - to accept and pay at maturity Draft(s) drawn by the Beneficiary on the Issuing Bank in the event the drawee bank stipulated in the Credit does not accept Draft(s) drawn on it, or to pay Draft(s) accepted but not paid by such drawee bank at maturity;

iv) if the Credit provides for negotiation - to pay without recourse to drawers and/or bona fide holders, Draft(s) drawn by the Beneficiary and/or document(s) presented under the Credit. A Credit should not be issued available by Draft(s) on the Applicant. If the Credit nevertheless calls for Draft(s) on the Applicant, banks will consider such Draft(s) as an additional document(s).

b) A confirmation of an irrevocable Credit by another bank (the 'Confirming Bank') upon the authorisation or request of the Issuing Bank, constitutes a definite undertaking of the Confirming Bank, in addition to that of the Issuing Bank, provided that the stipulated documents are presented to the Confirming Bank or to any other Nominated Bank and that the terms and conditions of the Credit are complied with.

i) if the Credit provides for sight payment - to pay at sight;

ii) if the Credit provides for deferred payment - to pay on the maturity date(s) determinable in accordance with the stipulations of the Credit;

iii) if the Credit provides for acceptance:

a. by the Confirming Bank - to accept Draft(s) drawn by the Beneficiary on the Confirming Bank and pay them at maturity,

or

b. by another drawee bank - to accept and pay at maturity Draft(s) drawn by the Beneficiary on the Confirming Bank, in the event the drawee bank stipulated in the Credit does not accept Draft(s) drawn on it, or to pay Draft(s) accepted but not paid by such drawee bank at maturity;

iv) if the Credit provides for negotiation - to negotiate without recourse to drawers and/or bona fide holders, Draft(s) drawn by the Beneficiary and/ or document(s) presented under the Credit. A Credit should not be issued available by Draft(s) on the Applicant. If the Credit nevertheless calls for Draft(s) on the Applicant, banks will consider such Draft(s) as an additional document(s).

c) i) If another bank is authorised or requested by the Issuing Bank to add its confirmation to a Credit but is not prepared to do so, it must so inform the Issuing Bank without delay.

ii) Unless the Issuing Bank specifies otherwise in its authorisation or request to add confirmation, the Advising Bank may advise the Credit to the Beneficiary without adding its confirmation.

d) i) Except as otherwise provided by Article 48, an irrevocable Credit can neither be amended nor cancelled without the agreement of the Issuing Bank, the Confirming Bank, if any, and the Beneficiary

ii) The Issuing Bank shall be irrevocably bound by an amendment(s) issued by it from the time of the issuance of such amendment(s). A Confirming Bank may extend its confirmation to an amendment and shall be irrevocably bound as of the time of its advice of the amendment. A Confirming Bank may, however, choose to advise an amendment to the

Beneficiary without extending its confirmation and if so, must inform the Issuing Bank and the Beneficiary without delay.

iii) The terms of the original Credit (or a Credit incorporating previously accepted amendment(s)) will remain in force for the Beneficiary until the Beneficiary communicates his acceptance of the amendment to the bank that advised such amendment. The Beneficiary should give notification of acceptance or rejection of amendment(s). If the Beneficiary fails to give such notification, the tender of documents to the Nominated Bank or Issuing Bank, that conform to the Credit and to not yet accepted amendment(s), will be deemed to be notification of acceptance by the Beneficiary of such amendment(s) and as of that moment the Credit will be amended.

iv) Partial acceptance of amendments contained in one and the same advice of amendment is not allowed and consequently will not be given any effect.

Article 10

Types of Credit

a) All Credits must clearly indicate whether they are available by sight payment, by deferred payment, by acceptance or by negotiation.

b) i) Unless the Credit stipulates that it is available only with the Issuing Bank, all Credits must nominate the bank (the 'Nominated Bank') which is authorised to pay, to incur a deferred payment undertaking, to accept Draft(s) or to negotiate. In a freely negotiable Credit, any bank is a Nominated Bank.

Presentation of documents must be made to the Issuing Bank or the Confirming Bank, if any, or any other Nominated Bank.

ii) Negotiation means the giving of value for Draft(s) and/or document(s) by the bank authorised to negotiate. Mere examination of the documents without giving of value does not constitute a negotiation.

c) Unless the Nominated Bank is the Confirming Bank, nomination by the Issuing Bank does not constitute any undertaking by the Nominated Bank to pay, to incur a deferred payment undertaking, to accept Draft(s), or to negotiate. Except where expressly agreed to by the Nominated Bank and so communicated to the Beneficiary, the Nominated Bank's receipt of and/or examination and/or forwarding of the documents does not make that bank liable to pay, to incur a deferred payment undertaking, to accept Draft(s), or to negotiate.

d) By nominating another bank, or by allowing for negotiation by any bank, or by authorising or requesting another bank to add its confirmation, the Issuing Bank authorises such bank to pay, accept Draft(s) or negotiate as the case may be, against documents which appear on their face to be in compliance with the terms and conditions of the Credit and undertakes to reimburse such bank in accordance with the provisions of these Articles.

Article 11

Teletransmitted and Pre-Advised Credits

a)   i)   When an Issuing Bank instructs an Advising Bank by an authenticated teletransmission to advise a Credit or an amendment to a Credit, the teletransmissionwill be deemed to be the operative Credit instrument or the operative amendment, and no mail confirmation should be sent. Should a mail confirmation nevertheless be sent, it will have no effect and the Advising Bank will have no obligation to check such mail confirmation against the operative Credit instrument or the operative amendment received by teletransmission.

  ii)   If the teletransmission states 'full details to follow' (or words of similar effect) or states that the mail confirmation is to be the operative Credit instrument or the operative amendment, then the teletransmission will not be deemed to be the operative Credit instrument or the operative amendment. The Issuing Bank must forward the operative Credit instrument or the operative amendment to such Advising Bank without delay.

b)   If a bank uses the services of an Advising Bank to have the Credit advised to the Beneficiary, it must also use the services of the same bank for advising an amendment(s).

c)   A preliminary advice of the issuance or amendment of an irrevocable Credit (pre-advice), shall only be given by an Issuing Bank if such bank is prepared to issue the operative Credit instrument or the operative amendment thereto. Unless otherwise stated in such preliminary advice by the Issuing Bank, an Issuing Bank having given such pre-advice shall be irrevocably committed to issue or amend the Credit, in terms not inconsistent with the pre-advice, without delay.

Article 12

Incomplete or Unclear Instructions

If incomplete or unclear instructions are received to advise, confirm or amend a Credit, the bank requested to act on such instructions may give preliminary notification to the Beneficiary for information only and without responsibility. This preliminary notification should state clearly that the notification is provided for information only and without the responsibility of the Advising Bank. In any event, the Advising Bank must inform the Issuing Bank of the action taken and request it to provide the necessary information.

The Issuing Bank must provide the necessary information without delay. The Credit will be advised, confirmed or amended, only when complete and clear instructions have been received and if the Advising Bank is then prepared to act on the instructions.

C.   Liabilities and Responsibilities

Article 13

Standard for Examination of Documents

a) Banks must examine all documents stipulated in the Credit with reasonable care, to ascertain whether or not they appear, on their face, to be in compliance with the terms and conditions of the Credit. Compliance of the stipulated documents on their face with the terms and conditions of the Credit, shall be determined by international standard banking practice as reflected in these Articles. Documents which appear on their face to be inconsistent with one another will be considered as not appearing on their face to be in compliance with the terms and conditions of the Credit.

Documents not stipulated in the Credit will not be examined by banks. If they receive such documents, they shall return them to the presenter or pass them on without responsibility.

b) The Issuing Bank, the Confirming Bank, if any, or a Nominated Bank acting on their behalf, shall each have a reasonable time, not to exceed seven banking days following the day of receipt of the documents, to examine the documents and determine whether to take up or refuse the documents and to inform the party from which it received the documents accordingly.

c) If a Credit contains conditions without stating the document(s) to be presented in compliance therewith, banks will deem such conditions as not stated and will disregard them.

Article 14

Discrepant Documents and Notice

a) When the Issuing Bank authorises another bank to pay, incur a deferred payment Draft(s), or negotiate against documents which appear on their face to be the terms and conditions of the Credit, the Issuing Bank and the Confirming Bank, if any, are bound:

   i)   to reimburse the Nominated Bank which has paid, incurred a deferred payment undertaking, accepted Draft(s), or negotiated,

   ii) to take up the documents.

b) Upon receipt of the documents the Issuing Bank and/or Confirming Bank, if any, or a Nominated Bank acting on their behalf, must determine on the basis of the documents alone whether or not they appear on their face to be in compliance with the terms and conditions of the Credit. If the documents appear on their face not to be in compliance with the terms and conditions of the Credit, such banks may refuse to take up the documents.

c) If the Issuing Bank determines that the documents appear on their face not to be in compliance with the terms and conditions of the Credit, it may in its sole judgment approach the Applicant for a waiver of the discrepancy(ies). This does not, however, extend the period mentioned in sub-Article 13 b).

d) i) If the Issuing Bank and/or Confirming Bank, if any, or a Nominated Bank acting on their behalf, decides to refuse the documents, it must give notice to that effect by telecommunication or, if that is not possible, by other expeditious means, without delay but no later than the close of the seventh banking day following the day of receipt of the documents. Such notice shall be given to the bank from which it received the documents, or to the Beneficiary, if it received the documents directly from him

ii) Such notice must state all discrepancies in respect of which the bank refuses the documents and must also state whether it is holding the documents at the disposal of, or is returning them to, the presenter

iii) The Issuing Bank and/or Confirming Bank, if any, shall then be entitled to claim from the remitting bank refund, with interest, of any reimbursement which has been made to that bank

e) If the Issuing Bank and/or Confirming Bank, if any, fails to act in accordance with the provisions of this Article and/or fails to hold the documents at the disposal of, or return them to the presenter, the Issuing Bank and/or Confirming Bank, if any, shall be precluded from claiming that the documents are not in compliance with the terms and conditions of the Credit

f) If the remitting bank draws the attention of the Issuing Bank and/or Confirming Bank, if any, to any discrepancy(ies) in the document(s) or advises such banks that it has paid, incurred a deferred payment undertaking, accepted Draft(s) or negotiated under reserve or against an indemnity in respect of such discrepancy(ies), the Issuing Bank and/or Confirming Bank, if any, shall not be thereby relieved from any of their obligations under any provision of this Article. Such reserve or indemnity concerns only the relations between the remitting bank and the party towards whom the reserve was made, or from whom, or on whose behalf, the indemnity was obtained.

Article 15

Disclaimer on Effectiveness of Documents

Banks assume no liability or responsibility for the form, sufficiency, accuracy, genuineness, falsification or legal effect of any document(s), or for the general and/or particular conditions stipulated in the document(s) or superimposed thereon; nor do they assume any liability or responsibility for the description, quantity, weight, quality, condition, packing, delivery, value or existence of the goods represented by any document(s), or for the good faith or acts and/or omissions, solvency, performance or standing of the consignors, the carriers, the forwarders, the consignees or the insurers of the goods, or any other person whomsoever.

Article 16

Disclaimer on the Transmission of Messages

Banks assume no liability or responsibility for the consequences arising out of delay and/or loss in transit of any message(s), letter(s) or document(s), or for delay, mutilation or other error(s) arising in the transmission of any telecommunication. Banks assume no liability or responsibility for errors in translation and/or interpretation of technical terms, and reserve the right to transmit Credit terms without translating them.

Article 17

Force Majeure

Banks assume no liability or responsibility for the consequences arising out of the interruption of their business by Acts of God, riots, civil commotions, insurrections, wars or any other causes beyond their control, or by any strikes or lockouts. Unless specifically authorised, banks will not, upon resumption of their business, pay, incur a deferred payment undertaking, accept Draft(s) or negotiate under Credits which expired during such interruption of their business.

Article 18

Disclaimer for Acts of an Instructed Party

a) Banks utilizing the services of another bank or other banks for the purpose of giving effect to the instructions of the Applicant do so for the account and at the risk of such Applicant.

b) Banks assume no liability or responsibility should the instructions they transmit not be carried out, even if they have themselves taken the initiative in the choice of such other bank(s).

c) i) A party instructing another party to perform services is liable for any charges, including commissions, fees, costs, or expenses incurred by the instructed party in connection with its instructions.

   ii) Where a Credit stipulates that such charges are for the account of a party other than the instructing party, and charges cannot be collected, the instructing party remains ultimately liable for the payment thereof.

d) The Applicant shall be bound by and liable to indemnify the banks against all obligations and responsibilities imposed by foreign laws and usages.

Article 19

Bank-to-bank Reimbursement Arrangements

a) If an Issuing Bank intends that the reimbursement to which a paying, accepting or negotiating bank is entitled, shall be obtained by such bank (the 'Claiming Bank'), claiming on another party (the 'Reimbursing Bank'), it shall provide such Reimbursing Bank in good time with the proper instructions or authorisation to honour such reimbursement claims.

b) Issuing Banks shall not require a Claiming Bank to supply a certificate of compliance with the terms and conditions of the Credit to the Reimbursing Bank

c) An Issuing Bank shall not be relieved from any of its obligations to provide reimbursement if and when reimbursement is not received by the Claiming Bank from the Reimbursing Bank

d) The Issuing Bank shall be responsible to the Claiming Bank for any loss of interest if reimbursement is not provided by the Reimbursing Bank on first demand, or as otherwise specified in the Credit, or mutually agreed, as the case may be.

e) The Reimbursing Bank's charges should be for the account of the Issuing Bank. However, in cases where the charges are for the account of another party, it is the responsibility of the Issuing Bank to so indicate in the original Credit and in the reimbursement authorisation. In cases where the Reimbursing Bank's charges are for the account of another party they shall be collected from the Claiming Bank when the Credit is drawn under. In cases where the Credit is not drawn under, the Reimbursing Bank's charges remain the obligation of the Issuing Bank.

D.   Documents

Article 20

Ambiguity as to the Issuers of Documents

a) Terms such as 'first class', 'well known', 'qualified'. 'independent', 'official', 'competent', 'local' and the like, shall not be used to describe the issuers of any document(s) to be presented under a Credit. If such terms are incorporated in the Credit, banks will accept the relative document(s) as presented, provided that it appears on its face to be in compliance with the other terms and conditions of the Credit and not to have been issued by the Beneficiary

b) Unless otherwise stipulated in the Credit, banks will also accept as an original document(s), a document(s) produced or appearing to have been produced.

   i)   by reprographic, automated or computerized systems.'

   ii) as carbon copies;

   provided that it is marked as original and, where necessary, appears to be signed

   A document may be signed by handwriting, by facsimile signature, by perforated signature, by stamp, by symbol, or by any other mechanical or electronic method of authentication.

c) i)   Unless otherwise stipulated in the Credit, banks will accept as a copy(ies), a document(s) either labelled copy or not marked as an original - a copy(ies) need not be signed Credits that require multiple document(s) such as 'duplicate', 'two fold', 'two copies' and the like, will be satisfied by the presentation of one original and the remaining number in copies except where the document itself indicates otherwise.

   ii) Credits that require multiple document(s) such as 'duplicate', 'two fold', 'two copies' and the like, will be satisfied by the presentation of one original and the remaining number in copies except where the document itself indicates otherwise.

d) Unless otherwise stipulated in the Credit, a condition under a Credit calling for a document to be authenticated, validated, legalised, visaed, certified or indicating a similar requirement, will be satisfied by any signature, mark, stamp or label on such document that on its face appears to satisfy the above condition

Article 21

Unspecified Issuers or Contents of Documents

When documents other than transport documents, insurance documents and commercial invoices are called for, the Credit should stipulate by whom such documents are to be issued and their wording or data content. If the Credit does not so stipulate, banks will accept such documents as presented, provided that their data content is not inconsistent with any other stipulated document presented.

Article 22

Issuance Date of Documents v. Credit Date

Unless otherwise stipulated in the Credit, banks will accept a document bearing a date of issuance prior to that of the Credit, subject to such document being presented within the time limits set out in the Credit and in these Articles.

Article 23

Marine/Ocean Bill of Lading

a) If a Credit calls for a bill of lading covering a port-to-port shipment, banks will, unless otherwise stipulated in the Credit, accept a document, however named, which:

    i) appears on its face to indicate the name of the carrier and to have been signed or otherwise authenticated by:

        - the carrier or a named agent for or on behalf of the carrier, or

        - the master or a named agent for or on behalf of the master.

    Any signature or authentication of the carrier or master must be identified as carrier or master, as the case may be. An agent signing or authenticating for the carrier or master must also indicate the name and the capacity of the party, i.e. carrier or master, on whose behalf that agent is acting,

    and

    ii) indicates that the goods have been loaded on board, or shipped on a named vessel. Loading on board or shipment on a named vessel may be indicated by pre-printed wording on the bill of lading that the goods have been loaded on board a named vessel or shipped on a named vessel, in which case the date of issuance of the bill of lading will be deemed to be the date of loading on board and the date of shipment.

    In all other cases loading on board a named vessel must be evidenced by a notation on the bill of lading which gives the date on which the goods have been loaded on board, in which case the date of the on board notation will be deemed to be the date of shipment.

    If the bill of lading contains the indication 'intended vessel', or similar qualification in relation to the vessel, loading on board a named vessel must be evidenced by an on board notation on the bill of lading which, in addition to the date on which the goods have been loaded on board, also includes the name of the vessel on which the goods have been loaded, even if they have been loaded on the vessel named as the 'intended vessel'.

If the bill of lading indicates a place of receipt or taking in charge different from the port of loading, the on board notation must also include the port of loading stipulated in the Credit and the name of the vessel on which the goods have been loaded, even if they have been loaded on the vessel named in the bill of lading. This provision also applies whenever loading on board the vessel is indicated by pre-printed wording on the bill of lading,

and

iii) indicates the port of loading and the port of discharge stipulated in the Credit, notwithstanding that it:

    a. indicates a place of taking in charge different from the port of loading, and/or a place of final destination different from the port of discharge,

    and/or

    b. contains the indication 'intended' or similar qualification in relation to the port of loading and/or port of discharge, as long as the document also states the ports of loading and/or discharge stipulated in the Credit,

and

iv) consists of a sole original bill of lading or, if issued in more than one original, the full set as so issued,

and

v) appears to contain all of the terms and conditions of carriage, or some of such terms and conditions by reference to a source or document other than the bill of lading (short form/blank back bill of lading); banks will not examine the contents of such terms and conditions,

and

vi) contains no indication that it is subject to a charter party and/or no indication that the carrying vessel is propelled by sail only,

and

vii) in all other respects meets the stipulations of the Credit.

b) For the purpose of this Article, transhipment means unloading and reloading from one vessel to another vessel during the course of ocean carriage from the port of loading to the port of discharge stipulated in the Credit.

c) Unless transhipment is prohibited by the terms of the Credit, banks will accept a bill of lading which indicates that the goods will be transhipped, provided that the entire ocean carriage is covered by one and the same bill of lading.

d) Even if the Credit prohibits transhipment, banks will accept a bill of lading which:

i) indicates that transhipment will take place as long as the relevant cargo is shipped in Container(s), Trailer(s) and/or 'LASH' barge(s) as evidenced by the bill of Lading, provided that the entire ocean carriage is covered by one and the same bill of lading.

and/or

ii) incorporates clauses stating that the carrier reserves the right to tranship.

Article 24

Non-Negotiable Sea Waybill

a) If a Credit calls for a non-negotiable sea waybill covering a port-to-port shipment, banks will, unless otherwise stipulated in the Credit, accept a document, however named, which:

   i) appears on its face to indicate the name of the carrier and to have been signed or otherwise authenticated by:

   ● the carrier or a named agent for or on behalf of the carrier, or

   ● the master or a named agent for or on behalf of the master,

   Any signature or authentication of the carrier or master must be identified as carrier or master, as the case may be. An agent signing or authenticating for the carrier or master must also indicate the name and the capacity of the party. i.e. carrier or master, on whose behalf that agent is acting,

   and

   ii) indicates that the goods have been loaded on board, or shipped on a named vessel.

   Loading on board or shipment on a named vessel may be indicated by pre-printed wording on the non-negotiable sea waybill that the goods have been loaded on board a named vessel or shipped on a named vessel, in which case the date of issuance of the non-negotiable sea waybill will be deemed to be the date of loading on board and the date of shipment.

   In all other cases loading on board a named vessel must be evidenced by a notation on the non-negotiable sea waybill which gives the date on which the goods have been loaded on board, in which case the date of the on board notation will be deemed to be the date of shipment.

   If the non-negotiable sea waybill contains the indication 'intended vessel', or similar qualification in relation to the vessel, loading on board a named vessel must be evidenced by an on board notation on the non-negotiable sea waybill which, in addition to the date on which the goods have been loaded on board, includes the name of the vessel on which the goods have been loaded, even if they have been loaded on the vessel named as the 'intended vessel'

   If the non-negotiable sea waybill indicates a place of receipt or taking in charge different from the port of loading, the on board notation must also include the port of loading stipulated in the Credit and the name of the vessel on which the goods have been loaded, even if they have been loaded on a vessel named in the non-negotiable sea waybill. This provision also applies whenever loading on board the vessel is indicated by pre-printed wording on the non-negotiable sea waybill,

   and

   iii) indicates the port of loading and the port of discharge stipulated in the Credit, notwithstanding that it:

   a. indicates a place of taking in charge different from the port of loading, and/or a place of final destination different from the port of discharge, and/or

b. contains the indication 'intended' or similar qualification in relation to the port of loading and/or port of discharge, as long as the document also states the ports of loading and/or discharge stipulated in the Credit,

and

iv) consists of a sole original non-negotiable sea waybill, or if issued in more than one original, the full set as so issued,

and

v) appears to contain all of the terms and conditions of carriage, or some of such terms and conditions by reference to a source or document other than the non-negotiable sea waybill (short form/blank back non-negotiable sea waybill); banks will not examine the contents of such terms and conditions,

and

vi) contains no indication that it is subject to a charter party and/or no indication that the carrying vessel is propelled by sail only,

and

vii) in all other respects meets the stipulations of the Credit.

b) For the purpose of this Article, transhipment means unloading and reloading from one vessel to another vessel during the course of ocean carriage from the port of loading to the port of discharge stipulated in the Credit.

c) Unless transhipment is prohibited by the terms of the Credit, banks will accept a non-negotiable sea waybill which indicates that the goods will be transhipped, provided that the entire ocean carriage is covered by one and the same non-negotiable sea waybill.

d) Even if the Credit prohibits transhipment, banks will accept a non-negotiable sea waybill which:

i) indicates that transhipment will take place as long as the relevant cargo is shipped in Container(s), Trailer(s) and/or 'LASH' barge(s) as evidenced by the non-negotiable sea waybill, provided that the entire ocean carriage is covered by one and the same non-negotiable sea waybill,

and/or

ii) incorporates clauses stating that the carrier reserves the right to tranship.

Article 25

Charter Party Bill of Lading

a) If a Credit calls for or permits a charter party bill of lading, banks will, unless otherwise stipulated in the Credit, accept a document, however named, which.

i) contains any indication that it is subject to a charter party,

and

    ii) appears on its face to have been signed or otherwise authenticated by:

- the master or a named agent for or on behalf of the master, or

- the owner or a named agent for or on behalf of the owner.

Any signature or authentication of the master or owner must be identified as master or owner as the case may be. An agent signing or authenticating for the master or owner must also indicate the name and the capacity of the party, i.e. master or owner, on whose behalf that agent is acting,

and

    iii) does or does not indicate the name of the carrier,

and

    iv) indicates that the goods have been loaded on board or shipped on a named vessel.

Loading on board or shipment on a named vessel may be indicated by pre-printed wording on the bill of lading that the goods have been loaded on board a named vessel or shipped on a named vessel, in which case the date of issuance of the bill of lading will be deemed to be the date of loading on board and the date of shipment.

In all other cases loading on board a named vessel must be evidenced by a notation on the bill of lading which gives the date on which the goods have been loaded on board, in which case the date of the on board notation will be deemed to be the date of shipment,

and

    v) indicates the port of loading and the port of discharge stipulated in the Credit,

and

    vi) consists of a sole original bill of lading or, if issued in more than one original, the full set as so issued,

and

    vii) contains no indication that the carrying vessel is propelled by sail only,

and

    viii) in all other respects meets the stipulations of the Credit.

b) Even if the Credit requires the presentation of a charter party contract in connection with a charter party bill of lading, banks will not examine such charter party contract, but will pass it on without responsibility on their part.

Article 26

Multimodal Transport Document

a) If a Credit calls for a transport document covering at least two different modes of transport (multimodal transport), banks will, unless otherwise stipulated in the Credit, accept a document, however named, which:

    i) appears on its face to indicate the name of the carrier or multimodal transport operator and to have been signed or otherwise authenticated by:

- the carrier or multimodal transport operator or a named agent for or on behalf of the carrier or multimodal transport operator, or

- the master or a named agent for or on behalf of the master.

Any signature or authentication of the carrier, multimodal transport operator or master must be identified as carrier, multimodal transport operator or master, as the case may be. An agent signing or authenticating for the carrier, multimodal transport operator or master must also indicate the name and the capacity of the party, i.e. carrier, multimodal transport operator or master, on whose behalf that agent is acting,

and

ii) indicates that the goods have been dispatched, taken in charge or loaded on board.

Dispatch, taking in charge or loading on board may be indicated by wording to that effect on the multimodal transport document and the date of issuance will be deemed to be the date of dispatch, taking in charge or loading on board and the date of shipment However, if the document indicates, by stamp or otherwise, a date of dispatch, taking in charge or loading on board, such date will be deemed to be the date of shipment,

and

iii) a. indicates the place of taking in charge stipulated in the Credit which may be different from the port, airport or place of loading, and the place of final destination stipulated in the Credit which may be different from the port, airport or place of discharge,

and/or

b. contains the indication 'intended' or similar qualification in relation to the vessel and/or port of loading and/or port of discharge,

and

iv) consists of a sole original multimodal transport document or, if issued in more than one original, the full set as so issued,

and

v) appears to contain all of the terms and conditions of carriage, or some of such terms and conditions by reference to a source or document other than the multimodal transport document (short form/blank back multimodal transport document); banks will not examine the contents of such terms and conditions,

and

vi) contains no indication that it is subject to a charter party and/or no indication that the carrying vessel is propelled by sail only,

and

vii) in all other respects meets the stipulations of the Credit.

b) Even if the Credit prohibits transhipment, banks will accept a multimodal transport document which indicates that transhipment will or may take place, provided that the entire carriage is covered by one and the same multimodal transport document.

Article 27

Air Transport Document

a) If a Credit calls for an air transport document, banks will, unless otherwise stipulated in the Credit, accept a document, however named, which:

i)   appears on its face to indicate the name of the carrier and to have been signed or otherwise authenticated by:

● the carrier, or

● a named agent for or on behalf of the carrier.

Any signature or authentication of the carrier must be identified as carrier. An agent signing or authenticating for the carrier must also indicate the name and the capacity of the party, i.e. carrier, on whose behalf that agent is acting,

and

ii) indicates that the goods have been accepted for carriage,

and

iii) where the Credit calls for an actual date of dispatch, indicates a specific notation of such date, the date of dispatch so indicated on the air transport document will be deemed to be the date of shipment.

For the purpose of this Article, the information appearing in the box on the air transport document (marked 'For Carrier Use Only' or similar expression) relative to the flight number and date will not be considered as a specific notation of such date of dispatch.

In all other cases, the date of issuance of the air transport document will be deemed to be the date of shipment,

and

iv) indicates the airport of departure and the airport of destination stipulated in the Credit,

and

v)   appears to be the original for consignor/shipper even if the Credit stipulates a full set of originals, or similar expressions,

and

vi) appears to contain all of the terms and conditions of carriage, or some of such terms and conditions, by reference to a source or document other than the air transport document; banks will not examine the contents of such terms and conditions,

and

vii) in all other respects meets the stipulations of the Credit.

b) For the purpose of this Article, transhipment means unloading and reloading from one aircraft to another aircraft during the course of carriage from the airport of departure to the airport of destination stipulated in the Credit.

c) Even if the Credit prohibits transhipment, banks will accept an air transport document which indicates that transhipment will or may take place, provided that the entire carriage is covered by one and the same air transport document.

Article 28

Road, Rail or Inland Waterway Transport Documents

a) If a Credit calls for a road, rail, or inland waterway transport document, banks will, unless otherwise stipulated in the Credit, accept a document of the type called for, however named, which:

   i) appears on its face to indicate the name of the carrier and to have been signed or otherwise authenticated by the carrier or a named agent for or on behalf of the carrier and/or to bear a reception stamp or other indication of receipt by the carrier or a named agent for or on behalf of the carrier.

   Any signature, authentication, reception stamp or other indication of receipt of the carrier, must be identified on its face as that of the carrier. An agent signing or authenticating for the carrier, must also indicate the name and the capacity of the party, i.e. carrier, on whose behalf that agent is acting,

   and

   ii) indicates that the goods have been received for shipment, dispatch or carriage or wording to this effect. The date of issuance will be deemed to be the date of shipment unless the transport document contains a reception stamp, in which case the date of the reception stamp will be deemed to be the date of shipment,

   and

   iii) indicates the place of shipment and the place of destination stipulated in the Credit,

   and

   iv) in all other respects meets the stipulations of the Credit.

b) In the absence of any indication on the transport document as to the numbers issued, banks will accept the transport document(s) presented as constituting a full set. Banks will accept as original(s) the transport document(s) whether marked as original(s) or not.

c) For the purpose of this Article, transhipment means unloading and reloading from one means of conveyance to another means of conveyance, in different modes of transport, during the course of carriage from the place of shipment to the place of destination stipulated in the Credit.

d) Even if the Credit prohibits transhipment, banks will accept a road, rail, or inland waterway transport document which indicates that transhipment will or may take place, provided that the entire carriage is covered by one and the same transport document and within the same mode of transport.

Article 29

Courier and Post Receipts

a) If a Credit calls for a post receipt or certificate of posting, banks will, unless otherwise stipulated in the Credit, accept a post receipt or certificate of posting which:

  i)   appears on its face to have been stamped or otherwise authenticated and dated in the place from which the Credit stipulates the goods are to be shipped or dispatched and such date will be deemed to be the date of shipment or dispatch,

  and

  ii) in all other respects meets the stipulations of the Credit.

b) If a Credit calls for a document issued by a courier or expedited delivery service evidencing receipt of the goods for delivery, banks will, unless otherwise stipulated in the Credit, accept a document, however named, which:

  i)   appears on its face to indicate the name of the courier/service, and to have been stamped, signed or otherwise authenticated by such named courier/service (unless the Credit specifically calls for a document issued by a named Courier/Service, banks will accept a document issued by any Courier/Service),

  and

  ii) indicates a date of pick-up or of receipt or wording to this effect, such date being deemed to be the date of shipment or dispatch,

  and

  iii) in all other respects meets the stipulations of the Credit.

Article 30

Transport Documents issued by Freight Forwarders

Unless otherwise authorised in the Credit, banks will only accept a transport document issued by a freight forwarder if it appears on its face to indicate:

  i)   the name of the freight forwarder as a carrier or multimodal transport operator and to have been signed or otherwise authenticated by the freight forwarder as carrier or multimodal transport operator,

  or

  ii) the name of the carrier or multimodal transport operator and to have been signed or otherwise authenticated by the freight forwarder as a named agent for or on behalf of the carrier or multimodal transport operator.

Article 31

'On Deck', 'Shipper's Load and Count', Name of Consignor

Unless otherwise stipulated in the Credit, banks will accept a transport document which:

    i)   does not indicate, in the case of carriage by sea or by more than one means of conveyance including carriage by sea, that the goods are or will be loaded on deck. Nevertheless, banks will accept a transport document which contains a provision that the goods may be carried on deck, provided that it does not specifically state that they are or will be loaded on deck,

        and/or

    ii) bears a clause on the face thereof such as 'shipper's load and count' or 'said by shipper to contain' or words of similar effect,

        and/or

    iii) indicates as the consignor of the goods a party other than the Beneficiary of the Credit.

Article 32

Clean Transport Documents

    a)   A clean transport document is one which bears no clause or notation which expressly declares a defective condition of the goods and/or the packaging.

    b)   Banks will not accept transport documents bearing such clauses or notations unless the Credit expressly stipulates the clauses or notations which may be accepted

    c)   Banks will regard a requirement in a Credit for a transport document to bear the clause 'clean on board' as complied with if such transport document meets the requirements of this Article and of Articles 23, 24, 25, 26, 27, 28 or 30.

Article 33

Freight Payable/Prepaid Transport Documents

    a)   Unless otherwise stipulated in the Credit, or inconsistent with any of the documents presented under the Credit, banks will accept transport documents stating that freight or transportation charges (hereafter referred to as 'freight') have still to be paid.

    b)   If a Credit stipulates that the transport document has to indicate that freight has been paid or prepaid, banks will accept a transport document on which words clearly indicating payment or prepayment of freight appear by stamp or otherwise, or on which payment or prepayment of freight is indicated by other means. If the Credit requires courier charges to be paid or prepaid banks will also accept a transport document issued by a courier or expedited delivery service evidencing that courier charges are for the account of a party other than the consignee

c) The words 'freight prepayable' or 'freight to be prepaid or words of similar effect, if appearing on transport documents, will not be accepted as constituting evidence of the payment of freight.

d) Banks will accept transport documents bearing reference by stamp or otherwise to costs additional to the freight, such as costs of, or disbursements incurred in connection with, loading, unloading or similar operations, unless the conditions of the Credit specifically prohibit such reference.

Article 34

Insurance Documents

a) Insurance documents must appear on their face to be issued and signed by insurance companies or underwriters or their agents.

b) If the insurance document indicates that it has been issued in more than one original, all the originals must be presented unless otherwise authorised in the Credit.

c) Cover notes issued by brokers will not be accepted, unless specifically authorised in the Credit.

d) Unless otherwise stipulated in the Credit, banks will accept an insurance certificate or a declaration under an open cover pre-signed by insurance companies or underwriters or their agents. If a Credit specifically calls for an insurance certificate or a declaration under an open cover, banks will accept, in lieu thereof, an insurance policy.

e) Unless otherwise stipulated in the Credit, or unless it appears from the insurance document that the cover is effective at the latest from the date of loading on board or dispatch or taking in charge of the goods, banks will not accept an insurance document which bears a date of issuance later than the date of loading on board or dispatch or taking in charge as indicated in such transport document.

f) i) Unless otherwise stipulated in the Credit, the insurance document must be expressed in the same currency as the Credit.

ii) Unless otherwise stipulated in the Credit, the minimum amount for which the insurance document must indicate the insurance cover to have been effected is the CIF (cost, insurance and freight (... 'named port of destination')) or CIP (carriage and insurance paid to (...'named place of destination')) value of the goods, as the case may be, plus 10%, but only when the CIF or CIP value can be determined from the documents on their face. Otherwise, banks will accept as such minimum amount 110% of the amount for which payment, acceptance or negotiation is requested under the Credit, or 110% of the gross amount of the invoice, whichever is the greater.

Article 35

Type of Insurance Cover

a) Credits should stipulate the type of insurance required and, if any, the additional risks which are to be covered. Imprecise terms such as 'usual risks' or 'customary risks' shall not be used; if they are used, banks will accept insurance documents as presented, without responsibility for any risks not being covered.

b) Failing specific stipulations in the Credit, banks will accept insurance documents as presented, without responsibility for any risks not being covered.

c) Unless otherwise stipulated in the Credit, banks will accept an insurance document which indicates that the cover is subject to a franchise or an excess (deductible).

Article 36

All Risks Insurance Cover

Where a Credit stipulates 'insurance against all risks', banks will accept an insurance document which contains any 'all risks' notation or clause, whether or not bearing the heading 'all risks', even if the insurance document indicates that certain risks are excluded, without responsibility for any risk(s) not being covered.

Article 37

Commercial Invoices

a) Unless otherwise stipulated in the Credit, commercial invoices;

 i) must appear on their face to be issued by the Beneficiary named in the Credit (except as provided in Article 48),

and

 ii) must be made out in the name of the Applicant (except as provided in sub-Article 48 h)),

and

iii) need not be signed.

b) Unless otherwise stipulated in the Credit, banks may refuse commercial invoices issued for amounts in excess of the amount permitted by the Credit. Nevertheless, if a bank authorised to pay, incur a deferred payment undertaking, accept Draft(s), or negotiate under a Credit accepts such invoices, its decision will be binding upon all parties, provided that such bank has not paid, incurred a deferred payment undertaking, accepted Draft(s) or negotiated for an amount in excess of that permitted by the Credit.

c) The description of the goods in the commercial invoice must correspond with the description in the Credit. In all other documents, the goods may be described in general terms not inconsistent with the description of the goods in the Credit.

Article 38

Other Documents

If a Credit calls for an attestation or certification of weight in the case of transport other than by sea, banks will accept a weight stamp or declaration of weight which appears to have been superimposed on the transport document by the carrier or his agent unless the Credit specifically stipulates that the attestation or certification of weight must be by means of a separate document.

E.   Miscellaneous Provisions

Article 39

Allowances in Credit Amount, Quantity and Unit Price

a) The words 'about', 'approximately', 'circa' or similar expressions used in connection with the amount of the Credit or the quantity or the unit price stated in the Credit are to be construed as allowing a difference not to exceed 10% more or 10% less than the amount or the quantity or the unit price to which they refer.

b) Unless a Credit stipulates that the quantity of the goods specified must not be exceeded or reduced, a tolerance of 5% more or 5% less will be permissible, always provided that the amount of the drawings does not exceed the amount of the Credit. This tolerance does not apply when the Credit stipulates the quantity in terms of a stated number of packing units or individual items.

c) Unless a Credit which prohibits partial shipments stipulates otherwise, or unless sub-Article b) above is applicable, a tolerance of 5% less in the amount of the drawing will be permissible, provided that if the Credit stipulates the quantity of the goods, such quantity of goods is shipped in full, and if the Credit stipulates a unit price, such price is not reduced. This provision does not apply when expressions referred to in sub-Article a) above are used in the Credit.

Article 40

Partial Shipments/Drawings

a) Partial drawings and/or shipments are allowed, unless the Credit stipulates otherwise.

b) Transport documents which appear on their face to indicate that shipment has been made on the same means of conveyance and for the same journey, provided they indicate the same destination, will not be regarded as covering partial shipments, even if the transport documents indicate different dates of shipment and/or different ports of loading, places of taking in charge, or despatch.

c) Shipments made by post or by courier will not be regarded as partial shipments if the post receipts or certificates of posting or courier's receipts or dispatch notes appear to have been stamped, signed or otherwise authenticated in the place from which the Credit stipulates the goods are to be dispatched, and on the same date.

Article 41

Instalment Shipments/Drawings

If drawings and/or shipments by instalments within given periods are stipulated in the Credit and any instalment is not drawn and/or shipped within the period allowed for that instalment, the Credit ceases to be available for that and any subsequent instalments, unless otherwise stipulated in the Credit.

Article 42

Expiry Date and Place for Presentation of Documents

a) All Credits must stipulate an expiry date and a place for presentation of documents for payment, acceptance, or with the exception of freely negotiable Credits, a place for presentation of documents for negotiation. An expiry date stipulated for payment, acceptance or negotiation will be construed to express an expiry date for presentation of documents.

b) Except as provided in sub-Article 44 a), documents must be presented on or before such expiry date.

c) If an Issuing Bank states that the Credit is to be available 'for one month', 'for six months', or the like, but does not specify the date from which the time is to run, the date of issuance of the Credit by the Issuing Bank will be deemed to be the first day from which such time is to run. Banks should discourage indication of the expiry date of the Credit in this manner.

Article 43

Limitation on the Expiry Date

a) In addition to stipulating an expiry date for presentation of documents, every Credit which calls for a transport document(s) should also stipulate a specified period of time afier the date of shipment during which presentation must be made in compliance with the terms and conditions of the Credit. If no such period of time is stipulated, banks will not accept documents presented to them later than 21 days after the date of shipment. In any event, documents must be presented not later than the expiry date of the Credit.

b) In cases in which sub-Article 40 b) applies, the date of shipment will be considered to be the latest shipment date on any of the transport documents presented.

Article 44

Extension of Expiry Date

a) If the expiry date of the Credit and/or the last day of the period of time for presentation of documents stipulated by the Credit or applicable by virtue of Article 43 falls on a day on which the bank to which presentation has to be made is closed for reasons other than those referred to in Article 17, the stipulated expiry date and/or the last day of the period of time after the date of shipment for presentation of documents, as the case may be, shall be extended to the first following day on which such bank is open.

b) The latest date for shipment shall not be extended by reason of the extension of the expiry date and/or the period of time after the date of shipment for presentation of documents in accordance with sub-Article a) above. If no such latest date for shipment is stipulated in the Credit or amendments thereto, banks will not accept transport documents indicating a date of shipment later than the expiry date stipulated in the Credit or amendments thereto.

c) The bank to which presentation is made on such first following business day must provide a statement that the documents were presented within the time limits extended in accordance with sub-Article 44 a) of the Uniform Customs and Practice for Documentary Credits, 1993 Revision, ICC Publication No. 500.

Article 45

Hours of Presentation

Banks are under no obligation to accept presentation of documents outside their banking hours.

Article 46

General Expressions as to Dates for Shipment

a) Unless otherwise stipulated in the Credit, the expression 'shipment' used in stipulating an earliest and/or a latest date for shipment will be understood to include expressions such as, 'loading on board', 'dispatch', 'accepted for carriage', 'date of post receipt', 'date of pickup', and the like, and in the case of a Credit calling for a multimodal transport document the expression 'taking in charge'.

b) Expressions such as 'prompt', 'immediately', 'as soon as possible', and the like should not be used. If they are used banks will disregard them.

c) If the expression 'on or about' or similar expressions are used, banks will interpret them as a stipulation that shipment is to be made during the period from five days before to five days after the specified date, both end days included.

Article 47

Date Terminology for Periods of Shipment

a) The words to', 'until', 'till', 'from' and words of similar import applying to any date or period in the Credit referring to shipment will be understood to include the date mentioned.

b) The word 'after' will be understood to exclude the date mentioned.

c) The terms 'first half', 'second half' of a month shall be construed respectively as the 1st to the 15th, and the 16th to the last day of such month, all dates inclusive.

d) The terms 'beginning', 'middle', or 'end' of a month shall be construed respectively as the 1st to the 10th, the 11th to the 20th, and the 21st to the last day of such month, all dates inclusive.

F.   Transferable Credit

Article 48

Transferable Credit

a) A transferable Credit is a Credit under which the Beneficiary (First Beneficiary) may request the bank authorised to pay, incur a deferred payment undertaking, accept or negotiate (the 'Transferring Bank'), or in the case of a freely negotiable Credit, the bank specifically authorised in the Credit as a Transferring Bank, to make the Credit available in whole or in part to one or more other Beneficiary(ies) (Second Beneficiary(ies)).

b) A Credit can be transferred only if it is expressly designated as 'transferable' by the Issuing Bank. Terms such as 'divisible', 'fractionable', 'assignable', and 'transmissible' do not render the Credit transferable. If such terms are used they shall be disregarded.

c) The Transferring Bank shall be under no obligation to effect such transfer except to the extent and in the manner expressly consented to by such bank.

d) At the time of making a request for transfer and prior to transfer of the Credit, the First Beneficiary must irrevocably instruct the Transferring Bank whether or not he retains the right to refuse to allow the Transferring Bank to advise amendments to the Second Beneficiary(ies). If the Transferring Bank consents to the transfer under these conditions, it must, at the time of transfer, advise the Second Beneficiary(ies) of the First Beneficiary's instructions regarding amendments.

e) If a Credit is transferred to more than one Second Beneficiary(ies), refusal of an amendment by one or more Second Beneficiary(ies) does not invalidate the acceptance(s) by the other Second Beneficiary(ies) with respect to whom the Credit will be amended accordingly. With respect to the Second Beneficiary(ies) who rejected the amendment, the Credit will remain unamended

f) Transferring Bank charges in respect of transfers including commissions, fees, costs or expenses are payable by the First Beneficiary, unless otherwise agreed. If the Transferring Bank agrees to transfer the Credit it shall be under no obligation to effect the transfer until such charges are paid.

g) Unless otherwise stated in the Credit, a transferable Credit can be transferred once only. Consequently, the Credit cannot be transferred at the request of the Second Beneficiary to any subsequent Third Beneficiary. For the purpose of this Article, a retransfer to the First Beneficiary does not constitute a prohibited transfer.

Fractions of a transferable Credit (not exceeding in the aggregate the amount of the Credit) can be transferred separately, provided partial shipments/drawings are not prohibited, and the aggregate of such transfers will be considered as constituting only one transfer of the Credit.

h) The Credit can be transferred only on the terms and conditions specified in the original Credit, with the exception of:

- the amount of the Credit,
- any unit price stated therein,
- the expiry date,
- the last date for presentation of documents in accordance with Article 43,
- the period for shipment,

any or all of which may be reduced or curtailed.

The percentage for which insurance cover must be effected may be increased in such a way as to provide the amount of cover stipulated in the original Credit, or these Articles.

In addition, the name of the First Beneficiary can be substituted for that of the Applicant, but if the name of the Applicant is specifically required by the original Credit to appear in any document(s) other than the invoice, such requirement must be fulfilled.

i) The First Beneficiary has the right to substitute his own invoice(s) (and Draft(s)) for those of the Second Beneficiary(ies), for amounts not in excess of the original amount stipulated in the Credit and for the original unit prices if stipulated in the Credit, and upon such substitution of invoice(s) (and Draft(s)) the First Beneficiary can draw under the Credit for the difference, if any, between his invoice(s) and the Second Beneficiary's(ies') invoice(s).

When a Credit has been transferred and the First Beneficiary is to supply his own invoice(s) (and Draft(s)) in exchange for the Second Beneficiary's(ies') invoice(s) (and Draft(s)) but fails to do so on first demand, the Transferring Bank has the right to deliver to the Issuing Bank the documents received under the transferred Credit, including the Second Beneficiary's(ies') invoice(s) (and Draft(s)) without further responsibility to the First Beneficiary.

j) he First Beneficiary may request that payment or negotiation be effected to the Second Beneficiary(ies) at the place to which the Credit has been transferred up to and including the expiry date of the Credit, unless the original Credit expressly states that it may not be made available for payment or negotiation at a place other than that stipulated in the Credit. This is without prejudice to the First Beneficiary's right to substitute subsequently his own invoice(s) (and Draft(s)) for those of the Second Beneficiary(ies) and to claim any difference due to him.

G.   Assignment of Proceeds

Article 49

Assignment of Proceeds

The fact that a Credit is not stated to be transferable shall not affect the Beneficiary's right to assign any proceeds to which he may be, or may become, entitled under such Credit, in accordance with the provisions of the applicable law. This Article relates only to the assignment of proceeds and not to the assignment of the right to perform under the Credit itself.

ICC Arbitration

Contracting parties that wish to have the possibility of resorting to ICC Arbitration in the event of a dispute with their contracting partner should specifically and clearly agree upon ICC Arbitration in their contract or, in the event no single contractual document exists, in the exchange of correspondence which constitutes the agreement between them. The fact of issuing a letter of credit subject to the UCP 500 does NOT by itself constitute an agreement to have resort to ICC Arbitration. The following standard arbitration clause is recommended by the ICC:

'All disputes arising in connection with the present contract shall be finally settled under the Rules of Conciliation and Arbitration of the International Chamber of Commerce by one or more arbitrators appointed in accordance with the said Rules.'

ICC Uniform Customs and Practice for Documentary Credits - 1993 Revision
ICC Publication 500 - ISBN 92.842.1155.7
Published in its official English version by the International Chamber of Commerce, Paris
© 1993 - International Chamber of Commerce (ICC)
Available from: ICC Publishing SA, 38 Cours Albert 1ᵉʳ, 75008 Paris, France, and from: ICC United Kingdom, 14/15 Belgrave Square, London SW1X 8PS.

Appendix V

Uniform Rules for Bank-to-Bank Reimbursements under Documentary Credits

A. General Provisions and Definitions

Article 1

Application of URR

The Uniform Rules for Bank-to-Bank Reimbursements under Documentary Credits ('Rules'), ICC Publication No. 525, shall apply to all Bank-to-Bank Reimbursements where they are incorporated into the text of the Reimbursement Authorisation. They are binding on all parties thereto, unless otherwise expressly stipulated in the Reimbursement Authorisation. The Issuing Bank is responsible for indicating in the Documentary Credit ('Credit') that Reimbursement Claims are subject to these Rules.

In a Bank-to-Bank Reimbursement subject to these Rules, the Reimbursing Bank acts on the instructions and/or under the authority of the Issuing Bank.

These Rules are not intended to override or change the provisions of the ICC Uniform Customs and Practice for Documentary Credits.

Article 2

Definitions

As used in these Rules, the following terms shall have the meanings specified in this Article and may be used in the singular or plural as appropriate:

a) 'Issuing Bank' shall mean the bank that has issued a Credit and the Reimbursement Authorisation under that Credit.

b) 'Reimbursing Bank' shall mean the bank instructed and/or authorised to provide reimbursement pursuant to a Reimbursement Authorisation issued by the Issuing Bank.

c) 'Reimbursement Authorisation' shall mean an instruction and/or authorisation, independent of the Credit, issued by an Issuing Bank to a Reimbursing Bank to reimburse a Claiming Bank, or, if so requested by the Issuing Bank, to accept and pay a time draft(s) drawn on the Reimbursing Bank.

d) 'Reimbursement Amendment' shall mean an advice from the Issuing Bank to a Reimbursing Bank stating changes to a Reimbursement Authorisation.

e) 'Claiming Bank' shall mean a bank that pays, incurs a deferred payment undertaking, accepts draft(s), or negotiates under a Credit and presents a Reimbursement Claim to the Reimbursing Bank. 'Claiming Bank' shall include a bank authorised to present a Reimbursement Claim to the

Reimbursing Bank on behalf of the bank that pays, incurs a deferred payment undertaking, accepts draft(s), or negotiates.

f) 'Reimbursement Claim' shall mean a request for reimbursement from the Claiming Bank to the Reimbursing Bank.

g) 'Reimbursement Undertaking' shall mean a separate irrevocable undertaking of the Reimbursing Bank, issued upon the authorisation or request of the Issuing Bank, to the Claiming Bank named in the Reimbursement Authorisation, to honour that bank's Reimbursement Claim provided the terms and conditions of the Reimbursement Undertaking have been complied with.

h) 'Reimbursement Undertaking Amendment' shall mean an advice from the Reimbursing Bank to the Claiming Bank named in the Reimbursement Authorisation, stating changes to a Reimbursement Undertaking.

i) For the purposes of these Rules branches of a bank in different countries are considered separate banks.

Article 3

Reimbursement Authorisation Versus Credits

A Reimbursement Authorisation is separate from the Credit to which it refers, and a Reimbursing Bank is not concerned with or bound by the terms and conditions of the Credit, even if any reference whatsoever to the terms and conditions of the Credit is included in the Reimbursement Authorisation.

B.   Liabilities and Responsibilities

Article 4

Honour of a Reimbursement Claim

Except as provided by the terms of its Reimbursement Undertaking a Reimbursing Bank is not obligated to honour a Reimbursement Claim.

Article 5

Responsibilities of the Issuing Bank

The Issuing Bank is responsible for providing the information required in these Rules in both the Reimbursement Authorisation and Credit and is responsible for any consequences resulting from non-compliance with this provision.

C. Form and Notification of Authorisations, Amendments and Claims

Article 6

Issuance and Receipt of a Reimbursement Authorisation or Reimbursement Amendment

a) All Reimbursement Authorisations and Reimbursement Amendments must be issued in the form of an authenticated teletransmission or a signed letter.

When a Credit, or an amendment thereto which has an effect on the Reimbursement Authorisation, is issued by teletransmission, the Issuing Bank should advise its Reimbursement Authorisation or Reimbursement Amendment to the Reimbursing Bank by authenticated teletransmission. The teletransmission will be deemed the operative Reimbursement Authorisation or the operative Reimbursement Amendment and no mail confirmation should be sent. Should a mail confirmation nevertheless be sent, it will have no effect and the Reimbursing Bank will have no obligation to check such mail confirmation against the operative Reimbursement Authorisation or the operative Reimbursement Amendment received by teletransmission.

b) Reimbursement Authorisations and Reimbursement Amendments must be complete and precise. To guard against confusion and misunderstanding, Issuing Banks must not send to Reimbursing Banks:

   i)   a copy of the Credit or any part thereof or a copy of an amendment to the Credit in place of, or in addition to, the Reimbursement Authorisation or Reimbursement Amendment. If such copies are received by the Reimbursing Bank they shall be disregarded.

   ii) multiple Reimbursement Authorisations under one teletransmission or letter, unless expressly agreed to by the Reimbursing Bank.

c) Issuing Banks shall not require a certificate of compliance with the terms and conditions of the Credit in the Reimbursement Authorisation.

d) All Reimbursement Authorisations must (in addition to the requirement of Article 1 for incorporation of reference to these Rules) state the following:

   i)   Credit number;

   ii)   currency and amount;

   iii) additional amounts payable and tolerance, if any;

   iv) Claiming Bank or, in the case of freely negotiable credits, that claims can be made by any bank. In the absence of any such indication the Reimbursing Bank is authorised to pay any Claiming Bank;

   v)   parties responsible for charges (Claiming Bank's and Reimbursing Bank's charges) in accordance with Article 16 of these Rules.

Reimbursement Amendments must state only the relative changes to the above and the Credit number.

e) If the Reimbursing Bank is requested to accept and pay a time draft(s), the Reimbursement Authorisation must indicate the following, in addition to the information specified in (d) above:

   i)   tenor of draft(s) to be drawn;

   ii) drawer;

iii) party responsible for acceptance and discount charges, if any.

Reimbursement Amendments must state the relative changes to the above.

Issuing Banks should not require a sight draft(s) to be drawn on the Reimbursing Bank.

f) Any requirement for:

i) pre-notification of a Reimbursement Claim to the Issuing Bank must be included in the Credit and not in the Reimbursement Authorisation;

ii) pre-debit notification to the Issuing Bank must be indicated in the Credit.

g) If the Reimbursing Bank is not prepared to act for any reason whatsoever under the Reimbursement Authorisation or Reimbursement Amendment, it must so inform the Issuing Bank without delay.

h) In addition to the provisions of Articles 3 and 4, Reimbursing Banks are not responsible for the consequences resulting from non-reimbursement or delay in reimbursement of Reimbursement Claims, where any provision contained in this Article is not followed by the Issuing and/or Claiming Bank.

Article 7

Expiry of a Reimbursement Authorisation

Except to the extent expressly agreed to by the Reimbursing Bank, the Reimbursement Authorisation must not have an expiry date or latest date for presentation of a claim except as indicated in Article 9.

Reimbursing Banks will assume no responsibility for the expiry date of Credits and if such date is provided in the Reimbursement Authorisation it will be disregarded.

The Issuing Bank must cancel its Reimbursement Authorisation for any unutilised portion of the Credit to which it refers, informing the Reimbursing Bank without delay.

Article 8

Amendment or Cancellation of Reimbursement Authorisations

Except where the Issuing Bank has authorised or requested the Reimbursing Bank to issue a Reimbursement Undertaking as provided in Article 9 and the Reimbursing Bank has issued a Reimbursement Undertaking:

a) The Issuing Bank may issue a Reimbursement Amendment or cancel a Reimbursement Authorisation at any time upon sending notice to that effect to the Reimbursing Bank.

b) The Issuing Bank must send notice of any amendment to a Reimbursement Authorisation that has an effect on the reimbursement instructions contained in the Credit to the nominated bank or, in the case of a freely negotiable Credit, the advising bank. In the case of cancellation of the Reimbursement Authorisation prior to expiry of the Credit, the Issuing Bank must provide the nominated bank or the advising bank with new reimbursement instructions.

c) The Issuing Bank must reimburse the Reimbursing Bank for any Reimbursement Claims honoured or draft(s) accepted by the Reimbursing Bank prior to the receipt by it of notice of cancellation or Reimbursement Amendment.

Article 9

Reimbursement Undertakings

a) In addition to the requirements of sub-Article 6(a), (b) and (c) of these Rules, all Reimbursement Authorisations authorising or requesting the issuance of a Reimbursement Undertaking must comply with the provisions of this Article.

b) An authorisation or request by the Issuing Bank to the Reimbursing Bank to issue a Reimbursement Undertaking is irrevocable ('Irrevocable Reimbursement Authorisation') and must (in addition to the requirement of Article 1 for incorporation of reference to these Rules) contain the following:

   i) Credit number;

   ii) currency and amount;

   iii) additional amounts payable and tolerance, if any;

   iv) full name and address of the Claiming Bank to whom the Reimbursement Undertaking should be issued;

   v) latest date for presentation of a claim including any usance period;

   vi) parties responsible for charges (Claiming Bank's and Reimbursing Bank's charges and Reimbursement Undertaking fee) in accordance with Article 16 of these Rules.

c) If the Reimbursing Bank is requested to accept and pay a time draft(s), the Irrevocable Reimbursement Authorisation must also indicate the following, in addition to the information contained in (b) above:

   i) tenor of draft(s) to be drawn;

   ii) drawer;

   iii) party responsible for acceptance and discount charges, if any.

   Issuing Banks should not require a sight draft(s) to be drawn on the Reimbursing Bank.

d) If the Reimbursing Bank is authorised or requested by the Issuing Bank to issue its Reimbursement Undertaking to the Claiming Bank but is not prepared to do so, it must so inform the Issuing Bank without delay.

e) A Reimbursement Undertaking must indicate the terms and conditions of the undertaking and:

   i) Credit number and Issuing Bank;

   ii) currency and amount of the Reimbursement Authorisation;

   iii) additional amounts payable and tolerance if any;

   iv) currency and amount of the Reimbursement Undertaking;

   v) latest date for presentation of a claim including any usance period;

   vi) party to pay the Reimbursement Undertaking fee, if other than the Issuing Bank. The Reimbursing Bank must also include its charges, if any, that will be deducted from the amount claimed.

f) If the latest date for presentation of a claim falls on a day on which the Reimbursing Bank is closed for reasons other than those mentioned in Article 15, the latest date for presentation of a claim shall be extended to the first following day on which the Reimbursing Bank is open.

g) i) An Irrevocable Reimbursement Authorisation cannot be amended or cancelled without the agreement of the Reimbursing Bank.

ii) When an Issuing Bank has amended its Irrevocable Reimbursement Authorisation, a Reimbursing Bank which has issued its Reimbursement Undertaking may amend its undertaking to reflect such amendment. If a Reimbursing Bank chooses not to issue its Reimbursement Undertaking Amendment it must so inform the Issuing Bank without delay.

iii) An Issuing Bank which has issued its Irrevocable Reimbursement Authorisation Amendment, shall be irrevocably bound as of the time of its advice of the Irrevocable Reimbursement Authorisation Amendment.

iv) The terms of the original Irrevocable Reimbursement Authorisation (or an Authorisation incorporating previously accepted Irrevocable Reimbursement Authorisation Amendments) will remain in force for the Reimbursing Bank until it communicates its acceptance of the amendment to the Issuing Bank.

v) A Reimbursing Bank must communicate its acceptance or rejection of an Irrevocable Reimbursement Authorisation Amendment to the Issuing Bank. A Reimbursing Bank is not required to accept or reject an Irrevocable Reimbursement Authorisation Amendment until it has received acceptance or rejection from the Claiming Bank to its Reimbursement Undertaking Amendment.

h) i) A Reimbursement Undertaking cannot be amended or cancelled without the agreement of the Claiming Bank.

ii) A Reimbursing Bank which has issued its Reimbursement Undertaking Amendment shall be irrevocably bound as of the time of its advice of the Reimbursement Undertaking Amendment.

iii) The terms of the original Reimbursement Undertaking (or a Reimbursement Undertaking incorporating previously accepted Reimbursement Authorisations) will remain in force for the Claiming Bank until it communicates its acceptance of the Reimbursement Undertaking Amendment to the Reimbursing Bank.

iv) A Claiming Bank must communicate its acceptance or rejection of a Reimbursement Undertaking Amendment to the Reimbursing Bank.

Article 10

Standards for Reimbursing Claims

a) The Claiming Bank's claim for reimbursement:

i) must be in the form of a teletransmission, unless specifically prohibited by the Issuing Bank, or an original letter. A Reimbursing Bank has the right to request that a Reimbursement Claim be authenticated and in such case the Reimbursing Bank shall not be liable for any consequences resulting from any delay incurred. If a Reimbursement Claim is made by teletransmission, no mail confirmation is to be sent. In the event such a mail confirmation is sent, the Claiming Bank will be responsible for any consequences that may arise from a duplicate reimbursement;

ii) must clearly indicate the Credit number and Issuing Bank (and Reimbursing Bank's reference number, if known);

iii) must separately stipulate the principal amount claimed, any additional amount(s) and charges;

    iv) must not be a copy of the Claiming Bank's advice of payment, deferred payment, acceptance or negotiation to the Issuing Bank;

    v) must not include multiple Reimbursement Claims under one teletransmission or letter;

    vi) must, in the case of a Reimbursement Undertaking, comply with the terms and conditions of the Reimbursement Undertaking.

b) In cases where a time draft is to be drawn on the Reimbursing Bank, the Claiming Bank must forward the draft with the Reimbursement Claim to the Reimbursing Bank for processing, and include the following in its claim if required by the Credit and/or Reimbursement Undertaking:

    i) general description of the goods and/or services;

    ii) country of origin;

    iii) place of destination/performance;

and if the transaction covers the shipment of merchandise.

    iv) date of shipment;

    v) place of shipment.

c) Claiming Banks must not indicate in a Reimbursement Claim that a payment, acceptance or negotiation was made under reserve or against an indemnity.

d) Reimbursing Banks assume no liability or responsibility for any consequences that may arise out of any non-acceptance or delay of processing should the Claiming Bank fail to follow the provisions of this Article.

Article 11

Processing Reimbursement Claims

a) i) Reimbursing Banks shall have a reasonable time, not to exceed three banking days following the day of receipt of the Reimbursement Claim, to process claims. Reimbursement Claims received outside banking hours are deemed to be received on the next banking day.

    If a pre-debit notification is required by the Issuing Bank, this pre-debit notification period shall be in addition to the processing period mentioned above.

    ii) If the Reimbursing Bank determines not to reimburse, either because of a non-conforming claim under a Reimbursement Undertaking, or for any reason whatsoever under a Reimbursement Authorisation, it shall give notice to that effect by telecommunication or, if that is not possible, by other expeditious means, without delay, but no later than the close of the third banking day following the day of receipt of the claim (plus any additional period mentioned in sub-Article (i) above). Such notice shall be sent to the Claiming Bank and the Issuing Bank and, in the case of a Reimbursement Undertaking, it must state the reasons for non-payment of the claim.

b) Reimbursing Banks will not process requests for back value (value dating prior to the date of a Reimbursement Claim) from the Claiming Bank.

c) Where a Reimbursing Bank has not issued a Reimbursement Undertaking and a reimbursement is due on a future date:

    i)   The Reimbursement Claim must specify the predetermined reimbursement date.

    ii) The Reimbursement Claim should not be presented to the Reimbursing Bank more than ten (10) of its banking days prior to such predetermined date. If a Reimbursement Claim is presented more than ten (10) banking days prior to the predetermined date, the Reimbursing Bank may disregard the Reimbursement Claim. If the Reimbursing Bank disregards the Reimbursement Claim it must so inform the Claiming Bank by teletransmission or other expeditious means without delay.

    iii) If the predetermined reimbursement date is more than three banking days following the day of receipt of the Reimbursement Claim, the Reimbursing Bank has no obligation to provide notice of non-reimbursement until such predetermined date, or no later than the close of the third banking day following the receipt of the Reimbursement Claim plus any additional period mentioned in (a)(i) above, whichever is later.

d)   Unless otherwise expressly agreed to by the Reimbursing Bank and the Claiming Bank, Reimbursing Banks will effect reimbursement under a Reimbursement Claim only to the Claiming Bank.

e)   Reimbursing Banks assume no liability or responsibility if they honour a Reimbursement Claim that indicates that a payment, acceptance or negotiation was made under reserve or against an indemnity and shall disregard such indication. Such reserve or indemnity concerns only the relations between the Claiming Bank and the party towards whom the reserve was made, or from whom, or on whose behalf, the indemnity was obtained.

Article 12

Duplications of Reimbursement Authorisations

An Issuing Bank must not, upon receipt of documents, give a new Reimbursement Authorisation, or additional instructions, unless they constitute an amendment to, or a cancellation of an existing Reimbursement Authorisation. If the Issuing Bank does not comply with the above and a duplicate reimbursement is made, it is the responsibility of the Issuing Bank to obtain the return of the amount of the duplicate reimbursement. The Reimbursing Bank assumes no liability or responsibility for any consequences that may arise from any such duplication.

D.   Miscellaneous Provisions

Article 13

Foreign Laws and Usages

The Issuing Bank shall be bound by and shall indemnify the Reimbursing Bank against all obligations and responsibilities imposed by foreign laws and usages.

Article 14

Disclaimer on the Transmission of Messages

Reimbursing Banks assume no liability or responsibility for the consequences arising out of delay and/or loss in transit of any message(s), letter(s) or document(s), or for delay, mutilation or other errors arising in the transmission of any telecommunication. Reimbursing Banks assume no liability or responsibility for errors in translation.

Article 15

Force Majeure

Reimbursing Banks assume no liability or responsibility for the consequences arising out of the interruption of their business by Acts of God, riots, civil commotions, insurrections, wars or any other causes beyond their control, or by any strikes or lockouts.

Article 16

Charges

a) The Reimbursing Bank's charges should be for the account of the Issuing Bank. However, in cases where the charges are for the account of another party, it is the responsibility of the Issuing Bank to so indicate in the original Credit and in the Reimbursement Authorisation.

b) When honouring a Reimbursement Claim, a Reimbursing Bank is obligated to follow the instructions regarding any charges contained in the Reimbursement Authorisation.

c) In cases where the Reimbursing Bank's charges are for the account of another party, they shall be deducted when the Reimbursement Claim is honoured. Where a Reimbursing Bank follows the instructions of the Issuing Bank regarding charges (including commission, fees, costs or expenses) and these charges are not paid or a Reimbursement Claim is never presented to the Reimbursing Bank under the Reimbursement Authorisation, the Issuing Bank remains liable for such charges.

d) Unless otherwise stated in the Reimbursement Authorisation, all charges paid by the Reimbursing Bank will be in addition to the amount of the Authorisation provided that the Claiming Bank indicates the amount of such charges.

e) If the Issuing Bank fails to provide the Reimbursing Bank with instructions regarding charges, all charges shall be for the account of the Issuing Bank.

Article 17

Interest Claims/Loss of Value

All claims for loss of interest, loss of value due to any exchange rate fluctuations, revaluations or devaluations are between the Claiming Bank and the Issuing Bank, unless such losses result from the non-performance of the Reimbursing Bank's obligation under a Reimbursement Undertaking.

Appendix VI

Answers to Self-assessment Questions and Specimen Answers

Unit 2 - Answers to Self-assessment Questions

Answer 1
Transactions take place at current market prices with settlement within two working days of the deal being contracted.

Answer 2
The benefits of clean floating are:

- It provides an automatic adjustment mechanism for dealing with balance of payment problems.

- The authorities are not obliged to bring in trade restrictions to defend a particular exchange rate.

- International currency reserves should only be required on rare occasions for occasional exchange rate stabilisation,

Answer 3
The main criteria for economic convergence are:

- annual inflation to be not more than 1.5% higher than the average inflation rate of the three lowest inflation EU countries;

- annual budget deficit must not exceed 3% of gross domestic product;

- government debt must not to exceed 60% of GDP, unless the ratio is sufficiently diminishing at a satisfactory pace;

- the exchange rate must have been within the normal bands of the ERM for at least two years.

Answer 4
A single currency means inevitably a single general rate of interest in all participating countries. If countries are at different stages of the business cycle, they will tend to need different interest rates for the purposes of domestic economic policy.

Answer 5
The banking industry will lose in the short term from the closure of the currency exchange markets in the domestic currencies of the participating countries. However, this will be offset in the short term by the development of the spot, forward and futures markets in the euro, and in theory in the longer term the introduction of the euro

should increase trade with a consequent rise in the demand for banking services in general.

Answer 6
The savings on foreign exchange transaction costs for cross-border payments.

Answer 7
Relative interest rate differentials in the two countries. In the absence of any government restrictions, the forward currency of the country with the lower interest rates will be at a premium to spot (and vice versa). Remember the acronyms LIP & HID.

Answer 8
Real rates of interest are equalised between countries.

Answer 9
Normally a forward contract is settled by one transaction at maturity, whereas accrued futures gains and losses are settled on a daily basis by means of margin calls.

Answer 10
The initial margin is paid to the Clearing House by the buyer or seller of a futures contract at the outset. If the holder of the contract subsequently fails to settle any variation margin calls, then the contract will be closed out and the initial margin will ensure that funds are available to meet the default on the margin call.

Margin calls and the initial margin ensure that all parties to the futures contract honour their obligations. (The SIMEX futures exchange and the counterparties of Nick Leeson did not suffer any loss in the Barings fiasco because the exchange had funds to honour the obligations from the margin call and initial margin system.)

Unit 3 - Answers to Self-assessment Questions

Answer 1
Debit £16,286.64 (use 3.07, sell low). Remember, it is the bank which sells the DEM to the importer to enable him to settle the debt.

Answer 2
Credit £32,467.53 (use 3.08, buy high).

Answer 3

Spot buy	9.3055	Spot sell	9.2950
Less: Three months premium	0.0470	Less: Three months premium	0.0550
Three months forward fixed	9.2585	Three months forward fixed	9.2400

Answer 4

One to two months option forward buying rate

Spot buy	9.3055	Spot buy	9.3055
Less: One month premium	0.0140	Less: Two months premium	0.0325
One month forward fixed	9.2915	Two months forward fixed	9.2730

The bank will select 9.2915 as this is the better (higher) rate from its point of view.

One to two months option forward selling rate

Spot sell	9.2950	Spot sell	9.2950
Less: One month premium	0.0175	Less: Two months premium	0.0390
One month forward fixed	9.2775	Two months forward fixed	9.2560

The bank will select 9.256 (the lower) as this is the better rate from its point of view.

Note

For important customers the bank may compromise by quoting somewhere between the one- and two-month rates.

Answer 5

There is a firm and binding contract between the bank and the exporter, whereby the bank will buy FRF 50,000 from the exporter at 9.2915. The exporter must produce the currency some time between one and two months from the date on which the forward contract was agreed. When the currency is produced, the bank will credit the exporter's sterling current account with £5,381.26 (ignoring charges). The only 'optional' element is the exporter's choice of date within the one- to two-months period.

Answer 6

0.lpf = DEM0.001.

Answer 7

Spot buy	236.0	Spot sell	235
Less: One month premium	0.5	Less: One month premium	1
One month fixed buying rate	235.5		234

Answer 8

The buying rate for a spot to one-month option is 236. The selling rate for a spot to one-month option is 234. (This assumes that the bank does not need to 'shade' its rate because the customer is important.)

Answer 9

The exporter must fulfil his obligations. The only 'optional' aspect is the precise choice of date within the option period.

Unit 3 - Specimen Answer

Supply of 30 vehicles at DEM 10,000 each = DEM 300,000.

Purchase of 30 vehicles at US $3,500 = US $105,000.
US $ covered forward - spot to three months option forward choose between 1.7702 or 1.7702

$$-0.0340$$
$$\underline{1\ 7362}$$

Therefore, bank will choose 1.7362.

Transactions

US $105,000 at 1.7362	=	£60,476.90	Dr (10 November)
DEM 300,000 at 3.74	=	£80,213.90	Cr (20 February)
Profit		£19,737.00	

The DEM spot rate on 20 February is used as the deal was not covered forward.

Unit 4 - Answers to Self-assessment Questions

Answer 1
Close out.

Answer 2
The bank will sell the currency to the customer at the spot rate ruling on the date of the close-out. It will then buy back the currency at the agreed forward rate. The resultant difference will be debited or credited to the customer's sterling current account. Alternatively, if there is a reasonable period of time before the expiry of the original forward contract, the customer could arrange a matching forward contract with the same expiry date. This would fix the loss or gain on the close-out.

Answer 3
The bank will sell the currency at the agreed forward rate and will then buy it back at the spot buying rate ruling on the date of close-out. The resultant difference will then be debited or credited to the customer's sterling current account.

Answer 4
No. The only optional aspect of an option forward contract is the choice of date at which the customer must fulfil the terms. The customer could fix the date of close-out at any time during the option period, but he could not avoid the close-out.

Answer 5
The bank will mark a limit on the account, the amount of which will usually be between 10% and 20% of the sterling value of the forward contracts. Hence, the potential borrowing facilities will be reduced by the amount marked up as a limit under the forward contract.

Answer 6

(Dr) Sell DEM30,000 at 3.82	£7,853.40
(Cr) Buy back DEM30,000 at 3.80	£7,894.74
Net credit	£41.34

Answer 7

a) On date of default, close out as shown in Question 6. Credit the account £41.34.

b) On the same date, agree a new forward contract:

Spot close-out	3.800
Less: Premium	0.005
One month fixed	3.795

c) In one month's time debit the account:

DEM30,000 at 3.795 = £7,905.14

Answer 8

(Cr) Buy US $80,000 at 1.8875	=	£42,384.11
(Dr) Sell shortfall of US $20,000 at 1.88	=	£10,638.30
Net credit		£31,745.81

Answer 9

(Cr) Buy US $80,000 at 1.8875	=	£42,384.11
(Cr) Buy US $10,000 at spot 1.89	=	£5,291.00
Net credit		£47,675.11

Answer 10

a) Close out on date of default:

(Cr) Buy US $80,000 at 1.8875	=	£42,384.11
(Dr) Sell US $80,000 at 1.88	=	£42,553.19
Net debit		£169.08

b) Arrange extended forward contract on same date as the close-out:

Spot close-out rate	1.8800
Add: Discount	0.0048
	1.8848

c) One month later, credit customer:

US $80,000 at 1.8848 = £42,444.82

Unit 4 - Specimen Answer

1) When the customer buys goods from abroad, the bank sells him currency, thus the bank is selling DEMs. Conversely, when he exports goods, the bank buys the currency; hence, the bank buys Norwegian kroner.

2) The customer arranged his forward contracts on 1 July. The contracts were arranged on the basis of the receipts and payments which the merchant expected to receive on the information available on 1 July.

3) Forward contracts arranged on 1 July:

a) Bank to sell DEM47,900 (479 x 100) One-month forward fixed. (Payment to be made on a definite date.)

	Rate agreed
Spot	9.58
Less: Premium	0.02 (2pf is 0.02 of a DEM just as 2p is 0.02 of a £1)
	9.56

b) Bank to buy NOK 180,000 (900 x 200), one-to-two-month forward option. The earliest date he can expect payment is 1 August, one month ahead, and the latest is 31 August, two months ahead.

	Rate agreed		
Spot	17.0875		17.0875
Less: One month premium	0.0375	Less: Two months premium	0.0850
One month forward fixed	17.05	Two months fixed	17.0025

The bank chooses 17.05, being the most favourable rate to itself.

4) Actual currency transactions:

a) *1 July*

Sell DEM 47,900 at spot 9.58	=	(Dr)	£5,000.00
Add: Commission			7.50
		(Dr)	£5,007.50

b) *1 August*

Sell DEM 47,900 at spot 9.56	=	(Dr)	£5,010.46
Add: Commission			7.51
		(Dr)	£5,017.97

c) *6 August*

Buy NOK 90,000 at 17.05	=	(Cr)	£5,278.59
Less: Commission			7.91
		(Cr)	£5,270.68

Note

With an option forward contract, the total amount of currency in the forward contract can be dealt with in instalments, provided these instalments take place during the option period.

d) *1 September*

The bank will buy the DEMs at the spot rate ruling on that date, no forward contract having been arranged.

DEM47,900 at 9.56	=	(Cr)	£5,010.46
Less: Commission			7.51
		(Cr)	£5,002.95

e) *1 September*

Close out the balance of the forward contract:

Bank buys NOK90,000 at agreed forward rate of 17.05 = (Cr) £5,278.59
Bank sells them at spot rate on 1 September of 17.00   = (Dr) 5,294.12
Net   (Dr)   £15.53

Note

The only item which would appear on the customer's statement as regards the close out is a single debit of £15.53.

Net profit is total credits less debits = £232.63

Unit 5 - Answers to Self-assessment Questions

Answer 1

Importers require call options, since they need to buy foreign currency.

Answer 2

A UK exporter would require a put option, giving him the right to sell the underlying currency, DEMs, in exchange for sterling to be credited to his account b) is the correct answer).

Answer 3

American options can be exercised in whole or in part at any time up to the expiry date.

Answer 4

European options can only be declared on the stated expiry date, and the deal must then be settled within two working days.

Answer 5

Banks write OTC options. Exchange traded options are written on the Philadelphia Exchange in the USA, or on similar exchanges..

Answer 6

OTC options are arranged to meet the customer's needs, whereas exchange traded options are standardised.

Answer 7

American options give greater flexibility than European ones, and therefore, require a higher option premium.

Answer 8

The holder will exercise the option. He is selling DEMs to the bank. The strike rate gives a higher sterling credit.

100,000 DEMs at 3.40 = £29,411.76

100,000 DEMs at 3.50 = £28,571.42

Answer 9

The option should have an intrinsic value; therefore, the bank will be prepared to buy it back. If the bank refused, the customer could buy DEMs at spot and then sell them under the option.

Answer 10

The exporter will walk away and deal spot. He will receive £31,250 if he deals spot, rather than £29,411.76 via the option.

Answer 11

The option will not have any intrinsic value, and so it will be simply abandoned.

Answer 12

The importer will deal at 3.40, since he would be debited with a higher amount if he dealt at 3.10 on the spot.

Answer 13

The option would have an intrinsic value and could be sold to the bank.

Answer 14

Currency options eliminate the downside, but allow the holder to exploit the upside if spot rates move in his favour.

Answer 15

a) Both the put and call option values of the underlying DEMs are above the spot value in terms of sterling on maturity. The call will be abandoned, but the put will be exercised.

As the customer does not have any DEMs, he will buy them on the market at 2.95, and then sell them back to the bank at 2.80. The intrinsic value of the option will be

Market cost of DEM @ 2.95	£33,898.31
Option Value @ 2.80	£35,714.29
Net gain for customer	£1,815.98

Note

In practice, the option will probably be 'closed out' and the customer will not actually purchase the DEMs.

b) The customer will exercise the option and will sell the DEM at 2.80, receiving £35,714.29

c) At the time the options were arranged, there was a possibility that the spot rate on maturity could have been below 2.80 (say 2.70). Had this been the case, the customer would have abandoned the put, but the bank would have exercised its call at 2.90 since the call would have had intrinsic value.

The limit is marked up on the account to cover the bank in case the customer defaults in such circumstances. The principles are similar to those for marking up limits on forward contracts, and the contingent liability position for forwards and cylinder options is broadly similar.

Unit 6 - Answers to Self-assessment Questions

Answer 1
The UK exporter.

Answer 2
The Italian exporter.

Answer 3
Both parties run the risk, since US $ are 'foreign currency' to both. (In these circumstances the US $ are known as 'third-party currency', being the currency of neither the buyer nor the seller.)

Answer 4
The cross rate. (A cross rate is the rate of exchange of one foreign currency in relation to another foreign currency.)

Answer 5
Use the spot rate in this case. On the date of receipt, the amount of DEMs will be the equivalent of CHF 50,000, if converted at the spot cross rate.

Answer 6
No. All that will happen is that DEM balances will build up in the account. At some stage the UK exporter will need to convert the DEMs to sterling.

There must be receipts and payments in the same currency for a foreign currency account to be an appropriate means of reducing the exchange risk.

Answer 7
The advice is inappropriate, since an exchange rate exposure will have been created by the 'double cover' of currency borrowing and forward contracts.
Borrowing DEMs will eliminate the exchange risk, and the proceeds will be used to pay off the currency borrowing. If forward contracts are taken out as well as the currency borrowing, the bank will have to close out the contracts. (Note that it is possible to borrow slightly less than the full proceeds, so that the proceeds will pay off the principal and interest.)

Answer 8
When the currency was originally borrowed, the bank would have converted it to sterling at the spot buying rate, and credited the current account.

Now that the sale has fallen through, the only way that the currency can be repaid is for the bank to sell the currency at the day's spot selling rate. The sterling equivalent will be debited to the current account. Depending on the way the spot rate has moved, the resultant debit may be greater or less than the original credit.

Unit 6 - Specimen Answer

a) The risk is the exchange risk. The company is sterling-based and it has entered into commercial contracts to pay and receive dollars.

The exchange risk runs from the moment the commercial contract is signed until conversion of the receipts/payments into sterling. Nobody can predict the spot rate,

b) The company should open a US $ account and should arrange a forward contract to cover the anticipated net proceeds.

The forward contract is a firm and binding commitment on the part of Tiger Moth Ltd to deliver the agreed amount of US $ to the bank on a certain date (fixed forward) or any time between certain dates (option forward). The bank will convert the US $ to sterling at the agreed forward rate.

If Tiger Moth Ltd do not fulfil their obligations, the bank will close out.

c)   i) US $ Currency Account for Tiger Moth Ltd

Date	Dr	Cr	Balance	
1 June 1993	300,000		300,000	Dr
1 September		500,000	200,000	Cr
1 December	300,000		100,000	Dr
1 December		500,000	400,000	Cr
1 June 1994	300,000		100,000	Cr
1 June		250,000	350,000	Cr

ii) On 1 June 1993 the bank would have agreed a forward contract to buy the anticipated surplus of US $600,000 at:

Spot	1.3210
Plus: Discount	0.0105
One year fixed	1.3315

iii) On 1 June 1994, the bank will proceed as follows:

(Cr) Buy 600,000 at 1.3315	£450,619.60
(Dr) Sell shortfall 250,000 at 1.4610	£171,115.67
Net credit	£279,503.93

Unit 9 - Answers to Self-assessment Questions

Answer 1
Vostro account.

Answer 2
Nostro account.

Answer 3
Nostro account.

Answer 4
Vostro account.

Answer 5
There is no difference at all.

Answer 6

a) Debit customer   £10,000

    Credit vostro account   £9,970

    Credit UK bank's commission   £30

b) On receipt of advice the overseas bank will:

    Debit vostro account £9,970 (vostro account from point of view of UK bank)

    Credit beneficiary the currency equivalent of £9,970 less overseas bank's charges.

Answer 7
No. Please see 9.8.

Answer 8
No. Please see 9.9.

Answer 9
TTs are more expensive, but there is a saving in interest because of reduced float time.

Answer 10
Please refer to 9.3.

Unit 9 - Specimen Answer

a)   **Sterling Cheques**

  i)   The cheques are sent to the drawee bank who will:

      1) debit their customer with the currency equivalent of the sterling;

      2) credit their sterling account with the UK bank (a vostro account from the UK bank's point of view).

    The overseas bank will authorise the UK bank to debit the vostro account and the UK customer's account will be credited.

or

  ii) Sometimes the UK bank will send the cheques to its agent overseas who maintains a vostro account. The overseas agent will collect the sterling, place the funds in the vostro account and the UK bank can then debit this account and credit its customer.

Dollar cheques

The procedure is similar, but the overseas bank will credit the proceeds to the UK bank's nostro account. The UK bank then withdraws the dollars, converts them to sterling and credits the customer's account.

b)   Sterling Cheques

Ask the European buyers to pay by MT, since the funds would be treated as cleared as soon as they were received. Alternatively, TT may be better, provided the extra charges do not prove a stumbling block.

Dollar cheques

The bank could negotiate the cheques instead of collecting them. This would eliminate the exchange risk and the customer would know how much the sterling credit to his account was to be.

The disadvantages are:

    a)   No specific advice of fate;

    b)   Interest is charged;

    c)   A possible exchange risk if the cheques are unpaid.

The bank has lent dollars against the dollar proceeds. Hence, if the cheque is unpaid the bank must sell dollars at the spot rate ruling on that date. The customer could gain or lose.

In addition, it should be possible for our bank to set up a 'lockbox' facility whereby the American buyers would be asked to send their cheques to a postbox address in the USA. The lockbox would be opened by a correspondent bank on a daily basis. The corresponding bank could co-operate in arranging a negotiation facility by crediting the cheques to our bank's nostro account and advising our bank by SWIFT. Our bank could then negotiate the cheques as shown above.

Unit 10 - Answers to Self-assessment Questions

Answer 1
Please refer to 10.1.

Answer 2
The exporter, or his agent.

Answer 3
The shipper (exporter) must endorse the bill of lading on the back.

Answer 4
The shipping company will release the goods from the overseas port against production of any one original bill of lading. Hence, if a third party holds an original bill of lading, he may be able to obtain the goods before the importer arrives to claim them.

Answer 5

He should choose sea waybills. Please refer to 10.6.

Answer 6

This means that, as far as the shipping company is concerned, there is no apparent damage to the goods. Please see 10.4 for a more detailed explanation.

Answer 7

Bill of lading.

Answer 8

Generally speaking, the word **negotiable** indicates that a document is a document of title whereas **not negotiable** indicates that the transport document is not a document of title.

Answer 9

There is no problem. The airline will advise the importer of the arrival of the goods, and he will be able to collect them, provided he can produce identification.

Answer 10

The basic functions of a bill of lading are:

    a)   To act as a receipt for the goods;

    b)   To show evidence of the contract of carriage;

    c)   To act as a quasi-negotiable document;

    d)   To act as a document of title to the goods.

Only items (a) and (b) above apply to sea waybills and to air consignment notes.

Unit 11 - Answers to Self-assessment Questions

Answer 1

A pro forma invoice is issued before the buyer has agreed to purchase the goods, and thus goods have not been despatched.

Shipping marks are placed on the cases/boxes containing the goods and are also inserted on the relevant shipping documents.

Hence, there are no shipping marks in existence when a pro forma invoice is issued.

Answer 2

Unless there is a special agreement to the contrary, it is accepted that the standard Institute of London Underwriters clause A covers the **all-risk** obligation. Please refer to 11.4.

Answer 3

An insurance certificate.

Answer 4
Please refer to 11.7.

Answer 5
The TIR carnet ensures that no Customs duty is payable in the intermediate countries. Duty will only be payable in the country of the buyer. (Please refer to 11.7.)

Answer 6
A policy would be issued. Open cover and certificates only apply to regular exports of goods.

Answer 7
See if the shipping marks agree.

Answer 8
Third-party inspection certificate.

Answer 9
The sum assured is usually expressed in the same currency as that of the invoice, unless the buyer and seller have specifically agreed that this should not be the case.

Answer 10
On the face of it, the goods have been uninsured for two days. If the goods had been damaged during that period, no claim could have been made against the insurer.

Unit 12 - Answers to Self-assessment Questions

Answer 1
Incoterms, which were drawn up by the ICC, provide an internationally accepted set of standardised terms which set out where the exporter's responsibility ends as regards insurance and transport of goods.

Answer 2

   a) The exporter must pay the transport cost as far as Hamburg. Any extra costs incurred in unloading the goods from the ship at Hamburg will be at the buyer's expense.

   b) The exporter's responsibility as regards insurance ends when the goods have crossed the ship's rail at Hamburg.

Answer 3

   a) Seller's interest insurance (also known as transit insurance).

   b) If the importer knew about the seller's interest insurance, he would be tempted not to insure the goods for the sea voyage.

Answer 4
Under FOB UK port terms, the importer will be able to nominate any UK port for the delivery of goods by the exporter. Thus, the exporter cannot be sure of the costs he will incur in transport and insurance of goods to the nominated port.

With FOB Southampton, the exporter knows the port to which he must deliver the goods. He can therefore predict his costs of transport and insurance, and can therefore set accurate prices.

Answer 5

a) Cost and freight New York.

b) Cost, insurance and freight Hamburg.

Note
Never use the term carriage in relation to CFR or CIF.

Answer 6

a)   i)   An air waybill showing the importer as consignee.

           The air waybill will show that the goods have been loaded on board an aircraft at Heathrow.

           The details as regards airline, date and flight numbers will conform to those stipulated by the buyer.

     ii)   No insurance document is required from the exporter.

b)   i)   Full set of clean, shipped on board bills of lading, made out to order and blank endorsed by the exporter. The bills of lading will name the ship, the UK port of loading, and will show New Orleans as destination. The bills will be marked freight paid.

     ii)   The insurance document must be dated on or before the date of the bills of lading, and must cover the goods on their journey from the UK port as far as New Orleans.

Answer 7

a) The bill of lading would show the goods as being received for shipment by the port of Liverpool. It would be marked freight payable at destination.

b) As for (a) above, but the bill of lading would show the goods as shipped on board a named vessel at the port of Liverpool.

c) The bill of lading would show the goods as shipped on board a named vessel, destination Oslo, and would be marked freight paid.

Answer 8
The document required would be a combined transport bill of lading which showed the ultimate destination as the buyer's premises in Chicago. It would be marked freight paid.

Answer 9

a) All transport costs, once the goods have crossed the ship's rail at Hamburg, as far as his own UK premises.

b) All insurance costs for the above journey, i.e. from the ship's rail at Hamburg.

Answer 10
CIF Hamburg. Because the exporter must insure the goods as far as Hamburg under CIF terms, he will wish to charge a higher price. With CFR there is no obligation for the exporter to insure the sea voyage.

Unit 12 - Suggested Answer to Specimen Question

a)   Importing from Belgium
On the date of shipment, the importer would arrange a one-month forward fixed contract for the bank to sell BEF 1,103,000 at:

Spot	64.00
Less: One month's premium	0.15
One month forward fixed	63.85

In one month's time, the importer will make the following payments:

To the supplier, BEF 1,103,000 at 63.85	=	£17,274.86
To the shipping line, freight costs, £5 x 100	=	500.00
		17,774.86

This represents the CFR value To the insurance company:

$$17,775 \quad \text{x} \quad \frac{110}{100} \quad \text{x} \quad \frac{1}{100} \qquad = \qquad 195.53$$

Total cash paid one month after shipment	=	17,970.39

Plus. Two month's interest at 15%, for comparison purposes

$$17,970 \quad \text{x} \quad \frac{15}{100} \quad \text{x} \quad \frac{2}{12} \qquad = \qquad 449.25$$

$$18,419.64$$

Explanatory note not required in the answer
If we assume shipment is on 1 January, then the payments are due as follows:

Belgium	1 February
Spain	1 March
France	1 April

We are told to compare the quotes, and we must therefore take into account the fact that the Belgium payment will involve an extra two months' interest when compared to the French, whereas the Spanish will involve an extra one month's interest when compared to the French.

The solution for comparison purposes is to add two-months' interest to the Belgium payment and to add one month's interest to the Spanish payment.

b)   Importing from Spain

On the date of shipment the importer will arrange a two month fixed forward contract for the bank to sell ESB 2,650,000 at:

Spot	145.45
Plus: Two months' discount	2.20
Two months forward fixed	147.65

In two months' time the following payments will be made:

To the supplier, ESB 2,650,000 at 147.65 =		17,947.85
To the bank for collection charge =		44.87
To the insurance company:		

$$17,948 \quad x \quad \frac{100}{100} \quad x \quad \frac{1}{100} \quad = \quad 197.43$$

Total paid two months after shipment	18,190.15
Plus: One month's interest for comparison purposes	227.38
	£18,417.53

Explanatory note not required in the answer

The bank charge of 0.25% will be based on £17,947.85 as this will be the amount paid to the supplier by MT, TT or whatever settlement method has been agreed. Do not charge the 0.25% on the insurance premium as this will be paid as an entirely separate item by means of a domestic cheque.

c)   Importing from France

On the date of shipment, the importer will arrange a three months' forward fixed contract for the bank to sell FRF 169,700 at:

Spot	9.32
Less: Three months' premium	0.04
Three months forward fixed	9.28

In three months' time, the following payments will be made:

To the supplier FRF 169,700 at 9.28	=	£18,286.64
Plus: Documentary credits charges to bank at 0.75%	=	137.15
		18,423.79

Conclusion

The Spanish quotation is the cheapest if we take account of interest charges.

Unit 14 - Answers to Self-assessment Questions

Answer 1

Status enquiries and the NCM International Policy.

Answer 2

Study political and economic reports on countries and take out credit insurance.

Answer 3

a) Buyer Risk   -   90% cover (except non-acceptance of the goods - 72%)

b) Country Risk   -   95% cover

Answer 4

Credit insurance cover normally commences on despatch of goods. Where pre-credit insurance is held, the cover normally commences from the signing of the commercial sale contract.

Answer 5

Where the goods are of a specialised nature and when there are few alternative buyers for them.

Answer 6

No, it can only be used in conjunction with the ECGD's Supplier Credit Financing Facility.

Answer 7

90%.

Answer 8

This is an insurance policy which covers bad debts on export sales which arise through buyer default or country default.

Answer 9

Banks who have supplied funds at fixed rates where the cost of the funds is greater than the fixed rates.

Unit 14 - Suggested Answer to Specimen Question

a) The payment terms net cash one month after arrival of goods are open account terms. The exporter will ship the goods to New Orleans and will send any documents of title, such as bills of lading, directly to the buyer. ABC will also invoice the buyer, requesting payment on the appropriate date.

b) The credit risks are the buyer and country risk. It is safe to assume that country risk is not applicable in the case of the USA.

However, the buyer risk applies, because the exporter will lose control of the goods on shipment, and in this case the buyer will have had possession for one month before he need pay.

In the event of non-payment, it could be costly to sue the buyer, especially with the current high level of legal fees in the USA.

To sum up, the basic buyer risk with open account is that the exporter loses control of his goods without receiving any guarantee of payment.

c) The customer can guard against the exchange risk by:

   i) Forward contracts - fixed or option.

   ii) Borrowing currency now, converting the dollars to sterling, and repay the currency borrowing with the export proceeds. Allow for interest on the currency borrowing.

   iii) Purchasing a currency put option if the amount of the sale is large enough. This minimises any exchange loss, but still allows the exporter to take advantage of any upward valuation of the dollar.

   iv) Opening a dollar account, but only if ABC Ltd have receipts and payments denominated in dollars.

Unit 15 - Answers to Self-assessment Questions

Answer 1
The exporter will be the drawer, and the importer will be the drawee.

Answer 2
D/P.

Answer 3

Principal	-	Speirs and Wadley
Remitting Bank	-	Barclays
Collecting Bank	-	Hong Kong and Shanghai Bank
Presenting Bank	-	Downtown Trust Company

Answer 4
Please refer to 15.6.

Answer 5
Financial document - bill of exchange. Commercial document - bill of lading, insurance policy.

Answer 6
The drawee may well feel inclined to dishonour the collection because, in the absence of a full set of bills of lading, there is no guarantee that he will be able to obtain the goods.

Usually, there is a perfectly innocent explanation; for example, the exporter may retain a bill of lading in case the others go astray. If there is an explanation for the missing bill of lading, the drawee will be less inclined to refuse payment or acceptance.

Answer 7
See if the shipping marks tie up.

Answer 8
No. The exporter is not contractually bound to insure during the sea voyage, and therefore he would not be expected to produce an insurance document. (If he took out seller's interest insurance, the exporter would certainly not send the insurance document to the importer!)

Answer 9
D/P is more secure than D/A. The exporter retains control of the goods until payment under D/P terms.

Answer 10
Acceptance pour aval. The prior agreement of the drawee and his bank is needed.

Unit 15 - Suggested Answer to Specimen Question

If the air waybill shows the importer as consignee, then the documentary collection will be no more secure than open account. On arrival of the goods at the overseas airport, the importer will be notified and he will then be able to collect the goods simply by providing identification.

Thus, if the importer is shown as consignee, he will be able to obtain possession of the goods whether or not he pays the collection. This is because an air waybill is not a document of title.

In order to make these payment terms more secure, the air waybill should show the collecting bank as consignee. Under this arrangement, the collecting bank will not allow the goods to be released to the importer unless he pays for them.

The prior permission of the importer and the collecting bank is necessary, otherwise the collecting bank is entitled to refuse to have any dealings whatsoever with the goods. In practice, the collecting bank is unlikely to agree to act as consignee, unless its customer is of major importance.

One other possible way of increasing the security is for the exporter to have his name shown as consignee on the air waybill. The documentary collection is then sent in the usual way, but among the documents is a delivery order, signed by the exporter in favour of the importer. If the importer pays or accepts the bill of exchange, he will obtain the delivery order, which will authorise the air freight company to release the goods to him. Without the delivery order, the importer cannot obtain the goods.

Unit 16 - Answers to Self-assessment Questions

Answer 1
Please refer to 16.1.

Answer 2
A confirmed, irrevocable credit.

Answer 3

a)	Importer	-	Applicant (or opener or accreditor)
b)	Importer's Bank	-	Issuing Bank
c)	Exporter's Bank	-	Advising Bank
d)	Exporter	-	Beneficiary

Note

Documentary credits can be issued in favour of a beneficiary located in the same country as the applicant.

Answer 4

The exporter should receive a letter of advice from a bank in his country. If the advice purports to come directly from an unknown bank, the exporter should ask his own bank to check that the letter is genuine.

Answer 5

The creditworthiness of the issuing bank is substituted for that of the buyer. If the credit is confirmed, then there is a guarantee by two banks.

Answer 6

The exporter must despatch the goods, obtain the required documents, and present these documents to the place named in the credit on or before the expiry date.

Answer 7

Please refer to 16.4.

Answer 8

Under UCP 1993, banks deal in documents, not in goods, and banks are not directly concerned with the underlying sales contract. Hence, the bank will reject the presentation, since the documents do not conform to the credit.

Please refer to 16.8 for the various courses of action to take in this situation.

Answer 9

The exporter is entitled to payment. Under UCP 1993, banks are concerned with documents and not with goods. The bank must not become involved in contractual matters between buyer and seller. A contractual dispute does not constitute evidence of fraud.

Answer 10

No. A confirmed irrevocable documentary credit eliminates the buyer and country risk.

Answer 11

A claiming bank is one which pays, incurs a deferred payment undertaking, accepts drafts or negotiates under a documentary credit and presents a reimbursement claim to a reimbursing bank. This term also includes a bank authorised to present a reimbursement claim to a reimbursing bank on behalf of the bank which pays, incurs a deferred payment undertaking, accepts drafts or negotiates (Article 2(e), URBBR).

Answer 12

No more than three days following the day of receipt of the reimbursement claim (Article 11 (a) (i), URBBR).

Answer 13

P Bank can ignore the terms of the documentary credit, even if mention of them is made in the reimbursement authorisation (Article 3, URBBR).

Answer 14

An amendment to a reimbursement authorisation should either be in the form of an authenticated teletransmission or a signed letter (Article 6 (a), URBBR).

Answer 15

No (Article 7, URBBR).

Unit 16 - Suggested Answer to Specimen Question

a)   Are the Documents Acceptable?

All matters are governed by UCP 1993, unless the credit states otherwise. Points to note, re the combined transport document:

i)   UCP Article 26(a) indicates that a combined transport document is equivalent to a multimodal transport document.

ii) The description of the goods on all documents except the invoice need only be in general terms not inconsistent with the credit (Article 37). Therefore acceptable.

iii) Documents which indicate that transhipment may take place are acceptable, even if the credit forbids transhipment, provided one document covers the whole journey (Article 26(b)). Therefore acceptable.

iv) Article 39 permits a S% tolerance in amounts of goods, where goods are described by weight or volume. The monetary maximum has not been exceeded. Therefore the document is acceptable.

v)   The documents can be presented on the next business day when the expiry date is a non-business day. However, the combined transport document must indicate that the goods were received by the carrier on or before 24 February. The non-business day aspect refers only to presentation of documents. Therefore acceptable, provided the combined transport document is in order.

Invoice

It must describe the goods in exactly the same way as the credit. Therefore the invoice is not acceptable (Article 37).

Insurance document

Article 36 states that insurance documents which contain the Standard London Underwriters all-risk clause are acceptable. Hence, the clause is perfectly in order. However, broker's cover notes are not acceptable unless specifically authorised (Article 34).

b)   Action

i)   *Invoice*
This is a document which the beneficiary prepares; therefore, the customer can easily prepare a new one.

ii)   *Broker's cover note*
See if a policy or certificate can be obtained. The customer must contact the broker as a matter of urgency. If the documents can be amended locally on the day, all will be well. If not, cable the issuing bank for permission to pay despite the broker's cover note being submitted; **or** send the documents to the issuing bank on a collection basis. If the customer is creditworthy, pay against the customer's indemnity promising reimbursement if the issuing bank declines to pay.

Unit 17 - Answers to Self-assessment Questions

Answer 1
No. Please refer to 17.5 b).

Answer 2
The facilities may be marketed under a without recourse banner, but they are in fact with recourse. Please see 17.5 c).

Answer 3
a)   The customer has borrowed dollars. The interest rate is therefore based on dollar rates.

b)   The bank will convert the dollars at its spot buying rate.

Answer 4
a)   The presenting bank will not know about the negotiation aspect. The remitting bank will submit the documents and will use the normal collection order.

b)   The exporter will have signed a negotiation authority which will authorise the bank to amend his instructions on the collection order as it thinks fit.

Answer 5
Export factoring is totally inapplicable. The exporter must be established and must deal with a large range of reputable clients.

Answer 6
Export factoring. The factor collects the debt.

Answer 7
Red clause documentary credits, or assignments of proceeds of the credit.

Answer 8
The exporter could arrange for the confirming bank to issue a **letter of assignment**, which would bind the bank to pay over a stated amount from the proceeds, if any, received from the presentation under the credit terms.

A

Answer 9

Invoice discounting, export factoring, negotiation by the confirming bank of bills of exchange drawn under a confirmed letter of credit.

Answer 10

Liner waybills are not documents of title. The importer can obtain the goods without production of these documents, provided the importer is named as consignee. Hence, the documents do not give the negotiating bank any control of the goods.

Answer 11

With D/P collections, the negotiating bank retains control of the goods until payment, provided that a full set of documents of title are submitted. With D/A, control of the goods is lost the moment the importer accepts the bill of exchange.

Unit 17 - Answer to Specimen Question

There is only one answer, export factoring. Please refer to 17.8 for the details.

Unit 18 - Answers to Self-assessment Questions

Answer 1

When there are complicated or substantial contract obligations.

Answer 2

The ECGD Supplier Credit Financing facility; ECGD buyer credit facility and ECGD lines of credit.

Answer 3

£25,000.

Answer 4

The UK bank can claim from ECGD, who will be bound to pay under the terms of their guarantee. ECGD cannot claim from the exporter and this is why the facility is **without recourse**.

Answer 5

Export house facilities, whereby the UK export house buys the goods from the manufacturer.

Answer 6

Please refer to 18.6.

Answer 7

Forfaiting.

Answer 8

The buyer credit facility can only apply if the exporter's contract value is at least £5m. Lines of credit can be used for the sale of goods worth as little as US $25,000.

Unit 18 - Answer to Specimen Question

The ECGD SCF facility. Please refer to 18.3 for details.

Unit 19 - Answers to Self-assessment Questions

Answer 1
Travellers to the United States should always take US $ as opposed to sterling traveller's cheques.

Answer 2
Company credit card.

Answer 3
Please see 19.3.

Answer 4
Joint venture.

Answer 5
International licensing or international franchising.

Answer 6
All legal agreements should, if possible, state that they are governed by English law.

Answer 7
Chambers of Commerce, The Governments OTS (Overseas Trade Service) and the business section of most libraries.

Answer 8
Please see 19.4.

Answer 9
Loss or theft, inconvenience because of bulk, possible exchange control problems, surplus coins cannot be converted to sterling, any surplus notes which are converted back to sterling involve an exchange risk.

Unit 19 - Answer 1 - Special Optics Ltd

a)   Advantages and Disadvantages of Employing a Distributor
Special Optics would sell their goods to a distributor who then sells those goods on his own account. The distributor's profit is the difference between his selling price and the price paid to Special Optics, after allowing for expenses.

Advantages
The distributor is able to offer the following benefits:

1   Local knowledge of the market and conditions.

2   Able to converse with potential French buyers.

3   On the spot as a point of reference in the market place for pre- and after-sales service.

4   May be willing to promote, display and/or stock goods.

5   May more easily be able to assess and control the credit risk of trading with local buyers.

From the UK exporter's point of view the benefits are:

6   The exporter is able to deal with one party in the country which will reduce administrative costs.

7   There is only one credit risk to assess.

8.   The exporter can more easily develop/concentrate on the relationship with one party.

9   The exporter may develop more business because of points I to 8.

10   The legal position regarding distributors may well be much more favourable for Special Optics than that which applies in the case of agents.

Disadvantages
The distributor:

1   may have other clients to satisfy as well as Special optics;

2   may lack in credit standing;
     This means the UK exporter;

3   is reliant on someone else to be successful in the market;

4   could be put at arm's length from buyers;

5   may not gain sufficient knowledge of the market if the agreement with the distributor is terminated.

b)   Travel Services Offered by UK Banks that would Assist in Regular Overnight Trips to Paris
Mr Glass would need facilities that were readily acceptable and some of which might be retained for the next visit:

1   A small amount of foreign notes that may be used for taxis, etc., and an ATM card to obtain cash when needed.

2   Means of paying larger business expenses, e.g. hotel, business

     entertainment:

     ● personal credit cards and some debit cards;

     ● company credit cards.

3.   Because trips are made regularly:

     ● hotel account could be settled by bank transfer;

- Mr Glass might also take travellers cheques or eurocheques supported by a cheque guarantee card.

4. It may be appropriate to issue a letter of introduction to the bank's own Paris office or correspondent bank. If an account is warranted, specimen signatures may be provided.

5. In this case, a bank account in Paris may be appropriate, rather than an open credit, which some banks have discontinued.

6. The bank would be able to arrange travel insurance if required.

    In view of the small amount of expenditure, tying up funds in travel facilities and exchange risk are considerations, but relatively minor ones.

c) Advantages and Disadvantages of a Collection Account
Advantages

1. Beneficial to French importers who may be more willing to do business on this basis, i.e. easier and cheaper to make a domestic payment in French francs for which there is no exchange risk.

2. Special Optics may bulk up smaller payments to reduce charges on transfers to the UK.

3. They could use the account to make payments in France, e.g. Mr Glass's visits.

Disadvantages

1. Payments to the account are not necessarily cleared funds as bank transfers to UK would be:

2. Only suitable if adequate number of payments into account.

3. Would be required to keep an average balance on the account to provide remuneration or pay an account maintenance charge.

4. Would need regular reports to check receipt of funds.

    in the absence of balance and transaction reporting by electronic banking or fax, reconciliation of incoming funds and statements could be problematic.

5. The balance of the account is subject to exchange risk unless payments are made from the account.

6. Funds may be needed for UK cashflow reasons, e.g. the company may have a credit balance in the collection account and may be borrowing in £ in the UK.

Answer - Telecom Exports Ltd

a) **Although Telecom Exports Ltd is an experienced exporter, the company may still need help for trade promotion in unfamiliar markets.**

439

Examples of relevant services currently available from the OTS are:

i) Information on countertrade opportunities and on specialist countertrade brokers who may be able to set up a deal.

ii) Export data services, including access to data services from other organisations.

iii) Country profiles giving an overall view of the potential market. Sector reports on particular industries overseas.

v) A register of enquiries from the appropriate overseas sector concerning Telecom's product range.

vi) Specialist country desks, staffed by experts on a particular country.

vii) Help with language and cultural requirements of the target market.

viii) Attending trade missions, both inward and outward.

ix) Details of OTS-sponsored trade fairs.

x) Advice on names of suitable local representatives.

b) **If, and only if, market research indicates that there are profitable opportunities:**

● Employ as sales manager an expert on Eastern Europe who could visit the area to make contacts.

● Set up a local agency, using an agent recommended by the OTS.

● Attend trade missions and exhibit at trade fairs, so as to see the market at first hand and help assess the market's potential.

● Seek countertrade deals using specialist brokers.

● Seek arrangements with other European or UK companies who have expertise in this market. The companies could share costs and revenues, and reduce the risks of the new venture.

● Set up a joint venture with a local company to avoid import quotas or tariffs.

● Open an Eastern Europe representative office. This would employ local staff and would act as a focal point for potential enquirers.

Unit 20 - Answers to Self-assessment Questions

Answer 1
The exporter's bank.

Answer 2
A counter-indemnity.

Answer 3
If a valid claim is made, the exporter's bank must pay irrespective of whether its customer has funds.

Answer 4

A stand-by letter of credit is governed by a clear set of rules, UCP. In addition, there is a stated expiry date which cannot be amended without the exporter's consent and that of his bank.

Answer 5

Applicant:	UK exporter.
Issuing bank:	UK bank.
Advising bank:	US bank.
Beneficiary:	US importer.

Answer 6

The **contingent liability** will remain outstanding, and thus his borrowing facilities will continue to be curtailed. The annual bank charges will continue to be levied.

Answer 7

By incorporating a reduction clause and an operating clause. Please see 20.6 d).

Answer 8

The tender bond will almost certainly commit the UK bank to issuing a performance bond for, say, 10% of the contract value, if the contract should be awarded. The UK bank must also consider whether the customer will need extra loan or overdraft facilities to fulfil the contract. It would be totally illogical to issue a performance bond and then to refuse the finance to complete the contract.

To sum up, the UK bank when asked to issue a tender bond must consider:

a) The creditworthiness of the exporter. Is he good for the amount of any performance bond plus any other financial facilities required to fulfil the contract?

b) Is the exporter technically capable of fulfilling the contract?

c) Is there any bond support available from the ECGD?

Unit 20 - Suggestions for the Answer

a) The answer requires a résumé of the various bonds and stand-by letters of credit as set out in this unit. Mention of bank assistance in countertrade as shown in 20.8 could also be made.

In addition, students should make a comment along the following lines:

One major risk in connection with tender bonds is the exchange risk. Usually the contract will be denominated in foreign currency, and the exporter must cover the exchange risk unless he wishes to gamble. However, if forward contracts are arranged, and if the contract is not awarded, then the exporter can face a possible loss or a possible gain on the close-out. Currency put options give the right but not the obligation to the exporter to sell a set amount of currency to the bank at a pre-set rate. If the contract is not awarded, the exporter may be able to sell the option back to the bank for its intrinsic value. If the option does not have an intrinsic value, then the exporter can **walk away**.

When several UK contractors are bidding for the same overseas contract, the bank may be able to offer a special currency option facility whereby each contractor pays his share of the option premium for a single currency option, with an agreement that the successful bidder will reimburse the other bidders' option premiums via the bank, and will take over the option in full. Obviously, the bank must ensure strict confidentiality in such arrangements.

b) This part requires a description of the ECGD bond support facility set out in 20.6 a).

Do **not** make the mistake of listing the services, such as guidance on Incoterms, which banks give to small exporters. Large-scale contractors do not require such basic services.

Unit 21 - Answers to Self-assessment Questions

Answer 1

b) The collecting bank is employed by the remitting bank and must follow that bank's instructions.

Answer 2
The presenting bank will claim from the remitting bank, who will be responsible for reimbursement. The remitting bank will then debit the principal's account.

Answer 3
With the D/P collection, the goods would be on the quayside at the importing country's port (assuming they came by sea), and thus, insurance must be effected if the collection instruction so stipulates.

With the D/A collection, the goods will already have been released to the importer on acceptance. Hence, insurance is irrelevant as the goods are out of the control of the bank.

Answer 4
A UK presenting bank would note the bill, to preserve the right to protest at a later date.

Answer 5
UK practice is not to insure goods unless a specific **store and insure** clause appears on the collection instruction.

Answer 6
While there is no recognition of avalisation in the Bills of Exchange Act, the practical position is that the avalising bank guarantees payment at maturity.

Answer 7
The presenting bank should:

a) Take the £5,000 and pay it to the remitting bank;

b) Protest for the full amount of the bill if protest instructions apply;

c) Advise the remitting bank of the position.

Answer 8
A householder's protest will apply:

a) When an inward collection is dishonoured;

b) When protest instructions apply;

c) When there is no Notary Public available.

Answer 9
With noting, the Notary Public does not personally visit the drawee, but with protesting he does.

Answer 10
The bank will not accept the countermand because it has guaranteed payment at maturity. The customer will have signed an authority which precludes countermand of avalised bills.

Answer 11

a) An original bill of lading, made out to order and blank endorsed by the **shipper**.

b) Proof of identity only, provided the importer is the named consignee.

Answer 12
An indemnity.

Answer 13
A counter-indemnity.

Answer 14
The amount of the indemnity, the creditworthiness and integrity of the customer, whether the indemnity is in standard form.

Answer 15

a) When the importer deals on documentary collection terms.

b) When the overseas exporter has arranged for the collecting bank to be named as consignee on the air waybill.

c) When the goods arrive before the documents.

Unit 22 - Answers to Self-assessment Questions

Answer 1
The issuing bank guarantees to honour the credit, irrespective of whether the applicant has funds, provided the documents fulfil the terms of the credit. Hence, the bank treats the documentary credit facility as a lending facility.

Answer 2
The issuing bank must pay the credit. It will then obtain control of the goods, via the bills of lading, and will sell them in reimbursement. The bank has a right of action against the applicant as regards any shortfall in the sale proceeds.

Answer 3
The bank could use the documents to have the goods warehoused in its name. The bank could then apply the produce loan procedure (see 21.13).

Answer 4
Under CFR terms, it is the buyer's responsibility to insure the sea voyage. Hence, the credit must not call for an insurance document. The credit should only call for documents which are the responsibility of the exporter.

Answer 5
The issuing bank could take an authority from the applicant to debit his account and transfer funds to a special suspense account. This would be earmarked to meet payment as and when due under the credit. The amount transferred could be the full amount of the credit. However, it would be more usual to take an agreed percentage, say, 10%.

Answer 6
The importer, being named as consignee, will be able to obtain the goods without the co-operation of the issuing bank. As a result, the bank cannot look upon the goods as security.

Answer 7
Check the expiry date to ensure that there is adequate time for the information to reach the advising bank. (Banks nowadays prefer not to use airmail for transmitting documentary credit details, as this method is more conducive to fraud, so secure methods such as SWIFT are preferred.)

Answer 8
Chamber of Commerce located in the exporter's country.

Answer 9
The issuing bank must refer to its customer to see if he is prepared to pay despite the discrepancy. The issuing bank has no responsibility or duty to honour the credit, and will only pay if the importer authorises payment and if he has sufficient funds. The issuing bank must also immediately advise the advising bank of any discrepancy in the documents.

Answer 10
The commercial reliability and integrity of the beneficiary.

Unit 23 - Answers to Self-assessment Questions

Answer 1

Transferable credit. A back-to-back credit is not appropriate because the bank will be involved in a liability under such an arrangement.

Answer 2

The Australian is the applicant. Dealer is the first beneficiary. The Brazilian is the second beneficiary.

Answer 3

The Australian bank advises an amount of US $5,500 to our bank. Our bank advises US $5,000 to the Brazilian bank.

Answer 4

The Brazilian seller.

Answer 5

Our bank will substitute Dealer's invoice for the Brazilian exporter's invoice, and will substitute a bill of exchange for the full US $5,500.

Answer 6

a) Nostro accounts.

b) US $5,500 from the nostro account of the Australian bank.

c) We shall transfer US $5,000 to the nostro account of the Brazilian bank and shall transfer US $500 for credit to Dealer's account.

Answer 7

Buying rate.

Answer 8

US $500.

Answer 9

a) No.

b) No, apart from the bank charges involved in the transfer by ourselves to the second beneficiary.

Answer 10

a) Widgets.

b) From a Brazilian port.

c) To an Australian port.

Unit 23 - Solution to Question on Transferable and Back-to-back Credits

Neither back-to-back nor transferable credits are appropriate here because different transport documents are used.

The credit in favour of the Australian will call for bills of lading evidencing shipment of phosphate from Australia to the UK, whereas the other credit will call for bills of lading evidencing shipment of fertiliser from the UK to India.

Thus, the documents under the Australian credit will not be of any validity as regards the Indian credit.

Exam point

If transferable or back-to-back credits are applicable, the underlying transaction will involve transport of goods directly from the ultimate seller's country to the ultimate buyer's country.

Unit 23 - Model Answers to Revision Questions

Answer 1: Held & Sons

a) The basic definitions are covered in the Uniform Customs and **Practice for Documentary Credits.**

A **documentary credit** is a guarantee by the issuing bank (in this case ourselves) to a beneficiary (the French seller), that payment will be made if the correct documents set out in the credit are presented in the stipulated time. Held & Sons are the applicant.

Irrevocable means that the credit cannot be amended without the consent of all parties. Thus, our customer must realise that he is committed to paying for the goods provided that the correct documents are submitted.

Confirmed means that a bank in the beneficiary's country provides an additional guarantee that if the issuing bank defaults, they will honour the commitment, provided that the terms of the credit have been fulfilled. It would seem to be an unnecessary expense to have a credit which a UK bank has issued confirmed but, if the seller insists, then our customer must comply.

Transferable. The first beneficiary, the French seller, is authorised to transfer the credit to a third party, if he wishes. The first beneficiary will request the transferring bank to make the credit available to a third party.

The credit can be transferred only on the terms of the original credit, apart from amount, unit price, expiry date, and possibly insurance requirements.

Under UCP a credit must expressly state that it is transferable before it can be transferred.

b) The French seller is obviously obtaining the steel from another source and is acting as a middleman. A transferable credit enables the second beneficiary to have the benefit of a documentary credit without any liability on the part of the middleman or his bankers.

c) Our customers, Held & Sons, do not know who is actually supplying the steel. Thus, the credit should call for a third-party inspection certificate to ensure that the goods are of the proper quality.

Answer 2: Junk Galore

a) If the bank establishes an irrevocable letter of credit in favour of an overseas supplier, it is committed to making payment if the correct documents are presented within the stipulated time. This commitment applies irrespective of whether the bank's customer has funds to meet it.

Since the customer's facilities are fully extended, the only way to protect the bank is to use the calculators as security for the bank's liability under the credit. Because the bills of exchange are payable 90 days after sight, the calculators would normally have been released to the customer on presentation of the documents. Therefore, some form of produce loan procedure is required to protect the bank by giving the bank rights against the calculators, or their proceeds.

b) Preliminary checks to make are:

   i)   Status report on the supplier and ultimate buyer.

   ii) Are the calculators readily saleable if the deal falls through?

   iii) Is there a firm sale contract with the ultimate buyer?

If the above are satisfactory, proceed as follows:

1) The customer must sign a letter of pledge at the same time as he signs the application form for the documentary credit.

2) The credit must call for a full set of clean, shipped on board bills of lading made out to order and blank endorsed, and a third-party inspection certificate. As the sale contract is CIF, an insurance document must be called for.

3) On presentation of the documents called for under the credit, the bank's agent will arrange for the calculators to be warehoused in the bank's name, exchanging the bills of lading for warehouse keeper's warrants in the bank's name.

4) The goods will be insured at the customer's expense.

5) Release the calculators to the customer for delivery to the ultimate buyer. The customer must sign a trust receipt and the bank will issue a delivery order to the warehouse in favour of the customer.

6) The money is due one month after receipt of the goods in the UK. Payment under the credit is not due for three months. Retain the funds in a suspense account to meet the bank's liability under the credit.

Answer 3: Trees Cut and Sawn

(**Note** This is **not** transferable/back-to-back credits. With transferable/back-to-back credits, the original seller is the one who 'ships' the goods, not the middleman.)

A red clause documentary credit is required. The applicant is Trees Cut and Sawn, the issuing bank is ourselves and the beneficiary is the Norwegian company.

The credit will authorise the advising bank to grant an advance to the Norwegian company prior to shipment. The Norwegian company will use the money to purchase the timber; they will then ship the timber and obtain the necessary shipping documents.

On presentation of documents, the money will be paid over to the company under the terms of the credit, after deduction of the loan plus interest.

If the Norwegian company defaults, the issuing bank must repay the loan to the advising bank, debiting Trees Cut and Sawn.

A red clause documentary credit amounts to an unsecured loan to the beneficiary for which the applicant is liable.

Note
As an alternative to the red clause procedure, Trees Cut and Sawn may suggest that the Norwegian merchant tries to negotiate pre-shipment credit from its suppliers, by offering to assign a proportion of the proceeds of the credit to those suppliers (see Unit 17, 17.7 c)).

Appendix VII

Answers to Revision Questions

Revision Questions 1

Currency Option Test: Answers

Answer 1
Exercise the option.

Answer 2
Walk away and deal spot.

Answer 3
Sell the option to the bank at its intrinsic value.

Example, not required in the answer:

Say US $100,000 involved.

Exporter could buy dollars spot

(i.e. bank sells dollars spot) at 1.90	Debit	£52,631.58
Customer sells back at 1.80	Credit	£55,555.56
	Net credit	£ 2,923.98

Instead of going through the above, the bank would offer to buy back the option for round about £2,924, i.e. its intrinsic value.

Answer 4
Walk away/abandon the option. The right to sell at 1.80 is of no value, if spot deals are at 1.71.

Note
If the customer would have exercised if he had the underlying currency, then the option must have an intrinsic value, and can be sold back to the bank.

Answer 5

a)   Walk away and deal spot (e.g. if amount is US$100,000 he would rather be debited £52,631 at 1.90, than £55,555.56 at 1.80.)

b)   Exercise the option. (Choice Dr 58,823.53 at spot or £55,555.56 at 1.80.)

c)   Abandon the option.

d)   Sell the option for its intrinsic value.

General Revision Questions: Answers

Answer 1
Advise the customer that he has not been penalised because:

a)   Banks do not speculate on the foreign exchange market. When the bank arranges a forward contract with the customer, it will make a 'matching' contract in the foreign exchange market.

b)   If the customer cannot fulfil the forward contract , the bank will, nevertheless, have to fulfil its 'matching' forward contract in the market. Thus, the customer's forward contract must be honoured.

c)   The only way in which the original banker/customer forward contract can be fulfilled is for the bank to close out, i.e. carry out the original deal at the agreed forward rate. Sell or buy, as appropriate, the currency at the present spot rate.

d)   Any loss on the close out is passed on to the customer, but if a profit had been made, the customer would have been credited.

e)   A forward contract is a firm and binding commitment on both bank and customer.

Answer 2
The forward contract rate would be:

	3.927
Less	0.093
	3.834

At maturity bank	sells 400,000 at 3.834	=	£104,329.68
	buys 40,000 at 3.9415	=	£ 10,148.42
	Net Debit	=	£ 94,181.26

Answer 3

a)   The forward contract will be a two to three month option for the bank to buy $100,000. (The date of shipment is not known for certain, nor is the date of payment certain; it depends on shipment.)

Spot rate	1.7775	or spot rate	1.7775
Plus: Discount	0.0123	Plus: Discount	0.0245
Two months forward rate	1.7898	Three months forward rate	1.8020

The bank is buying so it will choose the rate most favourable to itself, i.e. 1.8020.

b) The forward contract is for $100,000 but the customer only receives $95,000. The bank must therefore carry out the close out procedure.

Credit customer with the full 100,000 at the agreed forward rate:

100,000 at 1.8020		=	£55,493.90
Debit him with shortfall at spot sell: 5,000 at 1.795		=	£ 2,785.52
Net credit			£52,708.38

Answer 4

The forward contract rate arranged would be:

Spot sell	3.9225
Less: Premium	0.0086
Six months forward	3.9139

On being asked to extend the forward contract the bank would act as follows:

a) Close out the original forward contract.

b) Arrange a new forward contract.

Close out

Sell DEM 400,000 at 3.9139		=	102,199.85
Buy them back at spot 3.9395		=	101,535.72
Net debit			664.13

Extension

The new rate would be based on the close-out rate: 3.9395

Less: Premium	0.0015
	3.9380

When the customer completes the deal the bank will debit him

400,000 at 3.9380 = £101,574.40.

Revision Questions 2

CIB Multiple-choice Test: Answers

Answer 1

  b)

Answer 2

  c)

Answer 3

  c)

Answer 4

  c)

Answer 5

  d)

Answer 6

  d)

Answer 7

  a)

Answer 8

  d)

Answer 9

  b)

Answer 10

  d)

Specimen Answer to Exam Question 1

a) Customer exports: bank buys

    i) Spot one-month   9.3055

        Less   0.0140

        One-month forward fixed   9.2915

        Bank chooses spot -   9.3055

        Expected sterling   £53.731.66

    ii) One-to-two-months' option - bank buys

                                  9.3055

        Less   0.0325

        Two months' fixed forward   9.2730

        Bank chooses one month rate (see above)

        Sterling proceeds expected   £53,812.62

    iii) Two-to-three months' forward option

        Bank will choose two months' rate   9.2730

        Sterling proceeds expected   £53,919.98

b) Under UCP banks deal in documents not goods. The credit is irrevocable, and cannot be cancelled without the agreement of all parties.

   As the documents are correct, and as we are the paying bank, we shall pay the credit.

c) The forward contract, option two to three months, is to be extended by one-month option. The extension occurs on 1 June, and the new forward contract will be a one-to-two month forward option as payment can occur any time in July.

   1 June

   Close-out

   (Notional credit) Buy 500,000 at forward rate of 9.2730   £53,919.98

   (Notional debit) Sell 500,000 at spot rate of 9.3100   £53,705.69

   Net credit   £214.29

   This amount, £214.29, is credited on 1 June.

d) Extension one to two month forward option buy.

Spot close-out rate	9.3100		9.3100
Less	0.0090	*Less*	0.0240
One month fixed	9.3010	Two months fixed	9.2860

Bank will choose 9.3010.

e) A currency option (put option in this case) gives the exporter the right but not the obligation to sell the francs to the bank at a pre-set rate.

The exporter would pay a premium to the bank for this right. The pre-set rate of exchange would usually be the spot rate at the time the option is arranged, but the rate can be subject to negotiation.

If the exporter has the underlying currency, he can either exercise the option, if the pre-set rate is better for him than the current spot rate, or he can 'walk away' if spot is better.

If the exporter does not have the underlying currency, he can sell the option back to the bank if it has an intrinsic value, otherwise he will abandon it.

Specimen Answer to Exam Question 2

i)   The Risks to the Company
Buyer risk

a) The buyer may not take up the documents. In this case, the exporter still retains legal control, but the actual goods are physically in the USA.

b) The buyer will obtain the documents, and hence the goods, once he accepts a bill of exchange. but there is no guarantee that the bill of exchange will be paid on the due date.

Country risk
The US government could impose exchange controls to prevent the buyer from paying. This is most unlikely to happen in the case of the USA.

Transit risk
The goods could be damaged on their journey to the USA.

ii)   Remedies
Buyer risk

a) Failure to take up goods. Insert a store and insure clause on the collection order, plus details of a case of need if the UK exporter has a reliable agent located near the buyer. The extent of the case of need's authority must be stated on the collection order.

b) Failure to pay the accepted bill. Reduce the risk by:

    1)   Inserting protest instructions on the collection order. If an unpaid bill is protested, it will cause severe damage to the credit of the US buyer.

2) Taking out insurance against non-payment.

3) Obtaining a status report.

4) Seeing if arrangements can be agreed for acceptance pour aval.

Country risk

Probably not applicable, but could be covered if insurance is held.

Transit risk

a) Insure the goods in accordance with the Incoterm.

b) Consider seller's interest insurance if FOB, etc. terms apply.

c) Use a reliable freight forwarder. The bank can recommend one.

Specimen Answer to Exam Question 3

a) i) First, one must address oneself to the terms of this specific question and bear in mind that the goods are sold on an ex **horticultural unit** basis, so that the buyer will arrange for collection of the goods.

The banking method by which the customer can obtain protection is to arrange for a documentary collection through the offices of the bank. By this method the customer could draw up a bill of exchange in the agreed terms, on the purchaser. Attached to this bill of exchange would be an invoice and **possibly** a forwarder's receipt, indicating the taking over of the goods for despatch to the purchaser in Holland. The bill of exchange and the documents would be presented for eventual payment through the banking system.

ii) The presentation would be subject to Uniform Rules for Collection,

Publication No. 522, and as such these international rules are recognised throughout most parts of the world, specifically in the UK and Holland. The customer would be assured that payment, given the goodwill of the buyers, would be made in 30 days' time.

b) The specific instruction which should be included to give some protection to the customer is a protest instruction. Such an instruction should be given to the collecting bank in Holland.

In the event of default or dishonour by the purchaser, this action taken on behalf of my customer, Flower Power Ltd, by the Dutch correspondent, might impinge upon the purchaser's creditworthiness.

c) 30 days' D/P terms (30 days' documents against payment). This means that the documents are to be released to the buyer 30 days after they had accepted a bill of exchange, indicating their willingness to pay in 30 days. The accepted bill of exchange and the underlying documents would be retained by my bank's Dutch correspondent until the due date in 30 days' time. Upon settlement of the bill, the documents will be released to the buyer.

30 days' D/A terms (30 days' documents against acceptance). Documents would be released to the buyers upon acceptance of the 30-day bill. The purchaser, nevertheless, gives their obligation to pay in 30 days' time by accepting the bill of exchange. The documents would be handed over immediately upon acceptance. The bill would be presented to the acceptor for payment on the due date.

In respect of this particular transaction, as the goods have been taken over for despatch by a forwarding agent on an ex-horticultural-unit (ex-works) basis, the control of the goods has passed to the Dutch purchaser. A document of title will not be attached to the bill of exchange. The customer will have lost control of the goods both actual and constructive. In these circumstances there is little difference between a 30-day D/P and a 30-day D/A bill of exchange.

d) In order to protect themselves from the exchange risk, the customer should open a Dutch guilder account with my bank. Half of the payments received in Dutch guilders would be used to pay the suppliers of the cloned material in the UK. The remaining Dutch guilders can be sold, out of the currency account, against forward contracts established at intervals, arranged to suit the customer's needs.

Revision Questions 3

Answers to Short-answer Test

Answer 1
The minimum amount for an acceptance credit facility is usually £100,000.

Answer 2
The buying rate.

Answer 3
Invoice discounting with bad debt insurance and a formal without recourse agreement.

Answer 4
A forfaiting facility normally relates to a single transaction with a minimum value of £100,000.

Answer 5
No. Commercial interest reference rates would apply.

Answer 6
Invoice discounting, since the exporter can manage his own sales ledger.

Answer 7
In the event of buyer default, the UK bank claims from the ECGD, whose sole recourse is against the buyer. This answer assumes that the ECGD has not insisted on a recourse bond from the exporter.

Specimen Answer to Exam Question 1

a)   i)   A letter of introduction addressed to the bank's branch in Beijing, or to our correspondent bank if there is no branch of our bank there.

       ii)   Information from International Division as to which Ministry would have the authority to enter into meaningful discussions.

b)   i)   A UK bank lends a sum of money to the appropriate Chinese government agency.

       ii)   The ECGD guarantees this loan.

       iii)   The Chinese government agency must use this money to pay cash for UK exports in connection with an agreed contract or project.

       iv)   Individual contracts for as little as US $25,000 qualify.

       v)   The Chinese must find 80% of the contract value from their own resources, with 80% being met from the ECGD-backed loan.

vi) Lines of credit provide without recourse post-shipment finance to the UK exporter.

vii) Lines of credit can be denominated in sterling, US $ or Deutschmarks.

viii) The UK exporter must pay a fee for the use of the facility.

c) The UK bank will introduce the exporter to its Countertrade Unit. This unit could help by:

    i)   finding potential buyers for the raw materials;

    ii)   advising on the likely net proceeds of the raw materials so as to assess the maximum price to allow for them in the deal;

    iii) providing bonds to cover the obligations under the counter-purchase agreement;

    iv) arranging insurance of the raw materials in transit;

    v)   advising on the availability of ECGD facilities such as the line of credit;

    vi) advising the exporter on the premium he should quote on the exported goods to offset the discount on the counter-purchase goods.

Notes on the Facilities Required by Questions 1 and 2

Question 1

a) The facility is the ECGD line of credit.

b) The minimum amount is too low for buyer credit.

Question 2

a) The facility required is forfaiting.

b) Leasing or hire purchase is not applicable, because these facilities do not involve a guaranteed payment from a European bank.

c) All ECGD facilities are excluded by the wording in the question.

d) The European bank is the **first-class institution** which has agreed to guarantee the Third World country's promissory notes or to avalise bills of exchange drawn on the exporter.

Note
The notes above on Questions 1-2 merely show which facility is required and why. The full details of the facilities are in the background reading.

Answer to XYZ Question

a) i) The customer's current account is credited at once with £52,219.32 and the negotiation account is debited US $100,000.

ii) In three months' time the negotiation account is cleared from the proceeds of the bill of exchange.

iii) Interest of US $4,437.50 is payable on the dollar loan. (100,000 at 17.75% for three months.)

iv) The customer's current account is debited with the sterling equivalent of £2,329.39.

v) Net proceeds   £52,219.32
    Less   £2,329.39
                         £49,889.93

b) i) Three months fixed forward contract is arranged at the outset.

        Spot   1.9150
        Plus: Discount   0.0254
                              1.9404

ii) The bank calculates the proceeds as £51,535.77.

iii) The bank credits the current account and debits the negotiation account with £51,535.77 at the outset.

iv) In three months' time the dollar proceeds are received, converted to sterling at the agreed forward rate, and used to clear the negotiation account.

v) Interest on the negotiation account is charged at 12.5%, and £1,610.49 is debited to the current account.

vi) Net proceeds   £ 51,535.77
    Less   £ 1,61 0.49
                        £ 49,925.28

vii) Method (b) is better.

Specimen Answer to Exam Question 2

a) i) The document required is an irrevocable documentary credit which should be confirmed by a UK bank. The parties to the credit would be:

        Applicant - Neptune Inc.

        Issuing bank - First-class bank in the USA.

        Advising/confirming/paying bank - Ourselves.

        Beneficiary - Ancient Mariners.

This credit provides a guarantee by two banks that Ancient Mariners will be paid, provided the correct documents are submitted at the right time (see part b) below for operation of the credit).

ii) Neptune Inc. will require an advance-payment guarantee issued by ourselves. Under the advanced-payment guarantee we, the UK bank, undertake to refund the advance payment, if the services subsequently turn out to be defective (see part c) below for safeguards).

b) The irrevocable credit issued by the US bank will guarantee payment in three stages, provided the correct documents are presented. Payment will be made by ourselves, being the nominated paying bank against presentation of stipulated documents. Our bank will then be guaranteed reimbursement by the issuing bank. The stages are:

i) 30% against a copy of the signed commercial contract, plus an advance-payment guarantee issued by ourselves in favour of Neptune.

ii) 35% against a document signed by a harbourmaster stating that the ship has sailed with Savannah as its destination (payment due ten days after the date of the document).

iii) 35% against a receipt, signed by the agents of Neptune, stating that the ship has arrived in Savannah.

c) i) **Liabilities under Advance Payment Guarantees**
The liability of Ancient Mariners under the advanced-payment guarantee is that they are liable to refund the money if the vessel is not delivered in accordance with the contract. Ancient Mariners will have to sign a counter indemnity giving the UK bank the right to debit the account for any payments made under the guarantee. The liability of the UK bank is that it must meet any valid claims under the guarantee, irrespective of whether the customer, Ancient Mariners, has funds to meet the obligation under the counter indemnity.

ii) **Safeguards under Advance Payment Guarantees**

1) The guarantee must state that it is to be subject to English law and it must include an expiry date. In other words it must be in standard form which is approved by our bank.

2) The guarantee should state that it will become operative only if an irrevocable credit with terms acceptable to both customer and UK bank is issued (see (b)(i) above).

3) The guarantee should contain an **operative clause**, making it effective only on receipt by Ancient Mariners of the advance payment. In other words, proof of first having made the payment must be shown before Neptune can reclaim it.

4) The guarantee should contain a **reduction clause** stating that the amount due can be written down in line with performance of the contract.

    5)   It may be possible to stipulate that an arbitration certificate be submitted to back up any claim. However, this may not be acceptable to Neptune Inc.

Notes for Students (Not Required in the Answer)

a) Do **not** refer to bills of lading. Goods are not being exported.

b) American banks are not allowed to issue advance-payment bonds or guarantees, and they would have to issue a stand-by letter of credit. However, this complexity would only occur if Neptune Inc. were the seller and Ancient Mariners were the buyer. Advance-payment guarantees issued by UK banks in favour of American exporters are perfectly acceptable in the USA.

c) A red clause documentary credit is not a valid alternative to an advance-payment guarantee. A red clause documentary credit would be issued by the US bank and would authorise us to make a pre-shipment advance to Ancient Mariners. The red clause documentary credit does not guarantee the refund of the advance payment should Ancient Mariners default.

Specimen Answer to Exam Question 3

a) The appropriate scheme is the Supplier Credit Finance Facility (SCF). It came into force on 1 July 1991, replacing the old Medium-term Supplier Credit Facility.

b) The main features of the scheme are as follows:

- The banks which have agreed to participate in the scheme have taken out with ECGD a Master Guarantee Agreement (MGA).

- The exporter will normally approach the bank, who will contact ECGD for an indication of premium, interest rate and any other details and terms. The exporter can apply direct to ECGD for cover, if he wants to. If he is successful in this application, ECGD may issue an offer of Support for Finance. This means that the exporter can shop around to find a financing bank, and can be issued with a Certificate of Approval, if that bank agrees to provide finance.

- ECGD, having considered the position, will issue an indication giving details of premium cost, interest rate and any other conditions of cover. The costs will be held for a period up to six months.

- The interest rate the exporter can offer his buyer will be based on the Commercial Interest Reference Rates (CIRRS). ECGD continues to provide interest make-up to compensate banks lending at fixed rates to an agreed rate of return.

- If cover is required, the supplier must complete a proposal form and submit it to ECGD, through the bank.

- If the transaction is acceptable, ECGD will respond by giving an offer of support (it may offer pre-finance cover to the exporter, if appropriate). At this stage the exporter will have to find a bank willing to provide finance, if a direct approach has been made by the exporter to ECGD.

● If the exporter agrees to the terms offered by ECGD, a declaration and acceptance form will be completed and sent to ECGD. Meanwhile, the financing bank will complete and send to ECGD a Financing Declaration and Acceptance stating that it is willing to provide finance.

● ECGD will issue a Certificate of Approval stating the terms and conditions of the cover. This is sent to the bank, which must acknowledge it. A copy of the certificate is sent to the exporter.

● In order to draw down, the exporter must obtain the security listed in the agreement and present it to the bank, together with any other documentation and warranty. This will consist of:

i) bills of exchange or promissory notes, guaranteed unconditionally by a third party, either by bank aval, endorsement on the bills of exchange or promissory notes (where 'public' bodies or sovereign buyers are involved, the Ministry of Finance is expected to back the instruments);

ii) evidence of delivery of the goods, or that the service(s) had been performed;

iii) a warranty from the exporter that the terms and conditions agreed between the parties have been fulfilled;

iv) any other documentation required by the financing bank which is laid down in the bank's facility letter.

● Having checked that the documents comply with the certificate of approval, meaning that the finance is available under the terms of the Master Guarantee Agreement, the bank makes the finance available by purchasing bills or notes for their principal value, without recourse to the supplier. The exporter receives cash and the bank becomes a holder for value of the bill or note.

Revision Questions 4

Answers to Multiple-choice Questions

Answer 1

The correct answer is b).

Article 39 of UCP states that where goods are described by weight or volume in the credit, the documents may indicate that 5% more or up to 5% less has actually been shipped. In addition, apart from the invoice, the other documents can describe the goods in general terms not inconsistent with the credit (Article 37, UCP).

Answer a) is wrong, because the invoice must describe the goods in exactly the same way as the credit. Hence, the goods must be described as 'Chilean full fishmeal' on the invoice.

A final point, the 5% tolerance only applies to goods described by weight or volume. It does not apply if the goods are described as a number of units or individual items.

Answer 2

The answer here is c).

When the expiry date of a credit is on a non-business day, the documents can be presented on the next business day. However, the transport document must still evidence that goods were taken in charge on or before the expiry date (Article 44, UCP).

Answer a) is ruled out because the bill of lading is dated too late. Answer b) is incorrect because the documents have to be presented on the next business day. You may have ticked answer d), but unfortunately the bill of lading is stale, having been issued more than 21 days before presentation (Article 43, UCP).

Answer 3

Answer d) is correct.

Briefly, the bank will arrange for the goods to be warehoused in its name, immediately the documents are presented. The customer will already have signed a letter of pledge, and this will bind him to pay the storage and insurance costs.

When the time comes for delivery to the ultimate buyer, the customer will sign a trust receipt and the bank will give him a delivery order. The customer delivers the goods to the ultimate buyer, who pays the bank directly. Answer a) is wrong because it is most unlikely that the ultimate buyer would wish to involve himself in a documentary credit; likewise, answer c) is inapplicable. Red clause documentary credits provide pre-shipment finance to the beneficiary of the credit, whereas our customer is the applicant. This excludes answer b).

You may feel that this is an obscure question, but students so often confuse the different types of credit. Writing about the wrong credit is fatal, and an understanding of this multiple-choice question will prevent you from making this very common error.

A

Answer 4

The answer is d) because they would be two separate documentary credits calling for different transport documents.

Transferable and back-to-back credits are not applicable, because there are two different shipments:

i)   Phosphate from Australia to the UK.

ii) Fertiliser from the UK to India.

The transport documents would therefore be entirely different, making back-to-back or transferable credits inapplicable. 'Revolving' credits apply where buyers and sellers regularly trade in the same goods and use documentary credits. To save the time and cost of applying for a new credit every time goods are shipped, the terms of a revolving credit state that it is automatically renewed.

A typical revolving credit would be one which was available for £10,000 per month for 12 months.

Answer 5

Answer a) is correct.

The only amount which concerns the first beneficiary is the profit. At some stage his bank will receive $35,000, which will be dealt with as follows:

i) $30,000 passed onto the second beneficiary;

ii) $5,000 passed onto our customer, the first beneficiary.

Since our customer is to receive currency, the bank will buy. Thus answer d) is wrong. Answers b) and c) are incorrect, although answer c) could have been correct if the deal had been operated under back-to-back credits.

Answer 6

Answer b) is correct.

The second beneficiary makes the first presentation to his bank. The documents are sent to the transferring bank which in turn submits them, duly amended, to the issuing bank.

Answer 7

The correct answer is d).

This covers (once again) UCP Article 37, which was mentioned in Question 1. The description of the goods in the invoice must conform exactly to that in the credit.

Answer a) is incorrect, because banks are concerned only with documents, not goods (Article 4), and answer c) is incorrect because such documents can now be accepted (Article 30).

You may have chosen answer b), but although this choice is a sensible one, it is incorrect. Article 36 expressly allows such an insurance document in these circumstances. (The reasoning behind this Article is that this wording occurs in the standard 'all-risks' clause for policies issued by the main underwriters on the London Insurance Market.)

Answer 8
The answer is d).

Taking a status enquiry should ensure that the beneficiary is respectable and will ship the correct goods. The third-party inspection certificate also gives an indication that the goods are of the correct standard. Likewise, the reduced amount will encourage the beneficiary to ship the correct goods, otherwise the remaining 20% will be at risk.

Answer 9
The answer is c).

Banks are concerned only with documents. They will not be bound by the credit if the documents are incorrect, because the documents are part of the credit terms. Banks are not concerned with the commercial contract, thus d) is eliminated. Answers a) and b) are not applicable, because the confirming bank has added its own guarantee.

Answer 10
The answer is a).

Under an FOB contract, the seller is only responsible for the goods until they are loaded on board the ship. Thus the buyer (i.e. applicant) is responsible for payment of freight.

Answer b) is not quite correct. The time lag will allow for documents to be presented in time even if shipment is not made until the latest date. Thus, there will be no problems arising from the point set out in this answer.

Under a CFR contract, the seller is responsible for freight costs, but the buyer is responsible for the insurance. Hence, answer c) is not correct as the credit will be perfectly workable.

There is no need to stipulate a latest date of shipment, and so you should not have quoted answer d).

Specimen Answer to Exam Question 1

a)   i)   *Irrevocable credits and sub-standard goods*
               An irrevocable credit is one which cannot be cancelled or amended
               in any way without the consent of all parties to the credit. There is
               nothing to prevent Automart from asking the issuing bank to cancel
               the credit, but the proposed amendment can simply be rejected by
               the beneficiary. The position is set out in Article 9 of UCP.

        ii)   *Fraud and irrevocable credits*
               Automart would not have to pay if the fraud was evidenced by the
               documents, for example if the documents evidenced goods shipped in
               a dock strike, or if they evidenced a voyage which was not listed in

the Lloyd's register of shipping. Automart could also take legal action to prevent further shipments of goods. otherwise the position is as shown above.

b) The credit should have a six-month expiry date and should describe the goods, unit price and total amount in the usual way. It should then state that part shipments are allowed. However, under UCP Article 40, partial shipments and/or partial drawings are allowed anyway, unless the credit states otherwise.

The credit could set out a shipment's schedule showing the instalments along with the latest shipment date for each instalment. Under Article 41 of UCP, if any instalment is not drawn or goods are not shipped by the stipulated period, then the credit ceases to be effective as regards that instalment and any other instalment, unless otherwise stipulated in that credit.

c) The credit could call for a third-party inspection certificate, issued by a reputable organisation in the seller's country, stating that the goods are of a specific standard. Under Article 21 of UCP, the credit must state by whom the document is to be issued and must specify the wording or data content, otherwise banks will accept such documents as presented, provided they are not inconsistent with the other documents as presented.

The credit could also call for a certificate signed by Automart that it had accepted and approved a sample of the goods within a given number of days prior to shipment. Alternatively, the credit could call for a certificate signed by Automart, or its named agent, stating that the goods had been inspected and approved within a given number of days prior to shipment.

Much depends on the respective bargaining power of the two companies as to which type of document, if any, could be stipulated.

d) *How to reword the credit to provide greater protection to Automart (the applicant)*

  i) Call for third-party documents (see c) above).

  ii) State that documents must be presented strictly in accordance with the credit and that banker's indemnities are not allowed.

  iii) Nominate an office or subsidiary of the issuing bank as negotiating/ paying bank.

  iv) Show the amount of goods and money as that of the first shipment only. If that shipment is satisfactory, the credit could be amended to cover further shipments.

  v) Issue the credit with an expiry date six months hence, but show the amount as one sixth of the full amount. The credit could then say that the value of any documents drawn in accordance with the terms of the credit could be re-instated, provided Autocars agree (re-instatement documentary credit).

  vi) Issue the credit as a stand-by letter of credit for one sixth of the full amount. The credit could guarantee payment against a copy invoice and copy bill of lading, together with a signed certificate from the named beneficiary to say payment had not been made.

The beneficiary would then trade on open account terms, but would use the stand-by credit as a back-up to guarantee one month's payment.

Alternatively, the beneficiary could trade on documentary collection terms, and the credit could call for a dishonoured, protested bill of exchange.

vii) The credit could call for a retention monies guarantee which, while not allowing Autocars to revoke the credit, would subsequently allow them to claim reimbursement if the goods were proved sub-standard in accordance with the terms of that guarantee.

viii)The amount could be for, say, 70% of the value of the goods, with the remainder being on open account terms.

Note

Much depends on the respective bargaining powers as to what wording can be agreed.

Specimen Answer to Exam Question 2

a) Alternative payment terms

i) Open account or documentary collection terms, supported by stand-by letters of credit (see Question 1). Alternatively, UK factors may be prepared to provide post-shipment advances to the suppliers, possibly without recourse.

ii) Documentary collection with certain variations:

- bills of exchange to be avalised by Automart's bank either before shipment, or on presentation. These bills provide the supplier with an unconditional bank guarantee of payment, once they have been avalised. Automart's bank would need to be satisfied as to the creditworthiness of Automart.

- The supplier could obtain credit insurance and could then, possibly, obtain without recourse post-shipment finance from his bank.

- The collection could be D/P or D/A. D/P is more secure for the supplier.

iii) Payment in advance. Automart should compare the interest cost with the costs of avalisation.

b) Secure payment terms from the supplier's point of view are provided by:

i) Open account supported by stand-by letter of credit, or by factored invoices so long as without recourse factoring applies.

ii) Documentary collection with avalised bills, from the time of avalisation of the bill of exchange.

iii) Credit insurance to the extent of the cover provided, provided the supplier fulfils the underlying commercial conditions.

iv) Without recourse post-shipment finance against documentary collection.

v) Payment in advance.

c) The terms which would avoid the need for handling shipping documents are:

i) Open account. Once the stand-by letter of credit has been set up, normal open account terms apply so long as payment is made. As far as factoring is concerned, the supplier is responsible for organising that aspect.

ii) Documentary collection with avalised bills of exchange (prior to shipment). The supplier would be happy to use documents such as waybills once he had an avalised bill of exchange.

iii) Payment in advance.

Specimen Answer to Exam Question 3

a) Alternative Methods of Settlement:

- Telegraphic Transfer

- Mail transfer

- SWIFT transfer

- Giro payments into the overseas supplier's vostro account for sterling payments

- bank draft

b) Developments in Europe Regarding Streamlining of Payments:

i) Desktop terminals can be used by corporate treasurers to initiate TTs, bank giro payments or SWIFT transfers. Bank computers can retain payment details on file so that for regular suppliers, the treasurer simply needs to input the amount, value date, and relevant security code.

ii) The direct debit system, whereby the debtor can authorise his bank to accept claims from creditors with reimbursement from the debtor's bank account, is being extended into the EU and can be used internationally.

iii) Where two trading companies and their banks are linked by EDI, it is possible for the debtor to initiate a direct payment into the creditor's account with simultaneous advice being given to the debtor. Automatic reconciliations with the supplier's invoice reference is possible.

iv) Different giro systems are being linked throughout the EU to speed up international transfers.

v) Credit cards are being developed to facilitate person-to-person and person-to-company transfers.

vi) Banks in different EU countries are seeking to develop new networks and links to speed up payment.

c) **Potential benefits:**

i) Cost reduction.

ii) Payment and reconciliation/advice of payment is speeded up.

iii) EDI reduced the number of times the data concerning an order is input into the computer. This reduces the scope for errors.

iv) The desktop terminal system can be built into existing cash management systems.

v) If a potential purchaser has an EDI system, the supplier who has a compatible EDI network will gain a competitive advantage.

vi) Expensive management time can be devoted to aspects such as marketing, rather than to managing and reconciling payments, outward and inward, once EDI systems are used.

Specimen Answer to Exam Question 4

a) i) URC state that a bank has no responsibility at all to deal with goods which have been consigned to it without authority. It could tell the local airport to refer to the shipper (exporter) if it wished.

ii) Documents can only be released on payment if the collection order does not quote 'D/P' or 'D/A'.

iii) Part payments can be accepted in the case of clean collections, but cannot be accepted with documentary collections (unless the collection order so specifies).

iv) Our bank will treat the collection as honoured if the charges are merely stated on the collection instruction without any clause such as 'do not waive if refuse'.

If the charges are incorporated into the financial document (i.e. bill of exchange), refusal by the drawee to pay charges will amount to dishonour.

b) We are the presenting bank acting as agent for the remitting bank under URC. Our duty is to the remitting bank. We would accept the part payment, and either remit it to the overseas bank, or hold it to their order under advice. The collection is now 'clean' as the commercial documents will have been released on acceptance.

Receipt the bill of exchange for the amount paid and protest for the full amount if the collection instruction says to protest. Tactfully explain to our customer that we have no alternative but to protest the bill of exchange, if the instructions say protest.

Specimen Answer to Exam Question 5

a) **Today 1 April**
Forward contract 1-3 months option buy arranged.

Spot	1.7775	Spot	1.7775
Plus: Discount	0.0041	*Plus*:	0.0245
	1 7816		1.8020

300 FINANCE OF INTERNATIONAL TRADE

The bank chooses the 3-month rate: 1.8020

15 May
The actual profit is $760,000 ÷ 3 = $253,333
Converted as follows:

250,000 at agreed forward rate 1.8020	=	£138,734.74
3,333 at spot 1.80	=	£ 1,851.66
Net credit	=	£140,586.40

b) **Uniform Customs and Practice**

a) Rules are UCP 1993.

b) The rules cover all aspects except those expressly covered by the terms of the credit.

c) All authorities stipulate 'subject to UCP 1993'.

d) Transferable credits are covered in Article 48.

e) Credit can only be transferred if it is expressly stated to be transferable.

f) First beneficiary can only request his bank to transfer. His bank is not obliged to do so.

g) First beneficiary must pay all charges. His bank need not effect the transfer until charges paid.

h) The credit can be transferred only on the terms and conditions specified in the original credit except for lower amount, lower price per unit, earlier expiry date/date of shipment.

i) The first beneficiary can call for the second beneficiary to provide the full amount of insurance, based on the price paid by the applicant.

Specimen Answer to Exam Question 6

a) The spot rate would be used for a transfer to be value-dated two working days into the future. Bank sells US $250,000 at 1.5590 = £160,359.20

b) Bank buys DEM2m and sells US $ at cross rate of DEM 1.5725 = US $1 =
   $\frac{2,000,000}{1.5725}$ = US $1,271,860.09

Note
Use the cross rate. Do **not** convert DEM to GBP and then convert £ to US $.

c) *Details agreed in a forward exchange contract.*

   - date of contract;

   - customer's name;

   - currencies being purchased and sold;

   - amounts of currencies being purchased and sold;

   - exchange rate agreed at time contract established;

   - when currencies are to be exchanged;

     i) either on a fixed dated;

     ii) or during an agreed period of time at the customer's option.

Conditions of contract

   1. Confirmation usually required from customer signed in accordance with mandate.

   2. It is a firm and binding contract, i.e. it is a contract which covers the customer's exchange risk however much the rates fluctuate, and the customer is required to utilise the contract even if rates have since moved in their favour or the underlying transaction has been cancelled or postponed.

   3. Unless an element of cash cover is required, no sterling or currency is exchanged until the contract is utilised or closed out.

   4. The customer is required to provide instructions two working days before utilisation.

   5. One contract may cover a number of transactions.

   6. If a balance is left on the contract at maturity, it must be closed out and where appropriate extended - the close-out may result in a profit or loss to the customer.

   7. Because of the risk of non-delivery, some banks write a limit of 10%-20% of the amount of the contract.

d) *Approximate cost in sterling of payment of US $2m in three months time..*

Bank sells three months forward at 1.5444 calculated as:

Spot US $	1.5590
Less	0.0146
3 month forward	1.5444

US $2m at l.5444 = 1,295,001.29

e) 4.23% p.a. quoted in the FT market report is one month's forward cover expressed as a percentage per annum. It is the cost/profit as against spot and is in effect the difference between interest rates for two currencies. Formula for calculating the cost of covering forward p.a.:

$$\frac{\text{Premium or Discount} \times 360 \times 100}{\text{spot rate} \times \text{number of days for which premium/discount is quoted}}$$

Cost of covering forward one month forward is:

$$\frac{0.0056 \times 360 \times 100}{1.5590 \times 30} = 4.31\% \text{ p.a., i.e. approximately } 4.23\%.$$

Note

There are some distortions to the calculation rergarding the difference in the annual interest rates. These are caused by the effect of compounding on adjustment of monthly rates to an annual basis and the fact that sterling interest calculations work on a year having 365 days, while for the dollar a year is taken as having 360 days.

Specimen Answer to Exam Question 7

a) i) Mr Money was pleased at the dollar's weakness as it will mean that Euro Multinational will be able to buy more US $ per £1 and the cost of remittance to their parent company in the USA will be cheaper.

   ii) The main factors that affect the sterling/US $ exchange rates are:

Speculation

Speculation may have a dramatic effect on the value of a currency and may take various forms: for example, speculators may sell a weakening currency and/or hold a strengthening currency awaiting market movements in their favour. Hot money may be moved from one currency to another looking for future currency movements, or some commercial companies will 'lead' or 'lag', securing their exchange rate, anticipating a movement of rates in their favour.

Interest rates

A government/central bank may influence the value of its currency by raising or lowering interest rates.

Investors may buy or sell currencies to obtain the best return on their deposits.

Central bank intervention

A central bank may on its own or in concert with other central banks buy or sell currencies to stabilise rates (and when appropriate replenish the country's reserves of foreign currency).

When supporting a fixed value of its currency, it may be necessary to realign a currency, i.e. devalue/revalue.

Market news

World and/or home events, political or economic, positive or negative, will be analysed by the market-makers, and future trends will be anticipated and reviewed as news comes in, particularly economic indicators.

Bad news may affect confidence and unsettle the market and dealers will adjust rates. Currencies may also be bought and sold as funds are moved to perceived safe havens.

Such news could be the political strength and stability of the government, interest rates, inflation, balance of payments, government borrowing.

When markets are relatively quiet, supply and demand play an important part and large transactions may have an impact.

All things being equal, a country with, say, current and continuing low inflation, economic and political stability, a balance of trade surplus and high interest rates should have a strong currency that would be in demand.

iii) There would be factors affecting the sterling/DEM rate in addition to the above:

- Both currencies (sterling and DEM) are part of the EMS.

- Both countries are part of the EU, in which there is officially a high level of co-operation. Members aim for exchange rate stability and may take action in concert to achieve this.

In the longer term, the aim is that the economic performance of member states should 'converge'.

When the UK was a member of the ERM, it was necessary for the value of the pound to be maintained within a fixed band, with economic policy and central bank intervention necessary to keep the currency within these levels.

At present, the pound floats freely, although it could join the Euro in 1999.

b) i) Many large UK companies are happy to be invoiced in US $ because they have US $ receivables. To ensure that there would be no exchange risk if they invoiced Regional Distribution in US $, Euro Multinational could:

1. Open a US $ account to enable payments and receipts to be matched.

2. In view of the possible time delay, request an overdraft facility in US $. Interest would be based on Euro $ rates. As payments and

receipts would be value-dated, the overdraft may be less than seven days. There would still be an exchange risk if Regional Distribution did not pay, as Euro Multinational would at some stage need to purchase US $ at the spot rate to repay the overdraft.

    ii)   To pay US $ to Euro Multinational, Regional Distribution could:

        1.   Obtain the banking details of Euro Multinational's account.

        2.   Provide instructions to their bank, preferably completing the bank's form, which contains terms and conditions, to make a bank transfer by telegraphic or SWIFT transfer depending on the urgency.

        3.   Provide US $ in reimbursement from either a US $ account or a spot or forward booking or a currency option.

Alternatively, Regional Distribution could obtain a banker's draft from their bank or issue a cheque in US $ on one of their accounts if this was acceptable to Euro Multinational.

With a bank transfer, payment would be made on a value date by way of cleared funds through the network of nostro accounts.

With a banker's draft or cheque, the instrument would have to be presented for payment: Regional Distribution's cheque could be cleared through the currency clearing in London.

Specimen Answer to Exam Question 8

    a)   i)   Advantages and disadvantages of exporter remitting the bill directly to the overseas collecting bank in comparison to use of irrevocable documentary credit terms (LC)

Advantages

1. Documentary collections are more acceptable than documentary credits from the buyer's point of view. The buyer will save by:

    ●   reduced costs;

    ●   less administration (no need to request the issue of a credit);

    ●   no effect on bank facilities, whereas LCs will be treated on a par with borrowing facilities.

  This will make the deal more attractive.

2. The exporter will pay reduced bank charges because he cuts out the UK remitting bank by sending the collection direct and because there is no need for the bank to make a careful check of the documents.

3. The exporter decides what documents to send without having to refer to the conditions in the LC.

4. Time will be saved as the documents can be remitted directly to the collecting bank without the need for a UK bank to be involved.

Disadvantages

1. Greater credit risk as there is no conditional bank guarantee of payment. The buyer may refuse to accept the bill of exchange or he may refuse to pay it at maturity.

2. The direct collection method will mean that there is no check of the documents by a UK bank. Thus any documentary problems will only come to light once the documents have reached the German bank.

3. All follow-up correspondence will have to be done by the exporter, as opposed to his bank.

4. It may not be possible to negotiate this collection, whereas LCs can usually be used to provide post-shipment finance.

ii) Advantages and disadvantages of avalised promissory notes, as opposed to LCs

Advantages

1. Since the notes are to be received prior to shipment, the notes could be discounted (forfaited) to raise pre-shipment finance. A documentary credit can normally only raise post-shipment finance, since the required documents are normally only available on shipment, unless red clause or assignments can be applied.

2. The aval of the German bank means that payment is unconditionally guaranteed by that bank on the due date. Thus, provided that bank is sound, the exporter can be sure of payment.

3. Bank collection charges will be lower than for the LC because there is no need for a careful examination of documents.

Disadvantages

This method is less acceptable than the LC from the buyer's point of view. There is no 'documentary protection' to ensure receipt of the correct goods, the aval will tie up facilities with the German bank, and the commitment fee may be greater than for the LC.

Thus much depends on the relative bargaining power of the two parties.

b) Differences in the Procedures to Obtain Payment after Shipment

1. With direct collections, a UK bank is not involved in handling the documents, i.e. once the shipping documents are collated, the collection is sent to the German bank directly by the UK exporter.

    ● The UK bank could collect the proceeds of the avalised bill at maturity.

2. With the direct collection, the German bank presents the bill for acceptance.

    ● With the promissory note, acceptance and avalisation have already been achieved.

3. The German bank would hold the accepted bill until maturity and seek the drawee's authority to make payment.

    ● The promissory note would be held by the exporter and sent for collection in plenty of time before maturity.

4. The German bank is acting as the UK exporters' agent in collecting payment from the importer.

    ● With the avalised promissory note, the German bank has guaranteed payment and must pay at maturity whether it can recover the funds from the importer or not.

5. Subsequent correspondence on the collection, including advice of payment, would be sent to the UK exporter direct.

    ● With the promissory note, there will be an advice of payment only and that would be sent to the UK bank or exporter as appropriate.

c) **Main Features of the Accelerated Bills Service Provided by some UK Banks**

1. The UK exporter prepares the collection on their UK bank's paper with the UK bank's bill reference. This may be achieved by using an automated system like SITPRO's SPEX for preparing both the shipping documents and collection instruction.

2. Because the UK exporter prepares and sends the collection abroad in the bank's name, the bank charges are less.

3. Because the UK exporter sends the documents abroad, processing time is reduced, which means payment may be received more quickly.

4. The exporter has a helpline to the bank for general assistance.

5. After despatch of the documents, details of the transactions are passed to the UK bank in paper or data format.

6. Any subsequent correspondence is handled by the UK bank.

7. Payment is received by the UK bank through the international banking system, quoting the bank's bill of reference.

8. If the bills are prepared on a data link to the bank, details of the bills despatched are retained by the bank. The exporter has access to the bank's list of outstanding bills for information purposes. Advices including advices of acceptance and payment may be sent electronically via the data link rather than by paper.

Specimen Answer to Exam Question 9

a)   i) The basic instrument is a transferable letter of credit.

        ii) Under UCP Article 48, only credits which expressly state that they are transferable can be transferred.

        iii) The overseas buyer will be the applicant, and it is he who must agree that the credit can be transferred.

        iv) Our customer will be the first beneficiary, and he has the right to request our bank to transfer the credit to a second beneficiary. A transferable credit can be transferred only once, but it can be split up amongst a number of second beneficiaries.

        v) The credit will be transferred on the same conditions as were originally set up, except for:

            1) Expiry date - earlier;

            2) Amount - lower;

            3) Unit prices (if specified) - lower;

            4) Insurance cover. The amount called for can be whatever is required by the second beneficiary.

        vi) The suppliers know that they have a secure method of payment, provided the credit is irrevocable.

        vii) There will be no cash-flow problem for our customer, since the only item on his bank account will be a credit for the profit (apart from bank charges!).

b) Under Article 48, the amount transferred by the first beneficiary's bank must be in the same currency as the original amount. Hence, transferable credits cannot be used here, as the 'second beneficiary' wants DEMs.

c)   i) The only compromise available is a back-to-back credit.

        ii) The original buyer is the applicant and our customer is the beneficiary of the first credit. Our customer is the applicant for the second credit and the German supplier is the beneficiary.

        iii) These are two separate credits, and we rely on the documents presented under the second credit to fulfil the requirements of the first credit.

        iv) The problem is that our bank will be liable to honour the second credit if the correct documents are submitted. This applies even if the documents do not fulfil the requirements of the first credit.

            Hence, if we are not willing to issue the second credit on its own merits, we would be unlikely to agree purely because of the 'comfort' given by the first credit.

v) Cash-flow problems could also arise. Our customer will be debited with the full amount of the second credit and credited with the full amount of the first one.

If the terms of the two bills of exchange are the same (e.g. sight), our customer will be out of funds for a time. This never happens with transferable letters of credit.

vi) There is an exchange risk which our customer should cover. Suggest forward contracts or currency options as appropriate.

Specimen Answer to Exam Question 10

a)   The Definition of a Documentary Credit is found in Uniform Customs and Practice (1993).

A 'documentary credit' is a guarantee by the issuing bank (ourselves) in favour of a beneficiary (the Australian). The bank guarantees payment will be made against specified documents presented within a stipulated period.

'Irrevocable' means that the credit cannot be modified without the consent of all parties. From the point of view of our customer, it means that once the credit has been issued, he is committed to being debited if the conditions have been fulfilled, since we, his bank, are bound to honour the credit.

b)   The Credit should Call for:

i) **Bills of lading (B/Ls).** A complete set of clean, shipped on B/Ls, made out to order and blank endorsed.

The B/Ls must name the vessel and must show the destination as the UK port agreed by the parties.

The B/L should be marked 'freight paid', if the invoice shows the underlying contract to be CFR or CIF.

The B/L must be dated on or before the latest permitted date of shipment if one is shown in the credit. The B/L must describe the goods in general terms not inconsistent with the credit.

ii) **Invoice**, which describes the goods in exactly the same way as the credit, is made out in the name of the applicant (except for transferable credits), and is for the correct amount.

iii) **Insurance document**, which covers the goods and risks as specified in the credit. The certificate will be in the same currency as the credit and must be for the CIF value of the goods, plus 10%.

Cover must be effective from the date of shipment.

iv) If the goods were to come by air freight, an air waybill, as opposed to a B/L, showing the goods consigned to the bank (i.e. ourselves).

c) Precautions

i) Our customer could stipulate that one of the documents would be a third-party inspection certificate, issued by a reputable agency in Australia, certifying that the materials were up to standard.

If the documents presented include such a document, the applicant, our customer, can be sure that the goods are in order.

If the document is not presented, the credit is void since the documents do not conform to the credit.

ii) Do not establish the credit until a suitable status report is held on the general commercial integrity of the seller.

iii) It may be possible for our customer to arrange for the amount of the credit to be, say, 80% of the full value. The remaining 20% could be paid on open account after the goods had been received. This is an incentive to the seller to send materials of the correct standard.

iv) See if the seller will agree to a revocable credit. (This is unlikely, in practice.)

v) The credits should, wherever possible, be arranged through the correspondent or office of our bank abroad. This will ensure that the advising bank is trustworthy.

vi) The credit should clearly state that the documents must be presented strictly in accordance with the credit and that banker's indemnities are not allowed.

vii) The credit should restrict payment or negotiation to the advising or issuing bank.

Specimen Answer to Exam Question 11

a) If the sellers require secure methods of payment, documentary collections are totally inappropriate. The solution is an irrevocable documentary credit in favour of the sellers.

Notes

    i) Our customer, the applicant, must be creditworthy.

    ii) The credit should call for drafts drawn at 90 days' sight on us as the drawee if in sterling, or on the Manila bank as drawee if currency.

    iii) Once the documents had been presented and the bill of exchange had been accepted, the Manila seller could discount the bill at a fine rate.

    iv) The buyer and seller must agree beforehand who will meet discount charges, and instruct the banks.

    v) Our customer will not be debited until 90 days after he has accepted the bill of exchange. Hence, he receives 90 days' credit.

vi) If the bank wished to retain control over the goods after their arrival in the UK, a produce loan facility could be considered.

b) Documents called for would be the same as in Exam Question 10 above.

Specimen Answer to Exam Question 12

a) i) Because bills of exchange are sent direct to the buyer, the exporter is selling on open account. We are told that documentary credits are unobtainable. Hence the only available method is documentary collection.

The exporter is the principal and drawer of the bill.

We are the remitting bank.

The overseas bank is the collecting/presenting bank.

The buyer is the drawee of the bill of exchange.

Documents of title are attached to the bill of exchange, and the presenting bank will release the documents against payment or acceptance, depending on the terms of the collection instruction.

ii) For the French collection, the exporter will draw bills of exchange due 30 days after sight, and will authorise release of documents against acceptance.

The buyer will therefore obtain the goods 30 days before he needs to pay for them.

The collection instruction could say: 'If unpaid protest' and 'Remit proceeds by TT'.

This will ensure that if the buyer does not pay on the due date, the bill will be protested. If he does pay, cleared funds will be remitted at once.

An alternative guarantee of payment would be to call for acceptance pour aval. In this case the French bank would endorse the bill and add its own guarantee of payment on the due date.

The prior approval of the buyer and his bank would be required for acceptance pour aval.

iii) The principles would be similar for the German buyer, but the collection would include sight drafts and would be on a D/P basis.

This would ensure that the importer would have to pay before he could obtain the goods.

b) i) In the case of both France and Germany, the buyers should be happy to pay on the documentary collection basis.

This method is governed by Uniform Rules for Collections, which are an internationally accepted set of rules drawn up by ICC, governing the rights and duties of all parties to collections.

ii) Protection to the exporter will come from:

1) Protest instructions (see part a)).

2) Acceptance pour aval if available (see part a)).

3) Store and insure clause in case the German refuses to pay or the French buyer refuses to accept the bill of exchange.

4) A case of need clause, but only if our exporter has a reliable agent in France or Germany.

In addition, the exporter should take out a status report, and could insure against bad debts.

Specimen Answer to Exam Question 13

a) i) We are the presenting bank and our customer is the drawee. our bank's primary duty is to the remitting bank and not to our customer.

ii) The whole transaction is governed by Uniform Rules for Collections, except where the collection order, or UK law, contradict URC.

iii) Under URC, the presenting bank must advise the remitting bank without delay of non-acceptance.

iv) In any case, our bank should not have released the documents until the customer had accepted the bill of exchange.

v) It is now too late for the bills of exchange to be protested, since this must be done within 24 hours of dishonour. Thus, the remitting bank cannot now sue our customer on the bill of exchange itself (Bills of Exchange Act 1882). The overseas supplier's only remedy is to sue our customer on the contract.

vi) Our bank has wrongly released the documents and thus is a party to allowing control of the goods to pass from the seller.

vii) Our bank is liable to the remitting bank, having failed to act on the instructions in the collection instruction.

viii) The terms of the trust letter must be examined. Usually these letters bind the customer to:

1) Hold the documents as trustee for the bank;

2) Return the documents to the bank or (in this case) accept the bill of exchange;

3) Be debited for any breach of trust.

b) The action required is:

i) Remit the funds to the remitting bank.

ii) Politely but firmly explain the position to the customer and request his authority to debit his account in reimbursement.

iii) If the customer refuses to authorise a debit to the account, see if the trust letter authorises the debit. If so, debit the account. However 'good' the customer, our bank would not wish to stand the loss caused by our customer's breach of trust.

iv) If we have no agreement or authority to debit the account, we must see if our bank can take over the goods and subsequently sell them to reduce the loss.

v) Whatever the position between our bank and the customer, we must remit the funds to the remitting bank.

Specimen Answer to Exam Question 14

a) 90 days Sight Draft D/A

The documents will be released to the customer as soon as he accepts the bill of exchange.

The customer will be legally bound to pay the bill of exchange 90 days after the date on which it was accepted.

In effect, he receives 90 days' credit.

CFR UK Port
This is an Incoterm, short for cost and freight UK port.

The seller will pay the freight costs to the UK port.

Insurance of the goods on the sea voyage will be the responsibility of our importer customer, as will all costs and risks once the goods pass over the ship's rail at the UK port.

b) 90 days' Sight Bill

i) Release documents against acceptance.

ii) Whether to protest in the case of non-acceptance or non-payment.

iii) Method of advice of dishonour (cable, telex, etc.).

iv) Store and insure clause (optional).

v) Case of need and the extent of his powers (optional).

vi) Payment of charges and whether they may be waived.

vii) Method of remittance of proceeds (airmail, SWIFT, etc.).

viii)Can acceptance be deferred, pending arrival of goods?

c) **The position of the Drawee when an Inward Collection is Drawn on him on D/A terms**

i) The documentary collection will be in accordance with URC.

ii) We as presenting/collecting bank must follow these rules, as our duty is to the remitting bank.

iii) 'D/A' means that our customer must accept the bill of exchange before he can obtain the documents of title. We, the presenting bank, are not allowed to release the documents unless our customer has accepted the bill of exchange. Thus, customer cannot obtain the goods or examine them unless he accepts the bill of exchange.

iv) By accepting the bill of exchange, our customer becomes legally liable to pay on the due date.

v) The customer can 'stop' payment if he wishes, and we, his bank, will comply. However, we shall have to protest the dishonoured bill if the instructions tell us to do so. Protest could damage our customer's credit.

vi) The exporter could then sue our customer on the dishonoured bill of exchange. It would be up to the court to decide whether dishonour was justified.

How the drawee can obtain a measure of protection with D/A or D/P collections

i) Take a status enquiry on the supplier (as to his general integrity).

ii) Ask for a third-party inspection certificate to be included with the documents.

Additional Points (not required in answer)
The general conflict of interest for the bank when inward collections are drawn on its customer:

a) If the customer dishonours an inward collection we, his bankers, must protest the bill if the collection instruction so states.

    The customer may well object to this, but we have no choice as we act for the remitting bank.

b) In general, there is a possible conflict of interests between our duty as agent of remitting banks and our need to help our customer.

However, we must act in accordance with the instructions of the remitting bank, although we shall try, where possible, to help our customer.

Specimen Answer to Exam Question15

a)   i)   In accordance with Article 9 of URC the bank should act in good faith and exercise reasonable care at all times. This means that the bank in the circumstances described in the question should have acted in accordance with the instructions contained in the collection instruction. We should check that the documents received under the collection instruction are disposed of in accordance with those instructions.

ii)   In accordance with Article 6, the bank should have ensured that, where an acceptance was called for, the bill of exchange was accepted. Presentation should have been made and payment claimed not later than the appropriate maturity date, i.e. 60 days after the date of the appropriate invoice.

iii)   In accordance with Article 24, the collection order should have given specific instructions concerning protest but, as protest instructions were not given, the bank was under no obligation to have the bill of exchange protested for non-payment or non-acceptance (or noted in the UK). This is the general rule accepted in many parts of the world and embodied in the above Article.

b)   The bank's position under UK banking practice may be somewhat different from that described above. However, the bank in the circumstances described in the question would not have exercised reasonable care and it could be claimed as not acting in good faith and has been and is negligent. It has ignored in some measure part of the terms laid down by Uniform Rules and has not acted in accordance with normal UK banking practice. (Having said that, the collection instruction was incomplete and the bank was under no legal obligation to have the bills protested/noted.)

In accordance with standard UK banking practice, the British bank (my bank) has not exercised care and should have noted/protested the bill of exchange to obtain the protection offered under the Bills of Exchange Act, s. 51(2) and (4) for the benefit of the remitting bank and its customer. It may be difficult to give an appropriate satisfactory answer to the remitting bank concerning the delays in remitting payment other than to claim that full protest or noting instructions were not given. This might be regarded as a lame excuse. However, as documents of title were not attached to the bill of exchange, this method of selling and obtaining payment is principally the equivalent of an open account sale.

c)   As far as the claim for interest is concerned, a collection instruction must state clearly if interest is to be collected, and indicate if this is a mandatory instruction (Article 20).

This claim for interest is principally for overdue interest from the date of maturity of the bill of exchange until the date of the claim, and this is outside any terms of reference covered by URC.   Morally, the customer may be liable to pay the interest claim but, legally, any such claim would have to be made under the terms of the commercial contract if this covered interest claims. The customer can ignore the claim unless a mandatory instruction was included in the invoice, which in the circumstances described in this question would be difficult to include in a bank collection instruction. In commercial practices, many invoices do state that overdue interest may be claimed in the event of a delay in settling the amount covered by the invoice. In the event of such an instruction being included in the collection instruction, my bank should have told the customer of the potential interest claim at the time the bills of exchange were presented for acceptance, but in any event this should have been clearly covered by the collection instruction.

In the circumstances described in the question, this is a matter to be settled between the banks as correspondent banks and it is for them to settle the claim amicably or otherwise.

Most banks would refuse to pay interest in the circumstances described but such a refusal may jeopardise the relationship between the two banks. Because the bank has been rather negligent and has not exercised reasonable care, it might be felt prudent to pay the claim to its German correspondent. It is impossible to lay down a hard-and-fast rule, which is unusual in this type of question!

d) The change in instructions which might assist the supplier in Germany and be clearly in accordance with the 'instructions' covered by Uniform Rules and be in accordance with UK banking practice, would be for the German bank to give specific protest and/or noting instructions in the event of dishonour either upon presentation for acceptance or payment.

In the event of the change of instruction, my bank would clearly have to act in accordance with UK banking practice and protest or note the bills of exchange within 24 hours of dishonour in order to obtain the full protection of the Bills of Exchange Act, s. 51(2) and (4). Further, the bank would also be acting in accordance with URC, Article 24.

If there is an intention to claim interest in respect of a delay in payment or otherwise, this must be stated on the invoice and probably the bill of exchange, as well as in the collection instruction (Article 20).

Specimen Answer to Exam Question 16

a) The fact that the customer has been asked to give a guarantee means that the customer's facilities would be severely curtailed and they would not be able to finance this operation. The question does say that the customer's balance sheet has insufficient strength to finance an operation of this nature. Therefore, one has to suggest a banking instrument which would cater for the needs of all parties bearing in mind the customer's financial position. This is an irrevocable letter of credit which should be transferable in whole or in part.

A transferable letter of credit, issued subject to Uniform Customs and Practice for Documentary Credits, Publication No.500, Article 48, would satisfy the needs of all parties. It is an unalterable undertaking of the issuing bank which would guarantee the supplier that payment would be effected, providing the documents were presented strictly in accordance with the terms of the credit.

b) The terms and conditions that I, acting as the banker to Far East Traders Ltd, would 'insist' upon are as follows:

    i) The letter of credit should be confirmed by my bank and be payable at my counters.

    ii) The transferred part of the credit would be issued in the name of my customer, Far East Traders Ltd, as openers.

    iii) The transferred credit would be for a lesser amount, if appropriate for a smaller unit price, a shorter shipment date, and would expire earlier than the 'original' credit.

    iv) As the goods are to be sold on an ex-works basis, the shipping document would almost certainly have to be a forwarding agent's receipt/trucker's receipt, indicating that the forwarders/truckers had taken over the goods for irrevocable despatch or that they had in fact been despatched. If a name is to be shown on the forwarder's/trucker's receipt, it should be the name of FET Ltd, namely the middleman (my customer). The name of the supplier and purchaser should not be shown on this or any other document. Neither should the name of the manufacturer.

    v) Any other document should be issued in the name of Far East Traders Ltd or, alternatively, the documentation could possibly be issued in neutral names.

    vi) Suggest that when the letter of credit is opened it should be claused 'Discrepant documents are not acceptable and Banker's Indemnities are prohibited'.

Index